THE YEAR BOOK OF WORLD AFFAIRS 1979

VOLUME 33

Editors:

GEORGE W. KEETON

AND

GEORG SCHWARZENBERGER

Managing Editor:

C. G. BURNHAM

AUSTRALIA

The Law Book Company Ltd.
Sydney : Melbourne : Brisbane

INDIA

N. M. Tripathi Private Ltd.
Bombay
and
Eastern Law House Private Ltd.
Calcutta
M.P.P. House
Bangalore

ISRAEL

Steimatzky's Agency Ltd.
Jerusalem: Tel Aviv: Haifa

MALAYSIA : SINGAPORE : BRUNEI

Malayan Law Journal (Pte.) Ltd.
Singapore

NEW ZEALAND

Sweet and Maxwell (N.Z.) Ltd.
Wellington

PAKISTAN

Pakistan Law House
Karachi

U.S.A. AND CANADA

Westview Press, Inc.
Colorado

THE YEAR BOOK

OF

WORLD AFFAIRS

1979

Published under the auspices of
THE LONDON INSTITUTE OF WORLD AFFAIRS

WESTVIEW PRESS, INC.
Boulder, Colorado

All editorial communications should be addressed to the Director, London Institute of World Affairs, Thorne House, 4–8 Endsleigh Gardens, London, WC1H 0EH.

Published in 1979 by Stevens & Sons Limited of 11 New Fetter Lane, London and printed in Great Britain by The Eastern Press Limited of London and Reading

Published in the United States of America in 1979 by Westview Press, Inc., 5500 Central Avenue, Boulder, Colorado 80303

Frederick A. Praeger, President and Editorial Director

Library of Congress Catalog Card Number 47–29156

ISBN: 0-89158-551-6

Printed in Great Britain

CONTENTS

v

TRENDS AND EVENTS

THIS annual survey is intended to serve three purposes:

(1) With every additional volume of the *Year Book*, it becomes increasingly difficult for new readers to derive the fullest benefit from the material available in earlier volumes. This survey brings together references to themes examined in the past which have particular current relevance.

(2) The specific object of an annual publication is to make possible analyses in a wider perspective and on the basis of more mature reflection than may be possible in a quarterly or monthly journal. Thus, it is not the object of this *Year Book* to provide instant information on current issues of world affairs. Yet, international affairs have a stereotyped and, largely, repetitive character, so that, frequently, a " new " happening, or " modern " development has been anticipated in one or more of the earlier volumes of the *Year Book. Trends and Events* provides evidence of some such continuity as may be traced over a span of years.

(3) Reference to earlier contributions also offer readers an opportunity to judge for themselves the adequacy of the conceptual and systematic frameworks chosen or taken for granted in the papers selected:

(A) THE CONTROL OF STRATEGIC ARMAMENTS

Boardman, R.: *China's Rise as a Nuclear Power* (25 Y.B.W.A., 1971)

Boyle, Sir Dermot: *Thoughts on the Nuclear Deterrent* (16 *ibid.* 1962)

Bull, H.: *Two Kinds of Arms Control* (17 *ibid.* 1969)

Coffey, J. L.: *The Limitation of Strategic Armaments* (26 *ibid.* 1972)

Erickson, J.: *The World Strategic Balance* (23 *ibid.* 1969)

Joynt, C. B.: *Arms Races and the Problem of Equilibrium* (18 *ibid.* 1964)

Lee, R.: *Safeguards Against Nuclear Proliferation* (23 *ibid.* 1969)

Martin, L. W.: *Ballistic Missile Defence and the Strategic Balance* (21 *ibid.* 1967)

Millar, T. B.: *On Nuclear Proliferation* (21 *ibid.* 1967)

Radojkovic, M.: *Les Armés Nucleaires et Le Droit International* (16 *ibid.* 1962)

Ranger, R.: *Arms Control in Theory and Practice* (31 *ibid.* 1977)

Smart, I.: *Alliance, Deterrence and Defence* (26 *ibid.* 1972)

Williams, G.: *The Strategic Nuclear Balance and the Defence of Europe* (27 *ibid.* 1973)

1

(B) TERRORISM

Foot, M. R. D.: *Resistance, War and Revolution* (31 Y.B.W.A., 1977)

Kittrie, N. N.: *Reconciling the Irreconcilable: The Quest for International Agreement over Political Crime and Terrorism* (32 *ibid.* 1978)

Smith, W. H.: *International Terrorism: A Political Analysis* (31 *ibid.* 1977)

(C) THE FOREIGN POLICIES OF THE POWERS

1. *Foreign Policy Analysis*

Auma-Osolo, A.: *Rationality and Foreign Policy Process* (31 Y.B.W.A., 1977)

Doxey, M.: *International Organisation in Foreign Policy Perspective* (29 *ibid.* 1975)

Frankel, J.: *Rational Decision-Making in Foreign Policy* (14 *ibid.* 1960)

Morgenthau, H. J.: *The Moral Dilemma in Foreign Policy* (5 *ibid.* 1951)

Williams, P. and Smith, M. H.: *The Foreign Policies of Authoritarian and Democratic States* (30 *ibid.* 1976)

2. *Canadian Foreign Policy*

Doxey, M.: *Canada's International Connections* (32 Y.B.W.A., 1978)

MacDonald, R. St.J.: *Fundamentals of Canadian Foreign Policy* (12 *ibid.* 1958)

3. *Chinese Foreign Policy*

Boardman, R.: *China's Rise as a Nuclear Power* (25 Y.B.W.A., 1971)

Katona, P.: *Sino-Soviet Relations* (26 *ibid.* 1972)

— and Jotischky, L.: *New Patterns in Inter-Communist Relations* (17 *ibid.* 1963)

Lindsay, Lord: *Chinese Foreign Policy: Recent Developments* (15 *ibid.* 1961)

Mahajani, U.: *Sino-American Rapprochement and the New Configurations in South-East Asia* (29 *ibid.* 1975)

—: *Sino-Soviet Conflict and Rivalry in South-East Asia in the Post-Vietnam Phase* (32 *ibid.* 1978)

Meissner, B.: *The Political Treaties of China and the Soviet Union in East Asia* (27 *ibid.* 1973)

4. *Indian Foreign Policy*

Levi, W.: *The Evolution of India's Foreign Policy* (12 Y.B.W.A., 1958)

5. *Indonesian Foreign Policy*

Angel, J. R.: *Indonesian Foreign Policy Since Independence: Changing Preoccupations in Pursuit of Progress* (31 Y.B.W.A., 1977)

6. *Japanese Foreign Policy*

Green, L. C.: *Making Peace with Japan* (6 Y.B.W.A., 1952)
Grieve, M. J.: *The Foreign Policy of Japan* (28 *ibid.* 1974)
Mendl, W. M. L.: *Japan's Defence Problems* (22 *ibid.* 1968)
Nish, I. H.: *Is Japan a Great Power?* (21 *ibid.* 1967)
—: *Japan Among the Powers* (28 *ibid.* 1974)
Northedge, F. S.: *The Divided Mind of Japan* (11 *ibid.* 1957)
Whyte, Sir Frederick: *Japan* (2 *ibid.* 1948)

7. *Soviet Foreign Policy*

Burnham, C. G.: *Czechoslovakia: Thirty Years After Munich* (23 Y.B.W.A., 1969)
Gascoigne, Sir Alvary: *Soviet Foreign Policy* (9 *ibid.* 1955)
Ginsburgs, G.: *Soviet Internationalism and State Sovereignty* (25 *ibid.* 1971)
Gurian, W.: *Permanent Features of Soviet Foreign Policy* (1 *ibid.* 1947)
Hanek, H.: *Soviet Foreign Policy Since Khrushchev* (20 *ibid.* 1966)
Katona, P.: *Sino-Soviet Relations* (26 *ibid.* 1972)
— and Jotischky, L.: *New Patterns in Inter-Communist Relations* (17 *ibid.* 1963)
Lapenna, I.: *International Law Viewed Through Soviet Eyes* (15 *ibid.* 1961)
—: *The Soviet Concept of Socialist International Law* (29 *ibid.* 1975)
Mahajani, U.: *Sino-Soviet Conflict and Rivalry in South-East Asia in the Post-Vietnam Phase* (32 *ibid.* 1978)
Meissner, B.: *The Political Treaties of China and the Soviet Union in East Asia* (27 *ibid.* 1973)
Northedge, F. S.: *America, Russia, and Europe* (28 *ibid.* 1974)
Shapiro, L. B.: *Soviet Participation in International Institutions* (3 *ibid.* 1949)
—: *The Post-War Treaties of the Soviet Union* (4 *ibid.* 1950)
Schwarzenberger, G.: *An Inter-Camp Agenda* (18 *ibid.* 1964)

8. *United Kingdom Foreign Policy*

Frankel, J.: *East of Suez: The Aftermath* (23 Y.B.W.A., 1969)
Keeton, G. W.: *The Future of British Foreign Policy* (2 *ibid.* 1948)
Northedge, F. S.: *Parties and Foreign Policy in Britain* (14 *ibid.* 1960)
Strange, S.: *British Foreign Policy* (9 *ibid.* 1955)
Younger, K. G.: *Britain's Point of No Return* (22 *ibid.* 1968)

9. *United States Foreign Policy*

Bonn, M. J.: *The Foreign Policy of the United States* (2 Y.B.W.A., 1948)
Graber, D. A.: *United States Intervention in Latin America* (16 *ibid.* 1962)

Houghton, N. D.: *Social Structure and Foreign Policy of the United States* (15 *ibid.* 1961)

Johnson, J. T.: *Just War, the Nixon Doctrine and the Future Shape of American Military Policy* (29 *ibid.* 1975)

Livingston, G. S.: *The Indo-China War and American Values* (25 *ibid.* 1971)

Mahajani, U.: *Sino-American Rapprochement and the New Configurations in South-East Asia* (29 *ibid.* 1975)

Morgenthau, H. J.: *United States Foreign Policy* (9 *ibid.* 1955)

Nicholas, H. G.: *The New Administration and United States Foreign Policy* (11 *ibid.* 1957)

—: *The Nixon Line* (25 *ibid.* 1971)

Smith, M. H. and Carey, R.: *The Nixon Legacy and American Foreign Policy* (32 *ibid.* 1978)

Taylor, T.: *President Nixon's Arms Supply Policies* (26 *ibid.* 1972)

Vincent, R. J.: *Kissinger's System of Foreign Policy* (31 *ibid.* 1971)

10. *West German Foreign Policy*

Burmeister, W.: *Brandt's Opening to the East* (27 Y.B.W.A., 1973)

Morgan, R. P.: *The Scope of German Foreign Policy* (20 *ibid.* 1966)

(D) Africa

Bissell, R. E.: *The Ostracism of South Africa* (32 Y.B.W.A., 1978)

Butterworth, R.: *The Future of South Africa* (31 *ibid.* 1977)

Doxey, G. V. and M.: *The Prospects for Change in South Africa* (19 *ibid.* 1965)

Doxey, M.: *The Rhodesian Sanctions Experiment* (25 *ibid.* 1971)

Elias, T. O.: *The Economic Community of West Africa* (32 *ibid.* 1978)

Hudson, D.: *The World Council of Churches and Racism* (29 *ibid.* 1975)

Legum, C.: *South Africa: The Politics of Détente* (30 *ibid.* 1976)

—: *The Future of Ethiopia* (28 *ibid.* 1974)

Lloyd, P. C.: *The African Elites* (22 *ibid.* 1968)

Longmore, L.: *The South African Dilemma* (8 *ibid.* 1954)

Mayall, J.: *African Unity and the OAU* (27 *ibid.* 1973)

Shaw, T. M.: *Southern Africa: From Détente to Deluge?* (32 *ibid.* 1978)

Spence, J.: *The Strategic Significance of South Africa* (27 *ibid.* 1973)

Stent, G. D.: *Colour Problems of South Africa* (2 *ibid.* 1948)

Taylor, T.: *President Nixon's Arms Supply Policy* (26 *ibid.* 1972)

(E) The Middle East

Frankel, J.: *The Middle East in Turmoil* (10 Y.B.W.A., 1956)

James, A.: *Recent Developments in United Nations Peace-keeping* (31 *ibid.* 1977)

Kirk, G.: *The Middle Eastern Scene* (14 *ibid.* 1960)
Mitchell, C. R.: *Peace-keeping: The Police Function* (30 *ibid.* 1976)
Neumann, R. G.: *The Near East After the Syrian Coup* (16 *ibid.* 1968)
Parkinson, F.: *Bandung and the Underdeveloped Countries* (10 *ibid.* 1956)
Rodinson, M.: *Israel: The Arab Options* (22 *ibid.* 1968)
Rosenthal, E. I. J.: *The Role of Islam in the Modern National State* (16 *ibid.* 1962)
Roth, S. J.: *World Jewry and Israel* (28 *ibid.* 1974)
Strange, S.: *Palestine and the United Nations* (1 *ibid.* 1949)
—: *Suez and After* (11 *ibid.* 1957)
Troutbeck, Sir John: *Stresses Within the Arab World* (12 *ibid.* 1958)

(F) WORLD TRADE AND FINANCE

Alexandrowicz, C.: *The Study of International Economics* (4 Y.B.W.A., 1950)
Desai, R. R.: *World Monetary Reform* (20 *ibid.* 1966)
Fisher, A. G. B.: *The Future of International Economic Institutions* (1 *ibid.* 1947)
Goodwin, G. L.: *GATT and the Organisation for Trade Co-operation* (10 *ibid.* 1956)
—: *United Nations Conference on Trade and Development* (19 *ibid.* 1965)
Harrod, J.: *Non-Governmental Organisations and the Third World* (24 *ibid.* 1970)
Kaplan, G. G.: *Equality and Discrimination in International Economic Law (II): The UNCTAD Scheme for Generalised Preferences* (26 *ibid.* 1972)
Kojanec, G.: *Recent Developments in the Law of State Contracts* (24 *ibid.* 1970)
Modelski, G.: *The Corporation in World Society* (22 *ibid.* 1968)
Nussbaumer, A.: *Industrial Co-operation and East-West Trade* (32 *ibid.* 1978)
Penrose, E.: *Monopoly and Competition in the International Petroleum Industry* (18 *ibid.* 1964)
Ramcharan, B. G.: *Equality and Discrimination in International Economic Law (III): The Commonwealth Preferential System* (26 *ibid.* 1972)
Robertson, D.: *Proposals for a North Atlantic Free Trade Area* (23 *ibid.* 1969)
Ross, L. W.: *The Washington Monetary Agreement* (26 *ibid.* 1972)
Scamell, W. M.: *International Economic Co-operation and the Problem of Full Employment* (6 *ibid.* 1952)

Schwarzenberger, G.: *An International Investment Insurance Agency* (23 *ibid.* 1969)

—: *Equality and Discrimination in International Economic Law (I)* (25 *ibid.* 1971)

Strange, S.: *The Commonwealth and the Sterling Area* (13 *ibid.* 1959)

—: *Changing Trends in World Trade* (16 *ibid.* 1962)

Sutton, A.: *Equality and Discrimination in International Economic Law (VI): Trends in Regulation of International Trade in Textiles* (31 *ibid.* 1977)

Verdross, A.: *Quasi-International Agreements and International Economic Transactions* (18 *ibid.* 1964)

Wells, S. J.: *The Kennedy Round* (20 *ibid.* 1966)

(G) WORLD OIL RESOURCES

Brown, E. D.: *Deep-Sea Mining: The Legal Régime of " Inner Space "* (22 Y.B.W.A., 1968)

Frankel, J.: *The Anglo-Iranian Dispute* (6 *ibid.* 1952)

Odell, P. R.: *The International Oil Companies in the New World Oil Market* (32 *ibid.* 1978)

Penrose, E.: *Monopoly and Competition in the International Petroleum Industry* (19 *ibid.* 1964)

(H) INTERNATIONAL AID
AND THE DEVELOPING STATES

Brennan, G. A.: *The United Nations Development Programme* (24 Y.B.W.A., 1970)

Burns, C. L.: *The Colombo Plan* (14 *ibid.* 1960)

Cox, R. W.: *The Pearson and Jackson Reports in the Context of Development Ideologies* (26 *ibid.* 1972)

Dickson, A. G.: *Technical Assistance and Idealism* (12 *ibid.* 1958)

Donelan, M. D.: *The Ideas of United States Economic Aid* (20 *ibid.* 1966)

Gergen, K. J. and M.: *International Assistance in Foreign Policy Perspective* (25 *ibid.* 1971)

—: *Understanding Foreign Assistance Through Public Opinion* (28 *ibid.* 1974)

Levi, W.: *Are Developing States More Equal than Others?* (32 *ibid.* 1978)

Mahajani, U.: *Foreign Aid at the Operational Level in South-East Asia* (19 *ibid.* 1965)

Parkinson, F.: *Bandung and the Underdeveloped Countries* (10 *ibid.* 1956)

Parkinson, F.: *Social Dynamics of Underdeveloped Countries* (14 *ibid.* 1960)
—: *Soviet Aid to Underdeveloped Countries* (11 *ibid.* 1957)
—: *The Alliance for Progress* (18 *ibid.* 1964)
—: *The Politics of Underdeveloped Countries* (17 *ibid.* 1963)
Stokke, B. R.: *Soviet and East European Development Aid: An Economic Assessment* (21 *ibid.* 1970)
Streeten, P. P.: *Aid to India* (24 *ibid.* 1970)
Syz, J.: *Recent North-South Relations and Multilateral Soft Loans* (29 *ibid.* 1975)

(I) HUMAN RIGHTS

Honig, F.: *Criminal Justice in Germany Today* (5 Y.B.W.A., 1951)
Martin, A.: *Human Rights and World Politics* (5 *ibid.* 1951)

(J) THE COMPARATIVE APPROACH TO INTERNATIONAL LAW

Bredima, A.: *Comparative Law in the Court of Justice of the European Communities* (32 Y.B.W.A., 1978)
Butler, W. E.: *East European Approaches to Public International Law* (26 *ibid.* 1972)
—: *Methodological Innovation in Soviet International Legal Doctrine* (32 *ibid.* 1978)
Connelly, A. M.: *The History of International Law: A Comparative Approach* (32 *ibid.* 1978)
Lapenna, I.: *International Law Viewed Through Soviet Eyes* (15 *ibid.* 1961)
—: *The Soviet Concept of Socialist International Law* (29 *ibid.* 1975)
Schapiro, L. B.: *The Soviet Concept of International Law* (2 *ibid.* 1948)
Schwarzenberger, G.: *Civitas Maxima?* (29 *ibid.* 1975)

(K) INTERNATIONAL STUDIES

Alexandrowicz, C.: *The Study of International Economics* (4 Y.B.W.A., 1950)
Banks, M. H.: *Two Meanings of Theory in the Study of International Relations* (20 *ibid.* 1966)
Boardman, R.: *Comparative Method and Foreign Policy* (27 *ibid.* 1973)
Burton, J. W.: *Recent Developments in the Theory of International Relations* (18 *ibid.* 1964)
—: *The Analysis of Conflict by Casework* (21 *ibid.* 1967)
Curle, A.: *Peace Studies* (30 *ibid.* 1976)

Fawcett, C. B.: *Maps in the Study of International Relations* (6 *ibid.* 1952)

Goodwin, G.: *International Relations and International Studies* (27 *ibid.* 1973)

Goormaghtigh, J.: *International Relations as a Field of Study in the Soviet Union* (28 *ibid.* 1974)

Kaplan, M. A.: *New Approaches to International Relations: Progress or Retrogression* (22 *ibid.* 1968)

Kimminich, O.: *International Relations and International Law* (27 *ibid.* 1973)

Lasswell, H. D.: *The Scientific Study of International Relations* (12 *ibid.* 1958)

Midgley, B.: *National Law and the Renewal of the Philosophy of International Relations* (29 *ibid.* 1975)

Nicholas, M. B.: *Mathematical Models in the Study of International Relations* (22 *ibid.* 1968)

Pentland, C. C.: *Neofunctionalism* (27 *ibid.* 1973)

Rosecrance, R. N. and Mueller, J. E.: *Decision-Making and the Quantitative Analysis of International Relations* (21 *ibid.* 1967)

Rosenau, J. N.: *International Studies in the United States* (27 *ibid.* 1973)

Schwarzenberger, G.: *The Study of International Relations* (3 *ibid.* 1949)

Siotis, J.: *Social Science and the Study of International Relations* (24 *ibid.* 1970)

Vincent, R. J.: *The Functions and Functionalism in International Relations* (27 *ibid.* 1973)

Yalem, R. J.: *The Decline of International Relations Theory* (30 *ibid.* 1976)

—: *The Level of Analysis Problem Reconsidered* (31 *ibid.* 1977)

It may also be helpful to remind readers of the Cumulative Index to Volumes 1 to 25 in the 1971 Volume of the *Year Book of World Affairs—Managing Ed.*, Y.B.W.A.

A LIVING AND EXPANDING LIBRARY
OF WORLD AFFAIRS

The London Institute of World Affairs is pleased to announce that, in co-operation with the Institute Publishers, arrangements have been made for a micro-film edition of the previous volumes of the Year Book of World Affairs until Vol. 29 (1975) with Oxford Micro-film Publications. As a Preface to this micro-film edition, prepared by the Managing Editor of the Year Book, may be of interest also to readers of the Year Book, it is reproduced in this volume—The Editors, Y.B.W.A.

THE *Year Book of World Affairs* appears as an annual which, since 1947, has been published by Stevens, London, under the auspices of the LONDON INSTITUTE OF WORLD AFFAIRS, an independent, inter-national research and teaching organisation for the study of world affairs. As stated in an introductory note to the first volume by George W. Keeton and Georg Schwarzenberger—the joint editors throughout the whole of this period—the purpose of the Institute and the *Year Book* has been " to provide an independent international forum for the constructive criticism of, and research into, world affairs." The *Year Book of World Affairs* has sought to fulfil this function ever since.

Concentrating on serious analysis rather than reportage, the editorial policy of the *Year Book* has been, and is, to trace those trends and events which are likely to be of permanent significance. Thus, the significance of the *Year Book* is its object to constitute a living library of world affairs.

The scope of an annual devoted to world affairs is necessarily wide. It includes, but is not limited to, international affairs. Thus, we accept the definition of world affairs as " the relations between groups, between groups and individuals, and between individuals, which substantially affect international society"[1]; determining which matters at any time are relevant for purposes of the *Year Book* is essentially a question of touch and common sense.

Each of the first 25 volumes of the *Year Book* comprises about 12 papers on different aspects of world affairs and up to eight reports on different aspects of the literature of world affairs. In the subsequent seven volumes, the number of papers has been nearly doubled if at the price of excluding the reports.

I—EDITORIAL POLICY

The *Year Book of World Affairs* is planned with a mixed readership of specialists and interested laymen in mind. While it tends to avoid

---

[1] G. Schwarzenberger: *Power Politics* (3rd ed., 1964), p. 4.

9

the fancies of passing fashions in the study of relevant disciplines, it treats them, like other pertinent phenomena, as objects of sympathetic but critical analysis.

From the outset the Editors were conscious of the need to maintain and guard jealously the intellectual and financial independence of the Institute and *Year Book*. The *Year Book* espouses no ideology, nor any utopia or " establishment " of any sort. By its settled policy of not accepting funds from governments, corporations or foundations, the Institute tries to preserve complete freedom of expression for itself and its contributors. In this way, it has, for instance, been possible for contributors such as Paul P. Streeten,[2] Kenneth J. Gergen [3] and Werner Levi [4] to write on a controversial subject like international aid from unusual angles.

In order to fulfil its aims the *Year Book* has turned to a variety of contributors with a wide range of backgrounds and experience. Many of those who have been established authorities in their fields have honoured the *Year Book* with contributions. They include Max Beloff, Alastair Buchan, Hedley Bull, John Burton, Richard A. Falk, Morton A. Kaplan, Harold Lasswell, George Modelski, Hans J. Morgenthau, James N. Rosenau and Richard N. Rosecrance.

It has been a consistent line of editorial policy to provide opportunities for young scholars who, frequently, are in difficulties about finding a medium through which they can express themselves. Most of these have, long since, joined the ranks of leading scholars. To mention but a few of these: Arthur L. Burns, W. E. Butler, E. D. Brown, B. Cheng, Margaret Doxey, Joseph Frankel, Geoffrey Goodwin, Leslie C. Green, Alan James, D. H. N. Johnson, Roger Morgan, H. G. Nicholas, F. S. Northedge, Leonard Shapiro and J. E. Spence. It may also be mentioned that Susan Strange contributed to the first volume and appeared in each of the subsequent 12 volumes.

At the outset of the second Alastair Buchan Memorial Lecture of the International Institute for Strategic Studies, Chancellor Helmut Schmidt made a reference to Alastair Buchan's paper, published in the same volume of the *Year Book of World Affairs* as one by himself.[5] Others among eminent public figures include ambassadors and members of the International Court of Justice.[6] Sir John Cowley

---

[2] P. P. Streeten: *Aid to India* (24 Y.B.W.A., 1970).

[3] K. J. and Mary Gergen: *International Assistance in Psychological Perspective* (25 *ibid.* 1971); —: *Understanding Foreign Assistance through Public Opinion* (28 *ibid.* 1974).

[4] W. Levi: *Are Developing States More Equal than Others?* (32 *ibid.* 1978).

[5] A. Buchan: *An Expedition to the Poles* (29 *ibid.* 1975); H. Schmidt: *New Tasks for the Atlantic Alliance* (29 *ibid.* 1975).

[6] Sir John Troutbeck: *Stresses Within the Arab World* (12 *ibid.* 1961); Lord Gladwyn: *Britain and Western Europe* (15 *ibid.* 1961); E. Hambro: *The Human Environment: Stockholm and After* (28 *ibid.* 1971); —: *Permanent Representatives to International Organisation* (30 *ibid.* 1976).

contributed when Master-General of the Ordnance,[7] Sir Dermot Boyle when Marshal of the Royal Air Force [8] and Sir Francis Vallat when Legal Adviser to the United Kingdom Foreign Office.[9] Kenneth Younger, then Director of the Royal Institute of International Affairs, wrote a paper for Volume 22 (1968),[10] and David Owen, having been Minister of State at the Navy, looked to the future of naval power in the 1980s shortly before taking office as United Kingdom Foreign Secretary.[11]

Increasingly, journalists are in positions which enable them to unearth information otherwise not readily available. Those who, in addition, are serious analysts of world affairs, have unique contributions to offer, for which their newspapers could not readily find commensurate space. To this category belong the splendid contributions we owe to Colin Chapman, Charles Douglas-Home, Colin Legum, Richard Lowenthal and David Wilson.[12] Occasionally, the *Year Book* has been able to attract other trained observers of high-class calibre such as Charles Levinson, Secretary-General of the International Federation of Chemical and General Workers' Union,[13] and C. T. H. Plant, General Secretary of the United Kingdom Inland Revenue Staff Federation,[14] on subjects like labour and the multi-national enterprises, and matters of environmental concern.

II—AN EXPANDING LIBRARY OF WORLD AFFAIRS

The *Year Book of World Affairs* has been developing over a period of more than 30 years. Examination of past volumes provides insights into approaches which are appropriate only occasionally, such as concentration on various aspects of the single theme of the United Nations in Volume 8 (1954). The one clear break in continuity came with Volume 26 (1972) which adopted a new structure.[15] Increasingly, the *Year Book* has become a living library of world affairs. To make this clearer for users of the *Year Book*, since 1972 each volume opens with a section on *Trends and Events*, in which still significant papers

---

[7] Sir John Cowley: *Future Trends in Warfare* (14 *ibid.* 1960).

[8] Sir Dermot Boyle: *Thoughts on the Nuclear Deterrent* (16 *ibid.* 1962).

[9] Sir Francis Vallat: *International Law—A Forward Look* (18 *ibid.* 1964).

[10] K. J. Younger: *Britain's Point of No Return* (22 *ibid.* 1968).

[11] D. Owen: *Western Naval Strategy for the Eighties* (28 *ibid.* 1974).

[12] C. Chapman: *Towards a New Pacific Alliance* (29 *ibid.* 1975); C. Douglas-Home: *The Arms Sales Race* (23 *ibid.* 1969); C. Legum: *The Future of Ethiopia* (28 *ibid.* 1974); —: *Southern Africa: The Politics of Détente* (30 *ibid.*) 1976; R. Lowenthal: *The Ideological Crisis of International Relations* (12 *ibid.* 1958); D. Wilson: *Space Business: The History of INTELSAT* (25 *ibid.* 1971).

[13] C. Levinson: *Labour in the New Global Economy* (27 *ibid.* 1973).

[14] C. T. H. Plant: *The Relationship Between Multi-National Enterprises and Social Policy* (28 *ibid.* 1974).

[15] See the introductory section to this paper, above.

from past volumes are arranged into groups under headings of current relevance. A series entitled *Equality and Discrimination in International Economic Law* was introduced in the 1971 volume with a paper by Georg Schwarzenberger. By 1978, this paper has been followed by seven specialised papers on equality and discrimination in UNCTAD, the Commonwealth, the European Communities, the international textile trade, multi-national enterprises and the United Nations Regional Economic Commissions. Commencing with three papers in each of the first two volumes on the foreign policies of the Soviet Union, the United States and the United Kingdom, further papers have appeared at regular intervals on the foreign policies of the major Powers. There have also been regular contributions on the themes of international institutions, international law and inter-disciplinary aspects of world affairs. The *World Portrait* series also deserves to be mentioned.[16]

Each volume is thoroughly indexed, and a cumulative index in Volume 25 (1971) serves as a guide to earlier volumes. In addition, *Trends and Events*—since Volume 26 (1972)—can be used as an additional thematic index.

III—An Inter-Disciplinary Approach

The study of as complex a subject as world affairs calls for a synoptic approach which draws together the disciplines of sociology, history, law, economics, geography, psychology, anthropology and the natural sciences. Thus, a series of papers on the human environment includes those by specialists in archaeology, biochemistry, biology and investigative medicine.[17]

IV—A Relativist Approach

On matters of international planning, value-judgments are hard to avoid. In this field, " there is always a choice of several possibilities. The student of international relations must be willing to deal fairly with all of them. A relativist approach to questions of this type and the judicious use of patterns of possible and likely developments in international society make it possible . . . to keep on the right side of the borderline between detached study and politics." [18]

The dominant values and structures of the contemporary world are treated in a number of papers, with particular reference to topics

---

[16] For the *World Portrait* series, see *e.g. Trends and Events* (30 *ibid.* 1976), p. 3.

[17] G. W. Dimbleby: *Restoring the Ecological Balance* (23 *ibid.* 1969); C. Gorinski: *Cultures in Conflict* (24 *ibid.* 1970); H. Kalmus: *Living Together Without Man* (25 *ibid.* 1971); H. L. Penman: *International Hydrological Decade* (26 *ibid.* 1972); I. H. Mills: *The Biological Factor in International Relations* (27 *ibid.* 1973); C. H. Shaw: *Dilemmas .of Super-Growth* (30 *ibid.* 1976).

[18] *Op. cit.* in note 1, above, pp. 10–11.

such as race, transnational relations, bipolarity and tripolarity.[19] Where value-judgments cannot be avoided it is important to face them openly. Thus Kenneth W. Thompson presents a worldwide review of values and education,[20] while Roy Preiswerk has considered the significance of intercultural relations.[21]

Relativism encourages a comparative approach. It is characteristic of papers dealing with the Soviet Union and Eastern Europe, with particular emphasis on the economic and trading systems,[22] on Soviet concepts of international law and State sovereignty,[23] and on international law across the ages.[24]

The analysis of ideologies has recurrently been taken up in the pages of the *Year Book*. We understand by this term cover-up notions of any sectional interest which pretends to speak for a larger whole, whether this has occurred in the context of the pervading political ideologies of the twentieth century,[25] or those related to economic-interest groups [26] or social-attitude groups.[27]

---

[19] A. R. Preiswerk: *Race and Colour in International Relations* (24 *ibid.* 1970); D. Hudson: *The World Council of Churches and Racism* (29 *ibid.* 1975); A. Buchan: *An Expedition to the Poles* (29 *ibid.* 1975); J. Harrod: *Transnational Relations* (30 *ibid.* 1976); R. J. Yalem: *Transnational versus International Politics* (32 *ibid.* 1978); —: *Tripolarity and World Politics* (28 *ibid.* 1974).

[20] G. S. Livingston: *The Indo-China War and American Values* (25 *ibid.* 1975); K. W. Thompson: *Values and Education in a Worldwide Review* (31 *ibid.* 1977).

[21] A. R. Preiswerk: *The Place of Intercultural Relations in the Study of International Relations* (32 *ibid.* 1978).

[22] A. Nussbaumer: *The Economic Systems of Socialist Eastern Europe: Principles, Development and Operation* (29 *ibid.* 1975); —: *Western Market Economies* (30 *ibid.* 1976).

[23] G. Ginsburgs: *Socialist Internationalism and State Sovereignty* (25 *ibid.* 1971); —: *The Constitutional Foundations of the " Socialist Commonwealth "* (27 *ibid.* 1973).

[24] L. B. Shapiro: *The Soviet Concept of International Law* (2 *ibid.* 1948); W. E. Butler: *Methodological Innovations in Soviet International Legal Doctrine* (32 *ibid.* 1978); A. Bredima: *Comparative Law in the Court of Justice of the European Communities* (32 *ibid.* 1978).

[25] G. Schwarzenberger: *An Inter-Camp Agenda* (18 *ibid.* 1964); G. S. Livingston: *The Indo-China War and American Values* (25 *ibid.* 1971); E. F. and Edith Penrose: *The Third World in International Politics* (25 *ibid.* 1971); R. A. Remington: *The Warsaw Pact* (27 *ibid.* 1973); S. J. Roth: *World Jewry and Israel* (28 *ibid.* 1974); I. Lapenna: *The Soviet Concept of Socialist International Law* (29 *ibid.* 1975); A. Nussbaumer: *The Economic Systems of Socialist Eastern Europe* (29 *ibid.* 1975); F. A. M. Alting von Geusau: *Détente After Helsinki* (32 *ibid.* 1978).

[26] A. G. Dickson: *Technical Assistance and Idealism* (12 *ibid.* 1958); G. Modelski: *Corporations in World Society* (22 *ibid.* 1968); R. W. Cox: *The Pearson and Jackson Reports in the Context of Development Ideologies* (26 *ibid.* 1972); C. T. H. Plant: *The Relationship Between the Multi-National Enterprise and Social Policy* (28 *ibid.* 1974); I. Seidl-Hohenveldern: *Multi-National Enterprises and the International Law of the Future* (29 *ibid.* 1975).

[27] A. M. Chirgwin: *The World Church* (1 *ibid.* 1947); I. Ledermann: *The International Red Cross* (1 *ibid.* 1947); B. Tunstall: *The Papacy and World Peace* (5 *ibid.* 1951); B. G. Ivanyi: *Church and State in Eastern Europe* (6 *ibid.* 1952); E. I. J. Rosenthal: *The Role of Islam in the Modern Nation State* (16 *ibid.* 1962); Sir Kenneth Grubb and A. R. Booth: *The Church and International Relations* (17 *ibid.* 1963); J. D. Wood: *The World Council of Churches* (26 *ibid.* 1972); D. Hudson: *The World Council of Churches and Racism* (29 *ibid.* 1975).

V—HISTORICAL INSIGHTS

Inevitably, a number of papers have dealt with events which, at the time of publication, were of considerable current significance. Thus, it is possible now to look back more or less with detachment on evaluations made in the immediate aftermath of the Suez Crisis (1956), the Syrian *coup* (1961), the Cuba Crisis (1962), the Czecho-slovak Crisis (1968) and the Chilean *coup* (1973).[28]

It is evident on other occasions that some writers have shown remarkable perspicacity, as, for example, when in 1948 George W. Keeton looked ahead to the days when " the terms on which raw materials will be obtained will no longer be so favourable to Great Britain as they were before 1939." [29]

VI—TIMELESS THEMES

World affairs have a stereotyped and, largely, repetitive character, so that, frequently, a " new " happening, or " modern " develop-ment has been anticipated in one or more of past volumes of the *Year Book*. Moreover, there are themes which, within the foreseeable future, are likely to retain a good deal of their contemporary relevance. In this category are nationalism, sovereignty, neutrality and neutral-ism, hegemonial intervention, imperialism, the balance of power,[30] bipolarity, tripolarity, regionalism and federalism.[31]

VII—THE SHAPE OF THINGS TO COME

Consistently, the Editors of the *Year Book* have encouraged the study of trends pointing to the future developments of world society and the relativist study of models [32] for its reform. After all, the fact that a certain state of affairs has existed or exists does not postulate that it must continue indefinitely.[33]

Colin Burnham,
Managing Editor, Y.B.W.A.

---

[28] S. Strange: *Suez and After* (11 *ibid.* 1957); —: *Cuba and After* (17 *ibid.* 1963); R. G. Newman: *The Near East After the Syrian Coup* (16 *ibid.* 1962); C. G. Burnham: *Czechoslovakia: Thirty Years After Munich* (23 *ibid.* 1969); H. Blakemore: *Chile: The Critical Juncture?* (27 *ibid.* 1973).

[29] G. W. Keeton: *The Future of British Foreign Policy* (2 *ibid.* 1948), p. 2.

[30] H. J. Morgenthau: *Neutrality and Neutralism* (11 *ibid.* 1957); J. Frankel: *National-ism on Trial* (11 *ibid.* 1957); G. Schwarzenberger: *Hegemonial Intervention* (13 *ibid.* 1959); —: *The Scope for Neutralism* (15 *ibid.* 1961); —: *Beyond Power Politics* (19 *ibid.* 1965); M. A. Kaplan: *Theoretical Inquiry and Balance of Power* (14 *ibid.* 1960).

[31] G. Schwarzenberger: *From Bipolarity to Multipolarity?* (21 *ibid.* 1967); G. Ginsburgs: *Socialist Internationalism and State Sovereignty* (25 *ibid.* 1971); F. A. M. Alting von Geusau: *The European Communities After the Hague Summit* (26 *ibid.* 1972); M. Seara Vazquez: *Zones of Influence* (27 *ibid.* 1973); F. S. Northedge: *America, Russia and Europe* (28 *ibid.* 1974); R. J. Yalem: *Tripolarity and World Politics* (28 *ibid.* 1974); A. Buchan: *An Expedition to the Poles* (29 *ibid.* 1975); R. J. Vincent: *The Idea of Concert and International Order* (29 *ibid.* 1975).

[32] G. Schwarzenberger, *op. cit.* in note 1, above, p. 10.   [33] *Ibid.* p. 521.

THE THIRD WORLD
AND INTERNATIONAL SOCIETY

By

HEDLEY BULL

THE issue I propose to explore in this paper—without any expectation of arriving at firm conclusions about it, but in the hope of achieving some clarification—is that of the impact of the States and peoples to which we loosely and in some ways unsatisfactorily refer as the Third World on the common rules and institutions of international society. The following questions invite attention.

First, when we speak today of the Third World what we chiefly have in mind is a number of States and peoples that form a coalition or political combination, at least for certain purposes: the Bandung Conference of 1955; the Non-Aligned Conference that assembled at Belgrade in 1961; " The Group of 77 " formed at the first United Nations Conference on Trade and Development (UNCTAD) in 1964; the sponsors of the New International Economic Order in 1974. How far does the Third World in this sense really exist? To what extent is it united and what is it united about?

Secondly, the demands put forward in the name of the Third World are sometimes described—both by supporters and by opponents of them—in terms of a struggle to destroy the old international order and establish a new one, to shake off the rules and institutions devised by the old established forces (in Sukarno's phrase) and create new rules and institutions that will express the aspirations of the new emerging forces. To what extent are the demands of the Third-World coalition revolutionary in relation to the existing rules and institutions of international society and to what extent are they reformist? Can these demands be accommodated within the framework of international society as it is now constituted, or do they imply its overthrow?

Thirdly, the coalition or political combination we call the Third World is only a particular expression of something more basic in the present international system, something that would still be with us even if that coalition ceased to exist. This is the expansion of the originally European or Western society of States to embrace the world as a whole. Only five Asian and no African States attended the Hague Conferences of 1899 and 1907; only seven Afro-Asian States were original members of the League of Nations; only 12 of the United Nations. Today, it is the European or Western States (using these terms in the broadest sense to include the Soviet Union and the extra-European States of European settlement), the principal architects of the old international society, that are in a minority. What are the long-term implications for the rules and institutions of international society of its expanded membership? Has the geographical expansion of the membership of international society been accompanied by a contraction of the area of consensus about its rules and institutions? What degree of commitment to common rules and institutions do the new member States accept in their dealings not only with the older member States but with one another? Has international society outgrown the European or Western culture on which it was once founded, and if so what cultural foundations, if any, can it be said to have now?

I—THE THIRD WORLD AS A COALITION

The diversity of the Third World is apparent the moment we try to say what it is. We may begin, for example, by defining it negatively, as those countries that do not belong either to the group of industrialised, capitalist States or to the group of socialist countries. Yet Japan, the second greatest of the former, and China, the second greatest of the latter, must for certain purposes be counted as part of the Third World. Both were represented at the Bandung Conference. Japan, whatever its present political alignments and economic entanglements, is the country which more than any other is responsible for the military destruction of European imperial power, and which originated the policy, to which much of the Third World is now dedicated, of building strength in imitation of the West, and then using that strength to confront the West. China seeks to play the role of leader or champion of the Third World, in a struggle against the hegemonism of the super-Powers.

Nor will it do to treat the Third World as the group of countries that are " non-aligned " in the sense of not being participants in military pacts with one or other of the super-Powers. It is not merely that we can point to many States that are in one way or another " aligned " in this sense and yet have strong credentials as members of the Third World—Iran, Pakistan, the Philippines, North Korea, Cuba, Iraq and others. Given the complicated patterns of alignment and antagonism that have marked international politics in the 1960s and 1970s, " non-alignment " as it was understood in the 1950s has been drained of meaning. The alignments (or non-alignments) of Third World countries in relation to the super-Powers are today shifting and uncertain, as is shown by the recent history of Ethiopia and Somalia, and the posture of these countries as members of the Third World is maintained independently of them.

It may seem tempting to define the Third World as the countries of Asia and Africa, or more inclusively (to take account of areas such as Oceania and the black Caribbean) as the countries that are not predominantly European or Western in population and culture. But here we encounter the difficulty that at least in relation to the protest against economic injustice and dependence, the countries of Latin America have to be counted part of the Third World. We also have to face the difficulty, to which I shall return later, of saying what it is to be European or Western in culture and population.

In the first two decades of the United Nations, when many of what we now call the Third World States were first taking their places at the United Nations there was a tendency to speak of them as " the new States." The great majority of Third World States have indeed had no previous formal existence as such, and as Peter Lyon has shown, there are important similarities (and differences) as between them and the two previous groups of new States that entered international society at roughly the same time, those that emerged from the collapse of the Spanish and Portuguese empires in Latin America early in the 19th century, and those that emerged from the four dynastic empires that collapsed in the First World War.[1] We have to note, however, that by the time they became associated with the Third World the States of Latin America were not new, but old States; and that the Third World contains States such as China, Thailand, Ethiopia, Egypt, Liberia and Haiti which are not new-comers to the present international society, even if it is only quite recently that they have been accorded full equality of status in it. There is, moreover, something ludicrous about referring to the heirs of the Chinese, the Egyptian and the Persian empires as the representatives of " new States."

In the era of the " North-South Dialogue " and the debate on a New International Economic Order the essential characteristic of the Third-World countries might be thought to be their poverty or their position as exporters of food and raw materials or their lack of a strong industrial base, but there are notorious difficulties about these propositions also. Saudi Arabia and Kuwait are among the top half-dozen countries in the world in terms of *per capita* income. The United States, Canada and Australia are also major exporters of food and raw materials; indeed, if oil is excluded, it is the developed market economies, not the Third-World countries, that are the world's chief exporters of primary products. Industrialisation in some Third-World countries—in Brazil, Mexico and Argentina, and in the Asian-Pacific " mini-Japans "—is considerably advanced, and the

---

[1] P. Lyon, " New States and International Order," in A. M. James (ed.), *The Bases of International Order* (1973).

competition it provides has become a source of concern in the advanced countries. The Third-World countries are in fact extremely diverse in their economic characteristics, many of them have characteristics that place them closer to the advanced countries than to other Third-World countries, and it can be shown that in relation to some indices of economic performance (including growth rates and investment rates) there is no particular reason to group them together at all.[2]

But there is an idea of the Third World, a notional unity of the proletarian countries to which they all appeal. Whatever the lack of common objective characteristics, they share a consciousness of historic subjection to Western power in one form or another: to colonial rule, to quasi-colonial tutelage and hegemony, to economic domination or racial discrimination. Deep though the divisions are among them, and true as it may be that many Third-World States regard other Third-World States as their principal antagonists, the idea of a common struggle to end this historic subjection plays a part in the political rhetoric of all of them. Nor is the unity of the Third World wholly notional or rhetorical. In relation to certain specific, but very basic issues—the abolition of colonialism, the abolition of white supremacist governments and the redistribution of wealth from rich States to poor—actual unity has been achieved to a remarkable degree. The historical roots of this unity lie in the conferences and congresses earlier in the century that sought to assert common opposition to colonialism in Africa and Asia: the series of Pan-African Congresses that began in London in 1900, the Congress against Colonial Oppression and Imperialism held in Brussels in 1927, the League of Peoples against Imperialism established in Paris in 1948. In the course of the past three decades, using the United Nations as their vehicle (although the General Assembly's declarations are less a cause than a result of the change that has taken place) they have challenged and to a considerable degree altered the prevailing norms of the previously Western-dominated international order. Their solidarity survived the challenge of 1973–74 OPEC oil price increases, when, although the economies of the so-called Fourth-World countries were damaged more seriously than those of the West, they nevertheless supported the oil-producing countries, in whose policies they saw long-term hope for the Third World as a whole. In the welter of conferences about redistribution of wealth that have taken place since then (notably the 1974 Special Session on Raw Materials and Development, the 1975 Special Session on Development and International Economic Co-operation and the 1976 Fourth UNCTAD), as in relation to the Law of the Sea

---

[2] See C. Wolf, Jr., *A Dialogue on the North-South Dialogue* (1977), p. 5896.

Conference, a broad solidarity has been maintained and has shown increasing signs of institutionalisation.

If the Third-World countries are united, at least on certain basic issues, it is worth asking who it is that they are united against. We often encounter the notion that the other party in the conflict is not the West, but the North: that the revolt of the so-called South is directed against the advanced, industrialised countries as a whole, including the Soviet bloc as well as North America, Western Europe and Japan. This is a notion which derives some of its force from the roots of the present movement of Third-World solidarity in the non-aligned movement of the 1950s, which expressed dissent from Soviet policies as well as Western ones, and which, as the Soviet Union and the West found common ground in the 1960s, gave rise to the fear among Third-World countries that bargains would be struck at their expense. The idea that the sins attributed by the Third World to the West are attributable to the Soviet Union also is the theme not only of Western critics of the " new imperialism " of the Soviet Union in Eastern Europe, or of the "salt-water fallacy" that ignores the history of Russian expansion in Asia; it is also the thesis propounded by China. It is true that on some issues the Soviet Union has aligned itself with the Western countries against the Third World. On the question of nuclear proliferation, for example, which both China and India have sought to present as a battleground of the struggle between Haves and Have-Nots, the Soviet Union has adopted the position of a Have. On some of the issues that have arisen at the Law of the Sea Conference the Soviet Union stands aligned with the big maritime States against Third-World positions. The Soviet Union's pursuit of détente with the United States has at various times imposed on it the need to moderate its support of Third-World causes, such as the struggle of Arab States against Israel, of black African States against South Africa or of the Indochinese communists against the United States. The position in the Soviet Union of the various non-European nationalities, and the definition of its Asian borders by so-called " unequal treaties," are points of vulnerability underlined by Peking.

But it is the West and not the North that has been the principal target of the Third-World *animus*. In the eyes of those who speak for the Third World it is the Western Powers which imposed colonial domination on them; which in the post-colonial era hold them in the new form of subjection represented by neo-colonialism; which provide Israel and South Africa with the bulk of such international support as they have; and which, through their dominant position in the international politics of money, trade, aid and investment, hold the keys that determine how rich or poor they will be. As Western observers remarked painfully during the cold-war period, the

Third World was not neutral or impartial between the West and the Soviet Union, but tended to lean towards the latter. This the leaders of Third-World countries did because they perceived, correctly, that in the struggle to eliminate colonialism, to combat neo-colonialism and dependence and to redistribute wealth, the Soviet Union on the whole played the part of an ally of the Third World against the West for these limited purposes. The alliance of the Soviet bloc and the Third-World States against the West was a natural combination of the two weaker sections of international society against the section that was economically and militarily the strongest.

The unity of the Third World relates only to a limited range of objectives. There has been much discussion in the West of how to subvert it—whether by " co-opting " the resource-rich or industrial-ising countries of the Third World into the West, by " creaming off the élites " of Third-World countries as the élites of the working class in Western countries have been recruited into the middle classes, or by convincing the so-called Fourth-World countries that it is not the resource-rich, Third-World countries but only the West that will give them aid and succour. It is easy to envisage that the Third-World coalition might collapse, even without this outside encouragement, through the divisions within it. Even if it does not, it will presumably fall apart if and when in due course it is successful in achieving its objectives: colonial rule, after all, has already virtually disappeared, the days of white supremacist rule in Africa appear to be numbered, and even in relation to the still very distant goal of international economic justice one can say that, viewed in a long perspective, a certain movement has taken place. Nevertheless, the revolt of oppressed States and peoples has a momentum behind it that will surely carry it further before it is spent.

II—REVOLUTION OR REFORM?

The question whether the impact of the Third World on the rules and institutions of international society is to revolutionise or merely to reform and develop them is not an easy one with which to come to grips. That the presence in international society of a multitude of States and peoples whose voice has not previously been heard or heeded, and which now represents the great majority of the member-States of international society and of the world's population, should result in some changes in the rules and institutions, goes without saying. The rules and institutions of international society, for all that they contain elements of continuity that can be traced back over several centuries, have never been static, and would be undergoing change and development quite apart from any effect the presence of the Third World might be having on the process. Indeed, it is by no means clear that the contribution of the Third World to this process of institutional and normative change is as great as that of certain other factors that are at work: the ideological schism among the older States in the system, the impact of developing military technology on attitudes to the use of force, the march of economic and technological " interdependence."

There is also the difficulty of knowing what a genuinely revolutionary change in the rules and institutions of international society would look like if one encountered it. The term " revolutionary " has been debased, and today a change is often said to be revolutionary merely because it is basic or profound. If we use the term in this way the distinction between a change that is revolutionary and one that is not is a matter simply of degree. The change, for example, that has taken place from an international society in which colonial empires were extended the protection of the rights of sovereignty to one in which this protection has been withdrawn may be a basic one, but there is no clear reason for saying that this change is revolutionary whereas other changes are not.

A distinction can be drawn in kind rather than degree if we look not to the extent of the change but to the way in which it is made: a revolutionary change is brought about by defiance of the old rules and institutions and the creation of new ones; a reform is a change brought about by procedures which are available under the old rules and institutions. But while in a modern State it may be easy to say whether a change has been brought about by defying existing rules or by resort to legislative procedures, in international society the distinction is harder to apply because of the uncertainty as to what the legislative procedures of international society are, and indeed as to whether there are any procedures to which this name can be properly applied. Defiance of the existing rules and the assertion of new ones, if it becomes general enough and persists over time, can give rise to new " customary law," and may itself be regarded as a recognised procedure for changing the rules. Moreover, the adoption by a State or group of States of a revolutionary attitude or posture towards the existing rules or institutions, will not necessarily result in the carrying through of revolutionary changes. International society has displayed a remarkable capacity to "socialise" revolutionary forces with which it has been confronted, to absorb them and mould them to its purposes, even at the price of itself subtly changing in the process.

The attitude of Third-World countries towards some parts of international law inherited from the period of European or Western ascendancy has been to assert that they are not bound by it and to seek to change it. In relation to colonialism they have sought through the Declaration on the Granting of Independence to Colonial Peoples of 1960 and comparable resolutions to bring it to an end, and by interpreting prohibitions on the use of force so as to permit force used against colonialism and to disallow force used in defence of it, they have sought to facilitate the process. The Third-World States have also sought to condemn so-called racist or white supremacist government as illegitimate, while seeking to deny them the protection of rights of sovereignty or domestic jurisdiction, and to invoke collective action against them by arguing that they constitute threats to the peace. Finally, the Third-World States have sought to establish that rich States have duties to assist the economic development of poor States, and poor States rights to pursue their development without external interference, most notably through the Declaration on the Establishment of a New International Economic Order and the Charter of the Economic Rights and Duties of States of 1974. In the course of promoting these latter rights they have attacked those parts of existing law which have provided obstacles—a doctrine of the responsibilities of States that favoured the security of foreign investors, a doctrine of succession that committed new governments to inherited obligations, a doctrine of treaties that held so-called unequal treaties to be valid, a law of the sea that reflected the special interests of the great maritime States.

But these attacks on elements of previously existing international law held to embody discrimination against themselves have taken place against the background of the acceptance by Third-World States of the prevailing framework which international law provides. They have not sought to reject the international legal order as a whole, or to contend that they must be presumed to be outside the system, apart from specific rules to which they have given their consent; on the contrary, by assuming the rights and duties of States, they have established a presumption of participation in the system, apart from specific rules to which they may raise objections. Moreover, in raising objections to legal rules that they conceive to be contrary to their interests, and in seeking to establish new rules that will take account of them, they are following the normal practice of the older States within the system.

It is notable also that the attacks launched by Third-World countries on elements of the old international legal order themselves embody attempts to accommodate to it. The arguments presented in support of anti-colonialism, anti-white supremacism and economic independence and development do not take the form simply of an argument in the name of justice against law. There is an attempt to show that the positions supported by Third-World countries represent the true interpretation of existing law: that rights of self-determination or racial equality or economic and social welfare are recognised in the U.N. Charter or in the Declaration of Human Rights or in subsequent resolutions of the General Assembly. The idea that international law is not a static body of rules but a body of rules in constant development, and subject to continuous interpretation in the light of changing conceptions of justice, is one that is calculated to avoid a direct appeal to violate legality in the name of justice. When Third-World States have argued that colonialism is illegitimate, not because it is morally wrong or unjust but because it is an example of " aggression," or that armed resistance to colonialism is legitimate, not because it is just offensive war but because it is an example of " self-defence," then they are demonstrating the will to conform to the prevailing norms of the system.

Just as the Third-World countries have sought to play a role within the international legal order rather than to attack it from outside, so they have become part of the international system of diplomatic and consular relations: the conventions and usages governing immunities and precedence and methods of communication and negotiation that were evolved principally (although not exclusively) in Europe are now those of the world as a whole. We do not yet have any adequate study of the impact it has had on them: such a study might help to isolate those parts of Asia nor African diplomatic practice that embody indigenous traditions from those that take inherited Western practice as their point of departure and those that have been improvised to meet the requirements of the contemporary world. But on the face of it what is most striking in the attitudes of Third-World countries to European or Western diplomatic practice is the eagerness with which they have embraced it: it provides for them part of the symbolism of statehood and independence, along with the machinery of access to other governments that they have found it essential to use.

The clearest indication of the willingness of Third-World countries to pursue their objectives within the framework of common rules and institutions has been the importance they have attached to the United Nations. So central has the United Nations been in the diplomacy of Third-World States, and so much has it come in the late 1960s and 1970s to be perceived as their instrument that it is easy to forget that the People's Republic of China was excluded from the organisation up to 1971, that Indonesia left in 1963—to return in 1965, and that for a brief period it seemed as though a rival organisation, based on the confrontationist notion of the " new emerging forces " might get under way.

As the organs of the United Nations have fallen under the sway of Third-World majorities and the Western Powers have found themselves a beleagured minority the charge has been laid by Western spokesmen that majorities are being used " irresponsibly " or that such developments as the exclusion of Taiwan, the granting of observer status to the Palestine Liberation Organisation, the " Zionism is racism " resolution or the politicisation of the Specialised Agencies represent the perversion of the original objectives of the organisation. But in making use of the majorities they command to pass resolutions that embody their own values and priorities the Third-World States are not acting differently from the way Western countries acted when they were in a comparable position. Moreover, in challenging some of the common conventions and practices evolved by the United Nations and its Agencies during the period of Western ascendancy, the Third-World countries are not to be taken to be opposing common conventions and practices of any kind. The challenge put forward by Third-World countries does raise a question as to whether, in the light of the greater diversity of values now represented within the organisation, a framework of common conventions and practices can be preserved. But the answer to this question depends not only on the policies pursued by the Third-World countries but also on those of the Western countries and the Soviet bloc.

It is sometimes argued that the insistence of Third-World States— or of those of them that are new and weak—on what appear to be near-absolute rights of State sovereignty, and a near-absolute duty of non-intervention in the internal affairs of States, obstructs the progressive development of international society towards a more centralised form of world order, or even that it threatens to undermine the development of international society that has already taken place, and to restore a more fragmented or anarchical international system in which the sense of common interests, rules and institutions will have disappeared or will have been reduced to a minimum. If each State is to have " full permanent sovereignty " over its natural resources and an absolute right to determine the size of its population, it may be asked, how can a common, international approach to the management of the world's population and resources ever be developed? If the goal of international economic justice is to be expressed in a doctrine of the economic rights of poor States that reserves entirely to those States the distribution of wealth transferred to those States among the individual human beings that compose them, how can progress take place towards such goals as a world minimum standard of welfare? Are not the present moves unilaterally to enclose the seas and in the course of this to undermine the old law of the seas without putting any agreed, universal law of the sea in its place—moves in which the Third World has played a leading, even if not an exclusive role—signs of a disintegration of international society brought about by new assertions of State sovereignty? To be sure, the Third-World States are not consistent in their insistence on the rights of sovereign independence: while they insist on these rights for themselves it is the duties rather than the rights of the rich, industrialised States of the West that they seek to emphasise: in the campaign against colonialism, white supremacist rule and the " old international economic order " it has been the Third-World States that have led the assult on appeals to " domestic jurisdiction." Can there, however, be any development of limitations on State sovereignty if the limitations to be accepted are one-sided and not reciprocal?

But if the Third-World countries appear to be obstructing the " progressive development " of international society, or even to be reversing such development as has already taken place, it has to be remembered that from their perspective such " progressive development " means only the further consolidation of their relations of dominance and dependence from which they are seeking to free themselves. From their perspective the first priority is to work for a redistribution of power favourable to themselves. For so long as they are asked to negotiate about the strengthening of international society from a position of weakness their attitude towards it seems likely to be a negative one. It is not clear, however, that this would remain so if they were to achieve positions of strength.

It is not merely with the rectification of their distinctive grievance about colonialism, " racism " and economic justice that Third-World countries are concerned, but also with the redistribution of power, including military power. Since the 1973 oil crisis, Third-World statements have given a new prominence to the idea that it is by achieving positions of strength, rather than by appeals addressed to their opponents, that their grievances can be rectified. There is much evidence that can be adduced—the wealth of the oil-producing Third-World countries, the advance of the " new industrial " countries of the Third World, nuclear and conventional arms proliferation, the development in a number of Third-World countries of indigenous arms industries, the emergence of some major Third-World States as " regional hegemones," the institutionalisation of the Third World as a coalition—to show that some element of redistribution of power towards Third-World countries has already taken place.

We do not know what the effects on international order of a further redistribution of power will be. If there is one thing about which the Third-World countries are deeply divided it is as to how power should be distributed among themselves. The rise of new centres of power, in the Third World as elsewhere, is bound to be unsettling in its effects on established international relationships. But it is possible that the shift of power towards Third-World countries will cause those countries that benefit from it to be less sensitive about the defence of their sovereignty and independence, and more willing to believe that an international society that is " progressively developed " could be one in which they too had a stake.[3]

III—THE EXPANSION OF INTERNATIONAL SOCIETY

Whether or not the Third World endures as a political coalition, and whether its goals are best seen as revolutionary or as reformist, the formerly European international society has become a global one and the consequences of this expansion will be with us for a long time to come.

At first sight this expansion of the State system or international society represents a triumph of European or Western political thought and practice. In the course of this century non-European peoples and movements have carried out a successful revolt against colonial rule and other forms of European domination, but the object of this revolt has been to establish political forms in a European or Western image. Where once there was a great variety of political entities—oriental dynastic empires, Islamic sultanates and emirates, tribal societies with and without elements of government— there is now, at least in formal terms, a single kind of political entity, the sovereign State, whose model is European. Where once there was contact and systematic interaction only as between political entities in some parts of the world and others now there is interaction— economic, political, strategic—over the world as a whole: the sovereign States that are now the uniform kind of political entity are involved with one another in a global international system, and this too has as its foundation the world-wide networks of communication, trade, investment and military power built up by the European countries. Where once there was no universal structure of rules and institutions to express the political unity or identity of mankind as a whole, and to regulate relations among independent communities on a global scale, there is now a universal international society whose bases are the international law, the diplomatic machinery, the political and military conventions and the international organisations first developed by the European States to regulate relations among themselves.

But there is some question whether this triumph of European political thought and practice is not more apparent than real. Is it

---

[3] See H. Bull, *The Anarchical Society: A Study of Order in World Politics* (1977), Chap. 13.

not the case that the rules and institutions of the global international society have only the shallowest roots outside the European or Western cultural areas in which they grew? Is there not evidence, in many parts of Africa, Asia and Oceania, that as the indigenous élites trained by the former European rulers are replaced by élites more representative of local populations, and as the decline of Western power and privilege brings in its wake a decline in the authority once commanded by Western ideas and practices, a process of reversion has set in to indigenous political ways? Was not the old European international society founded on a common, European culture which it has now outgrown? And can the global international society of today be said to rest on any common cultural foundation at all?

Adda Bozeman's *The Future of Law in a Multicultural World* states a powerful thesis about these questions.[4] Her argument is that despite the unifying surface of technological and rhetorical arrangements the world is and will remain multi-cultural. The West is bemused by the culture-transcendent schemes of international law and organisation it erected in 1919 and 1945; and the United States, founded as it is on the attempt to deny cultural differences, fails to take account of them in its view of the world. But the reality, in Bozeman's view, is that law is the unique product of Western culture. It is only in the West, in her view, that law is recognised as a category of thought distinct from others such as custom or religion, or that there exists the belief in a structured universe of knowledge, and in the significance of the individual person apart from the group, which the idea of law presupposes. Outside the Western cultural zone, she contends, there is no conception of the State as subordinate to law, no tradition of " constitutionalism " to set against the view that the State is simply an expression of power. Nor can there be found beyond the bounds of Western culture, she claims, any belief that relations among States can be subject to law: there is no general agreement in the world today about notions so fundamental to Western thinking about international relations as that law can be distinguished from policy or morality, that peace is different from war and is the normal and preferable condition, that independent and territorially delimited States should co-exist and are able to undertake voluntary and binding obligations.

Dr. Bozeman is especially critical of the assumption that in China or India or the Islamic countries or black Africa it is not the traditional culture that determines political behaviour today but the culture transferred from the West. Words can easily be transferred from one

---

[4] Adda B. Bozeman, *The Future of Law in a Multicultural World* (1971). Some of the themes are elaborated further in her *Conflict in Africa: Concepts and Realities* (1976).

cultural context to another, but ideas only with difficulty: there is a tendency, Dr. Bozeman makes out, to borrow a word and fit it to a thought, rather than to borrow a thought and fit it to a word. As when Buddhism was transferred from India to China, resulting in a purely Chinese form of Buddhism, so Dr. Bozeman finds the cultural borrowing that is alleged to have taken place from the West in other parts of the world today to be largely spurious, as much when this borrowing is from Marxism-Leninism as when it is from democratic liberalism. The Western social sciences, she claims, perceiving the end of tribalism in Africa, the emergence of democracy in Ghana, the establishment of federation in East Africa, have described the extra-European world in terms of the crushing of tradition beneath the steam-roller of a uniform process of " development." " Today,' she writes, " when the myth of sameness is fast evaporating, and the rhetoric of unity ceases to screen existing discords as to the meaning and purport of internationally crucial concepts, it is important to identify the configuration of each active culture and political system as authentically as possible, and to locate its major and most trusted terms of reference. . . . Such an exploration may at times become a quasi-archaeological activity; for layer after layer of accrued borrowings may have to be analysed before it becomes possible to distinguish the genuine from the counterfeit, the constant and indestructible from the merely passing." [5]

Dr. Bozeman's thesis is stated specifically in relation to law, but it may be applied to the rules and institutions of international society as a whole. It deserves a thorough investigation, and I do not pretend to offer one here. In such an investigation, however, three questions are crucial.

First, is it possible to accept the assumption that within human society there are a finite number of cultures, each of which has at its core something indestructible or immutable? The theory that the rules and institutions of international society are the peculiar property of a particular culture, and that they are more or less permanently beyond the grasp or outside the experience of other cultures, depends heavily on this assumption.

Dr. Bozeman herself does not make this assumption. By way of providing a definition of culture she writes that " one culture is distinct from others when there is evidence that generations of people in a given area or human grouping have been unified by virtue of holding to certain specific modes of thought, patterns of behaviour and vocabularies of preferred norms and values." [6]

---

[5] *Ibid.* p. 33.
[6] Adda B. Bozeman, " Do Educational and Cultural Exchanges have Political Relevance?" *International Educational and Cultural Exchange* (1969), p. 7.

Dr. Bozeman acknowledges that there are " syncretic cultures," or cultures that combine the traits of several cultural centres. She concedes that cultures do not spring full-blown from the head of Zeus, and that each is in some measure the product of external influences. She even writes that " a culture is never quite still or immutable, and that the processes of growth, mutation and decline are more likely than not to bear the imprint of cultural borrowings." [7]

If, then, a culture does not contain a core that is in the strict sense permanent and indestructible, there is at all events no reason in principle why European or Western rules and institutions of international society cannot be transferred to cultures that are different and display some capacity for resistance. Moreover, if European or Western culture itself has no core that is strictly permanent or indestructible, but is itself an amalgam of different cultural components and influences—Greek, Roman, Jewish, Western and Eastern Christian, French, German, liberal, socialist, with uncertain geographical and chronological boundaries, and a restless and shifting character—then the notion that international law is uniquely associated with it takes on a looser meaning.

Secondly, how dependent is international law (and how dependent are other rules and institutions of international society) on the existence of a common culture? The argument that international societies in the past have presupposed some elements of a common culture is familiar enough. [8] Where there exists a common intellectual culture—for example, a common epistemology and cosmology, some common languages and literature—then communication within international society will be easier than when there is not. Where there exist also common moral values, religion or ideology, then the bonds of common interest by which international society is held together may be reinforced by a sense of moral obligation.

But it is also familiar that even where elements of a common culture are clearly present, this does nothing to remove conflicts of interest; as every undergraduate knows, some of the most bitter wars have been fought among States or among civil factions whose culture is the same. Moreover, it would be difficult to show that rules of international law or diplomacy or conventions of warfare or trade cannot be made to operate across cultural barriers. In the absence of unified " modes of thought, patterns of behaviour and preferred norms and values," common rules are sometimes improvised as a consequence of a perceived interest on both sides in having them. The " rules of the game " improvised by the United States and the Soviet Union to promote the interest both perceive in avoiding

---

[7] *Ibid.*
[8] See *e.g.* M. Wight, *Systems of States* (1977).

nuclear war, are an example. Furthermore, such improvised rules, if and when they are observed for long enough, come to be reflected in common "modes of thought, patterns of behaviour and preferred norms and values ": it is in this way that common culture arises.

Thirdly, how far is it true that in the global international society of today there is no common culture? If, as we have recognised, cultures are not permanent and indestructible, and are complex and divisible, it will be possible to take the view that underlying the contrast of cultures at the present time there are elements of common culture. The extra-European world in its political behaviour has indeed proved recalcitrant to many aspects of what is called " the Western model " (which on closer inspection proves to be a particular Western model, or a series of particular Western models). There is, however, a process of economic and technological unification and homogenisation at work in the world, for which " modernisation " is a possible name.[9] While there is abundant evidence that this process is not bound to bring social and political unification or homogenisation in its wake, it would be facile to imagine that it can take place without affecting the cultures of the societies in which it operates: underlying these economic and technological processes there are scientific method, technique, some chosen goals, a pattern of ideas, a view of the world. It is wrong, I believe, to treat " modernisation " as another name for " Westernisation ": the processes to which we refer by the former name do not involve emulation of the whole range of goals pursued by the Organisation for Economic Co-operation and Development (OECD) or by the Soviet bloc countries; and they have now a momentum of their own in the world quite independently of the support provided for them by the Western States.

One element in the complex cultural pattern of world society today is therefore the cosmopolitan culture, the culture of " modernity." It is a culture of the élite rather than of the masses, and in many Third-World countries, of the élite exclusively. It embraces more than merely a knowledge of gadgets or techniques: it presupposes a view of the world. It is consistent, however, with a wide range of moral or philosophical or religious outlooks: it does not bring in its wake any common moral code. In many countries there are reactions against it, partly provoked by its own élitist character: the reversion to " traditionalism " in many Third-World countries, like the rise of nationalist separatism in Western countries, are in this way connected

---

[9] For a critique of Bozeman, made out in terms of the effects of industrialisation, see J. Mayall, " International Society and International Theory," in M. Donelan (ed.), *The Reason of States* (1978).

with it. Yet it is a basic factor at work in world politics at present, and it facilitates the working of international society and its rules. It seems likely to be at work for a long time to come. The reactions against it, in the Third World and elsewhere, are perhaps ways of coming to terms with its progress.

THE FUTURE
OF THE EUROPEAN COMMUNITY

By

ULRICH SCHEUNER

IN Western Europe following the Second World War, as it was shaped by the division of the continent and its own military and economic links with the United States, the conception and realisation of the European Community [1] was one of the major factors in European recovery. The Community has grown into one of the greatest units in world trade, and has begun to exercise some influence in international affairs. When the transitional period after the conclusion of the Treaty of Rome in 1957 ended in 1969, the Common Market had become a living reality exercising a considerable power of attraction within Europe and beyond its borders. Surely the far-reaching expectations that economic unity would intrinsically lead to some sort of federal cohesion, widely entertained by public opinion in the Federal Republic of Germany and in the Benelux States, but certainly not shared in France, found no fulfilment. The customs union was completed, a free exchange of goods and capital secured, but the Luxembourg agreement of the member States of January 29, 1966, showed clearly that national sovereignty still remained an important factor, and that the building-up of supranational authority in the Community had reached its limits. Nevertheless, a new step in the process of economic integration was envisaged at the end of the transitional period. It was resolved to go beyond a customs union with closer economic co-operation in the form of an economic and monetary union. On December 1 and 2, 1969, the Conference of the Heads of States and Governments at the Hague commissioned a report on an Economic and Monetary Union (EMU), and on March 22, 1972, the ensuing " Werner Report " was accepted by the Council and set into motion. This ambitious aim did not achieve realisation. The development of the European Community in the 1960s had taken place in the favourable atmosphere of expanding world production and trade. With the beginning of the 1970s, however, the European Community had to face a world-wide recession which restricted further progress and tended to strengthen divergent national tendencies. In 1973 the monetary system of Bretton Woods dissolved and the currencies of the member States

---

[1] The official title is " European Communities," but as the organisation is practically a single unit since the merger of 1967, the singular is preferred here.

of the Community took a different course. It is a familiar pattern of experience that in a time of economic difficulties national interests come to the fore. Under the influence of the recession, the economic policy of the various member States showed considerable differences which inevitably set an end to the realisation of a closer economic union. Some countries followed Keynesian doctrines and sought to overcome recession and unemployment by an inflationary course; others, among them the Federal Republic of Germany, followed, with a measure of success, a course of greater monetary stability. Under these circumstances the idea of monetary union practically evaporated.

The 1970s, therefore, brought to the European Community a period of relative stagnation. Two main events dominated its activity during the first part of these years: the consequences of the world-wide recession which led to a practical renunciation of the project of economic and monetary union, and the accession of the United Kingdom, Ireland and Denmark to the Community. As to the first fact, the Council of Ministers still resolved, in April 1973, the transition to the second phase of economic union,[2] but the replacement of an integrated monetary system by a régime of floating currencies made further progress impossible. The goal was never given up, and, as we will see, it has been recently re-emphasised. It may be that in the entire programme for European Economic and Monetary Union (EMU) the amount of unifying activity necessary for the promotion of the scheme had been underestimated. Without directives from the Community relating to national budgets and the conjunctural policy of member States—areas still regarded as the nucleus of national independence—and without some strengthening of the legal framework of the Community the intended union cannot be realised.[3] The powers given to the Community in the Treaty of Rome are ample for the conjunctural policy (Art. 103), but not so extensive for the field of economic policy (Art. 105), and the Community can exercise no influence in an area so fundamental for the direction of the economy as negotiations in the field of industrial relations.[4] Is it possible to achieve a common economic policy for

---

[2] Bull. E.C. 4/73, p. 9.

[3] On the legal and institutional problems of EMU, see my contribution to P. D. Dagtoglou (ed.), *Basic Problems of the European Community* (1975), pp. 66 *et seq.* and 71 *et seq.*, and in the same volume, J. A. Frowein, pp. 127 *et seq.* See further L. J. Brinkhorst in P. J. G. Kapteyn (ed.), *The Economic Law of the Economic and Monetary Union* (1976), pp. 13 *et seq.*

[4] As national economic policy becomes more and more dependent on trade union influence in most of the West European countries, this leaves a fundamental issue to the national decision process. See my observations in Kapteyn, *op. cit.* in n. 3, above, p. 63, n. 2. A change could only be expected from a transnational concertation of the parties of national bargaining on wages and incomes.

the States of the Community which does not make provision for measures of central agreement in this sensitive area?

The second important event of the early 1970s, the enlargement of the Community from six to nine members,[5] raised no institutional difficulties. The British personnel acceding to the staff and to the leading positions of the Community, as well as those coming from the two other new members, fitted easily in the existing organisation. One can even say that the British members in the European Parliament brought a fresh impetus to the growing self-assertiveness of the Assembly. However, it was clear that the enlargement of the Community brought no reinforcement of the movement towards supra-national development. The British population gave its approval to accession in the referendum of June 5, 1973,[6] but the British Government made it quite clear that it accepted the existing situation of a community of independent national States and did not envisage a development to a supra-national unity. A similar opinion is prevailing also in Denmark. In a letter addressed to the Secretary-General of the British Labour Party in September 1977, the Prime Minister, Mr. Callaghan, openly stated that the United Kingdom Government would not support any federal development, stressing a demand for the preservation of national sovereignty and a large amount of national autonomy. On the other side, the United Kingdom Government assisted the demand for increased democratic control within the Community.

The movement towards an economic and monetary union and the enlargement of the Community did not lead to an intensification of the integrative process. The movement of the Community in this period slowed down. But it would be unjust to underestimate the fact that there has been always a certain progress in some areas and, moreover, that in recent years the activities of the Community have grown through the methodical extension of the former policy in a number of new directions. The main fields of new developments were the strengthening of the Community in the domain of external commercial policy, the evolution of a regional and social policy and the emergence of a system of consultation and co-operation of the member States in their foreign policy. There was, on the other hand, the danger that the divergent economic attitudes of the member States during the recession might generate protectionist tendencies and even lead to a weakening of the common structures already built. Perhaps the greatest achievement of these years of recession has been that this danger did not materialise and that the Community has succeeded in holding its ground and continuing its movement

[5] Treaty of Accession of January 22, 1972.
[6] Ninth General Report on the Activities of the E.C., p. 306.

towards integration. This proves that the system of a Customs Union with strong central management and direction, which was created in the first 12 years of the Treaty of Rome, can subsist even over a period when no great advances towards a closer economic unity of the member States can be undertaken.

There has been no standstill in other directions. During recent years considerable attention has been given to the institutional problems of the Community and to the improvement of its functional structure. In the second half of the 1960s, after the Luxembourg agreement, the role of the Council of Ministers had won ascendancy over that of the Commission. Decisions were reached more by negotiation and bargaining between the representatives of the member States than by a common spirit transcending the national interest. The style of the Community changes from a dynamic advance on the lines of a common policy shaped by the Commission to a situation where, according to the Treaty, the initiative still stays with the Commission, but the adoption of measures by the Council of Ministers is slow and often the result of protracted and difficult negotiation. A first step to institutional reform was taken by the Budgetary Treaty of April 22, 1970, which reinforced the budgetary powers of the European Parliament at the moment when the Community won resources of its own. In the following years the organs of the Community commissioned studies on the evolution of a more efficient institutional framework. In 1971 a group of experts, under the direction of Georges Vedel, studied the possibilities of enlarged powers of the European Parliament and recommended the strengthening of the democratic element and control in the Community by an allocation of wider budgetary powers to the Parliament and by participation of the Assembly in important legislative measures.[7]

It stressed also the demand for general direct elections of the European Parliament according to Article 138 of the EEC Treaty. The report had no immediate results. A new impulse to institutional improvement was initiated by the mandate given to Prime Minister Tindemans of Belgium for a report on the European Union by the Conference of the Heads of States and Governments of December 11 and 12, 1974, in Paris. In his report Tindemans [8] defined the goal of a European Union not in a federal sense but as an economic force with an effective solidarity between its members and a common policy in economic, monetary and industrial matters as well as in its

---

[7] Report of the Working Party (Vedel Report) Bull, E. C. Supplement 4/72. See J. A. Frowein in P. D. Dagtoglon, *op. cit.* in n. 3, above, p. 127, n. 2 and in the same volume, Fuss, pp. 143 *et seq.*

[8] Bull. E.C. Supplement 1/1976. The report was transmitted to the Council on December 29, 1975. See this writer, " Perspektiven einer Europäischen Union " 11 *Europarecht* (1976) 193 *et seq.*

external relations. To strengthen the institutional framework the report proposed the determination of matters of general policy by the European Council as the leading organ for decisions relating to the Community as a whole as well as those concerning the political co-operation of its members. The Assembly should arrange for periodic debates on fundamental problems of the Community as a consequence of direct elections and as an expression of democratic legitimacy. It seems that the Tindemans report will share the fate of many such documents: to be approved, only to be shelved. Nevertheless, the value of such proposals should not be underestimated. They influence the direction of later evolution and form a useful bank of ideas for future development.

A decisive turning-point in the evolution of the institutional structure of the Community came with the decision of the Paris Conference of 1974 to institute general direct elections in 1978.[9] After difficult negotiations, the Council of Ministers reached agreement on the distribution of seats among the member States on July 17, 1976.[10] The relation between the main organs of the Community will be strongly influenced by this change. It is an open question whether an Assembly, elected directly will secure, with increased legitimacy, a stronger position within the Community.

At the present moment a second new problem of great importance for the future of the Community has arisen with the application of Greece, Portugal and Spain for membership. Politically, the affirmative attitude of the Community towards these new accessions, is more or less taken for granted.[11] But the time and the conditions of the accession remain an object of negotiation and are also open to the consequences which the enlargement would have on the whole economic and institutional structure of the Community. Both these coming events, the introduction of direct elections and the extension of the Community to the Mediterranean area, will exercise an important influence on the future of the Community.

With regard to future developments, we shall turn first to the main areas of the activity of the Community giving particular attention to those where a degree of progress has already been attained: for example, in the concentration of external economic policy in the hands of the organs of the Community. Turning to the institutional problems, the closer co-operation of the member States in matters of foreign policy is the most significant feature of recent years. It will be

---

[9] Bull. E.C. 12/1974, Nr. 12 of the communiqué of the Conference.
[10] Bull. E.C. 7–8/1976, Nr. 1101.
[11] In this sense, see the Marshall Plan Memorial Lecture, delivered by the President of the European Commission, the Rt. Hon. Roy Jenkins, at Bonn on June 3, 1977, and the debate in the European Parliament of October 12, 1977 (O.J. Supplement, Nr. 221, pp. 95 *et seq.*).

necessary also to consider the relationship between the organs of the Community as they presently exist and their future evolution. Here the consequences of direct elections to the European Parliament pose the most important problem. The life of the Community will be fundamentally influenced by its enlargement through the accession of the Mediterranean countries. This may deeply affect expectations concerning the further development of the Community. Finally, we shall have to give attention to the possible influence on the Community of internal changes in the politico-economic outlook and practice of member States. The European Community is increasingly being drawn into international discussions between the industrial Powers of the North and the developing countries of other parts of the world.

I—THE COMMON MARKET:
PROGRESS OF INTEGRATION

By the end of the transitional period in 1969 the main features of the Common Market had been established. The free exchange of goods, especially industrial products, and of capital had been guaranteed, while the agricultural market was organised on the lines of a strict regulation of prices and qualities. However, in some other areas such as admission to the professions and transport policy, the aims of the Treaty had not yet been fully realised. The mutual recognition of diplomas and certificates and the possibility of common organisations for the professions across the different countries advanced at only a slow pace. The market in agricultural products has taken a separate course. It did not follow the free-market principle, but showed a dirigistic orientation. Heavily subsidising the agricultural sector of the national economy, it became over the years a heavy financial burden to the community, while redistributing income among the member States on a considerable scale.[12] In recent years, efforts to implement a free market in industrial goods and capital have continued, but without promoting any substantial change. The foundations of a freely convertible currency system formerly built on stable currency relations between the member States were deeply affected by the monetary crisis after 1973, which left only a much reduced area of interrelated currencies in the form of the " snake," consisting of those of the Federal Republic, the Benelux countries and Denmark. The Community adapted to meet the situation, but some repercussions on the free flow of goods were inevitable. Meanwhile, the Community offered assistance in the form of substantial loans to countries struggling against unfavourable

---

[12] In the fiscal year 1976, the appropriations for agriculture in the budget of the Community amounted to 5·8 billion units of account (u.a.) out of a total expenditure of 8·9 billion u.a. See *Tenth Annual Report* 1976, p. 51.

trade balances and inflation. On the whole, the Community has so far succeeded in preserving the system of the Common Market. One can but hope that this will be possible also in the future.

In some areas of common policy, the advance is difficult and slow. The harmonisation of the tax systems of the member States is not made easier by the financial position of most of them. With regard to transport, a common policy can only be shaped to increase the flexibility of road transport and river navigation, whereas ports, shipping and aerial transport are so intimately connected with general international developments as to escape the regulation of the Community. The principle of the free movement of labour received significant reinforcement through a decision of the European Court of Justice which, invoking the principles of fundamental freedoms recognised in the member States, removed the requirements in law of a member State imposing regional limitations on the residence of a foreign worker.[13] In practical terms, however, only Italian workers make any substantial use of the freedom of workers to move to other countries of the EEC. Another area where slow progress can be observed, is the harmonisation of the laws of member States in matters which affect the functioning of the Common Market, the most important item here being the elaboration of European company law. In all these traditional fields of European activity, the future promises no dramatic break-through, but a continuous and patient process in which the existing structures are refined.

A new important advance towards economic integration can only result from a course of common political action, not to be expected during the present international stagnation and monetary instability. The resolution to enter into an Economic and Monetary Union, taken in 1972, has not been abandoned, but the international situation prevented any move in the direction of a uniform economic and conjunctural policy. It is important, however, to note that it was not legal obstacles which impeded the pursuance of closer economic integration. In the discussion over the measures necessary for the establishment of EMU, doubts were expressed whether the Treaty of Rome gave the Community sufficient legal powers for the imposition of the directives necessary for establishing control over the budgetary and economic policies of member States. The powers mentioned in Article 103 of the Treaty concerning conjunctural policy cover parts of the demanded unification, whereas Article 105 speaks only of a " co-ordination " of economic policy.[14] The question was raised as to whether the Community would need new

---

[13] Case 36/75 *Rutili* [1975] 17 C.M.L.R. 140; (1975) *Recueil* 1219.

[14] For those doubts see Everling, 11 *Europarecht* (1976) 16 *et seq.*: this writer in P. D. Dagtoglou, *op. cit.* in n. 3, above, pp. 70, 75; H. Maas, [1972] 9 C.M.L.R. 10 *et seq.*

and wider powers of control. The outcome of this debate, which was conducted in the early 1970s, has a great bearing on future developments. Many writers pointed to Article 235 of the EEC Treaty, which empowers the Council, if the objectives of the Treaty cannot be attained with the powers provided in it, to take the necessary measures and supply the powers. Article 235 is a provision common to international organisations but a legal way of augmenting the powers of the Community beyond the text of the Treaty and within the limits of its general aims, with particular reference to Articles 2 and 3. This authorisation is not unlimited, but is bound to the execution of the aims of the Treaty. Article 235 had already been applied in some cases before the 1970s.[15] A change was initiated in 1972, when the Paris Summit of the Heads of States and Governments recommended using the provision in its widest terms.[16] In recent years, Article 235 has served, therefore, in a wider range of cases as a basis for extending the work of the Community to new areas, such as the environment, research, energy, or the creation of a Regional Development Fund.[17] The result of this wider interpretation and application of Article 235 has given the Community greater freedom of movement in areas where its power was limited, together with new areas of activity. The importance of this Article is underlined by the expected unwillingness of member States to agree to alterations in the Treaty concerning allocation of powers. Thus far, the dynamic character of the legal institutions of the Community has been confirmed through this development.

If we look for areas in the activities of the Community where changes were more visible than in the traditional areas and where this tendency will probably continue in the future, one can point to four fields: Regional and social policy, development and a common commercial policy, especially *vis-à-vis* third countries.

Regional policy supports those regions in the countries of the Community which have lagged behind in their general development. It received a strong impulse in 1975 through the creation of a European Regional Development Fund.[18] Work is done mainly through assistance to national projects already receiving aid from national exchequers, and is concentrated on the infrastructure and industrial investment. The main recipients of assistance, the amount

---

[15] A survey of the regulations and directives of the Community applying Art. 235 is given by Everling, 11 *Europarecht* (1976), 22 *et seq.* It shows 16 cases between 1962 and 1968 and a further 78 up to 1975.

[16] Bull. E.C. 10/1972, pp. 15 *et seq.*, pt. 15. See Ehlermann, *Integration* (1971), p. 166; this writer in P. D. Dagtoglou, *op. cit.* in n. 3, above, p. 75; Everling, 11 *Europarecht* (1976) 6.

[17] To environment see Resolution of June 18, 1973, J.O. L. 189/43.

[18] Regulation 724/75 J.O. L. 73 of March 21, 1975.

of which was contested between Council and Parliament in December, 1977,[19] are Italy and Ireland.[20] The regional policy is still no more than a limited remedy to national regional problems, but it may further develop to provide limited equality in living standards between EEC countries in the future. Its importance will necessarily increase at the accession of the Mediterranean countries. Social policy supplements regional assistance in promoting vocational training, retraining schemes, housing and health protection.[21] Its role is likely to increase. The struggle against unemployment is still mainly a national responsibility. However, possible changes in the internal political outlook of some of the member States will probably have repercussions on this field of the Community's activity, and a greater influence of European parties in the European Parliament after direct elections will also reinforce the voices which are demanding a more active Community policy in social matters. A similar development can be expected in the field of development. Today, the considerable sums allocated for assistance to developing countries— 800 million u.a. in 1976 [22]—flow almost entirely to the 55 countries associated with the EEC through the Lomé Convention of February 28, 1975. These sums might rise if member States preferred to channel the aid presently donated through bilateral agreements, through the EEC. Also the very modest aid deployed to countries outside the Lomé area will certainly grow in the coming years. The policies of the Community which provide assistance to the weaker links within its own orbit, as well as to the developing countries, will gain in overall importance and occupy a higher place in the priorities of the Community.

An important extension of the powers of the Community has taken place in recent times regarding the external relations with third Powers. During the transitional period, the member States retained the right to enter into agreements of all sorts with the world outside the EEC. Since then the Community has gradually taken over responsibility for representation with third States, especially in commercial affairs. Generally, outside commercial policy, a judgment

---

[19] The heads of government fixed in December the amount of commitment appropriations to 580 million European Units of Account (EUA) and authorisations to 460 million EUA. The Assembly demanded sums of 750 million and 525 million EUA. After following the procedures according to Art. 203 EEC Treaty the final vote of the Parliament came to appropriations of 581 million for commitments and 525 million for appropriations for payments.

[20] See " European Regional Development Fund, First Annual Report," Bull. E.C. Suppl. 7/76, and " Community Regional Policy," Bull. E.C. Suppl. 2/77; Bull. E.C. 5/1977, Nr. 111.

[21] See, Annual Report E.C., p. 117; 10 *Annual Report*, p. 134.

[22] Bull, E.C. 3/1976, Nrs. 1104–1108. The allocation of means is carried out in relation with the United Nations, the World Bank and the International Development Association.

of the Luxembourg Court assigned to the Community exclusive treaty-making powers on the realisation of a common policy in the form of a common set of rules, even in cases where the EEC Treaty does not explicitly allocate such powers to the Community.[23] In the field of commercial policy, however, the external powers are provided explicitly in Articles 113 and 114 of the EEC Treaty without deference to any previous internal regulation. In recent years the Community has gradually superseded member States in its external relations, claiming an exclusive right to negotiate and conclude commercial conventions including also such arrangements as agreements on industrial co-operation and export credits.[24] Only in limited areas where its competence was not clearly established, has the Community entered into treaties in conjunction with the member States concerned. The external powers of the Community have been extended in other directions as well, including agreements with third countries on fishing rights and on the conservation of the resources of the sea.[25] Affirming this right the Council resolved in 1976 that member States should introduce an economic zone of 200 sea miles around their coasts in a pre-emptive move to adapt to the expected outcome of the Third United Nations Conference on the Law of the Sea.[26]

The widening role of the Community in its external relations is a function of its growing stature on the international economic scene. Increasingly, as one of the greatest entities in world trade, the Community is being drawn into discussions between the industrialised and developing States. The strengthening position of the EEC has led also to a change in the attitude of the East European Socialist States. For a long time they looked on the EEC with critical eyes. Now a growing interest in broadening the scope of economic and technological exchange with Western Europe has resulted in the tacit recognition of the existence of the EEC and the wish to enter into closer relations with it.[27] In September, 1977, the first official

[23] Case 22/70 E.R.T.A. (1971) 73 C.M.L.R. 335, and in 17 *Recueil* (1971), p. 263. See Donner in (1974) 16 C.M.L.R. 127 *et seq.*

[24] This practice was approved by the Court in its opinion 1/75 of November 11, 1975: see (1976) 17 C.M.L.R. 85; see also P. J. G. Kapteyn, " The Common Commercial Policy of the EEC," 11 *Texas International Law Journal* (1976), pp. 485 *et seq.*; see also H. H. Schümacher, 12 *Europarecht* (1977), pp. 26 *et seq.*

[25] The powers for this action derive from Articles 30, 37–47, EEC Treaty, and Article 102 of the Accession Treaty of January 22, 1972. The court recognised these powers in cases 3 and 4/76: see Kramer in (1976) 18 C.M.L.R. 440 and in *Recueil* (1976), p. 1279. The internal distribution of fishing grounds among the member States is still under debate; English demands for reserved zones around Great Britain have found resistance.

[26] Resolution of October 30, 1976, Bull. EEC 10–1976, Nr. 1503. Six member States acted accordingly and created a " European Economic Zone." See O. Rojahn, 19 *German Yearbook of International Law* (1976), p. 93; Bull. EEC 2–1977, Nr. 124, 125.

[27] See E. Schulz, *Moskau und die europäische Integration* (1977).

visit of a representative of the Council for Mutual Economic Assistance (COMECON) took place at Brussels.[28] Future developments may produce problems. Both the EEC and the individual East European States have a preference for bilateral conventions between the Community and each Eastern State. But the Soviet Union and the COMECON countries in concert may insist on the Eastern partner of the Community being COMECON itself.

The image of the Community in its earlier days was one of a dynamic movement. As we have seen, present efforts are rather directed towards the preservation of an open Common Market with only minor advances in new directions. In its present form, the EEC is no more than a customs union with strong elements of central direction. Is a substantial step towards closer integration possible in the immediate future? The President of the EEC Commission, the Rt. Hon. Roy Jenkins, returned to the theme of Economic and Monetary Union in October, 1977. He proposed as a first step the establishment of stable currency relations and a substantial increase of the resources available for regional adjustment.[29] Such an ambitious program, however, seems to exceed all realistic expectations, so long as deep differences of economic philosophy separate the European countries on such matters as economic policy, and their attitude towards inflation and budgetary deficits. Without greater uniformity in these fundamental issues a stable currency system is not attainable, as past events have shown.

The future may hold in store a difficult and testing time for the Community. If in some member States—Italy, for example—political change were to lead to far-reaching economic upheaval, the question could arise of whether the fundamental principles of the Rome Treaty had been affected. The EEC is founded on the model of a mixed economy with an open market system, free competition and private enterprise. A deviation from these lines, as laid down in the first articles of the Treaty, in some member countries would raise serious problems for the coherence of the Community.[30] One can but hope that the economic system of the EEC would survive such diversity in the economic orientation of its member States, which might in addition be reflected in the attitudes of the Parties of a directly elected Parliament. On the other hand, to the EEC falls the task of maintaining European co-operation even in such circumstances.

[28] On this first formal visit on September 21, 1977, see Bull. E.C. 9–1977, Nr. 1.2.1.

[29] Lecture at Florence on October 27, 1977, and further statements of the same content. See also the cautious paper of the Commission in the preparation for the session of the European Council of December 5 and 6, 1977: KOM (77) 620 (final).

[30] See my contribution in P. J. G. Kapteyn (ed.), *The Economic Law of the Member States in an Economic and Monetary Union* (1976), p. 49.

II—EUROPEAN POLITICAL CO-OPERATION

The slow pace of internal integration has been partially compensated in recent years by the evolution of closer political co-operation among the member States in foreign affairs. From a legal stand-point, this development lies outside the scope of the Treaty with its economic emphases; it is a complementary movement towards integration in the field of foreign policy. As economic affairs form an essential part of foreign relations in modern times, the interconnection of this new area of co-operation with the aims of the Community is very close. Proposals for co-operation in external politics were already being made in the 1960s (Fouchet Plans, I and II: 1961). The report, entrusted to Vicomte Davignon (at present a member of the Commission) by the summit of The Hague in 1969, renewed the idea, and the Conferences of the Heads of Governments and States at Paris in 1972 and 1974 established a European Union with regular meetings of the Heads of Governments as a European Council and of ministers of the member-governments. At first these meetings were kept separate—even in the choice of venues—from those at which the same individuals met as an organ of the Community. Today, meetings of the European Council are linked to meetings within the Community; the difference lies in the fact that the first kind of meeting is prepared through diplomatic channels, the latter by the Commission.[31]

The introduction of European political co-operation enables the Nine to agree on a common approach to some of the problem areas of foreign policy like the conflict in the Middle East. In the case of South Africa a common " code of conduct " has been elaborated for industrial holdings. Accord is not always found; sometimes a member State, especially France, prefers to act independently. The effect of this co-operation has been to elevate the stature of the Community in world politics. Political co-operation has extended to important international conferences—like those at Helsinki in 1975 and Belgrade in 1977—where the States of the Community spoke with one voice; it has led to common action within the framework of the United Nations and its General Assembly.[32]

III—INSTITUTIONAL PROBLEMS:
DIRECT ELECTIONS TO THE EUROPEAN PARLIAMENT

It has been argued that the negative influence of the prevailing world economic crisis outrules for the present the possibility of a significant advance towards closer European economic union. It is even doubtful

---

[31] See H. Portelli in *Pouvoirs*, Nr. 2 (1977), pp. 137 *et seq.*

[32] On the co-operation of the Nine within the United Nations and at the General Assembly, see B. Lindemann, *Die EG-Staaten und die Vereinten Nationen* (1978).

whether at the present time a forward move would receive sufficient support from either governments or public opinion in some member States. The enlargement of the EEC in 1972 in no way strengthened the cause for closer institutional or economic cohesion. After the referendum of 1975, the European membership is now officially accepted by the major parties of the United Kingdom Parliament if not necessarily by every Member of Parliament, but the general feeling in the United Kingdom is less in favour of closer integration than of retaining the present state of relative national independence in economic policy.[33] In recent years member States have also shown a marked tendency to give priority to their national interests in the Brussels deliberations. If there is no other strong dynamic within the Community for innovation, two important questions have already arisen which will demand new decisions and adaptations in its institutional and economic structure: the resolution to hold direct elections to the European Parliament in 1979, and the request for membership from the three Mediterranean countries of Greece, Portugal and Spain. At first sight, these two events point in contradictory directions. The direct elections raise expectations of an Assembly with strengthened democratic legitimacy becoming a new force of integration. On the other hand, a new Community of 12 members brings not only economic problems with regard to its agrarian and regional policies, but would also seem to lead to inevitable difficulties in its institutional structure. For an evaluation of the future of the Community, both these changes demand full attention. We shall turn first to direct elections which must be considered from the stand-point of their effect on the whole organisational infrastructure of the EEC. We need to look first at the existing relations between the main organs of the Community which have moved away from the original conception of their functions. Since the beginning of the 1970s, several studies have been undertaken aimed at producing proposals for a better functioning of the organisation of the EEC [34] but the only results have been to strengthen certain budgetary powers of the Parliament.

The Treaty of the Coal and Steel Community and the Treaty of Rome gave the Commission an essential role of initiative and decision-making. It is no wonder that the supporters of a federal Community regarded the Commission as the decisive organ, comparable to a European government. But events took another course. The task of uniting the member Governments to common action transferred the ultimate decision to the Council of Ministers, which

---

[33] See a speech of the United Kingdom Foreign Secretary, D. Owen, to deputies of the Labour Party at Brussels on February 6, 1978.

[34] The Vedel Report of March 25, 1972, Bull. E.C. Suppl. 4/72; Report of Belgian Prime Minister Tindemans of January 7, 1976, Bull. E.C. Suppl. 1/76.

became the leading organ of the EEC. Since the Luxembourg agreement of January 29, 1966, transition to a majority vote was set aside [35] and the working process of the Council came nearer to a negotiation between national interests than to a decision representing a common spirit. Today the decisive role of the Council is firmly established. A decision of 1974 limited the degree of unanimity necessary in minor matters. The meetings of the Council which summons in turn the ministers of different departments (for example, agriculture, economic affairs, finance), are prepared by the national representations of the member States at Brussels. Their heads, assembled in the Committee of Permanent Representatives (COREPER), seek to reach agreement before the session. If they succeed, the Council proceeds simply with formal adoption. If they cannot find a solution, deliberation and negotiation ensue in the Council. The Council is responsible for decisions relating to legislation and other legal acts of the Community. It regulates the budget, now with the growing participation of Parliament. The Council is often blamed for its slow pace, its readiness to allow bargaining between national interests, and its failure to adopt many of the Commission's proposals. However, so long as the member Governments defend their national interests and have to take the responsibility for common decisions before national, elected legislatures—and will that change with the introduction of direct elections to a European Assembly?—the leading position of the Council and the character of its deliberations will be preserved. The Community is not a federation with unified supranational powers of decision, but a looser form of co-operation which works through an evolving process of negotiating for unity.

The Commission, with its exclusive powers of legislative initiative and its recently enlarged brief to implement decisions, retains a peculiar and strong position exceeding that of the secretariat of an international organisation. But it has lost in stature over the years; many of its proposals are rejected by the Council, and the massive bureaucracy whose head it is, enjoys no visible popularity with public opinion. Nevertheless, the Commission and its big technocratic machine are still a strong driving force within the Community, responsible for the continuous elaboration of the EEC Treaty, its defence and the minor advances noted earlier. Every proposal for reform needs therefore to take account of this role of the Commission.

The organ of the Community which comes closest now to the initial concept of supranationalism, is the Court of Justice of the European Communities. One must not forget that important

---

[35] The legal conformity of the Luxembourg decision is in doubt. See Bellanger, *Nederlands Tijdschrift voor international Recht* (1968), p. 179; and H. Mosler 26 *Zeitschr. f. ausländ. öffentl. Recht u. Völkerrecht* (1966), p. 1.

extensions of the legal powers of the Community, the recognition of
the primacy of European legal enactments over national law,[36] the
application of European legal enactments within the legal systems
of the member States,[37] the constructive interpretation of Article 235
of the EEC Treaty, the elaboration of general principles of law
common to the European States (such as the recognition of fundamental rights), are due to the dynamic case law of the European
Court. This is now the bastion of supranationalism within the
Community; it embodies a dynamic judicial system as initally
conceived in the EEC Treaty.[38] Hitherto the work of the European
Court has progressed smoothly, but there could develop in the future
a certain gap between a strong affirmation of integration in the
Court and the more reserved attitude of some member States towards
any supranational trend.

The question further arises of whether the introduction of general
direct elections strengthens the position of the European Parliament
among the other organs of the Community. This is the hope of those
who support the implementation of Article 138, paragraph 3 of the
Treaty. In recent years the Parliament could extend its influence,
especially in budgetary matters, but its overall position remains weak.
The Community was founded by governmental actions and grew up
with the focus on bureaucratic apparatus at Brussels. To the Assembly,
which is regarded as a source of parliamentary legitimation, the
Treaty ascribes only powers of consultation and control (Article
137). ¡The Parliament is consulted in legislative matters, when the
Commission has sent its proposals to the Council, but it takes no
part in the later discussions between Council and Commission and
the ensuing alterations of the draft.[39] To a limited degree the Parliament participates now in the regulation of the budget, where its
powers have been extended by the budgetary treaty of April 22, 1970,[40]
and the treaty of July 22, 1975.[41] The draft budget is prepared by

[36] The primacy of Community law over municipal law has been formulated in the
Case 6/64, *Costa/ENEL*, 10 Recueil (1964), p. 1159. See P. J. G. Kapteyn and P.
Verloren van Themaat, *Introduction to the Law of the European Communities* (1973),
pp. 26 *et seq.* This doctrine is now accepted by the municipal courts of the member
States. See P. Pescatore, *The Law of Integration* (1974), pp. 33 *et seq.* and 94 *et seq.*

[37] Case 2/62, *van Gend & Loos*, 1963 *Recueil* p. 23; Case 29/72, *Marimex*, 1973
C.M.L.R. 476; 18 *Recueil* 1309; Case 87/75 *Bresciani*, (1976) 18 C.M.L.R.; 62 *Recueil*
(1976), p. 129. See R. Riegel, 102 *Archiv d. öffentlichen Rechts* (1977), pp. 411 *et seq.*

[38] Description of this judicial role is given by H. P. Ipsen, *Europäisches Gemein-
schaftsrecht* (1972), pp. 131 *et seq.*, and P. Pescatore, *op. cit.* in n. 36, above, at pp. 71
et seq. and 83 *et seq.*

[39] The Assembly wishes a second consultation if essential alterations of the draft
occur after its first deliberation by the Assembly.

[40] 2 J.O. L., of January 2, 1971, p. 1.

[41] See regarding these alterations, G. Strasser, 18 *Revue du Marché Commun* (1975),
pp. 75 *et seq.*; Anonymous, 19 *Revue du Marché Commun* (1976), pp. 277 *et seq.*

the Commission,[42] approved by the Council and placed before the Parliament. The Assembly can propose modifications which the Council can reject with a qualified majority. In a second deliberation the Assembly may carry the modifications with a vote taken by the absolute majority and three-fifths of the members present. For those expenditures which are not obligatory under the Treaty or other legal commitments,[43] the Parliament can increase the amount of the appropriations within the limit of a maximum rate of increase fixed annually by the Commission. In recent times the Council, Commission and Parliament have instituted a conciliation procedure for overcoming differences between them in the budgetary process.[44] This procedure may be adopted more generally for acts with considerable financial implications. The treaty of 1975 confirms the right of the Parliament to reject the whole of the budget and to ask for a new draft. Such a vote of no-confidence is an ultimate restraint, to be applied only in extreme cases.

The Parliament has achieved some slight improvement of its position in other directions. The President of the Commission reports regularly before the House on the work of the Commission with an ensuing debate. The Council accepts written questions from the members of the Assembly—who make full use of this opportunity —and answers them. In some cases the Assembly has expressed its feeling of neglect at the hands of the Commission through a motion for a vote of censure against it according to Article 144 of the Treaty of Rome.[45] The Assembly has further entered freely into discussions on questions of the external policy of the Community, such as the European-Arab dialogue, the preparation of the Helsinki Conference, the protection of human rights, Cyprus, or the North-South negotiations over a new international economic order.[46] In general, the Parliament has been able to extend its consultative activity in some directions, but, except in the budgetary field, it has not been able to win the right to participate in decision-making. Recommendations in the Vedel Report to provide the Assembly with decision-making powers in conjunction with the Council on essential legal questions, have borne no fruit. The question arises as to whether

[42] From January 1, 1978, the budget is established in the new European unit of account (EUA), created in 1975. See Bull. E.C. 7/8–1975, Nr. 2407, 2423, and J.-Ch. Leygues, 18 *Revue du Marché Commun* (1975), pp. 190 *et seq.*
[43] The non-obligatory expenditure forms a small part of the total amount of appropriations.
[44] Joint declaration of the three organs of March 4, 1975: 89 J.O. C. of April 22, 1975, p. 1; also, 9 *General Report of the Community*, p. 14.
[45] The motions were either rejected (as on June 16, 1976 J.O. 1976, Annexe 204, p. 123) or withdrawn (as on December 16, 1976, J.O. 1976, Annexe 210, pp. 8, 135 and 298); see also Bull. E.C. 6–1976, Nr. 2411, and 12–1976, Nr. 2403.
[46] Examples of such debates in 1976, in J.O. Annexe 202, p. 164; Annexe 204, p. 51, and Annexe 207, p. 155.

direct elections will so strengthen the position of the Parliament as to enable it to overcome the silent resistance of the Council of Ministers against an extension of its decision-making powers.

Since other recommendations for alterations in the functions of the leading organs of the Community have produced no results, the demand for direct elections to the European Parliament, supported in Article 138, paragraph 3 of the Treaty of Rome, offered the last possibility for institutional reform. A draft was worked out by the Parliament in 1975,[47] and after long debates on the distribution of seats among the member States—the distribution must give stronger representation to the smaller countries than the size of their populations would allow—the Council decided this question on July 13, 1976, and issued an Act concerning the elections by direct, universal suffrage on September 20, 1976.[48] This resolution demanded approval by the Parliaments of the member States and this was given in all countries.[49] It left the determination of the electoral system to national legislatures. The majority of these decided on a system of proportional representation, but in the United Kingdom the House of Commons decided on December 13, 1977 to use the traditional majority vote in single-member constituencies.

Some of the supporters of direct elections entertain great hopes that a more democratic, and consequently legitimised, Assembly will bring a new impetus to integration. I can share this opinion only with some reservations. Surely, direct universal suffrage will bring to the Assembly increased legitimation. If one examines the entire administrative framework of Community, the change will not be so visible. The leading organ, the Council of Ministers, draws its legitimation from the responsibility of the national governments to their own legislatures, and not from its position in relation to the European Parliament. This is operating as an indirect democratic foundation, analogous to a government concluding international agreements or the actions of the *Lander* governments in the *Bundesrat* of the Federal Republic of Germany.[50] The position of the Council is not immediately affected by the changed mode of the elections. The Parliament exercises no decisive influence on the major acts and resolutions of the Community. Its improved democratic basis will be of real importance only if the Assembly is able to acquire wider powers of decision-making or shared decision-making.

---

[47] Bull. E.C. 1–1975, Nr. 2501.

[48] J.O. 1976, L. 278, pp. 1 and 5. The distribution of seats is the following: The United Kingdom, France, Italy and Federal Republic of Germany each 81; Netherlands 25, Belgium 24, Denmark 16, Ireland 15, Luxembourg 6: Total 410.

[49] The last consent came on November 24, 1977 from the United Kingdom Parliament.

[50] On the question of legitimation, see P. Chr. Müller-Graff, *Die Direktwahl des europaischen Parlaments* (1977).

A positive effect of direct elections is the impulse they give the national parties for the creation of unified European parties. The Socialists came first (1974), the Christian-Democrats, the Liberals, the Conservatives, the Communists and some minor parties followed. Such a transnational reunion of the political forces of Europe can be regarded as a remarkable advance in European integration. Likewise, direct elections will bring the average citizen for the first time into immediate touch with European problems. It is widely held that a Parliament, supported by a direct popular mandate, will claim and win larger powers within the Community. Indeed, this provides the Parliament with an opportunity. It may try to obtain a share in essential decision-making with the Council—without weakening the responsibility of national ministers in the Council—and strive for a better means of control. Such changes will not be achieved without considerable effort. The important economic, financial and political decisions in the Community are taken by the ministers of the national governments with a view to their domestic responsibility to a national Parliament. The European Parliament cannot supersede this connection, the more so, as its political composition may differ from that of the national Chambers. It remains to be seen how far it will succeed in extending its powers. A serious obstacle for the European Assembly has consisted in its geographical distance from the adminstrative centre. The Assembly has met either at Strasbourg or at Luxembourg; only the committees meet sometimes at Brussels. To alter the situation is not easy, given the interests of France and Luxembourg. A continuation of this wandering existence, however, will weaken the position of the Parliament.

IV—THE ACCESSION
OF THE THREE MEDITERRANEAN COUNTRIES

The other development of the coming years, the entrance of three new members into the Community, will exercise a profound effect on the entire economic and social orientation as well as structure of the Community. The EEC will accept as members, States with a lower level of industrial development, and will consequently encounter considerable problems of adaptation and regional assistance. The increase of member States to 12 raises institutional issues for Commission and Council which are difficult to solve. An examination of the three applications of the years 1975–77 [51] from a purely economic point of view would have led to a cautious response.[52] However, the

[51] The applications for membership came from Greece on June 1975, from Portugal on March 18, 1977, and Spain on July 28, 1977. See Bull. E.C. 6–1975, Nr. 1201, 3–1977, Nr. 1.1.1, and 7/8–1977, Nr. 1.1.1. A discussion of the problems involved is to be found in 32 *Europ-Archiva*, Nr. 19 (1977), pp. 617 *et seq.*

[52] This is the impression one gains from " The Opinion on Greek Application for Membership," a report of the Commission of July 29, 1976, Bull. E.C. Suppl. 2/1976.

question of the accession was put to the Community in a predominantly political context. All three countries—Greece, Portugal and
Spain—have recently returned to a democratic régime and their
governments expect to gain political stability and economic aid from
membership of the EEC. The decision relating to their acceptance
was therefore a political one, as the United Kingdom Foreign
Secretary, Mr. Owen, put it, " historically inevitable and politically
desirable." [53]

The economic problems are easy to discern. The *per capita* income
of the three Mediterranean States is lower than in the EEC countries.[54]
A larger part of the population is still employed in agriculture. In
addition, the major agricultural products of these countries—wine,
citrus fruits, olive oil—raise serious problems for the agrarian
market. The Treaty of Rome includes the free movement of workers.
This could lead to migration problems, particularly in the light of the
high unemployment in the Iberian peninsula. Moreover, in the
background, there are also the former assurances given to Turkey
with regard to the admission of workers. Beyond these specific problems, the fundamental orientation of the Community will change.
From an association of highly industrialised States, it will become
an organisation which includes developing industrial States and gives
them assistance. The trend, begun with the chain of associations and
the Lomé Treaty, will extend in a new direction. No doubt, that
regional policy will have to play a considerable role. Under these
circumstances closer economic integration recedes into the background. On the other hand, the enlargement opens the greater part
of the Northern shore of the Mediterranean to the EEC and confirms
it as the dominant factor on the European scene.

Great difficulties are encountered in terms of the institutional
structure of the Community. The Commission cannot be extended
to 16 members without losing its efficiency and cohesion. The
question is whether the four leading States will relinquish their
second representative. In the Council of Ministers the increase is
inevitable, making the process of reaching agreement even more
cumbersome. Finally, some rationalisation of the language problem
must be envisaged. Already today, the percentage of headquarters
staff employed in the linguistic service is extremely high. However,
the Community has to answer the new challenge and even if its
general orientation changes in the direction of care for weaker
economies, this is a role which the Community will eventually have
to fulfil in a wider trans-European sphere.

---

[53] Speech at Brussels on February 8, 1978.
[54] In 1973 the average income in the EEC was over 3000 United States dollars, in
Greece 1790, Spain 1750, and Portugal 1250. See *op. cit.* in note 52, above, p. 23.

V—Prospects for the Future

In a final evaluation of the future development of the European Community, it seems appropriate first to underline its historic destination in post-war Europe. Conceived as a means of promoting reconciliation between former adversaries of the Second World War through economic co-operation, the institution has grown into an efficient economic unit, the nucleus of European recovery. The political division of Europe limited its activities to Western Europe, but the economic results of European co-operation are also attracting rising interest in the socialist States. Together with the Organisation for Economic Co-operation and Development (OECD) the Community has united the economic forces of the major industrial countries in Western Europe, created an open market for industrial goods, and—with much more central dirigism—for agrarian goods. The enlarged economic entity established by the EEC stimulated trade between the European countries and enhanced the welfare of all peoples of the area. The Community has helped to overcome past antagonisms, and has given to the inhabitants of Western Europe the feeling of living in a larger open society where a free movement of persons and ideas across borders is assured. The nations of Europe remain and wish to preserve their independence, but the old exclusiveness of the nation-State is weakened and, at least on the continent, the sense of a common destiny is appearing. To the external world the Community represents the industrial and commercial power of Europe. The common spirit, so much hoped for by the founders of the European Communities, has not extinguished national egoism, but the need to co-operate for the common benefit of all has found recognition. In the present economic crisis, with its strong temptations for protectionist practices and national separatism, the Community has maintained the open market and withstood disruptive tendencies. This alone is a great achievement. The existence and continuation of the Community is deeply rooted in the economic and political realities of contemporary Western Europe. The need to maintain and develop it further in the direction of a specific economic and political union is now recognised by all its members as well as by those West European countries which—for different reasons—have not acceded to it. Any crisis in the Community would have a disrupting effect for the whole of Western Europe. So it seems that the Community is now an established factor of the present European order.

It is necessary to look on the Community and its future realistically. Some of the great ideas and expectations which accompanied the work of Brussels at its inception have not been realised, and its development in the foreseeable future will be limited. In the Federal Republic of Germany and in the Benelux countries, the European idea is still widely connected with the conception of a European federation, a " *Bundesstaat* " as an ultimate goal.[55] This expectation no longer corresponds to reality. Even if the French Assembly has refrained from legislating to prevent direct elections leading to a substantial increase in the powers of the European Assembly, it is clear that the retention of national sovereignty and a consequent resistance to federal structures are cardinal principles of French policy. The British Prime Minister and some of his colleagues have bluntly stated that they do not envisage a development of the Community into a federation. The ideal of a federation of Western Europe will continue to be cherished in the Federal Republic of Germany [56] and elsewhere, but under the present conditions it is a question for the remote future rather than one of practical politics. While all member States accept that the Community may acquire new powers, the term " confederation " would appear to be the only appropriate concept from the tradition of political science to apply to it. It is probably better to avoid all the familiar descriptions of national or international law, and to recognise that the Community has to be understood on its own specific merits. From the beginning one characteristic feature of the Community was its dynamic character. It is an organisation with an inbuilt tendency towards integration beyond the constraints of the actual situation. Even now, when the process of integration has slowed down, the organisation is still on the move. As one point in the process of integration is reached, new tasks are undertaken: geographical growth is imminent. I have never shared the opinion that without constant advance the present achievement of the Community would be endangered. The experience of past years has shown that the Community can experience a period of relative stagnation without damage. The structure of the Community transcends a mere inter-governmental co-operation. There are central organs, the Commission, the Court of Justice and the Parliament, which represent transnational common interests and whose initiatives and actions form a general element.

The coming years will bring to the Community a number of new and important tasks and challenges. The accession of three Mediterranean countries, besides promoting the idea of economic aid to the weaker regions and encouraging social and economic adjustment between members at different stages of development, will also provoke a new debate on the Common Agricultural Policy, which has become a heavy burden to the Community. Today, the costs of the

[55] In his report, Belgian Prime Minister Tindemans speaks of " *le chemin de l'unification de l'Europe.*"
[56] A leader of the European movement strongly insists on the final aim of federation. See W. Hallstein, *Die Europäische Gemeinschaft* (1973), pp. 364 *et seq.*

agrarian policy amount to two thirds of the whole budget of the Community. However, strong vested interests in France and Italy stand in the way of a fundamental review. The agrarian problem will therefore accompany the Community into the next period. The greatest challenge faced by the Community in the coming years lies in another direction. The Common Market grew up at a time when the fundamental economic principle of a free market economy was accepted in all member States. More recently, socialist criticism has sometimes castigated the Community for espousing this economic philosophy and demanded greater commitment to social ends. The reproach is heard that the Community should be more active in the struggle against unemployment. In this particular respect, I believe the criticism to be unjust. So long as the member States stick to national decisions in their economic and monetary policy, the main responsibility for employment and investment must remain at the centres of decision. Meanwhile, internal political change may lead in the future to greater differences in the fundamental issues of economic and social policy between member States than in the past. The question also arises of majority opinion in the directly elected European Parliament. The Community may find itself challenged in some of its fundamental principles in the coming years. It may have to hold together States with a wider spectrum of economic orientation than formerly, and some changes in its own orientation may result. On the other hand, until now the system of social security has been an eagerly guarded domain of national politics.

The co-operation of member States in the domain of external policy—European Political Co-operation—is a development outside the legal framework of the Treaty. It has been an outstanding feature of recent years and will tend to grow in importance in the future. As the Community takes over the representation of its members in external commercial affairs and participates in negotiations and conferences, it is drawn into the international scene. Some of the tasks it faces, like that of pursuing a common energy policy, can only be performed through negotiating with the oil-producing countries and the United States. The policy adopted by the United States in the Nuclear Non-Proliferation Act (1978) [57], directed towards the firmer control of the peaceful uses of nuclear technology to prevent its use for military purposes, has important repercussions on the European countries, their nuclear policy and their export of nuclear technology. The Community, therefore, will continue to enact its role on the international stage. On the other hand, the limits of its activities are clearly discernible. The European nations will co-

---

[57] Nuclear Non-Proliferation Act (1978), *Public Law* 95–24L, 95th Congress of March 10, 1978. Text in I.L.M. (1978), p. 397.

operate, but will retain their position as independent States with the ability sometimes to take their own independent course.

The political co-operation of the member States will further be limited to matters of economic and foreign policy. Suggestions, which come from time to time, to extend this co-operation to questions of defence, seem to me to be unacceptable. The political evolution of Europe since the Second World War has produced different organisational structures for defence on the one hand, and for economic and political co-operation on the other. This division must be preserved because it makes possible the fostering of relations between the Community and the East European States as well as with the countries of the wider world. It is sufficient that the Community, by its sheer existence, contributes to the peace in Europe.

The difficulty of reaching unity in the central organs of the Community and the slowness of their procedure, has provoked recent proposals that *some* members of the EEC might be able to make their own separate progress towards a limited form of integration. The idea of two different levels of integration, however, has met with heavy criticism. The enlargement of the Community may reinforce a certain tendency on the part of the larger countries to seek arrangements amongst themselves as a preliminary to general discussions. Such meetings with restricted participation have encountered the resistance of the smaller countries. Sometimes, even the sheer economic weight and stability of the Federal Republic of Germany has produced an impression of imbalance in the minds of others. The equal participation of all members in decision-making is an essential principle of the European Community. It precludes any institutional development which would recognise the pre-eminence of some members. It does not exclude factual solutions which will be elaborated after an enlargement of the Community.

As we have already seen, the European Community now forms a settled institution and a constituent part of the European order. The limits of its aims and its immediate potential are more clearly recognisable than in former times when wide expectations were entertained. Europe continues to exist as a family of independent nations, but the Community now embodies the united strength of many of the nations of Western Europe. The European movement retains a dynamic element; it seems capable of meeting new challenges and of coping with the new tensions evolving within the social and political life of Western Europe. Looking to the future, it therefore seems probable that the European Community will continue to play a role of primary importance in the next period of European history.

E.E.C.
AGRICULTURAL POLICY

By

GAVIN STRANG

IT was inevitable for a variety of reasons that, if the Six[1] were serious in their intention to set up a customs union and common market,[2] agriculture could not be excluded, and would have a prominent part to play, if only by virtue of the importance of food products in the cross-frontier trade which was to be liberalised, and the complexity of the task of removing the barriers to free trade in food products compared with that of achieving free trade in the industrial sector—a complexity which stemmed largely from the extent and variety of support and protection methods in the Member States. In addition, the nature of international trade in foodstuffs made it necessary from the start for the European Economic Community (EEC) to set up a single agricultural trading policy towards the rest of the world.

I—THE AGRICULTURAL POLICY: ONE OF MANY COMMON POLICIES

The social and political importance of agriculture to the Six has certainly been a factor in making the Common Agricultural Policy the dominant feature of the Community. But it is perhaps well to recall that it was by no means the intention of the founders of the Community that its Common Agricultural Policy should become, and least of all, remain the centrepiece of effort—and expenditure—that it now is.[3] This development is a paradoxical one, for, while it

---

[1] The Six: The six countries—France, the Federal Republic of Germany and Italy and the Benelux countries Belgium, the Netherlands and Luxembourg—which formed the European Economic Community and Euratom instituted by the Treaties of Rome, signed in 1957. Discussions and negotiations which formed the basis of the Treaty of Rome establishing the EEC had taken place since 1955.

[2] Customs union: removal of trade barriers and the adoption of a common external tariff (common customs tariff): completed simultaneously on July 1, 1968 (18 months ahead of the schedule laid down in the Treaty). Common market: removal of all unnecessary restrictions on the movement of goods, people and resources; elimination of discriminatory conditions; common agricultural market, with common market organisation.

[3] The proportion has declined with the advent of embryonic regional, social and other spending policies. The 1970 EEC budget provided for agricultural expenditure of 3,049,224,680 units of account (u.a.) out of a total budget of 3,255,816,438. Agriculture took up 72·9 per cent. of the 1975 and 64·97 per cent. of the 1976 budgets, totalling respectively 6,268,300,000 u.a. and 8,470,609,608 u.a. (Net EEC farm expenditure as percentage of EEC gross domestic product has remained at around 0·3 per cent. to 0·4 per cent. since 1973.)

has helped to bring the agricultural policy into disrepute, it reflects more the failure of the Community to adopt or develop common policies in other fields specified or implied by the Treaty of Rome (notably economic and monetary policies), than it does its failure to deal with the problems of agriculture.

II—THE ONLY COMMON POLICY

Indeed, some of the more intractable difficulties that have beset the Community's agricultural policy in recent years have stemmed directly from a divergence in national economies and economic policies which is quite at variance with the assumptions made about the degree of future integration by the authors of the Treaty and the framers of the agricultural policy.[4] It is easy to forget that the establishment of a Common Agricultural Policy (CAP) was welcomed on the widest political grounds by those, both outside and inside the Community, who wished for a more united Europe, as a bold and serious attempt by the Six to meet a considerable challenge. It is debatable indeed whether the Six would have been able to make worthwhile progress in other fields had they not gone ahead with an agricultural common market—and it is arguable that, whatever the merits and demerits of the arrangements that they made for dealing with agriculture, the fact of politicians and officials being forced to continue to work hard at and within the only truly integrated EEC policy has virtually kept the Community from falling apart at various times of stagnation and crisis.

III—SETTING UP THE CAP:
NO EASY TASK FOR THE SIX

There has been a tendency when looking at the Six from Britain to think of their agricultures as considerably more homogeneous than they in fact were when the EEC agricultural policy was set up. There were important features which the Six had in common with each other and with all West European agricultures, notably the large numbers of people engaged in agriculture and its corollary, the small average size of holdings, and the degree and general methods of protection and support. But there were significant differences in the structure and very important differences in price levels: each of the Six had a quite distinct agricultural " profile " (see Tables 1 to 4).

---

[4] The Treaty is for the most part unspecific about the content of several policies to which it refers in the broader economic and social fields, being more concerned with the abolition of barriers to integration. It was widely assumed, for instance, that the achievement of free trade would of necessity be accompanied by efforts to co-ordinate economic and social development; and that the pricing arrangements adopted in the Common Agricultural Policy would make monetary co-operation essential.

It is also worth remembering that the Six's protective systems had worked as much against each other as against imports from elsewhere. In more respects the Six's agricultures indeed presented a very different picture from that of Britain in the 1950s, but it was Britain's which was unique.

Table 1

Numbers and Percentages of Populations Engaged in Agriculture, 1953–56*

Total population		Numbers engaged in agriculture†	As percentage of active population	As percentage of population
Germany	50·5m	6·5m	20	13
(Federal Republic)				
France	43·6	9·5	26·7	20
Italy	48·2	16·792	33	36
Belgium	8·8	1·1	10	12
Netherlands	10·6	1·55	12·3	15
Luxembourg	0·311	0·05	26	17
Community	162·011	35·492	24·7	—

* Not entirely comparable.
† Includes families.
Comparable percentages for United States and United Kingdom: 12 per cent. and 5 per cent. of active populations (1956) (1957).
Regional variations were wider, for example as between 73 per cent. of the working population in Basilicata, Italy, or the Department of Gers, France (70·8 per cent.) and 9·5 per cent. in the Department of Nord, France.
Decline in agricultural populations since before the Second World War.
In Netherlands: from 20 per cent. in 1947 to 12·3 per cent. in 1956.
In Italy: from 48·6 per cent. in 1936 to 32 per cent. in 1958.
In France: a 25 per cent. decline between 1929 and 1954.

Table 2

(information relates to 1958)

	Share of each member State in total of Six's agricultural production	Share of each member State in total of Six's active agricultural population	Share of each member State in total of useful agricultural land in Six
Germany	22·6	27·4	20·7
(Federal Republic)			
France	38·3	29·5	48·7
Belgium	4·6	2·2	2·7
Italy	29·4	37·8	24·5
Netherlands	5	3	3·3

Table 3

(information relates to 1958)

	Agricultural population as percentage of total working population	Agriculture's contribution to GNP*	Farm incomes as proportion of non-agricultural incomes (%)
Germany (Federal Republic)	18	9	56
France	27	12	57
Belgium	10	7	58
Italy	34	23	38
Netherlands	12	10	76
EEC	24	12	50

* Agricultural production declining as share of GNP in each of the Six between 1950 and 1959 (Germany from 10·4 per cent. to 6·9 per cent.; Italy from 28·2 per cent. to 18·7 per cent.) as industrial production grew.

Table 4

Price Differences among the Six 1958–59

(100=mean)

	Federal Republic of Germany	France	Italy	Belgium	Luxem- bourg	Nether- lands
Wheat	109·4	74·9	109·1	100·4	123·3	83·0
Rye	116·7	71·0	101·7	87·1	138·9	84·7
Barley	134·6	76·6	93·4	105·1	98·9	91·4
Oats	121·2	83·6	84·3	100·3	110·5	100·1
Sugar beet	122·3	81·5	103·9	92·8	—	99·1
Milk	101·6	92·1	98·7	94·3	116·1	97·8
Beef	101·3	87·8	113·7	89·5	105·9	101·8
Pigmeat	110·0	93·7	105·7	84·9	115·3	90·4
Eggs	109·4	89·8	113·1	94·5	119·9	73·2

German and United States prices 1959–60 *expressed in DM per* 100 *kg*

	Germany	United States
Soft wheat	42·4	27·16
Rye	38·5	16·37
Barley	42·2	16·4
Oats	34·2	18·52
Potatoes	18·5	31·95

Source: EEC Commission studies

IV—Technological Change,
Farming in the Six, and Support

In the 1950s nearly a quarter of the populations of the Six were still engaged in agriculture but the dramatic effects of the first wide-spread application of technology to farming were beginning to be felt to varying degrees in all the Six. Until the Second World War much of the Six's agriculture had been depressed, with low wages, low productivity and low investment: in France and Germany yields per acre were scarcely higher in 1939 than at the turn of the century. The 1950s saw a surge in productivity in many sectors of European agriculture as fertilisers, pesticides, improved crop varieties, seeding methods and so on were applied in farming.

(a) *Tradition of Protection*

Along with all other countries in Western Europe, except the United Kingdom, the Six had a long tradition of protection against imports (the Netherlands and Denmark being partial or temporary exceptions). It was largely the tariff walls set up in the nineteenth century against imports of North American grains which preserved intact European arable farming and rural populations (with the result that 40 per cent. of the French and German populations were still engaged in agriculture as late as 1900, compared with a mere 11 per cent. in the United Kingdom in 1910). It is debatable to what extent either the rural populations themselves, or the agricultures in Europe, lost or benefited from this protection; but in any case they were not to be preserved from the impact of the post-war technological revolution in agriculture.

(b) *Social Problem and Surplus Production*

One of the most pressing needs the EEC had to bear in mind when framing a Common Agricultural Policy was that of providing for a socially and politically acceptable rate of departure from the land—at the very least some way of providing a sufficient income for those thousands of small farmers who would, despite insufficient land and capital, have to remain in agriculture, to avoid an altogether disastrous haemorrhage of population from the countryside. Another aspect of the problem created by the upsurge in productivity was that of chronic over-production. This was a feature of most agricultures, but had particularly acute repercussions in the EEC, because of the situation of the small farmer on the margins of viability whose need was to produce more to keep up his income as he saw the returns per unit of production falling in real terms. The problem of structural surplus production of certain commodities which was to become such a significant feature of the CAP resulted in part from the technological revolution itself, but also, as we shall see, from some of the means the EEC chose to cope with its effects.

(c) *Demand*

It was to be greatly aggravated by the fact that overall demand for many of the basic foodstuffs was not keeping up with the increase in production.

(d) " *Market Management* " *Systems of Support*

Distinct as each of the Six's agricultures were, they all had systems of support which fell into the category of " market management " as opposed to—for instance—direct guaranteed prices. That is to say, the producer received a market price which governments attempted to manage in order, as a rule, to maintain an agreed level of return, through various mechanisms. These mechanisms would normally include a good measure of protection against imports through tariffs or quota restrictions, and in some cases intervention in the market—the buying up of produce when production levels were so high that market prices were failing to give producers an adequate return. The British system in post-war years was dominated, in contrast, by a generally open policy towards imports (on which the United Kingdom depended for more than half its total food requirement), and a guaranteed price—direct payments to producers to supplement when necessary the price they obtained from the market.

It was not surprising, therefore, that when the Six in the absence of the United Kingdom came to decide on the methods they would use to support agriculture, they opted for a market management system, to which protection—" Community Preference "—was central. The strong tendency among all West European countries at the time was to increase the degree of self-sufficiency in food. The Six as a whole were already approaching self-sufficiency for temperate foodstuffs (and, incidentally, enormously increasing the extent of their trade among themselves) well before the CAP began to take effect (see Table V). Self-sufficiency in wheat, for example, had increased from 88·7 per cent. in 1955–57 to 107·3 per cent. in 1969, the year when the major part of the CAP arrangements were in force. Similar increases were taking place in all the West European countries, while during the 1960s the United States' total world exports of wheat were to double to 51·5 million tons. The CAP came into being at a time of massive explosion in world productivity and of chronic world surplus in the markets for many primary products. Trade in agricultural products was rarely " free," but rather the bulk of commodities were traded under agreements of one kind or another, or were subsidised down or dumped on markets.

Table 5

Degree of Self-Supply in Certain Products in 1950s, 1960s *and* 1970s

Product	EEC Six			United Kingdom	
	1954–57	1968–69	1973–74	1968–69	1973–74
All cereals	84	92	98	63	68
Wheat	87	109	117	45	60
Rice	82	104	99	—	—
Maize	77	54	66	—	—
Sugar	98	103	112	34	30
Milk	101	100	100	100	100
Butter	100	112	119	11	14
Cheese	100	103	103	43	63
All meats	99	95	96	68	73
Poultry	92	99	101	99	98
Eggs	94	98	100	99	97
Wine	92	96	102	—	—
Fresh fruit	107	87	84	34	34
Potatoes	102	100	101	95	98
Other vegetables	102	100	97	78	75
Citrus fruit	53	55	47	—	—

Source: FAO EEC Commission

The Community had no choice but to protect its home market to a very considerable extent, as did most other countries, against low cost imports.

V—OBJECTIVES OF THE POLICY:
TREATY OF ROME

In forming the Common Market in food products the Six could not quickly abandon the various kinds of protection they had previously afforded their agriculture in favour of free trade among themselves. There had to be a gradual dismantlement of intra-community tariffs and other barriers, accompanied by a progressive merging of systems and price levels to form a single market, within common external tariffs and trade policy frameworks. The Rome Treaty had laid down only the broad principles and objectives the CAP was to pursue (leaving it up to the EEC Commission to prepare the ground for a policy in 1958). These objectives were: (a) to increase productivity by developing technical progress and ensuring the rational development of agricultural production and the optimum utilisation of the factors of production, particularly of labour; (b) to ensure a fair standard of living for the agricultural population particularly by increasing the individual earnings of people engaged in agriculture; (c) to stabilise markets; (d) to guarantee supplies; (e) to ensure reasonable prices to consumers.

The Treaty also laid down that there should be a common organisation of markets at a Community level, and excluded discrimination among producers and consumers anywhere in the Community. Three alternative systems for this market organisation were mentioned in the Treaty (Articles 39–40); the Six later opted for a system employing a separate market organisation for each main product. It laid down that there should be central financing, through a fund (FEOGA: *Fonds Européen d'Orientation et de Garantie Agricole*) which would pay for support interventions and export refunds (guarantee section) and for structural reforms (guidance section). All the arrangements which we now think of as the CAP were left to be negotiated among the Six and the Commission in the years to come.

VI—Arrangements Take Shape

The Common Market in agricultural products—free trade, common organisation of the market—was largely achieved by July 1, 1968 for all but a few major agricultural products. The work had begun in 1962 with decisions on regulations governing the markets for cereals, pigmeat, poultry, eggs, fruit and vegetables and wine. These were followed by decisions on milk and milk products, beef and veal, rice, sugar, oilseeds and olive oil. Prices for all products were to be aligned at a common level by 1969 to coincide with the attainment of a customs union. Alignment of support prices was to be reached through the fixing of upper and lower limits, spanning the wide variation in support levels among the Six—and the band between them narrowed each year.

(a) Cereals and the Variable Levy

Basic to the first set of 1962 regulations and to everything that came after them was the regulation for cereals. It was basic because its effects were far-reaching and because it was seen as the prototype for the Community's market organisations and, in effect, its philosophy. Cereals—central to world agricultural trade owing to the predominance of wheat and rice as food crops and to the extensive use of wheat and maize as animal feedingstuffs—were likewise the key commodity in the internal working of the CAP and in its trading policy. Very briefly, the prototype was the establishment of a target price (the price it is hoped producers will obtain from the market), supported by charges on imports from non-member countries and supplemented by a system of support-buying at intervention prices somewhat below the target price and the subsidisation of exports to other countries. In the case of cereals, the import charges are exacted in the form of a variable levy, representing the difference between the lowest offer price on world markets (actually, at the port of Rotterdam) and the threshold price—the target price minus costs of transport from port to centre of population. The levies are calculated daily and are payable on every consignment entering the Community —at whatever price. The point about the variable levy system is that it was designed to give European producers the maximum of protection. The fact that it has succeeded too well is very much a matter of the way it has been handled—and a factor of the community price.

Aside from the mechanisms which the Six chose was the crucial question of the level at which common prices would be pitched. Cereals were central, for trade in livestock products could not be freed until some equality of input costs in the shape of cereals had been attained. The lower the price of cereals, the lower the costs for a whole range of livestock products dependent on cereal feeds.

(b) *The Level of Common Prices*

The Six decided in 1964 to anticipate the timetable for the introduction of common cereal prices by two years: levies and duties were thus abolished from intra-community trade on July 1, 1967, for grains, pigmeat, eggs and poultry. It is worthwhile looking at the circumstances of the decision, for it was a fateful one and one which highlighted some of the perennial political problems affecting the CAP: the prices the Six decided for grains were high, not only in relation to those prevailing on the world market, which was to be expected, but higher than most of those obtaining in the member States—and inauspiciously high given the EEC's growing dependence on (largely imported) feedingstuffs.

(c) *General Decision in 1964*

It is an irony perhaps typical of the EEC that it was under pressure from the EEC Commission to clear the way for negotiations to move on at a crucial stage in the Kennedy Round in 1964 when the Germans eventually abandoned their resistance to deciding on a common cereals price. (Progress in the industrial sector of the talks had come to depend on the EEC finalising enough of its Common Agriculural Policy to be able to take a common position on the agricultural side.) The core of the irony—which persists in many respects today—was that the price the Germans exacted for agreeing to push ahead with the CAP was the high cereals price their farmers required. Much of the subsequent story of the CAP becomes clearer if it is remembered that the established truism of the Franco-German " trade-off," under which France consented to expose her industries to competition from Germany in return for an agricultural policy, did not mean that her farming was less efficient or prosperous than Germany's;

on the contrary, it was German producers who were among the least efficient in the Community. Cereal prices were pitched where they were, not to satisfy efficient French grain farmers—which they more than amply did—but to meet the needs of small German farmers. As it was as much as 200 million dollars were paid out of Community funds in the first year of operation of common prices, to compensate (mainly) German farmers for their losses.

The decision thus fixed the common prices towards the upper end of the range of national prices with the result that grain production in many areas of the Community, notably in France, received an unwarranted boost while the protectionist repercussions of the variable levy were fruitlessly increased.

For obvious reasons the Six's arrangements for agricultural trade have not pleased major world exporters, among them the United States, whose main aim throughout the 1960s was to expand market outlets for its own (lower-cost) surpluses and who consequently pressed hard in the General Agreement on Tariffs and Trade (GATT) and elsewhere for a liberalisation of trading policies in agricultural products. The Kennedy Round produced little in the way of solution to problems of agricultural trade, and in fact the years following 1967 were marked by generally illiberal policies and practices, outstanding among them being quantitative restrictions on imports and subsidisation of exports on a frequently massive scale (including the commodities, most often grains, deposited as food aid).

VII—BRITAIN'S AGRICULTURE AND TRADE POLICIES

The British system reflected conditions which were very different from those underlying the thinking of the Six. The United Kingdom had a much smaller degree of self-sufficiency. It allowed access for relatively cheap food imports from traditional suppliers, many of them in the Commonwealth, to whom it had traditionally supplied industrial goods; and a highly technologically-developed agriculture which employed a very much smaller proportion of the population than did those of the Six (see note to Table 1). The United Kingdom had, insofar as this is possible, a cheap food policy. The success of this depended on a situation of relative world plenty, and on suppliers' readiness to sell at prices which gave their producers a lower return than that guaranteed to United Kingdom producers, generally efficient though the latter were. United Kingdom policy assumed that it would often be the recipient of food dumped or subsidised.

The support system worked by guaranteeing a minimum income to the farmer irrespective of the state of the market through direct payments (later called " deficiency payments "). Low-cost exporters had relatively free access to British markets and the gap between market prices (generally low as a result of the admission of cheap imports) and the guaranteed price was made up by the deficiency payment, the bill for which was paid by the Exchequer. The system probably helped to increase the efficiency of British farming, subjected as it always was to competition from cheap imports. But it is arguable that agriculture should have been allowed to make a greater contribution to alleviating the balance-of-payments problems that have bedevilled Britain's post-war policy makers.

Problems of Open-Ended Support: Policy Changes

It would be a mistake in any case to suppose that during the 1960s and onwards the United Kingdom was immune to the effects of the technological revolution in agriculture, whose chief effects could best be described as the outstripping of outlets by increased production. The United Kingdom was vulnerable because the cost of maintaining the most liberal import régime in the world together with an open-ended deficiency payments system was becoming an intolerable financial burden, and out of proportion to the benefits afforded consumers. A watershed in British policy came in the mid-1960s when the cost of maintaining deficiency payments to beef producers in circumstances of world glut necessitated supplementary payments of £70 millions (1962–63) and £40 millions (1967–68). From this point there began a series of modifications to the system, which—though it retained many features of the deficiency payments method of operation—had parted company significantly from the early models. The United Kingdom began to seek on the one hand to limit the extent of the support it offered farmers, for example by introducing standard quantities and target prices; on the other, it began to step up restrictions on imports, bringing in a global quota for butter, voluntary restraint arrangements for cheese, quotas for bacon, apples and pears, and minimum import prices for cereals enforced by variable levies. A levy on beef imports was introduced in 1969, and a tariff on lamb in 1971. Imports of main-crop potatoes were banned and a form of " intervention " buying was operated to sustain market prices. Whatever the broad arguments for and against maintaining a policy along the lines of the United Kingdom's former food and agricultural systems there was no doubt that farmers' leaders were generally eager to take advantage of the higher returns held out by the CAP.

VIII—UNITED KINGDOM ENTRY AND WORLD EVENTS: 1970–75

Along with most of the other prognoses concerning the effects of membership on the United Kingdom—and the impact of the United

Kingdom on the Community—the belief that there could be a big expansion in British farming, whether it was right or wrong, was overtaken by the events of the early 1970s. The radical changes in the world's economic situation which have occurred since the time the United Kingdom began negotiations in 1970 all affected the CAP profoundly: the break-up of the Bretton Woods monetary system; the explosion in prices of a number of key commodities including oil; a rapid shift from a world foodstuffs market in chronic surplus to one of (temporarily) crucial shortage and longer-term instability when the world's stockpiles of grain nearly ran out; a period of recession accompanied by rapid inflation.

Green Currencies

As far as the United Kingdom agriculture is concerned, the divergencies in European currencies and the associated development of agri-monetary arrangements under the CAP have had the consequence that, even at the end of the transitional period, there remains a big difference in real terms between the level of United Kingdom support prices and those in others of the Nine and this, together with the impact of monetary compensatory amounts (MCAs) on agricultural trade, has had obvious effects on the competitive position.

The green currencies [5] have enormously complicated the day-to-day workings of the CAP and have introduced new complexities into the area of political decision-making, particularly as regards price-fixing. But by offering greater autonomy to individual Member States over the level of their national food and agricultural prices they have helped, though perhaps only temporarily, to diminish internal dissent about the correct level for CAP prices. They have enabled the United Kingdom at one end of the scale to compensate for the effects of inflation and a depreciating currency by holding down internal food prices; they have enabled Germany at the other end of the scale to retain farm support-price levels which would otherwise have been undermined by the appreciating market rate for the mark; and they have enabled Ireland and Denmark to optimise their returns as agricultural exporters. This has, however, only been achieved at the cost of creating new problems, particularly as regards the distortion of agricultural trade within the Community which the system of MCAs inevitably produced.

---

[5] Over the past 10 years EEC currencies have appreciated or fallen in relation to each other and some have been floated, making it impossible to apply common price levels. To translate common prices into national currencies " green " exchange rates are used which in effect give each country its own level of support. Price levels in many cases vary widely from those which would apply if the former fixed parities or current market exchange rates were used. Products imported from within the EEC or from outside it are subject to the payment of subsidies or levies called " monetary compensatory amounts," paid out of or into the FEOGA.

IX—UNITED KINGDOM MEMBERSHIP
AND COMMUNITY EXTERNAL POLICIES

In one area it would be true to say that United Kingdom membership has combined with the events of 1972–74 to change somewhat the EEC's outlook and behaviour. The Community has always tended to be more successful in an international arena—despite the well-documented difficulties of reaching a common position—than it has been in tackling some of its own problems. The Kennedy Round was an early example. It was always widely assumed that the United Kingdom's entry into the EEC would make the Community more " outward-looking " than it had hitherto succeeded in being. De Gaulle's paranoia about the United Kingdom's potential as an American Trojan horse exaggerated her " special relationship "— and fears that the Commonwealth ties would be a real impediment to Britain's participation in Europe proved ill-founded. But undoubtedly in matters of trade policy as well as politics enlargement has contributed to changes in the Community's stance. The Community has made some concession to Britain's traditional trade in Commonwealth produce.

(a) *Accession: butter*

The United Kingdom's partners have never been enthusiastic about the arrangements made in the entry negotiations, and subsequently modified in the course of the Labour Government's renegotiation in 1975, to assure preferential access on to the British market for certain quantities of New Zealand dairy products. They are tolerated by the rest of the Community as necessary exceptional treatment justified only because of New Zealand's particular dependance on the British market and on the products concerned. No such exceptions were made, or indeed sought by the United Kingdom, for exports from Australia or Canada. Nevertheless, these were hard-won concessions, constituting a breach in the hitherto impenetrable principle of Community preference, furthermore for a commodity whose structural surplus in the Community was already its most acute embarrassment.

(b) *Sugar and the developing countries*

The other major negotiating issue for United Kingdom entry in the agriculture sphere was also related to imports from the Commonwealth: the cane sugar from developing countries (mainly in the West Indies) under the Commonwealth Sugar Agreement (CSA). No precise details had been worked out for implementing the Six's pledge to " hold to the heart " the exporters' interests. The CSA was due to run until the end of 1974, and it was during that year that negotiations with the exporters on sugar arrangements were to take place. As late as the summer of 1973 there had been strong resistance within the EEC towards the undertaking demanded by the Commission that the Community declare itself a net importer with a commitment to take annually 1·4 million tons of cane sugar. (The EEC had only recently been instrumental in frustrating hopes for a new International Sugar Agreement.) In the event, the Community demonstrated a different frame of mind. By 1974 the fate of the sugar deal (quantities and prices) had come to be tied in with the negotiations between the Community and the 35 or so developing countries which were known as the ACP (African, Caribbean and Pacific countries). These were the 18 " French-speaking " African States already associated with the EEC under the Yaoundé Convention, together with the ex-Commonwealth developing countries of Africa, and the islands of the Caribbean and Pacific. Partly because of a world shortage of sugar which sent prices through the roof, but also because there was a genuine desire among the Nine (pushed hard by the United Kingdom, the Netherlands and the Commission) to conclude a fair deal with the ACPs, the terms of the sugar deal were very good indeed for the exporters: they were assured not only of access on to the Community market but also a price on a par with the EEC's own producer price for beet sugar. (Although the EEC were short of sugar themselves at the time, sugar is a commodity in which the Six were generally in surplus and which they subsidised down on world markets.)

(c) *Lomé Convention*

It would be fair to say that the entire trade and aid package negotiated with the ACPs (the Lomé Convention)—and the new configuration of relationships to which it gave rise—was a vast improvement on the previous association convention, and bore the marks of considerable efforts on the part of the United Kingdom, the Commission and others to change established patterns.[6] The EEC's much greater interest in the problems of the less developed countries—including those outside the scope of the association— reflects also a generally increased awareness of the interdependence of all world economies, which has affected also its trading policies in other areas.

---

[6] Virtually all the ACPs' food exports enter the Community duty free under the Convention; increasingly long lists of agricultural products are included in the generalised system of Tariff Preferences, duty-free quotas given to all other developing countries.

X—WORLD CHANGES:
EEC, UNITED STATES
AND GATT MULTILATERALS

The events of the early 1970s, in particular the spectacular increase in the world wheat price and depletion of stocks, in drawing sudden attention to the underlying instability in world commodity trade, have reduced some of the differences in approach which habitually divided the two major trading blocs, the United States and EEC. The Community has tended to advocate greater regulation of world grain markets through pricing, to complement the EEC's own system, so to speak, while the United States and others have complained that the CAP's success in insulating the Community market from both downward and upward movements in world prices has exacerbated those fluctuations: *i.e.* the greater the internal stability of a large trading bloc, the greater the degree of external instability (which has unfortunate repercussions for poor countries dependent on imported grains). While the United States has come closer to the EEC with its recognition of the dangers of excessive world price instability in key commodities, the EEC is now committed (in its negotiating mandate for the Commission in the GATT Tokyo Round) to see a greater integration of the CAP within the world trading system. The prospects for agreement on the methods of organising an internationally managed system of stockpiling for wheat, the major single agricultural issue in the Multilateral Trade Negotiations (MTNs), are promising.

CAP in Negotiations

The Community has always made it clear in such negotiations that the principles of the CAP are non-negotiable. (By mutual consent, countries do not expect to negotiate changes in each others' domestic support system as such in the MTNs, only their external trade effects.) The EEC is particularly sensitive in this respect, first because the CAP *is* the EEC's trading policy for temperate foodstuffs and consequently any concessions made on the trading front are immediately translatable in domestic policy; but also because of the delicate balance of national interests that go to make up the Community's policy.

XI—CAP MODIFICATIONS:
INTERNAL AND EXTERNAL PRESSURES

The most valid of the outsiders' complaints concerning the CAP are mirrored in the criticisms and attempts at reform from within the EEC. The Kennedy Round precipitated the putting together of the

CAP; now, in the light of the problems some elements of the CAP create for the Community itself, the Tokyo Round could well provide an opportunity, and if necessary a pretext, for improvements to it. Such changes could be illustrated briefly. The EEC's high level of protection for maize and high energy wheat, both of which it is obliged to import in large quantities (the EEC is less than 60 per cent. self-sufficient in maize) is a major source of friction; its effects on the Community, meanwhile, are to push up the costs of livestock production—pigmeat, poultry, eggs, but increasingly of dairy and beef cattle (which in turn necessitates greater protection for those products). As we have seen, the level of prices is the core of the problem but the variable levy mechanism itself is a source of annoyance to exporters to the Community: it tends to give an arbitrary, as well as excessive, protection (triggered off by the lowest, not an average, offer price). To add to the offence, a short period of " prefixation " creates unpredictability. Thus, the variable levy, through its method of operation, rather than its actual existence, is a cause of frustration to the EEC's trading partners while it has the effect of unduly raising internal prices. Similarly in the dairy sector: it is not so much the CAP's protection against dairy imports (which, by different means is paralleled in the United States) as the methods used to dispose of EEC surpluses on world markets. Its periodic dumping of butter, butter oil and skim milk powder on world markets already depressed has been a very real source of friction internationally. Whatever the difficulties and cost of alternative methods of disposal, the unrestrained use of export funds for dairy or, as in the past, cereals and sugar as well, is bad for the CAP's trading image; it is patently unsatisfactory inside the EEC politically. The international dairy trade is a messy and unsatisfactory one, but the EEC's murky profile is a just reflection of its unresolved internal problems.

XII—STRUCTURAL AND OTHER REFORMS: THE DAIRY SECTOR

The dairy sector is the Community's structural problem *par excellence* (though problems of a similar kind exist for " southern " agriculture).[7] As we saw, the CAP began life with levels of support prices for cereals which reflected the need of high-cost German producers. Milk prices were fixed at levels which represented considerable increases for French and Dutch farmers but which were not outrageously high. In fact the 1968 EEC guarantee prices were to be on a par with those then operating in the United Kingdom. The excessive

---

[7] See Section XVII, below.

intervention levels and surplus production which have marked the years since 1970 sprang from a succession of moves on the intervention price for butter which completely upset the balance of supply and demand.

It is the dairy sector which exemplifies the EEC's over-reliance on end-price support to achieve a basically social end, with unfortunate economic repercussions: prices were geared over a vital period to the needs of the small farmer, who typically relied on milk sales for his livelihood. High prices have had two main effects. On the one hand they greatly encouraged milk production by efficient farmers, with the result that even greater quantities of milk are produced; and, on the other, the repercussions on consumer prices of dairy products has led to a considerable fall in consumption. It will prove enormously difficult even with the progress now being made in redressing the balance of prices for the Community to achieve a matching of supply with demand within the next few years; and the dairy sector is likely to continue to be a very expensive item in terms of budget cost and consumer disadvantage.

XIII—THE EARLY 1970s

The Six had set up a part of the farm fund to be used for " structural " improvements, but it was under-endowed and under-used, and in any case structural reform—which is to say, broadly, farm amalgamation and the elimination of unviable producers—would be a long-term, slow business.[8] Between 1970 and 1972 the much-publicised Mansholt Plan occupied a central position in debate about the future of the CAP in negotiations, but this too was a long-term affair and while the need for the Community to assist in structural reform became accepted, the effects of other decisions by the Six— namely, the awarding of excessive price increases for many products —were immediate and manifest. (It can be pointed out, however, that the governments of the Six spent considerably more money on structural reforms of various kinds outside the framework of the CAP than was spent during the period on price support.) But even with a rate of departure from the land in the order of 5 per cent. every year since 1958, there were still by 1972 reckoned to be as few as 700,000 viable farms in the EEC out of a total of over 4 million (see Table 6) and the changed economic situation with reduced opportunities outside agriculture has affected the recent rate of movement).

---

[8] The point must be made that although the underlying problems of EEC agriculture are to do with the structure of farming, " structural reform " in no way represented or represents a solution to them in the short or medium term.

Table 6

Total Numbers Employed in Agriculture, Forestry and Fisheries Compared with the Total Population in Active Civil Employment (1968 *and* 1975)

Member State	Agricultural employment ('000s)		Total employment ('000s)		Agricultural employment as % of total employment	
1	1968	1975	1968	1975	1968	1975
	2	3	4	5	6	7
Germany (Federal Republic)	2,523	1,822	25,491	24,828	9·9	7·3
France	3,098	2,452[1]	19,749	21,166[1]	15·7	11·6[1]
Italy	4,173	2,964	18,607	18,818	22·4	15·8
Netherlands[2]	352	299	4,445	4,535	7·9	6·6
Belgium	201	136	3,614	3,744	5·6	3·6
Luxembourg	17	10[1]	139	151[1]	12·2	6·6[1]
Six	10,364	7,683[1]	72,045	73,242[1]	14·4	10·5[1]
United Kingdom	763	667	24,903	24,632	3·1	2·7
Ireland	310	252	1,055	1,030	29·4	24·5
Denmark	276[3]	228	2,282[3]	2,332	12·1	9·8
Nine	11,713[3]	8,830[1]	100,285[3]	101,236[1]	11·7	8·7[1]

[1] France and Luxembourg=1974.
[2] Man years.
[3] Denmark=1969.

Number of farm holdings in Community of Six: (1960) 6·4m; (1973) 5m.
Rate of reduction per year: 3·9 per cent. (1967–70).
Average size of holdings in the Community of Nine in 1973 (*hectares*):

Nine	Italy	Netherlands Belgium Federal Republic Germany	Denmark Ireland Luxembourg France	United Kingdom
17	7	13–14	22–23	62

(Regional variations considerably greater)

Source: EEC Commission.

XIV—CHANGES SINCE UNITED KINGDOM ENTRY

Significant developments have occurred since the United Kingdom became a member: the much firmer recognition by the EEC of the need to gear prices to the requirements of efficient farmers and restrict the rate of annual price increases for certain commodities is a key one; and recently, the acknowledgment that there should be more flexibility in the mechanisms for market management. Alongside these changes in attitude is the growing recognition that the problems of the small and disadvantaged farmer will never be satisfactorily resolved by paying economically unjustified support prices.

XV—MECHANISMS AND SOCIAL PAYMENTS

The United Kingdom has had considerable influence in bringing about the introduction of changes in these respects, notably (as far as mechanisms are concerned) in the intervention system for beef, to which has been added an element of direct payment to producers. An important innovation, stemming from the United Kingdom's request to continue to operate its system of hill-farming subsidies, is the Directive on Less Favoured Areas, providing for direct payments to farmers who, owing to the natural difficulties of the land they farm and other circumstances, cannot be expected to compete on equal terms with efficient producers, but whose farming activities it is desirable to maintain on wider social, environmental (or indeed economic) grounds. (This contrasts with the rather raw economic thinking behind the Mansholt Plan, which in any case has been largely overtaken by recent events: it can hardly be maintained in present circumstances of high unemployment that less efficient agriculture is using manpower and other resources that would better be used elsewhere in the economy; indeed, the many-fold increase in input costs for most types of *efficient* farming are making it necessary to look again at exactly what that term means.)

XVI—RECENT NEW SCHEMES:
DAIRY AND WHEAT

More recent changes have stemmed from the efforts of the Commission, fuelled by the 1975 " Stocktaking " exercise (though some of these measures have been advocated by the Commission for a number of years without success). Eventual agreement was reached in 1977 on a number of changes in the dairy sector, notably a " non-delivery premium " intended to encourage dairy farmers to quit dairying and take the land more or less permanently out of milk production. Changes in the intervention system for breadmaking wheat should serve to improve the price relationships between hard and soft wheat and reduce the importance of the intervention mechanism.

XVII—ENLARGEMENT TO THE MEDITERRANEAN

Certainly the issue which has the widest implications for the future of the Common Agricultural Policy, with that of the Community itself, is that of the enlargement of the EEC to include the countries of Portugal, Spain and Greece. Much of the EEC's future trading policy, as well as the prospects for improvements in the levels of support which are the key to the CAP problems, will depend on the solutions the Community finds to the difficulties of integrating these Mediterranean agricultures into the existing structure. The " southern " commodities—wine, olive oil, tobacco, rice, durum wheat—have not until very recently occupied a central place in the attention given agriculture; Italy, with by far the poorest and least developed agricultural sector among the Six, has benefited considerably less from the CAP than the richer countries of the north. The question is whether in seeking to accommodate the new southern states the EEC will resist the already strong pressure to strengthen the support mechanisms, and the protection, afforded the " southern " products. This it will have to do by enlisting the aid of strong regional and social policies, and continuing in the direction taken in such innovations as the Less Favoured Areas scheme which frankly recognises the difference between the economics and the social content of agriculture.

XVIII—FOR THE FUTURE

The United Kingdom, like other member States in the Community, has advocated, and in some areas secured, changes in the CAP to protect and further its national interest. But the changes for which the Labour Government has been pressing under the CAP are not simply in response to domestic political needs: they are important themes for the long-term development of the EEC and they represent valid social and economic objectives for the Community as a whole. The objectives of the CAP relate not only to the standard of living of farmers but also to improving the efficiency of agriculture and providing food for consumers at stable and reasonable prices. The Community therefore has to recognise the importance of a realistic pricing policy for agriculture and the need to take account of market realities. The Community needs to avoid the waste of resources which is involved in creating surplus production and selling at below cost on world markets—resources which could be better used providing employment or improved services in other areas. Equally, the Community must recognise that some foodstuffs can be produced more efficiently and competitively in third countries. Excessive protectionism cannot be in the general interest of the EEC. Perhaps the simplest summary of what United Kingdom Ministers have been seeking to achieve is to say that agricultural prices should not be burdened with the effects of social needs.There are no simple answers to the problem of unsatisfactory agricultural structure. Every country in the world to some degree has experienced, or is experiencing the strain which arises from the reduction in the numbers involved in agriculture. The CAP can play some part in easing these difficulties but they call for national rather than Community solutions. The circumstances vary enormously from country to country according to the historical and social background. What is clear is that postponing the evil day by boosting farm incomes through an over-protective price support system only adds to the problem.

CONTINUITY AND CHANGE
IN THE COMMONWEALTH

By

MARGARET DOXEY

IN the late 1950s and throughout the 1960s it was fashionable to forecast the demise of the Commonwealth and it was even labelled a " gigantic farce." In an earlier paper in this *Year Book* I commented that even if this were a fair description, one would have to admit that the farce had staged a very long run, and suggested that the Commonwealth deserved to be taken—and studied—much more seriously.[1] The continuing series of biennial Heads of Government meetings bears witness to sustained top-level interest in the Commonwealth. The most recent was held in London in June 1977, attended by representatives of 33 governments, among whom 26 were Presidents or Prime Ministers. In alternate years, senior government officials now meet to review the Commonwealth's work and maintain its momentum, and there are also numerous official and unofficial meetings and contacts between Commonwealth countries every year, some held on a regular basis, others organised *ad hoc*. Moreover, the Commonwealth Secretariat which was established in 1965 has proved its worth by giving focus and direction to the activities of the whole body. It provides a visible core to the Commonwealth and by emphasising the need for co-operative endeavour for the benefit of less privileged members, it has neatly reversed the principle underlying imperial relationships where the interests of the more privileged take precedence. In its first decade, under the Secretary-Generalship of Arnold Smith, the Secretariat established itself firmly as the nerve centre of the organisation, co-ordinating political, economic and social co-operation and giving a new impetus to developments in the field of technical assistance. Under Mr. Smith's successor, Mr. Shridath Ramphal, the Secretariat entered a new phase in which its existence, like that of the Commonwealth as a whole, is taken for granted and new and broader initiatives can be attempted.[2]

One of the two objectives of this paper is to consider the extent to

[1] " The Commonwealth in the 1970s," in this *Year Book*, Vol. 27 (1973), pp. 90–109. See too this writer, " The Commonwealth Secretariat," in this *Year Book*, Vol. 30 (1976), pp. 69–96. Research on the Commonwealth has been supported by grants from Trent University which are gratefully acknowledged.

[2] There is, however, no intention that the Secretariat shall expand into yet another sprawling international bureaucracy. Its staff in 1977 numbered 360; its budget for 1976–77 was £1·8 million.

which Mr. Ramphal can hope to develop and extend Commonwealth roles. The first objective is to review the usefulness of the contemporary Commonwealth for its own members, particularly in the practical sphere of functional co-operation.

I—THE COMMONWEALTH CONNECTION AND ITS VALUE FOR MEMBERS

There are, at the time of writing, 36 full members of the Commonwealth, with a population exceeding 900 million—one-quarter of the world's total. The Commonwealth also encompasses a number of self-governing States and dependent territories with a combined population of nearly 8 million, all of whom are eligible for Commonwealth assistance and participate in a variety of Commonwealth activities. This represents a complete change from 1945, when the Commonwealth had seven members, and even from 1960 when there were only 11 members. Table 1 gives details of the post-war expansion of Commonwealth membership.

Inevitably, diversity of geographical situation, race, religion, language and constitutional arrangements characterise the contemporary Commonwealth, and even the basic criteria for membership —to have been a part of the former British Empire, to recognise the Queen's symbolic status as Head of the Commonwealth and to be acceptable to all existing members, may be modified as time passes.[3] The Commonwealth has shown great flexibility in adapting to new circumstances—indeed this has been the secret of its survival—and changes in membership eligibility are not inconceivable. The artificiality of political boundaries in the Third World, which are the product of rival imperialisms, have already given way to some co-operation between neighbouring States, and the Commonwealth is more likely to facilitate such co-operation than to obstruct it.[4] But acceptability to all members will remain of crucial importance in an association which has fundamental norms of equality and consensus.

It is possible to identify more than one level at which the Commonwealth operates. On the first level it is a limited membership intergovernmental organisation with no specific security or welfare goals,

[3] One would not expect any objection to be raised if Namibia (South West Africa), which was mandated to South Africa after the First World War and whose international status has been hotly contested ever since the Second World War, were to seek admission after gaining independence.
[4] The Commonwealth Secretary-General notes developing relationships between Commonwealth Caribbean countries and Latin American States, between Commonwealth and non-Commonwealth African countries particularly in the OAU, and in the South Pacific Bureau for Economic Co-operation (SPEC) under the leadership of Australia and New Zealand. *Sixth Report*, 1977, pp. 11–12.

Table 1

The Post-War Expansion of Commonwealth Membership
(Date of membership in brackets)

1945—Total membership: 7	1960—Total membership: 11	1976—Total membership: 36
United Kingdom	United Kingdom	United Kingdom
Australia (1901)*	Australia	Australia
Canada (1867)*	Canada	Canada
Eire (Ireland) (1921) [1]	New Zealand	New Zealand
Newfoundland [2]	South Africa [3]	India
New Zealand (1907)*	India (1947)	Sri Lanka
South Africa (1910)*	Pakistan (1947) [4]	Ghana
* Dominion status	Ceylon (1948)	Malaysia
	(Sri Lanka)	Nigeria
	Ghana (1957)	Cyprus (1961)
	Federation of	Sierra Leone (1961)
	Malaya (1957)	Tanzania (1961) [5]
	(Malaysia)	Jamaica (1962)
	Nigeria	Trinidad and Tobago (1962)
		Uganda (1962)
		Kenya (1963)
		Malawi (1964)
		Malta (1964)
		Zambia (1964)
		The Gambia (1965)
		Singapore (1965) [6]
		Guyana (1966)
		Botswana (1966)
		Lesotho (1966)
		Barbados (1966)
		Mauritius (1968)
		Swaziland (1968)
		Tonga (1970)
		Western Samoa (1970) [7]
		Fiji (1970)
		Bangladesh (1972) [8]
		Bahamas (1973)
		Grenada (1974)
		Papua-New Guinea (1975)
		Seychelles (1976)
		Solomon Islands (1978)
		Special Member:
		Nauru (1968)

Notes

[1] Left 1949.   [2] Joined Canada 1949.   [3] Left 1961.   [4] Left 1972.
[5] Tanganyika (1961) and Zanzibar (1963) joined to form Tanzania in 1974.
[6] Seceded from Malaysia.   [7] Independent since 1962.   [8] Formerly East Pakistan.

Other former dependencies

Sudan—left the Commonwealth on attaining independence in 1956.

British Somaliland—joined the United Nations Trust Territory (Italian) Somaliland to form Somalia in 1960.

Southern Cameroons—joined the French Cameroons to form Cameroun in 1961.

The Maldive Islands ceased to be protected in 1963.

Southern Yemen became independent when the South Arabian Federation broke up in 1967.

but rather a general concern for maintaining open lines of communication and consultation on matters of common interest. On the second level, it sponsors a wide range of functional activities, encouraged and co-ordinated by the Secretariat. The " Commonwealth " also defines the scope of many non-governmental links in education, health, science, radio, the arts, sport and other fields, and there would seem to be mutually reinforcing effects between government and non-governmental linkages, which could be encouraged.

In his Sixth Report to Heads of Government, Mr. Ramphal identified " four themes which have dominated the collective work of the Commonwealth since the [1975 Heads of Government] Kingston meeting: liberation in Southern Africa, the restructuring of world economic relations, the more positive commitment of our association to the service of the world community, and the enlargement of its practical contribution to the economic and social development of its member-States." [5] While Southern African problems take first place in his list and may have dominated discussion at recent Heads of Government meetings, there can be no doubt that the Commonwealth's main achievement in an age when imperial relationships find little favour is the last of these " themes "; without it, survival would not have been possible. Within the Commonwealth the developing countries have provided the rationale for an extensive network of co-operation in technical assistance, health, education and related fields, and the financial support for these efforts has come from the four " developed " members, the United Kingdom, Australia, Canada and New Zealand. But all four of Mr. Ramphal's " themes " clearly indicate the extent to which the Commonwealth has come to reflect the main concerns of the overwhelming majority of its members.

In terms of a rough balance sheet of costs and benefits the Commonwealth connection seems to offer moderate benefits to members at a

---

[5] *Sixth Report of the Commonwealth Secretary-General* (1977), p. 1.

very low cost.[6] Materially, contributions to the Secretariat, scaled according to capacity to pay, are so small as to be derisory, while contribution to the multilateral Commonwealth Fund for Technical Co-operation (CFTC), and to various other programmes and scholarship funds are voluntary and also very small.[7] Affluent members would have to make some aid effort, irrespective of co-membership of the Commonwealth, and as bilateral aid is often associated with procurement and other benefits for the donor, it should not, in any case, be regarded wholly as cost.[8] But what of political costs?

There are no direct penalties for joining, or for not joining, but one may raise the question of whether membership places any restriction on foreign policy and, in particular, on freedom to join or remain outside other international organisations or groupings. The Declaration of Principles issued after the Singapore Heads of Government Meeting in 1971 specifically stated that it did not, but there have been three occasions when this question has arisen, two of major importance. The first possible incompatibility was India's desire to remain non-aligned, outside the western alliance system. This was successfully resolved, and India's concern over an independent foreign policy and Great Power dominance by the United Kingdom, proved needless.[9] The majority of other new members also opted to remain free of defensive alliances. The second was the question of a Communist State becoming a member, when the Ghana-Guinea union was apparently imminent in 1958. As the union proved abortive, the question did not really arise.[10] Today, such a development might not prove much of a problem. There is no defence aspect to Commonwealth activities and it seems capable of accommodating all types of political system.

The third question of incompatibility concerned the United Kingdom's membership of the European Economic Community (EEC). For as long as it suited her, the United Kingdom did not seek membership of the EEC, claiming that membership of the Commonwealth took priority in her foreign policy. Then, when the United Kingdom found it useful to assert that the two could be

[6] A framework for analysis of international organisation focusing on the uses of these bodies for member governments was developed in this writer's " International Organisation in Foreign Policy Perspective," in this *Year Book*, Vol. 29 (1975), pp. 173–195.

[7] See *Sixth Report of the Commonwealth Secretary-General*, App. III for rates of contribution to the Secretariat for 1976–77. The United Kingdom contributed 30 per cent. (£542,826); Canada 19·2 per cent.; Australia 8·73 per cent.; India 7·29 per cent.; New Zealand 1·69 per cent. All other members contributed either 1·5 or 0·75 per cent. of the total budget.

[8] Economic aid is discussed in more detail in subsections (d), (e) and (f), below.

[9] See N. Mansergh, " The Commonwealth and the Future," *International Studies* (New Delhi) 1967, pp. 4–5.

[10] See J. D. B. Miller, *Survey of Commonwealth Affairs: Problems of Expansion and Attrition 1953–1969* (1974), p. 392.

reconciled, President de Gaulle reiterated the theme of incompatibility, rejecting the United Kingdom's application and demanding that she become more " European " before seeking admission. At the same time, other members of the Commonwealth deplored the United Kingdom's decision to seek admission. But by the end of the 1960s, French objections to the United Kingdom's entry had disappeared and members of the Commonwealth were generally reconciled to it. Having made arrangements to cushion the impact for itself and for other Commonwealth members, the United Kingdom is now a member of both bodies.

The present nature of Commonwealth activities, therefore, does not set any restraints on simultaneous membership of other organisations. Costs here are nil.

One may doubt, too, whether membership of the Commonwealth establishes any constraints on domestic policy. South Africa's apartheid system did constitute a fundamental incompatibility between national and Commonwealth policy, and the " massive violation " of basic human rights in Uganda under President Amin provoked condemnation in " strong and unequivocal terms " at the 1977 Heads of Government meeting,[11] but these two cases are exceptions to the general rule that internal matters of a politically sensitive nature are not discussed at Commonwealth meetings. The occasion for discussion of South Africa's apartheid policies was provided by the South African government's application to remain in the Commonwealth as a republic in 1961, while some reference to Uganda was essential in 1977 if the Commonwealth was to retain credibility for its stand on human rights. Feelings of outrage were strongly expressed, particularly in the United Kingdom where the Heads of Government meeting coincided with the Queen's Silver Jubilee Celebrations.[12]

On the benefit side, the Commonwealth offers all its members advantages of status and role, communication and participation, while the majority also benefit directly from its programmes of economic and social co-operation.

(a) *Status and Role*

For the major members, Australia, Canada, India, Nigeria, and the United Kingdom, there are opportunities for constructive

---

[11] *Commonwealth Heads of Government Meeting 1977*, The Commonwealth Secretariat, p. 11.

[12] See Mr. Ramphal's guarded comments in his *Sixth Report* on the need to " strike the balance of political judgment between the two extremes of declamation and silence . . .", p. 13. President Amin had already been informed by the British government that he would not be welcome in London and he did not attend, although bizarre Press reports of his intention to enter the country by unconventional means were circulating immediately before the Heads of Government Meeting.

leadership which can bring enhanced prestige, while for the four " old " Commonwealth countries there is the special value of a network of links not only with each other but also with developing countries in Africa, Asia, the Caribbean and the Pacific.

In 1945, within the Commonwealth, the United Kingdom was the apex of the pyramid, enjoying unquestioned leadership and pre-eminent status. But the Commonwealth and the world have changed. Although it is true that successive British Governments were prepared to relinquish political responsibility for overseas dependencies, and with gathering enthusiasm and speed to launch them on the path to independence, there seems to have been a British expectation that this would reduce the burden of role, without sacrifice of status. Unfortunately, nations, like people, are not often able to enjoy the best of both worlds, and in the 1960s there were clear signs that instead of a pleasant retention of status without role, the United Kingdom would have to accept a continuing and burdensome role with few benefits of status. This situation arise particularly because of residual constitutional responsibility for Rhodesia.

In addition, despite its own economic difficulties, when compared with the new Commonwealth countries the United Kingdom is obviously a major Power with the ability, as well as the responsibility to play a leading part in setting standards and in meeting some of the urgent needs of the poorer members. At the same time, new members were anxious to assert their own sovereignty, and were not prepared to accord any special status to the United Kingdom which might seem to derogate from it. Tensions were inevitable, and they reached their peak in the period 1965–71, although there was an earlier and violent outbreak of criticism of British policy at the time of the Suez Crisis when India and Ceylon both contemplated leaving the Commonwealth. But whereas criticism of the Suez policy, and of the first application to join the EEC found support among sections of British government and public opinion, the pressure of African Commonwealth members for the United Kingdom to use force in Rhodesia did not. A general consensus within the United Kingdom would probably be that Labour and Conservative Governments have done all they could or should, to bring down the illegal Smith régime. As the main instigator of sanctions, and the main source of surveillance of their implimentation, it was not likely that policy towards Rhodesia would be seen in the United Kingdom in any sense as a betrayal of the Commonwealth, and the fact that other Commonwealth countries were not subjected to condemnation and pressure, even where their policies have obviously not been in accordance with the standards of multi-racialism which they support, made British resentment even sharper.

For many British people today, the Commonwealth may seem more an ironic reminder of past glory than an association relevant to the United Kingdom in the late twentieth century, and British contributions more a discharging of responsibility than a constructive role-playing exercise. But as expectations of status disappear, the role benefits of being an important member may be more generally appreciated, and the uneasy nature of Britain's membership in the EEC may also contribute to a positive view of Commonwealth membership. In any case, the United Kingdom does not now expect to be the prime mover in Commonwealth affairs or to enjoy pre-eminent status and, in return it does not expect to be called to account for its policies. The Singapore Declaration of Principles which noted that " each State was responsible for its own policies " applies to the United Kingdom as well as the rest of the Commonwealth. But although the feeling that the Commonwealth is, above all, British has certainly disappeared, it still cannot be said that the United Kingdom is just another member of the Commonwealth. Her political status has shrunk, but she is still the power who at one time was responsible for the government of all other members and her cultural contribution will remain immense. She also contributes a major portion of the budget of the Secretariat and, after Canada, is the main contributor to the Commonwealth Fund for Technical Co-operation.

For all other Commonwealth countries, initial membership of the Commonwealth has been equivalent to the attainment of independence. " Dominion status " was eagerly sought by Canada and South Africa and willingly accepted by Australia and New Zealand. As decolonisation spread through the Commonwealth after the Second World War, the requirement of common allegiance to the Crown was dropped, but the emphasis on the attainment of sovereignty remained. Joining the Commonwealth and attending Prime Ministers' meetings, like joining the United Nations, was a kind of graduation ceremony, and although United Nations membership is the greater prize, Commonwealth membership serves to reinforce status. In the cases of Sri Lanka and Bangladesh, where United Nations membership was not immediately attainable because of the attitude of the Soviet Union in the former case and China in the latter, Commonwealth membership was a temporary consolation prize. One may note, too, the negative aspect of this process. The Prime Minister of Rhodesia does not now enjoy the privilege of attending Commonwealth meetings, and the self-styled independence of Rhodesia has been recognised by no other member of the international community.

The " old " Commonwealth members, Australia, Canada and

New Zealand, form a distinct group, not only because of the longer period during which they have enjoyed independence, but also because of their affluence. They are rich, " middle Powers " and for such Powers membership of major international organisations can offer scope for enhancing the prestige both of the government and of the country as a whole.

Australia traditionally followed the United Kingdom's lead, and did not itself seek a distinctive political role within the Commonwealth.[13] More recently however, Australian Governments have laid far more stress on her regional position and when the Labour Party came to power in 1973, the new government introduced several changes in foreign policy designed to stress a new and constructive interest in Asia. This regional concern has been maintained and there is no doubt that the Commonwealth generally provides a useful context in which Australian external relations can be initiated and fostered.

To an even greater extent than Australia, New Zealand endorsed an imperial foreign policy and did not actively support Canada, South Africa and Ireland in their efforts to establish separate interests and identities. But as early as 1935, at the time of the first Labour Government in New Zealand, there were signs of greater independence After the Second World War, it was obvious that the United States had succeeded the United Kingdom as the provider of security, while economic links were to be undercut by the British application to join the EEC. Ties of sentiment with the United Kingdom have remained but the emergence to full statehood of the South Pacific territories of Western Samoa, Tonga, Fiji and Nauru, as well as the development of a special relationship with the Cook Islands, has meant that New Zealand has a new regional role of being the giant among minnows instead of itself being the minnow of the old Commonwealth. Its international status has been generally high as a result of enlightened racial policies and its opposition to nuclear testing, and it can make a distinctive contribution to the contemporary Commonwealth.[14]

---

[13] But see (Sir) P. C. Spender, *Exercises in Diplomacy* (1969), p. 200 *et seq.* Spender claims an important role for Australia in initiating the Colombo Plan while denying this role to Ceylon.

[14] The only cloud on this horizon relates to the issue of apartheid in sport which has complicated relations between New Zealand and the non-white Commonwealth countries. The New Zealand Government has permitted a rugby team to visit South Africa and this led to problems of boycotting at the Montreal Olympics which have been repeated at the 1978 Commonwealth Games in Edmonton. In an attempt to ward off further difficulties a special statement was appended to the communiqué issued after the Heads of Government meeting in London calling apartheid in sports " an abomination " and accepting it as the " urgent duty of each of their governments " to take every practical step to discourage contact or competition by their nationals with sporting organisations, teams or sportsmen from South Africa or any other country where sports are organised on the basis of race, colour or ethnic origin."

For Canada, too, the Commonwealth offers scope for role-playing. A persistent commitment on the part of the Canadian public to peacekeeping and internationalism means that an active and constructive role in international organisations has commended itself to successive Canadian governments. Throughout the post-Second World War period there was much evidence of Canadian support for the United Nations and for the Commonwealth. In 1947 the St. Laurent government gave a very warm welcome to the new Asian members and something like an Indo-Canadian entente developed.[15] And although diplomacy was concentrated at the United Nations, Canada played a useful role in holding the Commonwealth together during the Suez Crisis, and enhanced its status and that of Lester Pearson by so doing. As Minister of External Affairs and later as Prime Minister, Pearson continued to pursue internationalist policies in the United Nations and in other international bodies, including the Commonwealth. Pierre Trudeau, Pearson's successor initiated a reorientation of foreign policy which involved new emphasis on Canada's francophone connections and on national economic interest and although Mr. Trudeau attended the 1969 Prime Minister's Meeting, the Commonwealth did not appear then to weigh heavily in his priorities. But subsequent events suggest that the change in orientation was more apparent than real. The Canadian government continued to play an active part in international organisations and Mr. Trudeau declared publicly that he had been " converted " to support of the Commonwealth. The connection is still valued by many Canadians; moreover, it can offer useful benefits to the Canadian government. The Commonwealth has no hidden imperialistic core, and the United States is not a member. Commonwealth egalitarianism, multi-racialism, emphasis on practical co-operation and wide range of membership make it a useful framework for national leaders who wish to cut a good figure at home and abroad and sharpen a distinctively Canadian profile in the North American context.[16]

For the majority of Commonwealth members, once they have achieved the status of independence, the scope for sustained role-playing may be limited, although one may note the prominent role which India, under Nehru, played in Commonwealth affairs in the late 1940s and early 1950s. India's status in the new Commonwealth, and as leader of the non-aligned group of nations helped her government to project a strong image on the world stage. Nigeria, with

---

[15] See M. S. Rajan, " The Indo-Canadian Entente," *International Journal* 1962, pp. 358–384.

[16] See this writer " Canada's International Connections " in this *Year Book*, Vol. 32 (1978), pp. 43–63.

important oil resources, may come to the fore in the next decade of
Commonwealth relations. But Commonwealth egalitarianism is
reassuring for all new States, and particularly for the small ones.
Miller noted that Ceylon gained stature through membership which
other small Asian States such as Vietnam and Cambodia did not
possess; the prime benefit was " an artificial but useful equality with
India." [17] And as the Commonwealth provides no entrenched status
(even for the United Kingdom), it is possible for any member to
take the leading role on a particular issue.

(b) *Communication*

A further set of benefits which can be derived from membership of
international organisations can be collectively grouped under the
heading of communication, and here the Commonwealth is of special
value. One of its chief functions is to facilitate the transmission of
information, ideas and opinions among and between its members, and
often to a wider audience as well. The Commonwealth spans the
north-south chasm where most other international bodies simply
reproduce it, and set-piece speeches, *dialogues des sourds* and confrontation tactics are not characteristic of its meetings. Privacy,
informality and a willingness to listen are very helpful in facilitating
discussion at international meetings of political leaders, and there is
no doubt that the relatively small size of the association and the
availability of English as a working language have enhanced its value
as a communication network.

(c) *Participation and Legitimisation*

One may also consider whether the Commonwealth provides scope
for participation in policy-making and for legitimisation of national
policies. By participating in international organisations, new States
have asserted and tested their sovereignty; they have discovered, too,
the possibilities of collective pressure by banding together as a less-
privileged group to demand concessions from richer States. They are
also ready to dissociate themselves individually or as a group from
policies and decisions over which they were not consulted and with
which they do not concur. In this respect, they are merely following
the well-trodden path of older States, whose governments are fiercely
jealous of their right to participate in international decision-making
whether at the regional or global level.

In the context of Commonwealth relationships, participation means
the right to attend all meetings and to contribute to discussion and
debate; to contribute personnel to the Secretariat; to be involved in
programmes of mutual assistance. These may not be matters of high

---

[17] J. D. B. Miller, *The Commonwealth in the World* (1965), p. 220.

policy and participation in the Commonwealth could not be presented as a vital interest, but at the level of consultation and in programmes of functional co-operation, participation in planning and initiating Commonwealth policy is obviously useful.

International organisations may also offer their members scope for legitimising policies, giving them the stamp of international approval and respectability. As a spin-off from participation this has rather special connotations.

Legitimisation of policy is possible where a single Power dominates an organisation's decision-making processes or where a group of Powers in coalition can exert similar influence to achieve collective goals. Collective legitimisation reinforces national positions and delegitimises opposing policies.[18]

Historically, the United Kingdom dictated foreign policy for the Commonwealth and Empire, but the contemporary Commonwealth does not allow the United Kingdom, or any other single member, to legitimise its policies through the organisation. For one thing, there is little in the way of Commonwealth policy-making in matters of defence or economics; it is not an exclusive arrangement in which one dominant Power can set and enforce norms and control outcomes. For another, the present-day egalitarianism of the Commonwealth would not allow single-Power hegemony to develop. On the other hand, the enlargement of the Commonwealth to the point where, as in the United Nations, new States make up the overwhelming majority of members, means that the older members find it difficult to stand out against policy declarations which are enunciated and vigorously pressed by the majority, particularly where moral principles form the basis of such declarations. The Commonwealth, like the United Nations, has been used as a means of legitimising self-determination and multi-racialism, and as a means of delegitimising systems based on principles of white supremacy. It has also given collective endorsement to principles of economic and social justice and to the restructuring of the international economic order.[19] The danger is that these broad statements of principle which are not binding on individual governments may be pitched so far beyond the reality of existing situations—and the prospects for improving them —that they are heavily discounted and have little practical effect.

While it is clear that the Commonwealth today would not find a Heads of Government meeting worthwhile unless a high-sounding declaration was issued at its conclusion, the value of such statements is presumably in complementing similar declarations and resolutions

---

[18] See I. L. Claude Jr., *The Changing United Nations* (1967), pp. 73–103.

[19] See *Commonwealth Heads of Government Meeting* 1977, The Commonwealth Secretariat, pp. 11–18.

passed by the United Nations General Assembly, and other bodies, and in committing all members of the Commonwealth (old and new), at least morally, to the collective line. But those who abstain from voting at the United Nations, or give tacit approval to such statements in Commonwealth meetings—where votes are not taken—may not feel that their policy options are thereby unduly circumscribed.

(d) *Economic Assistance*

Finally, the Commonwealth offers practical benefits to the majority of its members through programmes of co-operation, particularly in the field of technical assistance—Mr. Ramphal's fourth " theme."

Economic aid in a variety of forms has figured prominently in international relations in the second half of the twentieth century and has become an important element of foreign and domestic policy both for donors and recipients. For the most part it has been offered bilaterally, on a government-to-government basis, as grants or easy-term loans. A small proportion is multilateral, given to international agencies who are then responsible for its disbursement. Much bilateral aid takes the form of military material, supplied to allies or potential allies, but as the process of decolonisation produced an ever-growing number of new States whose living standards were deplorably low, there was an obvious need for extensive economic aid. Rapid industrialisation was a major objective, but there was also a desperate need for improved agricultural techniques, better infrastructure and the initiation or improvement of basic social services.

For the major aid givers, humanitarian concerns have been reinforced by political and economic considerations. Foreign aid has been granted, withheld, and cut off as an instrument of policy and the widespread practice of tying it to the procurement of goods and services from donor countries helped them to support their domestic economies. The needs of developing countries were publicised by the United Nations' Development Decades for the 1960s and 1970s, the latter ushered in by the adoption in December 1970 by the General Assembly of a Development Strategy which looked to an annual rate of growth in *per capita* GNP in the developing countries of 3·5 per cent. and set a target of total aid from developed countries of 1 per cent. of GNP at market prices to be reached at latest by 1975. Of this 0·7 per cent. was to be in the form of official development assistance.[20] These targets have been met by few countries and in recent years the tendency has been for the value of aid, in real terms, to decline. The rise in oil prices since 1973 and the accumulating

---

[20] The Pearson Report *Partners in Development* (1969), also set this target.

burden of debt have also placed an impossibly heavy burden on the balance of payments of the developing countries.

The Commonwealth is not, and has never been, an exclusive aid system. Commonwealth donors give mainly but not exclusively to Commonwealth recipients, while Commonwealth recipients receive bilateral aid from Commonwealth and non-Commonwealth sources.[21] In the contemporary Commonwealth, the United Kingdom, Canada, Australia, and New Zealand are the aid givers, and the bulk of their aid is given bilaterally, on a government-to-government basis, to other Commonwealth countries.[22] In 1973, approximately 70 per cent. of official development assistance from these four countries went to Commonwealth recipients, and this amounted to approximately 36 per cent. of their total aid receipts. Table 2 shows the net official development assistance receipts for developing Commonwealth countries from these four donors in 1973 and 1974.

The United Kingdom has accepted in principle the target of 0·7 per cent. of GNP for official development assistance, although it has not achieved more than 0·4 per cent. to date. In 1975 a new aid strategy was announced " to give an increasing emphasis in . . . bilateral aid towards the poorest countries, especially those . . . most seriously affected by the rise in the price of oil and other commodities." [23] There was henceforth to be particular emphasis on rural development and food production, and it was also hoped to promote the matching of British concessional aid funds by similar funds from other countries and to encourage their deployment through bilateral and multilateral channels towards the poorest countries. Government-to-government aid to countries with a *per capita* income of less than 200 dollars is now given in grant form, while loans are usually made at concessionary interest rates (3 to 6 per cent.) with a grace period of three to six years before repayment begins. Average maturity is 25 years. Except in special circumstances where local costs may be met from aid funds, loans are generally tied to the procurement of goods and services from the United Kingdom.

Mention should also be made of the Commonwealth Development Corporation which permits government and private funds to work in partnership for development. Most of its capital is borrowed from

[21] In 1976 the United States accounted for nearly one-third of the total net flow of assistance to developing countries and multilateral agencies. Canada, Japan, the EEC and its members and other Western countries are also active in the aid business, as are the Soviet Union and Eastern Europe, China and, more recently, the oil-producing States of the Third World.

[22] Nigeria uses its oil resources mainly for its own development but in 1974 made grants to neighbouring countries totalling £12 million.

[23] *The Changing Emphasis in British Aid Policies: More Aid for the Poorest*, Cmnd. 6270, 1975, p. 70.

Table 2

Net Official Development Assistance receipts of developing Commonwealth from developed Commonwealth

Disbursements US $m. Developing Commonwealth by region	Britain		Canada		Australia		New Zealand		Total	
	1973	1974	1973	1974	1973	1974	1973	1974	1973	1974
Africa	104·78	108·41	52·10	76·49	1·92	3·30	0·07	0·22	158·87	188·42
of which:										
Ghana	4·06	1·22	6·71	11·78	0·20	0·23	0·01	0·2	10·98	13·25
Kenya	21·14	23·65	4·44	4·61	0·17	0·13	0·01	—	25·76	28·39
Malawi	14·80	16·64	0·91	1·83	0·10	0·09	0·01	—	15·82	18·56
Nigeria	11·95	3·61	10·34	10·64	0·26	0·21	0·01	0·02	22·57	14·48
Tanzania	2·06	2·02	11·08	31·62	0·15	0·79	—	0·03	13·29	34·46
Zambia	13·33	18·80	2·59	3·91	0·22	0·54	0·01	0·09	16·15	23·34
Asia	126·78	172·74	117·36	170·14	14·01	48·48	2·43	2·91	260·58	394·27
of which:										
Bangladesh	6·54	15·06	54·90	48·55	4·06	31·92	0·76	0·75	66·26	96·28
India	88·94	141·72	54·77	112·56	1·96	7·13	0·22	0·20	145·89	261·61
Sri Lanka	3·95	2·09	4·76	7·06	2·25	4·46	0·04	0·05	11·00	13·66
Malaysia	8·72	7·40	1·65	1·58	4·54	4·05	1·00	1·59	15·91	14·62
Caribbean	42·50	42·55	14·70	18·32	0·06	0·05	0·02	0·03	57·28	60·95
Europe	17·78	15·13	0·01	—	—	0·08	0·01	—	17·80	15·21
Oceania	33·3	30·43	0·05	0·04	196·36	261·03	9·63	14·08	239·37	305·58
of which:										
Papua New Guinea	0·02	0·03	—	—	192·64	254·15	—	0·28	192·66	254·46
Unspecified	23·37	43·38	—	—	—	—	0·54	0·95	23·56	44·33
Total	348·54	412·64	184·22	264·70	212·00	312·84	12·7	18·19	575·46	1,008·37
To all developing countries	602·9	730·9	514·9	713·4	285·9	430·3	29·1	39·2	1,432·8	1,913·8
% of disbursements to Commonwealth countries	57·8	56·4	35·8	37·1	74·1	72·7	43·6	46·4	52·9	52·7

Source: Overseas Development Institute (1976)

the British government and in 1975 its investment in a variety of projects in some 40 countries totalled £200 million.

In 1975, official British development assistance amounted to £432 million. Bilateral aid totalling £297 million was made up of £69 million in grants, £132 million in loans and £96 million in grants for technical co-operation. Commonwealth countries, including dependent territories, accounted for £233 million, or 78 per cent. of the total, and the new policy to help the poorest countries will mean that India, Bangladesh, Sri Lanka and many African countries will receive grant aid in future. Technical assistance, which is a growing feature of all aid programmes, accounted for 31 per cent. of all bilateral aid from the United Kingdom in 1975. Approximately one-half financed experts sent to developing countries and there was also support for students and trainees in the United Kingdom.

Multilateral agencies received £134 million or approximately 30 per cent. of official British aid, in 1975. These funds were shared between the World Bank and its affiliates—the International Development Association (IDA) and the International Finance Corporation (IFC); the International Monetary Fund (IMF) oil facility and its Special Account to help countries most seriously affected by the rise in oil prices; the United Nations Development Programme (UNDP) and other United Nations agencies such as the Food and Agriculture Organisation (FAO) and United Nations Children's Fund (UNICEF); and various development banks with mainly but not exclusively Commonwealth membership (Asian, African, Inter-American and Caribbean). As a member of the EEC since 1973, the United Kingdom is also a contributor to the European Development Fund. For the five-year period 1975–80, the British contribution is £355 million (18·7 per cent. of the total). Much of this EEC aid goes to the countries having a special relationship with the Community under the Lomé Convention, among whom are numbered Commonwealth countries in Africa, the Caribbean and the Pacific.

Historical reasons have also influenced the channelling of Australian, Canadian and New Zealand aid to Commonwealth recipients, but there are some competing demands. Canada as a bilingual, bicultural country, is anxious to support francophone countries through its aid programmes, and it also has regional links with non-Commonwealth as well as Commonwealth Caribbean countries. Most Canadian aid is on a soft loan basis, with zero interest, a 10-year grace period, and 50-year maturity. Australia and New Zealand have regional preoccupations: they are anxious to improve and develop their relationships in South-East Asia and the Pacific. All three countries are committed to the target of 0·7 per cent. of GNP: in 1974 Australia achieved 0·55 per cent., Canada 0·5 per cent. and

New Zealand 0·3 per cent. The proportion of Canadian aid given to multilateral agencies (24 per cent. in 1974) is comparable to the British figure, while Australia gives 15 per cent. in this form. But with few exceptions, Australian aid is given entirely in grant form, and New Zealand's aid follows the same pattern, with 30 per cent. provided through multilateral channels. Australian bilateral aid is concentrated on the Asian/Pacific region, with two-thirds going to Papua-New Guinea, and an increased flow to the Indian sub-continent, particularly food aid. New Zealand concentrates on neighbouring countries in the South Pacific: Fiji, Tonga, Western Samoa, the Cook Islands and Papua-New Guinea.

Bilaterally, it is clear that the Commonwealth provides a useful focus for aid disbursement, particularly as the total amount available for distribution is limited and cannot be spread too widely. Priority for rural development and food production has been generally accepted in recent years. Since the establishment of the Secretariat in 1965, however, and especially since the addition of the Commonwealth Fund for Technical Co-operation (CFTC) in 1971, there has been a small programme of multilateral Commonwealth aid, offering a broad range of technical assistance. This programme does not compare in scale with those administered by the United Nations and its agencies; although the CFTC has grown rapidly, its planned expenditure for 1976–77 (its sixth year of operation) totalled only £8 million. But it is significant because it is a genuine Commonwealth enterprise and because it has been highly successful.

(e) *The Commonwealth Fund for Technical Co-operation*

The basic structure and work of the Commonwealth Fund for Technical Co-operation (CFTC) were described in an earlier paper.[24] It contributes towards the realisation of the developing countries' economic goals by making available advice, experts and training facilities virtually free of charge. Australia, Canada, New Zealand, Nigeria and the United Kingdom—the " affluent " members of the Commonwealth—are the main contributors, but all members are encouraged to contribute on a voluntary basis and do so. Canada matches contributions by developing countries on a two-to-one basis while the United Kingdom has agreed to contribute 30 per cent. of total net expenditure. But there are no sharp lines dividing donor and recipient and, increasingly, experts are drawn from developing countries. In 1977 275 experts were sent out by the Fund, and of these over 100 came from developing Commonwealth countries. As Mr. Ramphal has pointed out, this ensures that the experts under-

---

[24] This writer, " The Commonwealth Secretariat," *op. cit.* in note 2, above, at pp. 88–93.

stand not only the technical problem at hand, but also the social and economic environment in which solutions must be found.[25]

The work of the CFTC is handled through three Divisions concerned with Technical Assistance, Education and Training, and Export Markets. One of its success stories has been the work of the Technical Assistance Group (TAG), a specialist consultancy team made up of economists, lawyers, fiscal specialists and a statistician, who respond quickly to requests from governments for help and can draw on outside resources when required. Thus the TAG has offered constitutional advice to the Seychelles during independence talks in 1975–76; advice to governments undertaking negotiations with multinational corporations and other investors over the exploitation of natural resources, particularly mineral resources (*e.g.*, Papua-New Guinea, Sierra Leone, Botswana and the Caribbean); help with the development of statistical systems on which successful planning depends (*e.g.*, Dominica).

The CFTC's annual expenditure now totals £8 million, compared with £0·2 million in 1971–72 (its first year of operation) while the proportion applied to administration has steadily declined from an initial 45 per cent. to under 9 per cent.[26] Economy and efficiency have been its hallmarks. The 1977 Heads of Government meeting approved its administrative integration into the Secretariat, but it retains full control over the recruitment of experts.

(f) *Other programmes*

Commonwealth co-operation has also continued to expand in fields of education, law, health, science, food production and rural development and youth affairs. Mr. Ramphal notes that in education " the Secretariat's responsiveness to the needs of member countries is informally guided by a vast network of personal contacts between administrators in all of them." [27] In March 1977, the sixth in a series of triennial Commonwealth Education Conferences was held in Accra, and the practical implementation of its recommendations, like those of the Fifth Conference, has been facilitated by the CFTC. The Accra Conference looked specifically at the economics of education, and pointed the need for universal primary education in all Commonwealth countries, for expansion of technical and vocational training, and the expansion of awards under the Commonwealth Scholarship and Fellowship plan. As usual with Commonwealth conferences, its work has been followed up through smaller scale workshops and seminars.

---

[25] *Sixth Report of the Commonwealth Secretary-General* (1977), p. 10.
[26] See *Commonwealth Skills for Commonwealth Needs*, The Commonwealth Secretariat (1977), p. 21.　　　　[27] *Op. cit.* in note 25, above, at p. 35.

Legal activities have also expanded, under the aegis of the Legal Division of the Secretariat. Assistance has been given with drafting; long-term training schemes in regional centres for draftsmen have been instituted; a *Manual* prepared and published. A Commonwealth *Law Bulletin*, launched in 1974, has been well received and is now published regularly three times a year, keeping members aware of legal developments in other parts of the Commonwealth.

A particularly useful Commonwealth undertaking which links the " political " and " technical assistance " aspects of its work has been the Special Programme for Rhodesians initiated in 1966. Exiles from Rhodesia (Zimbabwe) are assisted with education, training and employment and 2,800 have been helped in this way. The Secretariat acts as a clearing house in liaison with Commonwealth governments, the Organisation of African Unity (OAU), United Nations agencies, Zimbabwe nationalist bodies and voluntary organisations. Scholarships outside Rhodesia and correspondence courses for students in Rhodesia are also financed by the Commonwealth Rhodesia Scholarship Trust Fund. Since 1975 a similar programme has been in operation for Namibia, and the Commonwealth Secretary-General reported that in April 1977, 71 Namibians had been helped and 55 were currently studying in secondary schools in the Gambia, Ghana and Sierra Leone.

In health there have been notable developments. A Medical Adviser to the Secretary-General was appointed in 1969, and his office is now responsible for identifying problems of wide significance, and for organising follow-up action. Training of medical engineering technicians is one of the projects in this area: the development of community health services is another. There has also been a welcome emphasis on regional co-operation. Health Secretariats have been established in West Africa (Lagos 1972) and East, Central and Southern Africa including Mauritius and the Seychelles (Arusha, Tanzania 1975), while a health section has been added to the Secretariat of the Caribbean Community (CARICOM). The Commonwealth Secretariat gives financial support to these ventures, and also maintains liaison with the World Health Organisation to avoid duplication of effort.

The importance of science and technology in assisting developing countries in their struggle to improve living standards can hardly be overstressed and it is planned to integrate the Commonwealth Science Council into the Secretariat as a new division in order to tackle this area with the maximum efficiency. It is particularly relevant to food production and rural development which are basic to any rise in living standards, and which have been looked after by a special division of the Secretariat since the Kingston meeting.

The problems of youth continue to exercise Commonwealth governments, and three regional centres in Chandigarh, India, Lusaka, Zambia and Georgetown, Guyana provide training facilities for youth leaders and sponsor other youth-related activities.

All these programmes, which are also supported by non-governmental organisations, have helped to build a latticework of connections between Commonwealth countries which have positive results not only in bringing people in touch with each other, but in raising levels of performance through training schemes and helping to improve socio-economic conditions throughout the developing Commonwealth.

In general the Secretariat is ready to provide advice and assistance and follow-up action on a wide range of matters and its publications and special studies are most useful. Moreover, as part of its general service to members, it has also continued to watch the interests of those members of the Commonwealth who were adversely affected by the United Kingdom's entry to the EEC and the consequent loss of Commonwealth preference or duty-free entry to the British market. New Zealand still has some problems, but the worst hit are the Asian countries who did not qualify under Protocol 22 of the Treaty of Accession for association through the Lomé Convention, and who must rely on the rather insubstantial benefits of the EEC, and other General Systems of Preference.

II—PROSPECTS FOR THE FUTURE

The Commonwealth now has some solid achievements to its credit, and one can understand Mr. Ramphal's concern to maintain its momentum and to seek ways of fulfilling the objectives which he sees as crucial in the years ahead. It might be expected, too, that his background as a politician in Guyana, where he was Minister for Foreign Affairs before becoming Secretary-General of the Commonwealth, would draw him to develop the political aspects of his office, particularly as a firm groundwork had been laid by his predecessor for initiatives to be grasped by the Secretary-General wherever opportunities offered scope for him to do so. Moreover, Mr. Ramphal *is* a Third-World man, not just responsive to its needs, but sharing them, and he sees the Commonwealth as a group which must work in the wider global context for the realisation of economic and social justice.[28]

In considering his Commonwealth objectives of contributing to

---

[28] For an interesting discussion of political leadership by the United Nations Secretary-General, particularly through the vehicle of the Annual Report see R. Rieber, this *Year Book*, Vol. 30 (1976), pp. 62–68. Mr. Ramphal's *Sixth Report* suggests that he sees the value of this medium for direction as well as information.

the restructuring of international economic relationships and making a more positive commitment to the service of the world community, one applauds the intention not to be inward-looking or self-serving, and to maintain the vitality of the association by setting it new goals which are in tune with the times, even if one retains a certain scepticism about the chances for success of these new policy directions which may require from the Commonwealth a more politicised thrust than it is able to sustain.

There are certainly a number of areas in which the Commonwealth can be of service to the wider world, and its links with other international bodies are particularly useful in this context. The Commonwealth was granted official observer status at the United Nations in 1976, and permanent representatives of Commonwealth States now meet monthly at the United Nations on an informal basis. Formal or informal liaison is also maintained with bodies in the United Nations system (UNCTAD, UNESCO, FAO, WHO, GATT, the World Bank the IMF and IMCO) and outside it (OECD, the European Commission). The Secretariat is also in touch with L'Agence de Coopération Culturelle et Technique—a francophone grouping which would like to emulate the success of the CFTC—and links between the two associations could be productive in areas where their respective members are neighbours, as in West Africa.

The Commonwealth as a whole, encouraged by the Secretariat, has also tried to come to grips with the problems of the "New International Economic Order." A Commonwealth group of (10) experts, chaired by Mr. Alastair McIntyre, Secretary-General of the Caribbean Community, was appointed by the 1975 Heads of Government meeting to draw up proposals for bridging the gap between rich and poor nations as a contribution to the dialogue on this subject. Two interim reports were published, the first of which was made available first to the annual meeting of Commonwealth finance ministers in August 1975 and then to the Seventh Special Session of the United Nations General Assembly. The final report, which like the interim reports, reflected unaminity of the group, was presented to the Heads of Government meeting in London in June 1977.

The Group of Experts interpreted its terms of reference as requiring it to "approach the problem of poverty and deprivation in the developing countries from the standpoint of their fundamental requirements for economic development." [29] Their recommendations are intended to accelerate structural transformation, encompass "bold and complementary action on several fronts" and look to a

---

[29] *Toward a New International Economic Order: a final report by a Commonwealth Experts' Group*, The Commonwealth Secretariat (1977), p. 9.

" substantially different pattern of international economic relations " as well as " fundamental changes in the structure of production in developing countries." [30] The report notes the urgency of the problem, commenting that if present trends are not checked, " the balance of payments situation of developing countries will become progressively unmanageable " and calls for " concrete action " to match rhetoric. [31]

It is impossible to do justice to the report in a short paper of this kind. The main areas covered by its recommendations are commodity arrangements; food production and rural development; industrial co-operation and development; economic co-operation among developing countries; invisibles; international finance and international institutions. In commenting on the role which a new international economic order could play in transforming and developing the Third World, the Group notes that certain changes would be essential. First, there must be a radical and progressive change in the global distribution of economic activity. Secondly, there must be an improved volume and quality of financial flows and of technology; in fact, the transfer of technology should be " one of the central thrusts of the New International Economic Order," [32] and multinational corporations should be part of the new relationships. Thirdly, there must be emphasis on self-reliance; and, fourthly, universal husbanding of the world's resources.

In areas of this kind, where the Commonwealth provides a stimulating framework for research and policy-oriented planning, it is obviously desirable that findings should be made widely available; similarly the extension of Commonwealth co-operation in regions such as West Africa to include non-Commonwealth countries is to be welcomed. Few social or economic problems respect national boundaries. It is also important that the Commonwealth can provide a forum for constructive discussion, the results of which can be carried forward to other bodies. An example would be the establishment of a common position at a meeting of Commonwealth Finance Ministers prior to the annual IMF and World Bank meetings in Washington. It is in this context that Mr. Ramphal writes of the Commonwealth becoming a " catalyst in consensus formation " [33]; its unique make up and flexible procedures give it a role which he is anxious to develop.

But too much should not be expected of the Commonwealth even in this area. It is a microcosm of the world and, like other

---

[30] *Ibid.* p. 10.

[31] *Ibid.* pp. 10–11.

[32] *Ibid.* p. 21.

[33] S. Ramphal, " The Role of the Commonwealth in the Context of the New International Economic Order," *Commonwealth Record of Recent Events*, January–March 1976, p. 11.

international bodies, it reflects in its membership wide disparities in wealth, power, ideology and interests. A greater willingness to talk reasonably at Commonwealth meetings is valuable in itself and can produce limited agreement, but meaningful consensus, which leads to action, is likely to be elusive.

Once the early post-colonial (mainly British) rhetoric had evaporated, the level of Commonwealth aspiration became sensibly modest. Aspiration and achievement did not sharply diverge; expectations were not disappointed and the organisation's credibility was not depreciated. Indeed, in some areas the Commonwealth's success has produced pleasurable surprise. Nor can it be disputed that open relationships and an atmosphere conducive to communication are worth preserving in themselves. It is also true that the Commonwealth today tends to be supportive of governments. It confirms sovereignty and facilitates the tasks of governing which are becoming more difficult as governments are expected to play a greater role in managing the economic and social life of the country while, at the same time, it becomes increasingly difficult for them to do so because of interdependence with other economies.[34] The danger for the Commonwealth is that it could be seen by the majority of its members as a body which must present the developing countries' position strongly at all times. Its bridging role between different countries with different levels of achievement and aspiration could be threatened if it becomes yet another forum for indicting the affluent and if Commonwealth statements are transmitted to other bodies which do not reflect a genuine consensus among its own members. It is more important that the Commonwealth should preserve its cross-cutting links, and this requires continuing restraint in rhetoric as well as in goals. Moreover, a widening gap between pronouncements and outcomes must be avoided if the Commonwealth is to retain the confidence of all its members.

There is the further difficulty that the Commonwealth itself is not free from political strain. In the past, India and Pakistan were bitterly hostile and at times at war while both were members.[35] Nigeria suffered a protracted civil war in which different members of the Commonwealth took different sides. Cyprus, a Commonwealth member, was invaded and dismembered by Turkey in 1974, but the Commonwealth took no action. Above all, there have been continuing crises over Southern Africa. The major questions at issue have

---

[34] At the suggestion of the Canadian Prime Minister, a programme for Applied Studies in Government was initiated within the Secretariat in 1975, which has relevance to all members. See the *Sixth Report of the Commonwealth, Secretary-General* (1977), p. 43.

[35] Pakistan left the Commonwealth in 1972 when Bangladesh was recognised by the United Kingdom and other Commonwealth members.

been South Africa's continued membership of the Commonwealth and, later, British arms sales to the Republic; the independence of Namibia; the illegal declaration of independence by the Smith Government in'Rhodesia and the imposition of international sanctions. At the time of writing, Rhodesia presents an acute crisis; the situation has deteriorated to the point where guerrilla warfare is raging in parts of the country, supported by the " Front Line " neighbouring African States of Zambia, Tanzania, Botswana and Mozambique (three of whom are Commonwealth members, and the fourth, Mozambique, in receipt of special Commonwealth assistance) while strenuous efforts are being made by the United Kingdom and the United States to bring about a peaceful settlement and transfer of power to black Rhodesians. Their object is to avoid further bloodshed and an escalation of violence which could engulf the whole Southern African region. One major difference of opinion within the Commonwealth has already been mentioned; African States advocated the use of force by the United Kingdom to end the " rebellion " in Rhodesia, while the United Kingdom and other " old " Commonwealth members have preferred to work through diplomatic and economic pressure for a peaceful transfer of power. But, as time has passed and external circumstances have changed, the chances of salvaging a privileged, or perhaps even a protected position for Rhodesian whites have become slimmer, and a potentially very divisive issue in future Commonwealth relations looms larger. This is the question of emotional affinity between whites in Southern Africa and whites in the United Kingdom (which in many cases involve family ties) and indeed with whites in Australia, Canada and New Zealand as well. Increasing guerrilla activity and acts of black terrorism, or an extremist black government in Rhodesia (Zimbabwe) could make this issue even more sensitive and Commonwealth unity could be imperilled.

Both Mr. Ramphal and his predecessor Mr. Smith have been involved in " quiet diplomacy " on all these issues, but there has been a reluctance to involve the Commonwealth politically, except in support of United Nations initiatives where these have been possible. It may be enough for the Commonwealth to provide moral support for majority rule in Rhodesia and independence for Namibia, and to offer practical assistance in training and education rather than attempting a distinct political role of its own which would strain Commonwealth unity.

But if there are dangers in the Commonwealth attempting too much, there are also dangers in attempting too little. This dilemma confronts Mr. Ramphal as it confronts executive heads of other international bodies, tempting the activists like Dag Hammarskjöld to press to the limits of their office and beyond, and encouraging the less venturesome to stay within " acceptable " and neutral boundaries.[36] While functional co-operation can expand and the shared background and style of many Commonwealth administrators provides some " cement," one has the sense that something more will be needed to hold the organisation together in the future. The Commonwealth does need to present an identifiable international image and this requires that there be activities which are known to have a Commonwealth " stamp " and occasionally the Commonwealth must act collectively as a group. The Commonwealth might for instance, have taken a firm stand on issues such as the resources of the deep sea bed, the preservation of the environment, the declarations of " zones of peace " in the Indian Ocean and elsewhere, the slackening of the arms race and a total ban on nuclear testing, and the support of human rights. This would require more than agreement on brief statements of principle at biennial Heads of Government meetings: the Commonwealth position would have to be presented vigorously in other forums, particularly the United Nations, and the Secretariat would be required to co-ordinate effective follow-up activity.

It is also important that the public in Commonwealth countries should be much better informed about the work of the association. Although its programmes of co-operation bring people together at official and unofficial levels, so that an increasing number of people meet their Commonwealth counterparts and may therefore be expected to have some sense of the value of Commonwealth links, reports of such meetings usually have little media appeal. The role of the Information Division of the Secretariat can be important here, and it has greatly improved the quality and range of its publications. A new and interesting service which reaches out to a mass audience is the monthly service of taped programmes on Commonwealth current affairs provided by the Secretariat free of charge to more than 50 radio stations throughout the Commonwealth. There are also plans for a " bank " of radio and television material. Governments, too, could do more to publicise the Commonwealth in their own countries.

The Commonwealth has shown great adaptability in changing its structure and focus in response to environmental needs and the Secretary-General, with the confidence and support of member governments, can now exercise a strong leadership role within the association which can contribute to its continued vitality. If the

---

[36] For discussion of the " minimalist " and " maximalist " theories concerning the Secretary-General of the United Nations see S. Schwebel, *The Secretary-General of the United Nations* (1952), pp. 3–12; O. Young, *The Intermediaries* (1967), pp. 265–271.

Commonwealth were more central to the foreign policies of its members, it would be more likely to die suddenly as a result of political crises blowing it apart. As it is, it may be some time before it dies of old age. In the meantime, its value as a set of connections, building on common historical and cultural experience, cutting across lines of colour and wealth, meeting current practical needs and transcending the nation-State is not to be gainsaid.

INDIRA GANDHI

AUTOCRATIC DEMOCRAT

By

HUGH TINKER

THE political career of Indira Gandhi has unfolded as a serial story of the unexpected. Chosen as India's Prime Minister because her backers judged her to be a political lightweight who would be malleable in their hands, she turned out to be tougher than them all. Her first general election as national leader was a near-disaster, in which the Congress Party, the unchallengeable " Freedom Movement," came near to losing its parliamentary majority. Within four years, Mrs. Gandhi had gained an unrivalled position of national regard by her courageous handling of the long crisis out of which East Pakistan emerged as Bangladesh. Yet, within a short time her popularity was ebbing and she was again under pressure.

Unexpectedly, her whole position became vulnerable when a judge, hearing an election petition brought against her, ruled that she was not entitled to her seat in Parliament—and therefore could not, legally, remain Prime Minister. Mrs. Gandhi replied by assuming autocratic powers even beyond those wielded by the British Viceroys. She manipulated Parliament, the Press, and the judiciary. Her " Emergency " distorted and seemingly transformed India's system of government. Observers deduced that the last great democracy in Asia had now gone the way of all the others and surrendered popular government for a ruthless personal authority.

Then, quite against the trend of her announced programme, she decided to ask the electorate for a mandate on her record of rule. Observers inferred that this would be a rigged election, carefully orchestrated to provide her with even greater personal power. In perhaps the greatest upset ever experienced by a solidly-established leader in an appeal to previously solid electoral support, Mrs. Gandhi was decisively rejected by the Indian people: her own constituency providing a personal humiliation. It appeared as though her political career was finished. Gradually, however, she began to receive support from groups disillusioned with the uncertain performance of her successors. In order to check her rise, the new government brought charges against her, once again citing electoral irregularities. She was brought before a magistrate, who dismissed the case. There followed a surge of public sympathy, which seemed to be sweeping Indira Gandhi back into a commanding position. Yet all did not go her way, and, although it seems probable that she will make a return to power and influence one day, that day does not yet seem imminent.

After her defeat, without a seat in Parliament or a position of power within the Congress Party, Mrs. Gandhi still remains the most talked-about politician in India. The weeklies constantly run features about her; the Prime Minister is quizzed about his intentions towards her at his press conferences; whenever she chooses to make a public appearance, all others present are up-staged. And yet she is the opposite of a charismatic leader. Her personality has always appeared withdrawn, " up-tight," in current jargon. Her utterances seldom depart from the trite; it is only the conviction with which she speaks that saves her pronouncements from the trivial. Her ideas are not her own; at best they are taken from the thoughts of her father and of Mahatma Gandhi. It is only in her actions that she is impressive; and she therefore requires a political arena, before she can demonstrate her capacity for decision-making.

Daughter of a man who was an enigma, she is even more an enigma. Nehru was always able to articulate his doubts and ambiguities in language of haunting persuasiveness. Indira Gandhi seems unaware that she is so baffling to other people. Moreover, while Nehru—like his daughter—was aloof, imperious, and scarcely bothered to conceal the impatience and contempt which he so often felt for his importunate admirers, he could also be charming, gay, warmhearted, and sympathetic to all manner of persons, high and low. Those who manage to please or even to interest Mrs. Gandhi seem to be very few indeed.

Thus, in treating Indira Gandhi as one who deserves to be regarded as a major figure in the world's forum, certain difficulties arise. She does not lend herself either to a " hard " presentation, as a political leader with a coherent philosophy and programme which is amenable to intellectual analysis, nor to a " soft " presentation as the subject of a human drama. Several studies have portrayed her merely as a tyrant; but this is too easy. She is a strange mixture of the dictator and the tribune of the people. Like Nehru, she has a demi-mystical vision of India's millions as her own family. She believes that she is acting on behalf of the Indian people because she and they want the same objectives. When she is accused of seeking personal power, or power for her son, Sanjay, she seems unable to comprehend how she could be so misunderstood. In her own estimation she has always behaved as the servant of the people. And, indeed, she has been misrepresented and perhaps misunderstood by certain opponents whose motives are even more mixed than her own. Perhaps the key to her story is provided by one of Oliver Cromwell's sayings: " He goes furthest who knows not whither he goes." It is impossible to believe that Indira Gandhi deliberately planned the Emergency, with all its grim constraints on liberty and the rule of law. Now that it is past, she seems not to realise fully what was done in her name.

She will be chiefly remembered by her ruthless exercise of supreme authority. Yet, under no pressure save from within herself, she submitted her whole Emergency system to the verdict of the people —and lost. She accepted the verdict without argument. She is indeed a strange mixture of the democrat and the autocrat. Perhaps the confused, contradictory circumstances of her upbringing helped to make her so.

I—A REMOTE CHILDHOOD

Indira was born in 1917, at her grandfather's palatial residence, Anand Bhavan, the " Heavenly Mansion " in Allahabad. Jawaharlal was his imperious father's only son, and before this birth a son had been ardently desired. Kamala, Indira's mother, was made very conscious of her shortcomings, which were added to the educational deficiencies and physical frailty which (so she sensed) had made her an inadequate wife for Jawaharlal in others' eyes. Soon after her daughter was born, symptoms of congenital illness were manifested. When she again conceived, the child was stillborn. That it was a manchild made this all the more tragic.

Soon after Indira's fourth birthday, her father was arrested and sentenced to imprisonment. Thus began the long sequence of political campaigns, followed by jail sentences, which were to be the background to Indira's girlhood. At Anand Bhavan, the life of luxury was somewhat modified to meet the dedication to working for India's freedom which Jawaharlal and his father had embraced; yet it was still a wealthy household, where the only child of the Nehrus was at the centre of the continuous coming and going. Her most perceptive biographer has observed of this period that Indira was " alternatively petted and abandoned by those around her." [1] Her own recollections of this time centred upon the deprivations rather than the indulgences. " My own childhood was an abnormal one, full of loneliness and insecurity," she later recalled.[2]

Following her father's instructions, she was packed off to a boarding school at Poona run on lines of cultural nationalism, not those of a Western syllabus leading to British-type examinations. Subsequently, Indira was sent to the academy presided over by the poet Rabindranath Tagore at Santiniketan, the " Abode of Peace."

---

[1] Z. Masani, *Indira Gandhi; a biography* (1975), p. 33.
[2] Indira Gandhi, *India: Speeches and Reminiscences* (1975), p. 42.

Under the towering influence of the poet, her life began to have some meaning. But her ailing mother was now very sick indeed, and Indira was taken away to be at her side.

Meanwhile, Nehru from his prison cell had seemed to view his daughter as a symbol of the new India, rather than as a child in need of affection and support. He addressed a series of reflective, philosophical essays to her, subsequently published as *Letters From a Father to a Daughter*, and he eventually composed for her a series of Toynbeean vignettes, entitled *Glimpses of World History*. It must have been both flattering and daunting for the rather ill-educated Indira to be the recipient of these cosmic reflections. On a personal level, the father was unhappy about his daughter's development. Her replies to his communications were perfunctory and infrequent. To his beloved sister, Nan (Mrs. Pandit), Jawaharlal complained: " If there is one type I dislike it is the languishing type which lounges through life undecided as to what to do, but expecting everybody to minister to his or her comforts. Indu has already developed many characteristics of this type. Then again she is remarkably casual and indifferent to others . . . Indu, however, revolves around herself; self-centred, she hardly thinks of others." [3] This was the girl who now accompanied her parents to Europe in search of treatment which might arrest the disease—tuberculosis—which was killing Kamala Nehru. For nine months, Indira was at her mother's side while she slowly declined. During this time, Indira's understanding of her mother's sense of frustration, and of her unrealised aspirations as a woman drew them close together. Jawaharlal was frequently away from his wife's bedside, making contacts among European socialists and other potential allies. Typical of this time was a letter of December 6, 1935, which Jawaharlal sent to an English friend, Agatha Harrison, wherein he reports that " Kamala's temperature again shot up," though he insists, "at least she is holding her own." Planning to return to India, he declares, " I should very much like to join her in Switzerland before I go, but how can I say if this will be possible." Indira would be with her mother for Christmas: meanwhile, " a young friend of ours had visited Kamala: Feroze Gandhy," described by Nehru as " a bright lad, and one of our best workers in Allahabad."

Feroze Gandhy had been accepted by Kamala as a friend in Allahabad. The fact that he was a member of another religious community—the Parsis—was not a barrier; for Kamala's most intimate friend (closer to her, perhaps, than her husband) was a Muslim, Syed Mahmoud. Now, as they sat by the dying Kamala, the casual relationship which Feroze and Indira had accepted in

---

[3] B. N. Pandey, *Nehru* (1976), p. 182.

Allahabad grew into something deeper. Feroze went off to study at
the London School of Economics; Indira was placed in a girl's
school in Switzerland (where she acquired a good knowledge of
French in a Swiss accent). So it remained, until on February 28,
1936, Kamala Nehru died in the presence of husband and daughter.
Indira returned to her Swiss school; Jawaharlal returned to India.
" No longer inhibited by her physical presence, Jawaharlal was able
to feel a deeper love for Kamala now than ever before ": so concludes
Nehru's biographer. The same might be said of his relationship with
Indira.

Oppressed by her mother's death, the girl was sickly and sad.
Agatha Harrison was deeply distressed by her unhappy condition.
When, some months later, she sat for the entrance examination to
Somerville College at Oxford she was not accepted. Intensive coaching
followed, and in February 1938 she was admitted at Somerville. She
was now 21, but still immature and quite unable to respond to the
intellectual demands of Oxford. In October 1939, she contracted
pleurisy; naturally, it was feared that she might follow her mother's
unhappy course. Agatha Harrison took her back to Switzerland,
where she spent a year while Europe moved from phoney war to
Nazi hegemony.

In February 1941, she managed to get a passage from Britain to
India. Accompanying her on the ship was Feroze Gandhy, whose
academic career had been as successful as hers had been dismal.
They regarded themselves as betrothed to be married.

II—A WILL OF HER OWN

This news was received with dismay by the Nehru family. It has been
argued that opposition to Feroze Gandhy was not based on his
belonging to a different religion and caste, but on his social inferiority.
Nehru's sister, Krishna Hutheesing (herself married outside the clan
of the Kashmiri Brahmans) put it very bluntly: his background was
" so different from Indira's. He came from a middle class Parsi
family of modest means. He may have felt ill at ease in the midst of
social formalities." [4] It is therefore necessary to add that the Gandhy
family, long domiciled in Allahabad, were actually as cultured as
the Nehrus. The sister of Feroze, Tehmina Kershap Gandhy,
possessed a Cambridge diploma and had a senior position in the
education service while D. J. Gandhy, of the agricultural service, had
an American M.A. (like the Nehrus, the Gandhys straddled nationalist
politics and service in the British administration). What was different
was that the Gandhy family was less wealthy than the Nehrus.

---

[4] *Op. cit.* in note 1, above, at p. 95.

Jawaharlal turned to Mahatma Gandhi to dissuade the wayward girl from this *mésalliance*. Gandhi was always ready to urge young people not to marry until the day that India was free. But now, for the first time, Indira demonstrated that she was a woman with a backbone. She resisted all pleadings. The young couple agreed that they would wait a year to see how their feelings developed under the conditions of home life. Seeing that they remained determined, the family consented to their marriage at the end of March 1942. Indira's childhood was over.

The year 1942 saw the " Quit India " movement and the subsequent incarceration of Nehru for almost three years. In the wake of her father's arrest, Indira was interned, though she was released after nine months in jail. Feroze was also quickly released (politically, he was not important). In 1944, their first son, Rajiv, was born. The birth of the second son, Sanjay, followed in December 1946: by then, Jawaharlal was leader of the interim government and independence was only nine months distant.

After independence, the Viceroy's House in New Delhi—as large as Versailles—became the President's official residence; the second largest mansion in the capital—formerly occupied by the Commander-in-Chief—was taken over by the Prime Minister. Indira Gandhi (as she was now known) became mistress of this mausoleum. Here she brought up her little boys, and here her husband resided; but rather as the lodger. Increasingly, Indira became involved in the ceremonial and protocol of high politics. Feroze disliked his own position, neither in nor out of the Prime Minister's menage. In 1950, he was found a constituency at a by-election, and increasingly he went his own way, staying at the flat which went with his job as Member of Parliament. But there was no formal change in the marital status of Indira and her husband.

Besides accompanying Nehru on his political tours, Indira began to emerge as a peripheral political figure. She made speeches during the general election campaign of 1952, and it was noticeable that her shyness and awkwardness disappeared as the crowd responded to her appeal. She did not seek to enter parliament, but she did begin to participate in party politics. In 1955 she was elected a member of the Working Committee of the All-India Congress Committee: the so-called " High Command." Then, in 1958, she was promoted to the Congress Parliamentary Board, the key group which supervised the functioning of the Congress ministries in the States. Also, in 1958, Feroze broke away completely from his wife and came no more to the Nehru home. Indira did not accept that the break was final; somehow, she hoped to reconcile her growing political career with her marriage. As Nehru observed: " She couldn't make up her mind one way or the other, and it only caused more suffering all round." [5] Unexpectedly, in 1959, she was nominated President of the Congress. This promotion was as much an acknowledgment of the standing of Nehru as of the ability of his daughter. In her new role Indira proved to be " as much a source of embarrassment as of pride " to the ageing Prime Minister.[6] Later, Indira was to observe: " My father was a saint who strayed into politics: I am a politician." Whether or not Nehru was a saint, he was certainly an intellectual; one who saw several sides to every question. Indira saw only the need to produce an answer to a question: *one* answer. She was not interested in discussing alternatives.

During her time as Congress President the explosive situation in Kerala—where a Communist government confronted an agitation stirred up by Congress in opposition—came to crisis point. Nehru was disposed to accept the Communist government as an element in the Indian political set-up; Indira was resolved to bring it down. The President of the Indian Union was endowed with emergency powers whereby the State government could be suspended and the administration taken under direct " president's rule." Indira Gandhi urged this course on President Rajendra Prasad, and when he hesitated she publicly called for action: " Central action in Kerala is already long overdue," she urged; adding in prophetic tones, " If the Constitution has no remedy for the people of Kerala, the Constitution should be amended." Six days later the president fell into line and dismissed the Communist government.

Her second intervention concerned the State of Bombay which was torn apart on linguistic lines by those who spoke Marathi and those speaking Gujarathi. Nehru tried to minimise the dispute in the interests of preserving a bilingual State, believing that both groups needed to retain their links with the great city of Bombay. Indira paid a whirlwind visit to the Marathi districts of the State, addressing 150 meetings within six days. She returned convinced that the linguistic division must be recognised, or else Congress would lose ground to the opposition parties. Her argument was accepted; the Congress Working Committee endorsed the partition of Bombay State, and parliament carried through the necessary legislation.

However, the strain of the Congress presidency proved too much for Indira's indifferent health. Instead of completing the normal two-year term, she resigned after one year, pleading that she needed complete rest. An added factor was the breakdown in the health of Feroze, which temporarily served to bring him together again with his wife. In September 1960 Feroze died, after his second heart

---

[5] *Ibid.* p. 96.
[6] *Op. cit.* in note 2, above, at p. 396.

attack; he was only 48. Indira was shocked and shattered. Nevertheless, within a year she was back in active politics.

Internal events now became secondary to the gathering border dispute with China; a dispute which Nehru attempted to minimise and shrug aside, much influenced by his Defence Minister, V. K. Krishna Menon. At last, in November 1962, his policy collapsed. Under pressure from public opinion, he ordered the Indian army to eject the Chinese from their front-line positions. The offensive failed, and the Chinese attacked, laying open the Assam valley to invasion. At this moment, when the government was almost paralysed and local defences had collapsed, Mrs. Gandhi flew to the most threatened point in Assam, Tezpur, to assess the situation for herself. Almost as she arrived China announced a cease-fire, and Indira's resolve was not finally tested.

The Indo-China war had undermined the Indian people's faith in Nehru's leadership. There were demands for the dismissal of some of his protégés, notably Krishna Menon, and some talk of bringing Indira into the Cabinet to strengthen the younger, progressive element. Nehru rejected pleas by T. T. Krishnamachari, the confidant of his later years, to make Indira a Minister on the grounds that he must not favour his own family.[7] The argument was unconvincing, considering the favours he had shown to others—Mrs. Pandit, especially, who had been given the highest diplomatic appointments, though Nehru's own sister.

Whatever Nehru's reservations about his daughter's political style, he came to depend on her to take most of the burden of office from him during the last two years in which his powers rapidly went into decline. One who saw him frequently at this time commented: " The Prime Minister's schedule, his appointments, the papers to be shown him—all came under her scrutiny and control. And while she may not have played a substantive [political] role, with influence on basic governmental decisions, she was an important element in the power structure by virtue of her unique access to the Prime Minister, still the seat of ultimate decision." [8]

When Nehru died there was no designated heir-apparent, and the Congress leaders, the so-called " Syndicate," looked for a successor among a small group of candidates. All were seasoned politicians—except for Mrs. Gandhi, who was named publicly and privately. Jagjivan Ram, leader of the former Untouchable community, made an attempt to induce the other candidates to stand down in her favour, though this manoeuvre failed to interest the other leaders.

---

[7] *Ibid.* p. 397.

[8] M. Brecher, *Succession in India: a study in decision-making* (1966), p. 25.

No evidence emerges to indicate that she herself was behind Jagjivan Ram's ploy.[9]

However, after Lal Bahadur Shastri had been unanimously chosen by Congress, as the new Prime Minister, Indira accepted his offer of a post in the new Cabinet. Thus, within two weeks of her father's death she had moved into the position denied her during his lifetime. She was not a Member of Parliament, and the Constitution of India requires that all Ministers must become M.P.s within six months of taking office (or else forfeit their posts). A place was found for her in the Upper House, the *Rajya Sabha*, whose members are nominated or indirectly elected. Hence, she did not have to win a constituency.

Her parliamentary performance as Minister of Information was somewhat faltering. It was in accord with her record that she made a greater impact outside parliament. When the long-standing agitation in Madras for the rights of the Tamil-speakers reached a dangerous level of conflict, Mrs. Gandhi suggested that a member of the Cabinet ought to visit Madras in order to demonstrate the concern of the central government. As no-one else volunteered, she made the journey. She was several times exposed to personal danger, but she carried through her programme.

III—THE UNEXPECTED PREMIERSHIP

Then, unexpectedly, the whole question of the national leadership arose again after the sudden death of Shastri at Tashkent. This time, the President of the Congress, the powerful southern leader, Nadar Kamaraj, put all his authority behind the nomination of Mrs. Gandhi. Kamaraj could well have had the premiership for himself; for his power in the Congress machine was so wide-ranging that he could have fixed a majority of supporters behind him. Having a poor knowledge of English, and conscious of the difficulty facing a leader from the South in controlling northern India, he picked on Indira as the only personality who could appeal to the masses in the impending election while (so he judged) she posed no threat to his overall control, possessing no personal power base within the Congress machine. Kamaraj was able to persuade almost all the premiers of the States—men whose chief concern was to preserve their own kingdoms from central pressure—that Indira would suit them best of all. Twelve of the fourteen premiers announced that they were for her. However, in contrast to the choice of Shastri in 1964, unanimity could not be attained because Morarji Desai of Gujarat insisted on coming forward as a rival. The contest was not without personal bitterness, but, when the vote of the eligible Congress Parliamentary

---

[9] *Ibid.* pp. 50–51.

Party members was counted, 169 had voted for Morarji and 355 for Indira.

Mrs. Gandhi's debut as Prime Minister was uncomfortable. She read out her first speech " with a somewhat monotonous and school-girlish sing-song intonation," and she was so often heckled by the opposition that the Speaker had to threaten discipline.[10] Soon after-wards, the decision to devalue the Indian rupee was taken and responsibility for this calamity was assigned to her; even supporters like Kamaraj blamed her for the move, so disastrous in view of the impending election. Attempts to reshuffle the Cabinet, and to give prominence to Mrs. Gandhi's main allies, C. Subramaniam and T. B. Chavan, were thwarted by Kamaraj and the established Congress leaders. In a state of personal and party political weakness, Mrs. Gandhi faced the general election of 1967.

No-one could accuse her of shrinking from the contest. Like her father, she undertook a gruelling all-India tour, travelling 15,200 miles to reach the electorate. For the first time she directly contested a constituency—for the House of the People (*Lok Sabha*)—Rae Bareli (where Nehru launched his first campaign among the peasants in 1921). Speaking to her constituents she declared: " My family is not confined to a few individuals. It consists of crores [hundreds of thousands] of people. . . . Crores of my family are poverty-stricken, and I have to look after them."

The opposition used smear tactics against her. A song was sung in the Rae Bareli villages: " At Delhi, there is the reign of a widow; Above all there is *Kamraj* [' the reign of lust ']; How can you expect *Ramraj*? [' the reign of God ']." The villagers were being reminded that, according to Hindu belief, widowhood is an affliction incurred because of sins committed in a previous incarnation.[11] However, the rural voters saw through the attempt to deceive them.

When the result was announced, she had scored a dramatic personal success at Rae Bareli; but the all-India result was nearly disastrous. Congress strength in parliament fell from 371 to 281, with 150 of the seats won by a margin of 500 to 1,000 votes in constituencies with an average electorate of 500,000.

When parliament re-assembled it was not even certain that Mrs. Gandhi would be re-elected as leader of Congress. The leaders tried to make her accept their men as Ministers; she fought back, but was compelled to appoint Morarji Desai as Deputy Prime Minister and Finance Minister. The internal party wrangling came to a head over the choice of a new President. Indira wanted the scholarly veteran

[10] *Op. cit.* in note 1, above, at p. 151.
[11] V. P. Vatuk, *Thieves in my House: studies in Indian folklore of protest and change* 1969), p. 30.

Nationalist Muslim, Dr. Zakir Hussain. Kamaraj and the leaders objected to a Muslim and wanted the strong-minded Radhakrishnan to be given a second term as President. This time, Indira won the argument; she had now acquired her own following within the Congress Parliamentary Party and she was demonstrating a new strength. Zakir Hussain died after two years in office, and again her Congress opponents tried to override the Prime Minister. Sanjiva Reddy, a southern conservative was selected as presidential candidate with tacit support from opposition members. Mrs. Gandhi fought back. She could not openly challenge Reddy's nomination, but she encouraged the Vice-President, V. V. Giri to stand, and she used her influence to secure a free vote.

There was another audience, wider than the party faithful, waiting to see the consequences of the growing struggle. Mrs. Gandhi sensed that the public had withdrawn support from Congress in 1967 because it was no longer " their " party. They looked for some demonstration that India belonged to the people, not to those with power and influence. She took bold actions. First, she outlined a radical programme of economic reform which she placed before the Working Committee. Predictably, they reacted adversely. She responded by sacking Morarji Desai, and then announced that 200 of India's banks were to be nationalised. One observer noted: " Almost overnight the political climate changed in her favour and she became the people's heroine." [12]

Now she could take the offensive. With her backing, V. V. Giri was elected president, with a majority of the Congress M.P.s voting against their official nominee. The Prime Minister was now assured of the support of the President should she want to invoke the emergency powers of the Constitution. Next, she moved to oust the reigning Congress president; S. Nijalingappa; he countered by arranging her expulsion from the party hierarchy. She retaliated by getting 441 of the 750 members of the All-India Congress Committee to meet together and pass a No-Confidence motion against Nijalingappa. A similar move to get the Congress M.P.s to stand up and be counted produced support for Indira from 222 of the 281 elected members of the *Lok Sabha*. Soon the break was complete, with the old guard Congress leaders, led by Morarji, joining the opposition under the name of Congress (O) and with Mrs. Gandhi's 220 supporters governing as Congress (R) backed by 43 members of the Communist Party.[13]

Mrs. Gandhi continued to implement measures which dramatised

[12] D. Hiro, *Inside India Today* (1976), p. 77, quoting Ranajit Roy.
[13] O stands for " Organisation " (which the old guard still controlled) and R stands for " Ruling " Congress.

the contrast between rulers and ruled. Before independence, one-third of India remained under the rule of feudal princes. As the price of acceding to the New India, 500 princes received guarantees which confirmed many of their privileges under the new Constitution. It was now decided to liquidate these privileges; but this required a two-thirds vote in both houses of parliament. The necessary percentage was given by the *Lok Sabha*, but was denied in the *Rajya Sabha*. Mrs. Gandhi thereupon carried through her move against the princes by presidential ordinance. The action was appealed in the Supreme Court, which, in December 1970, ruled that it was unconstitutional. Faced with this crisis, Mrs. Gandhi announced that she would take the issue to the people in a general election to be held in March 1971.

This was the first national election to be held out of the regular five-year sequence. Most regarded it as a desperate gamble, and most of the professional political analysts forecast that Indira would not win: many gave her only 230 and 270 seats, and there was a tendency for the figure to fall as polling day drew nearer.[14] The Congress (O) combined with all the Rightist parties and the United Socialists to form a Grand Alliance; electoral pacts were arranged whereby one combined opposition candidate faced the Congress (R) nominee. As these ill-assorted allies possessed no common ground, their campaign revolved around the slogan *Indira Hatao* (" Get Rid of Indira "). Mrs. Gandhi's only allies were the Communist Party of India (the Moscow-oriented Communists) and the Tamil *Dravida Munnetra Kazhagam* (DMK) confined to one State. The campaign owed almost everything to Indira Gandhi's personal leadership— she covered 33,000 miles on her nation-wide tour. The slogan she employed was a direct reply to that of her enemies: *Gharibi Hatao* (" Get Rid of Poverty ").

IV—ENEMIES DEFEATED

Mrs. Gandhi succeeded in convincing the electors that just as before independence Congress had challenged the forces of authority so now she was combating entrenched interests: in a sense, she succeeded in reversing roles, portraying herself as the leader of the " Have-Nots " challenging the " Haves." The result was as amazing as it was unexpected. The Congress (R) won 350 seats in the *Lok Sabha*

---

[14] Thus, Kuldip Nayer, one of the most experienced analysts of the Indian political scene (author of *The Judgement: the Inside Story of the Emergency*, and other political studies) declared on the eve of poll that according to Mrs. Gandhi's most optimistic supporters she would only get 261 seats: 10 less than a majority! See W. H. Morris-Jones, " India Elects for Change—and stability," *Asian Survey*, August 1971, for a fascinating analysis of the 1971 results which in many respects anticipates the 1977 election.

(total, 520). Congress (O) was almost obliterated, retaining only 16 seats. Even giants like Kamaraj were defeated. The Rightist Swatantra Party was reduced to eight seats from 60, and the Socialists fell from 23 to a total of three seats. Yet all this was achieved on a low poll (55 per cent.) with only a 3 per cent. improvement (40 to 43 per cent.) in the Congress vote.

How far was the result due to what was described as " New-Type Politics "? This was supposed to be the overturning of " old " politics based on patronage and casteism, by the " Indira-Wave," a direct appeal to the masses. Perhaps more important, was the behind-the-scenes decision of Indian big business that Indira Gandhi meant stability and continuity, and hence came a massive financial boost for her party funds. A " modest estimate " put their contributions at Rs. 250 million (£14 million) and in a campaign that was " nasty, brutish and short," the capacity to mobilise resources fast was of decisive importance.

Mrs. Gandhi saw the result as a vindication of her own personal appeal to the masses. She felt that she owed little or nothing to her principal supporters like Jagjivan Ram and Chavan. Writing immediately after the event a wise foreign observer concluded: " There persists a suspicion that a leadership which found *party* at worst a source of trouble, and at best inessential, may prefer the freedom of courtly rule to the necessity of institutional organisation." [15]

What was certain was that Indira Gandhi had changed the rules of the game of Indian politics. Mahatma Gandhi and Jawaharlal Nehru could both be ruthless when occasion demanded, but they liked to set the stage for an *inclusive* system of politics in which all political elements had a place. Both were, on occasions, nonplussed by evidence that some elements (notably the Muslims) were determined to play an *exclusive* form of politics. Mrs. Gandhi determined that henceforward the *exclusive* model would prevail. Some have called this *realpolitik* or pure politics, and have denounced the style as un-Indian.[16] National styles can change; and time has shown that India has no special affinity with non-violence, *ahimsa*; Indira Gandhi participated in this process of change, substituting confrontation for consensus as the national model.

Indeed, the times were changing. The Indo-China war of 1962 had ended (perhaps forever) the conception of brotherhood,

---

[15] Morris-Jones, *op. cit.* in note 14, above, at p. 741.

[16] For a percipient study of the impact of Indira Gandhi on the Indian political mode, arguing that her effect was " un-Indian," see A. Nandy, " India's Political Culture," (1) The Lessons of Mrs. Gandhi's Rule, (2) How Freedom Came to be Devalued, (3) The " Us " and " They," and (4) Ploys that Failed, *Times of India*, May 13, 14, 16 and 17, 1977.

" peaceful co-existence " as the international framework within which India's posture was assumed. After the " invasion " of India's north-east borderlands the mood changed from the bland and blind assumption of a mutually sympathetic Asia, united in shaking off the bonds of Western colonialism, into a new, more narrow nationalism in which India was seen to be threatened by forces of destruction, external and internal. Indira Gandhi personified this new mood of defensive nationalism or chauvinism.

Almost immediately she faced up to the two threats, internal and external. Throughout the twentieth century, politics in Bengal had been shaped by the cult of violence and revolution. Assassination was the preferred political weapon of extremist Bengalis. The State of West Bengal had rejected Congress government for a Marxist, Communist régime. The State election of March 1971 left the Marxist/ Maoists in a majority; but Mrs. Gandhi patched up a coalition government of Congress and the Moscow Communists. Lacking a majority, this soon collapsed and West Bengal came under central rule. Calcutta, and several rural districts, were moving towards guerrilla warfare. The peaceful campus of Santiniketan was wracked by arson and murder. Mrs. Gandhi took personal charge of the rescue operation. Vacillating district officers and police chiefs were replaced by tough men of action. Reinforcements of the central armed police moved in. The Youth Congress was given a role as the intelligence and liaison arm of the administration. Hundreds of activists were jailed without trial. Mrs. Gandhi had justification for these strong-arm methods inasmuch as next door, in neighbouring East Bengal, the people were resisting the efforts of the central Pakistan government to suppress the Bangladesh movement.

India watched the campaign of brutality of the Pakistan army with apprehension. The Hindu population was particularly vulnerable to Pakistani repression, and a flood of refugees began to cross into West Bengal. Eventually, the refugee camps on the Indian side were sheltering 10 million victims of army tyranny. Mrs. Gandhi strove to alert international opinion to the nightmare, travelling to London, Washington, and other capitals to plead for a restraining influence on Pakistan. She was received with polite indifference. At length, the decision was taken to intervene. Unlike the situation in 1962 when India confronted China, or, in 1965, when India was challenged over Kashmir, this time the army commanders received the strongest support from their political masters. When the army moved on December 4, 1971, the country was united and determined as never before. Twelve days later Mrs. Gandhi was able to announce the unconditional surrender of all the Pakistan forces in what was now Bangladesh. Her triumph was complete. In the United States, a

Gallup Poll, to discover the woman most admired in all the world, came up with the name of Indira Gandhi.

Not surprisingly, the Prime Minister exploited her crest-of-the-wave popularity by holding State-elections in 16 States in March 1972. Her Congress (R) won over 70 per cent. of the seats, while the Congress (O) could cling to a mere 3·4 per cent. of the total. These elections provided the opportunity to resolve the vexed problem of West Bengal. The objective was to give Congress a stable majority for the next five years. The strategy was to concentrate efforts in the 113 constituencies where the Maoist-Communists had won before. The operation was entrusted to the innocuous-sounding Research and Analysis Wing of the central Cabinet office, directly controlled by Mrs. Gandhi. The Maoist cadres, spearhead of the movement, were penetrated and many activists were jailed or forced to move out. Pressures were brought to bear upon working class voters. As a result nearly 100 seats in the West Bengal legislature were lost to Congress by the Maoist-Communists: only a rump of 14 remained.[17] The politics of confrontation and manipulation had triumphed.

And yet, according to some, despite her hold over politics throughout India, Indira Gandhi still remained insecure: " She knew, even if others had forgotten it, that her victory . . . was not based on numbers [*i.e.*, popular support] but good timing, imaginative public relations, and inspired management of the various communications media. . . . She could not forget the elaborate ploys through which she had consolidated her power within the Congress party, and she always feared the possibility that others would do to her what she, given a chance, had always done to others. It is this fear which had made her a lonely, imperious leader and induced her to discourage the emergence of even subsidiary centres of power within her party." [18]

All might have been well, but for the explosion in oil prices which hit India worse than any other country and accelerated long-term inflation into a crazy spiral. Demands for wage increases came from all sections of the workforce. Demands were reinforced by massive strike action in industry and in public transport. The government replied by punishing the strikers, consigning hundreds of union leaders to jail. Counter-inflationary measures revolved around the introduction of new restrictions. The Congress system in India had been called *Permit Raj*; now trade and industry were cocooned in regulations, the economy slowed down, and a gigantic illegal operation involving smuggling from overseas and black-market operations

---

[17] A full account of how the West Bengal election was rigged is provided by D. Hiro, *op. cit.* in note 12, above, at pp. 173–180. The author makes no secret of his own ideological motivation, but his account is confirmed by those of others less ideologically committed.

[18] A. Nandy, " Ploys that Failed," *loc. cit.* in note 16, above.

began to affect almost everyone in the land. Many officials were mixed up in the operation. Discontent grew ever louder and the call to clean up public life and government was led by Jayaprakash Narayan (JP), the veteran socialist and worker for *sarvodaya* (the Welfare of All). Massive anti-government rallies were held in the States and in Delhi. Mrs. Gandhi retaliated by ordering pro-government rallies (which all too often assumed a " rent-a-crowd " appearance) and by ordering tough police action against JP's followers. Repression succeeds more often than idealists will admit; by mid-1975 the movement to oust Mrs. Gandhi's administration was faltering. Then, in June, in the mid-term State elections in Gujarat the Congress government was toppled out by a united opposition coalition. There followed a blow directed straight at Indira Gandhi. After the 1971 election her socialist opponent at Rae Bareli had lodged a petition, alleging improper use of government vehicles and personnel by the Prime Minister. The appeal had been grinding along for four years; then on June 12, 1975, the High Court Judge announced his finding. Mrs. Gandhi had been guilty of electoral improprieties; therefore her election was void; therefore she was not an M.P. Further he declared she was disqualified from office for six years: the question was, therefore, was she, properly speaking, Prime Minister?

V—EMERGENCY

The High Court Judge granted a request from Mrs. Gandhi's legal adviser that the court order should not be enforced for 20 days to allow time for the Congress Party to appoint someone to function as Prime Minister while the case went up on appeal to the Supreme Court. The immediate response of those close to Mrs. Gandhi was to declare that she would step down; at any rate for a time.[19] The opposition announced a nationwide campaign to put pressure on the Prime Minister to step down. If she needed an excuse to fight the court and the constitution, this was now provided. On June 26, 1975, the President declared a state of emergency throughout India on the grounds that national security was threatened. The presidential action was taken, formally, on the advice of the Cabinet; but the decision was that of Indira Gandhi alone—according to her own statement.[20]

---

[19] For example, the recently-retired Secretary to the Cabinet, who knew Mrs. Gandhi intimately, wrote a postscript to his book on Cabinet and Prime Minister in June 1975, following the judgment: " the point is made, and has been acclaimed by all, amongst them even senior members of the Prime Minister's own party: the rule of law is supreme; all are equal before the law, whatever be their status." See S. S. Khera, *The Central Executive* (1975).

[20] Mrs. Gandhi's first press interview after her electoral defeat was given two weeks later. In response to the suggestion that some important decisions had been taken

Some of the actions that followed had a familiar, " imperial " air about them. Thousands of politicians were arrested (including some of the " Young Turk " Congress M.P.s) and interned without trial (veteran freedom fighters complained that conditions were stricter than under the British). Others were novel, such as the blanket censorship of all news items. Recalcitrant editors had their leading articles written for them.[21] The justification for all this, never publicly stated, but privately disseminated by hundreds of Indira's supporters, was that the agitation by JP and the militant trades unionists, Young Turks, and all the other malcontents, was being fomented by a gigantic Central Intelligence Agency (CIA) operation designed to bring down the government which was to be replaced by one which would identify with United States interests.

Mrs. Gandhi announced a new programme of radical reform. The black market would be cleaned out, prices would be stabilised and the administration required to work for the people. As a result of the sweeping powers assumed under the Emergency regulations, inflation was halted, strikes ceased, trains ran more punctually, and civil servants arrived at the office on time. Meanwhile, Mrs. Gandhi pushed through a series of decrees through the now subservient Parliament which made her position secure. Her own election was confirmed, and any future attempt to remove the Prime Minister was made impossible. She was even given immunity from legal proceedings for life! The power to challenge constitutional amendments was limited. The life of Parliament was extended: elections (due in 1976) were postponed to 1978. And the whole system of parliamentary government was placed under review. Recalcitrant State governments were eliminated. President's rule was imposed in Gujarat and in Tamil Nadu where her allies, the DMK, were dismissed from office.

In her Emergency decrees, Indira was sustained by many of the senior politicians who had followed her into Congress (R) in 1969; notably by Chavan and Jagjivan Ram. Increasingly, they were ignored and Indira governed through her own " court." Sanjay Gandhi was looked upon as his mother's heir (Rajiv, the eldest son, an airline pilot, had displeased his mother by wanting to marry an Italian girl, and the stalemate which preceded Indira's own marriage was repeated). Sanjay was the favourite. He had launched a vast project to build a new Indian car, the *Maruti*, and had been given extraordinary concessions: foreign exchange, land grants, govern-

secretly she replied: " Whatever decisions were taken regarding government policy were in Cabinet.... Except for Emergency ... or, for instance, devaluation." *Statesman*, April 6, 1977.

[21] The full extent of the suppression of all free reporting and the substitution of pro-government propaganda was revealed when the Shah commission heard evidence: see *Statesman*, September 28, 29, 30, 1977 and November 1, 2, 3, 1977.

ment-sanctioned bank loans. The *Maruti* had never come off the production line (it is not clear whether even a few were assembled from imported parts), but certain individuals acquired great wealth: or so rumour insisted. Sanjay now transferred his talents to politics, becoming leader of the all-India Youth Congress, which assumed a major role in " selling " the Emergency to the public.

Mrs. Gandhi also relied heavily on her private secretary, R. K. Dhawan, who became her hatchet man in all the fixing and framing which was essential to the Emergency system of control. Then, out of the Cabinet, one minister became the main agent for the Prime Minister and her son: Bansi Lal (former Chief Minister of Harayana), a second-rank politician now participating in the most confidential operations of the Emergency. Indira-Sanjay-Dhawan-Bansi Lal—to those who whispered their opposition to the régime—became known as " The Gang of Four," in reference to those in China who had conspired with Mao's widow.

Sanjay Gandhi announced a Five-Point programme. These policies had long appeared in Congress manifestos, but now two projects were given top priority and implemented with ruthless efficiency. Delhi, Calcutta and the other great cities had long harboured shantytowns where urban squatters—many refugees from the partition of 1947—had made their homes. Under Sanjay's direction, the Delhi squatters were moved out to new locations beyond the far fringes of the city and their former habitations were bulldozed out of existence. Even more far-reaching was the mass sterilisation programme. Family planning had been official policy for 20 years, and had achieved nothing among the millions of India's poor. Now, Sanjay decided that population control would be made effective by sterilising men with three or more children. Towns and districts were allotted quotas, and teams of health workers, assisted by " persuaders," went into action. The sterilisation was supposed to be voluntary, but the whole of northern India buzzed with stories of men who had been cajoled, deceived, or bullied into undergoing the operation.

Sanjay Gandhi exhibited a ruthlessness normally foreign to Indians. Allegations were made concerning the death of people supposed to know too much about his operations: none of these appears to stand up to close investigation.[22] However, ample evidence emerges concerning other exactions. Sanjay's mother-in-law owned a textile firm called " Indira International." When some Customs inspectors began to look into illegal exports by the firm, 12 inspectors

---

[22] V. Mehta, in " Letter From New Delhi," *New Yorker*, October 17, 1977, examines some of these allegations, finding that the death of Sanjay's father-in-law, Lieut. Col. T. S. Anand, had the most sinister overtones.

were arrested and held in jail. The wife of one of the prisoners, Yadav, pleaded with the Delhi police chief. He told her: " No person other than Mr. Sanjay Gandhi could help in the matter since Mr. Yadav had annoyed him." [23] They remained in jail from June 1, 1976 until the general release of *détenus* in February 1977.

Occasionally, Rajiv Gandhi came into these behind-the-scenes deals and fixes. Thus, without warning, Air India (the national airline) was instructed to purchase three Boeing 737 aircraft, with Rajiv as intermediary. When senior officials and cabinet ministers queried the deal, R. K. Dhawan intervened and ordered them to expedite the matter. Three ministers lost their posts at Dhawan's behest. " Whatever Mr. Dhawan said, went," observed Raghu Ramaiah, Minister of Civil Aviation and Tourism, who was sacked over this affair.[24]

In weeding out any who were " unreliable," Mrs. Gandhi did not hesitate to tamper with the Supreme Court. A " reliable " judge was promoted above others as Chief Justice. The weakening of the judiciary was intensified by a sweeping change in the Constitution: by means of the 42nd Amendment, most of the Fundamental Rights guaranteed to all citizens were revoked.

This increasingly arbitrary and authoritarian rule was broadly accepted by India's politically conscious professional upper middle class—with little protest and a wide measure of approval. One respected Indian commentator makes this assessment: " In the twenty-one months of Emergency rule, not only did small time bosses and political upstarts come close to the centre of power in India, sycophants barged into prominence in a wide variety of fields in the bureaucracy, the academia, and even in the creative arts . . . Mrs. Gandhi, often anti-intellectual, but always deeply sensitive to the opinion of the intellectuals, wanted the support of respected scientists and artists as an indicator of the support of the intelligentsia. The natural scientists and artists . . . easily gave her their support in return for patronage. That is why some of the finest minds in these two spheres unashamedly gave her their support. The social scientists and those in the humanities . . . could not produce for her a single first-rate mind willing to collaborate. Only the second-raters in these fields tried to obtain through sycophancy what they could never hope to get through academic performance." [25] Support for Mrs. Gandhi was even more solid amongst the business community. Why, then, did she announce in February 1977 that a nationwide election

[23] Evidence to Shah Commission, *Statesman*, November 4, 5, 1977.
[24] Evidence to Shah Commission, *Statesman*, November 6, 1977.
[25] A. Nandy, " Ploys that Failed," *loc. cit.* in note 16, above.

would be held in six weeks' time, followed by a massive jail-delivery, in which almost all her political opponents were again set free?

The pundits have been busy discovering reasons. Some appear bizarre. It is said the astrologers warned her that astral forces were becoming increasingly unfavourable. It is said that Michael Foot, on a visit during the Emergency, was secretly informed that an election would follow and in return presented a favourable picture of Indira's India to the British public. It is said that Mrs. Gandhi was piqued by Bhutto's announcement of elections in Pakistan, with the implication that his régime was more democratic than hers. More plausibly, it is suggested that she was increasingly haunted by her father's ghost, rebuking her for betraying the democracy he had nurtured.

Others see her decision as a preliminary move towards legitimising an even more authoritarian structure in which Sanjay would be given a recognised position as heir-apparent. According to this argument, she wanted an election in which the only issue was to endorse her leadership. This would entail her parliamentary supporters making a total commitment to her. The strategy, then, was to implement a thorough shake-up among the Congress (R) parliamentarians, " to clear out some of this not totally loyal membership, ' to be replaced by Sanjay's followers; for when the 500, or so, " tickets " were distributed to Congress candidates, 200 would go to leaders of the Youth Congress.[26]

Perhaps Indira knew she was taking a gamble; but she was always a gambler, and in the past it had paid off. This time things began to go wrong. First, the various Rightist and Centrist opposition parties quickly came to an arrangement to campaign as one organisation, the Janata Party. Secondly, Jagjivan Ram, after supporting Indira throughout the Emergency, announced that he was leaving the government to form another Congress, the Congress for Democracy (CFD).

These moves threw the government unexpectedly onto the defensive. The plan to make radical changes among the candidates had to be scrapped. It was too dangerous to alienate sitting M.P.s with their network of supporters. Hence, only about 12 Youth Congress leaders (including, of course, Sanjay) were given the " ticket." This meant that some of Indira's most committed workers lost their incentive to support her cause.

Although radio and television were still completely at the disposal of the government, the Press soon rediscovered its traditional freedom of comment. At this election there could be no doubt who were the

---

[26] W. H. Morris-Jones, " The Indian Elections and their Aftermath," *Asian Affairs*, October 1977.

Haves and who the Have-Nots. Most of the Janata candidates emerged straight from prison with the aura of " jail graduates " as Mahatma Gandhi and Jawaharlal Nehru had done. Their claim to the oppositional role was unchallengeable; and the electors were in an oppositional mood.

Sensing danger, most Congress leaders stuck to their own bailiwicks; perhaps realising that Sanjay had become a liability, Indira confined him to his own constituency (where an attempt was made to assassinate him). Gallantly, Indira took the now-familiar campaign trail, exposing herself to the accusations of the multitude.

VI—DISASTER

Only when at last the vote was counted did the full extent of Mrs. Gandhi's *débâcle* emerge. Janata fielded 404 candidates; 270 were successful; the CFD, with 50 candidates, won 29 seats. Congress (R) put up 493 candidates, of whom only 153 were returned. In South India (where the impact of the Emergency was slighter), the Congress retained much of its strength; 92 of the new Congress M.P.s came from the four southern-most States. Throughout the huge area of the four northern, Hindi-speaking States, plus Delhi, only two constituencies remained loyal to Congress.[27] Sanjay was massively rejected; worst of all, Indira lost her Rae Bareli seat by a margin of more than 50,000 votes.

When she knew the extent of her defeat, Mrs. Gandhi arranged for the last remnants of the Emergency to be lifted and withdrew from office without hesitation.[28] Asked if she perceived a role for herself in opposition she replied: " I am out of politics just now." [29] In a message to Congress, she declared: " I should like to make it clear that as one who led the Government I unreservedly own full responsibility for this defeat. I am not interested in finding alibis or excuses for myself." Congress had been expected to repudiate their ex-leader; instead, there was a tearful reconciliation.

VII—LADY IN WAITING

Lacking employment, Indira seemed to have lost all her old direction and drive. During the summer of 1977, she was observed on one of her rare appearances at a dinner party: " When she wasn't picking at her food, she was nervously folding and unfolding a small handker-

[27] M. Weiner, " The 1977 Parliamentary Elections in India," *Asian Survey*, July 1977.

[28] Many alleged that, at the last moment, she plotted a pre-emptive strike against her opponents: see R. Manoff, " The Coup that Failed: Indira was willing," *Nation*, May 7, 1977. All Delhi appears to believe that she used the interregnum before the new Cabinet took over to move truckloads of documents from her residence to safe hiding places.

[29] " Mrs. Gandhi, With No Regrets," *Statesman*, April 6, 1977.

chief, cupping and twisting it with her hands. She kept blinking as if she had something in her eye or had developed a twitch. She seemed bored and lonely and quite tense. Conversation was hesitant. . . . She talked mostly about how difficult it was for her to find a good cook."[30]

There were occasional political conversations; with Chavan, and even with the new Prime Minister, Morarji Desai, but these did not seem fruitful. Then, quite suddenly, she was back at the centre of the stage: on October 3, 1977, the police arrived at her New Delhi home, charged her under the Prevention of Corruption Act, and took her into custody.

Some Janata ministers—notably George Fernandez—had been pressing for her arrest since March; but Morarji had insisted that before action was taken the charges against her must be absolutely watertight. Now, the carefully-planned arrest was made. Alert to this move, Sanjay informed the press and mobilised Indira's still numerous supporters. She emerged: " Where are the handcuffs? " she demanded, " I am not going without handcuffs." The embarrassed police refused her demand. In court, next morning, charges were brought, but no evidence was offered. The magistrate ordered Mrs. Gandhi's release; and her return home was a public triumph.

In the wake of her " martyrdom," Mrs. Gandhi tried to launch her political comeback. She attempted to repeat her 1969 tactic of taking over the leadership of Congress by mobilising her supporters to vote out the Congress President. The first shock-action failed, and Indira departed on a national tour to demonstrate her hold over the masses. A trip around Gujarat was a triumph, but when she visited Tamil Nadu (her dismissal of the DMK government not forgotten), she received a rough reception. Even in neighbouring Karnataka, where the Chief Minister was her personal protégé, she was greeted with black flags.[31]

Indira's aunt, the formidable Mrs. Pandit, warned: " I don't think she's aiming at anything except to get back in power. . . At present, I don't think she has very many friends. She always had a definite streak of obstinacy." Asked if Indira had been influenced by Nehru, Mrs. Pandit answered: " He was not the type of person who would train anybody and she was not the kind who would be trained. He was an idealist. . . . She is ruthless." [32]

---

[30] V. Mehta, " Letter From New Delhi," *loc. cit.* in note 22, above. I am grateful to Ved Mehta's brother-in-law, Art Helweg, for providing me with written and other materials which enabled me to keep abreast of developments in Delhi towards the close of 1977.

[31] The régime of Chief Minister Urs " dwarfed all previous régimes in the scale of its corruption," using " illegal and brutal methods " to fill its party coffers, a commission of inquiry was told: see J. Manor, " Structural Changes in Karnataka Politics," *Economic and Political Weekly*, October 29, 1977.

[32] *Times of India*, November 1, 1977.

Late in 1977 it appeared that Indira's moment had not yet arrived. She had to withdraw from the struggle to oust the Congress President and was content to be called " one of our respected leaders." But her spirit appeared unbroken. Summoned before the Shah Commission, charged with investigating Emergency excesses, she declined to appear personally. She described the commission as " politically inspired inquisitorial proceedings." She asserted once again that her Cabinet had acted collectively. " In marked contrast," she added, to that of Harold Wilson who had acted in presidential style: " Yet no-one in Britain, not even Crossman, has suggested that concentration of so much power in the Prime Minister was designed to subvert democracy or to establish any personal dictatorship." [33]

Having failed in her first attempt to take control of the Congress, Mrs. Gandhi organised her own faction, the " Indira Congress," which proceeded to field its own candidates in competition with the main Congress, Janata, and other parties, in the elections held in February 1978 for the legislatures of five States which had previously been governed by Congress ministries. In two States, Karnataka and Andhra Pradesh, the Indira Congress gained an absolute majority and were able to form governments. In Maharashtria the Indira Congress was able to match the success of the old Congress and Janata, though no party had an absolute majority. In none of these States did the old Congress emerge as the winner, and in recognition of the failure of the campaign to halt Indira Gandhi the president of the main Congress, Brahmananda Reddy, promptly resigned.

Mrs. Gandhi issued a statement claiming recognition as the national leader of the opposition to the ruling Janata Party. She added that she had no plans to return to parliament " in the near future." Beside all this, the move to prosecute her for refusal to give evidence before the Shah Commission, also initiated in February 1978, seemed more likely to contribute to her resurgence of popularity than to damage her reputation. More in exasperation than in admiration, the leading liberal newspaper called her " the cleverest politician in the country." [34]

During the following months, the Janata Cabinet was harshly divided over the question of prosecuting Mrs. Gandhi. Two prominent hardliners left the Cabinet one being Charan Singh, the Home Minister. This split nearly tore the coalition apart. Eventually, the decision was taken to proceed against her, and the long, leisurely judicial process began affording her more publicity. Prime Minister Desai was plagued by persistent demands that the activities of his son, Kanti, be investigated. The allegation was that Kanti Desai

---

[33] *The Times,* November 22, 1977.
[34] *Statesman,* February 28, 1978.

had solicited massive contributions to the Janata funds in his father's name and had appropriated these funds for himself. Morarji Desai rejected the demands for an inquiry on the grounds that the stories were false: and, anyhow, he was not responsible for his son's actions. Mrs. Gandhi compared this rejection of an inquiry with the Janata enthusiasm for the Shah tribunal's investigations of her own record, while the cover-up of Kanti by Morarji seemed to absolve her from the actions of Sanjay (now relegated to the background by his mother as she breasted the new Indira wave).

By the autumn of 1978 (when this paper was finally revised) Mrs. Gandhi judged it was time to make a parliamentary comeback. Her client-patron, Chief Minister Urs, was able to find her a safe seat in Karnataka, and the sitting M.P. obligingly resigned to make way for her return. Indira Gandhi had never made parliament her forum; it always eluded her. But it was a symbol of her move back into the centre of Indian politics. She awaits the moment when Janata's mistakes open the way for her restoration. Perhaps with some reason, she firmly believes that the Indian people want her back. She is prepared for the most extraordinary political comeback in modern history.

EDUCATION IN JAPAN

By

BRIAN HOLMES

THE Japanese take justifiable pride in the fact that they have been able to incorporate modern technology into their economic system without destroying long-cherished traditions. Two periods in their recent history exemplify the truth of this claim.*

I—THE FIRST ECONOMIC REVOLUTION
1868–1941

(a) The Meiji Restoration

During the first of these periods from 1868, when the government established after the restoration of Imperial rule set up a system of government along Western lines, to 1945, when the Japanese forces surrendered unconditionally to the Allied Powers, the country's economy was transformed. Feudal controls of commerce and industry were abandoned. Foreign trade was encouraged. Silk, tea and the products of other traditional industries were exported. Cotton yarn and goods were imported. A fundamental task of the new government was to introduce modern machinery and mass methods of production. Western machines transformed Japan's silk and cotton industries. Modern heavy industries were created for armaments, iron, ship-building, chemicals, and machinery. Engineers from England, America, France and Germany helped the government to develop and operate coal and other mines.[1] Government initiative preceded private enterprise so that by the end of the 1930s, under the *Zaibatsu*, or family economic companies, Japan's industrial potential in spite of world-wide depressions matched that of the United States.

Against these successes should be placed attempts to transform the political situation after the Meiji Restoration. Members of the democratic movement (*Jiyu Minken Undo*) based their case on the supremacy of the natural rights of man. Their proposals to establish a system of government based on the principles of Western *laissez-faire* liberalism were challenged and the Meiji Constitution

---

* The author is extremely grateful to Kazuko Nagamatsu for undertaking the research on materials in Japanese. She selected relevant books and articles, translated appropriate parts of them and discussed the general views advanced by the author with him in the light of contemporary Japanese debates.

[1] Keizo Shibusawa (ed.), *Japanese Society in the Meiji Era* (1958) (translated and adapted by A. H. Culbertson and Mikuru Michiko).

(*Dai-Nippon Teikoku Kenpô*), promulgated in 1889, limited the power of the national assembly and conferred on the Emperor (Articles I, III, IV, V, X and LV) legislative and executive responsibilities and a divine authority which, in the event, made it possible for the Emperor to act as an absolute monarch, whether in accordance with his own ambitions or as a figurehead controlled by powerful cliques. After the assassination of Prime Minister Tsuyoshi Inukai in 1932, economic (the *Zaibatsu*) and military (the *Gunbatsu*) cliques were responsible for the ultra-militaristic and imperialistic policies which culminated in the Second World War and ultimate defeat. Among the material losses which led to that defeat was the destruction of some 4,000 schools. Some 40,000 buildings were unusable. Educational activity with 18 million students idle [2] was at a standstill.

The contribution of the schools to economic success and ultimate national disaster during the first period should be mentioned. R. P. Dore [3] has described education in the period which immediately preceded the Meiji Restoration. It consisted of a dual system of high schools for the *samurai* and literacy schools for the commoners. Chinese classics and strict codes of behaviour informed the education of the *samurai* while a considerable proportion of town-dwellers and some farmers were literate. Nevertheless the successful expansion of schooling after 1872 throughout Japan is worthy of note. In 1873 there were some 12,000 public and private elementary schools, 10 years later the number had more than doubled. During the same decade the number of private and public secondary schools rose from 20 to some 200 and at the end of it there were five times as many institutions of higher education as 10 years previously. Pupil numbers rose even more rapidly so that by 1900 the proportion of school-age children enrolled in elementary schools was more than 80 per cent. The growth in secondary school enrolments was even more impressive and by the turn of the century there were thirteen times as many students in institutions of higher education as in 1873. [4]

What is striking about the Fundamental Code of Education of 1872 is that it established the beginnings of a unified and universal school system for both *samurai* and commoner. It owed much to foreign example. The French administrative system was copied.

---

[2] R. King Hall, *Education for a New Japan* (1949). See also, by the same author, *Shushin: The Ethics of a Defeated Nation* (1949). Also, R. King Hall (ed.) *Kokutai no Hongi* (1949); (translated by J. O. Gauntlett).

[3] R. P. Dore, *Education in Tokugawa Japan* (1965), examine the concepts of moral education and the provision of schools during the two centuries prior to the Meiji Restoration. Like other writers he emphasises the contributions made to the modernisation of Japanese society during the Ecdho period and the Western innovations which had been introduced prior to 1868.

[4] See Historical Statistics in, Government of Japan, *Education in Japan* (Annual Report of the Ministry of Education), Research Bureau, Ministry of Education, Tokyo.

There were eight academies,[5] each sub-divided into 32 secondary school districts and 210 elementary school districts. In a powerful Ministry of Education there were, by 1937, eight permanent bureaux in charge of General Education, Higher Education, Technical Education, Social or Adult Education, Thought Supervision, School Books, Religious and Educational Research. Imperial universities of which there were six in 1922 were set up. Technical secondary schools, of which by 1900 there were some 200, were established. Normal schools for teachers, women's colleges, youth schools and schools for the deaf, dumb and blind completed a system of pre-1945 education that was similar in many respects to those in Western Europe and North America. The schools with desks, chairs and Western teaching materials helped to create the impression that a cultural transformation had been brought about.

Not so; the reaction to political radicalism which culminated in the Imperial Constitution of 1889 found expression in many aspects of Japanese life. The Meiji government was able to introduce Western style military and school uniforms, but it was not able to transform family life. Many people initially resisted official attempts to introduce Western style clothes, hats and footwear and continued to live in houses with matted floors and no chairs, and to wear comfortable traditional Japanese clothes.[6] Eventually changes in clothing styles and hair styles were numerous. Willingness to adopt them was related to the social status, occupation, place of residence and personality of individuals. In general, however, people developed the habit of wearing Western clothing to work and Japanese clothing at home. Some, perhaps older people, still do. This situation serves to illustrate the strength of outward manifestations of an earlier culture.

(b) *The Imperial Rescript and Moral Education*

Equally important, if modern Japan is to be understood, are the constraints placed upon the emancipation of former attitudes by the Imperial Rescript on Education promulgated in 1890.[7] It laid down a pattern of moral behaviour which owed much to Chinese Confucianism and Japanese Shintoism by stressing filial piety, familial affection, friendship, modesty and moderation. Aesthetic, moral and intellectual development was stressed in the interests of the common good, the Constitution and the State. Since these were inextricably linked with

---

[5] Each academy was to have an Imperial university and to be sub-divided into 32 secondary and 210 elementary school districts.

[6] Keizo Shibusawa, *Japanese Life and Culture in the Meiji Era* (1958) (translated and adapted by C. S. Terry).

[7] For a full English version of the Rescript, see *e.g.*, B. C. Duke, *Japan's Militant Teachers* (1973), p. 11.

a divine, all-powerful Emperor the schools were, in effect, to inculcate obedience to the Emperor and his spokesmen.

Moral education (*Shushin*) as a compulsory subject in pre-war Japanese schools had as its aims clarification of the fundamental concepts of the national political and imperial systems and respect for hierarchical human relationships particularly between the Emperor and his people. In pursuit of these aims the content of moral education closely followed the precepts laid down in the Imperial Rescript of 1890. Parents, brothers and sisters, marriage partners and friends and relationships between them dominate the stories through which attitudes were to be inculcated. Virtues such as thrift, endeavour and generosity, knowledge and skills were to be developed so that individuals and families could contribute to the welfare of society and respect its laws. The origins of these beliefs lie in *Shintoism*, with its many sects, which was fused with Confucianism and then Buddhism to provide a religion characterised by nature and ancestor worship. The Imperial Constitution and Rescript on Education helped to transform this system of family ethics into National or State Shintoism (*Kokka* or *Jinja Shinto*) the essential feature of which [8] was made manifest in the unique spirit of national service possessed by the Japanese people. It became more than a code of ethics, but a religion based on the divinity and sovereign power of the Emperor as head of the national family who had inherited his position from a Divine Ancestor. In brief, codes of behaviour appropriate to family life in Japan were incorporated into national systems of morals and ethical behaviour.

The ultra-nationalists went further. In a fundamental policy statement in 1937 (*Kokutai no Hongi*), issued by the Ministry of Education differences [9] between Western parliamentary democracies and the Imperial Diet were made clear. The latter had one function to perform in Japan, that of assisting the Emperor's direct rule. The Cardinal Principles of the National Entity of Japan went even further: the mission of the Japanese people was to build up a new culture by adopting and sublimating Western cultures so as to sustain nationalism and bring the benefits of the Japanese way to countries in East Asia. Robert King Hall [10] comments that had Japan's Divine Mission of world leadership been based on that nation's pre-eminence in science, industry, ethics and the arts it might well have succeeded. Its pre-Second World War failure was a consequence of the methods adopted. The subordination of individuals to the authority of persons within a

---

[8] R. King Hall, *Education for a New Japan* (1949), p. 113.
[9] See Hall (ed.), *Kokutai no Hongi*; and *op. cit.* in note 8, above, at p. 116.
[10] *Op. cit.* in note 8, above, at p. 123.

tight mesh of relationships in a State system and the belief in militarism, were the seeds from which failure grew.

II—THE SECOND ECONOMIC REVOLUTION
1950–?

(a) *The Allied Occupation*

The second period of economic growth [11] since about 1950 can hardly be understood without reference to the successes and failures of the first period. One major difference is that, whereas after 1868 initiatives were taken by Japanese leaders, reform was introduced into post-1945 Japan by members of the Headquarters of the Supreme Commander for the Allied Powers (SCAP) under chaotic conditions. Yet at first, in defeat, the Japanese people seemed as superficially willing to accept all that was new and discard all that was old as they had been in the early years of the Meiji Restoration.[12] SCAP issued a number of directives between October 1945 and January 1946 [13] which were designed to destroy militarism and the authority of the Emperor. Official support for State Shintoism was abolished and the dissemination of militarism through Shintoism, or other religions,

---

[11] See G. C. Allen, *A Short Economic History of Modern Japan* (1962); OEDC, *Japan: Economy Survey* (1973; 1975; 1976 and 1977); and OECD, *Manpower Policy in Japan* (1973).

[12] See, T. Doi, *Amae no Hakken*, in T. Wakamori (*et al.*), *Nihonjin no Sai-Hakken* (1972). Takeo Doi, a Japanese psychoanalyst, points out that history exemplifies a tendency among the Japanese to reveal in the face of a new situation previously unsuspected characteristics which enable them to put the past behind them and " restart in a fresh mood " (*Shinki Makinaoshi*). He cites the manner in which during the 19th century when the country was opened up the Japanese adopted a policy of seeking " enrichment and strength " from foreigners who had previously been excluded with great determination. Again, though shocked by defeat, once the war was over, it was psychologically easy for the Japanese to accept that peace-loving policies should replace aggressive militarism. These responses to a new situation are, according to Takeo Doi, typical of a temperament which finds expression in individual and national behaviour patterns. " New Year's Day " is welcomed as an occasion on which individuals and the nation can start afresh and cast the old year from their thoughts. K. Kobori suggests, moreover, that the Japanese tend to avoid intellectual conflict and confrontations and are prepared to compromise for rather vague reasons.

[13] The year 1945 was devoted to liquidating unacceptable features of the pre-war education system. The initiatives taken by the Ministry of Education in its *Educational Plan for Building the New Japan*, announced on September 15, 1945 did not satisfy the occupying Powers. Although the Ministry ordered the removal of war-time material from textbooks and formulated a new policy towards religious education, General Headquarters of SCAP clearly wished to see more fundamental changes and issued a series of Directives to the Japanese Government. The first, *Administrative Policy Concerning the Japanese Education System* of October 22, 1945, dealt with textbooks, research and the control of teachers. The second Directive of October 30, 1945 was designed immediately to purge the system of militarists and ultra-nationalists and subsequently to prevent retired soldiers from teaching. The third Directive of December 15, 1945, dealt with *Shintoism* as a State religion and the teaching of it in schools. The fourth Directive of December 31, 1945 was designed to eradicate subjects and textbooks which had promoted ultra-nationalism and militarism, *e.g.* history and geography.

was prohibited. Public educational institutes devoted to the study of Shintoism and the training of priests were abolished. Shinto textbooks were censored and volumes dealing with the Fundamental Principles of the National Structure (*Kokutai no Hongi*) could not be circulated. Courses in morals (*Shushin*), Japanese history and geography, were suspended. Textbooks were drastically censored. Teachers and educational officials were screened. How far these purges succeeded in their aim, namely the eradication of all aspects of ultra-nationalism, has been debated. Certainly, in contrast to the vigour of the attack on National Shintoism, the Imperial Rescript on Education which had been committed to memory by millions of school children before the war, carefully guarded in every school and read publicly from time to time, was not banned, although its ceremonial reading was not allowed. In spite of the use to which it had been put by the ultra-nationalists it was preserved inviolable thus providing a traditional statement to which some scholars in Japan could appeal when the reaction to American educational policies set in.

On the positive side a revised Constitution [14] published by the Japanese Government in April 1946 dealt in a somewhat ambiguous way with the status and powers of the Emperor who, after voluntarily denying his divinity, became merely a symbol of the State and the unity of its people. This most important step in the establishment of a new democracy, together with the renunciation by the Japanese of any attempt to rebuild an army, constituted for the Allies the most important foundations on which a post-war democratic system could be built. The ambiguity [15] which surrounds the Japanese text, and the failure of the Emperor to clear it up, presents some people in Japan with the chance to see some continuity between the old and new political systems. Certainly, cultural traditions die hard and initial attempts to disperse the *Zaibatsu*, redistribute the land, achieve sex equality, free young people to marry whom they wish, revise the laws of inheritance and democratise education have met with variable success.

(b) *The American Education Mission*

Superficially, Japan's education system was democratised. The principles of its post-war reform were outlined in a report prepared

---

[14] See, English version, *The Constitution of Japan: Effective May* 3, 1949, Government Printing Office, Washington (1947). See, G. F. Hudson (ed.) *Reform and Revolution in Asia* (1972).

[15] The precise meaning of the Japanese text of the Emperor's denial of his Divinity and the establishment of government in accordance with the will of the people is less clear than the American version. Commentators have noted that various interpretations have been given by the Japanese to these important pronouncements.

by 27 educationists under the leadership of Dr. George D. Stoddard,[16] who visited Japan as members of a United States Education Mission in March 1946. With the help of a Japanese Committee, members of the Mission toured the country interviewing people in an attempt to identify the problems of education. In a statement on " The Aims of Education," the Mission's report emphasised the need to clarify the foundations of a philosophy of education in a democracy. They included recognition of the worth and dignity of individuals, the need to prove equality of opportunity in accordance with the abilities of each person, and the preparation of young people to become responsible members of society. To achieve these aims the Report suggested that a central authority should not prescribe content, methods of teaching or textbooks. On the contrary, teachers should be free to develop their own methods and adapt them to the needs of students at different stages of their development. Methods of free inquiry were consequently advocated. Examinations should not stifle inquiry and so dominate the system as to create conformity among teachers and students.

Ironically,[17] the Report proposed major and specific reforms. The system of administration should be decentralised by establishing elected school boards in the prefectures, towns and villages. Instead of a differentiated post-elementary system of schools, a 6-3-3 " comprehensive " structure of primary, junior high and senior high schools was proposed. Social studies were to replace moral education (*Shushin*). Physical and vocational education were to receive more attention. Adult education was to be developed and more universities established. Teacher training was to be broadened and provided in

---

[16] The group visited Japan at the request of G.H.Q., Supreme Commander, for the Allied Powers. The ground was prepared by the special section of the Military Government called Civil Information and Education (C.I.E.). The American Mission had the help of the Japanese Education Committee (the name was subsequently changed to the Japanese Education Reform Council). A substantial level of agreement between the two groups was apparently reached. Most of the proposals stemmed from American concepts of child-centred education and the role the school should and could play in the reconstruction of society. John Dewey's democratic philosophy of education aroused interest in Japan and the theories and techniques associated with it were accepted without hesitation. Active " problem solving learning " in discussion groups and from experience was encouraged. The optimism of American progressive educationists was infectious. The image it produced was of an individual who speaks out without fear and works cheerfully, in co-operation with others in a changing democratic society. The interest taken by American educationists in their own social problems had convinced them that schools should develop critical thinking, an understanding of society and an ability to solve its problems. Many Americans were convinced that these hopes could best be realised in co-educational schools and through " social studies."

[17] It did not escape the notice of the Japanese that the Allied Powers were at one and the same time prepared to criticise authoritarianism while issuing clear directives to the Japanese Government and its agencies. Nevertheless the Report of the American Mission accepted by SCAP and given wide publicity in April 1946 was a starting point for postwar educational reform.

four-year courses. Methods of student guidance were to change. Finally, the American Education Mission was disturbed by the complexities of the Japanese language with four ways of writing it, four types of style—familiar, epistolary, literary and classical—and by a grammar which takes account of the respective rank of the speaker, the person spoken to and the persons spoken about. The Mission suggested that instead of Chinese ideograms, or either of two native phonetic systems (*hiragana* and *katakana*), the Latin alphabet (*romaji*) should be used exclusively.[18]

In the event some features of this comprehensive educational reform were quickly put into practice. In November 1946 the Constitution guaranteed fundamental human rights, freedom of thought, conscience and religion, academic freedom and the right of all people " to receive an education correspondent with their ability." [19]

The Fundamental Law of Education passed in March 1947 stressed rights rather than duties and made the full developmentof personality and independence of spirit the goals of the new education. Academic freedom, equal educational opportunity and free compulsory education for nine years were stressed. The School Education Law, passed during the same month, laid down how the new aims were to be achieved. In that year compulsory attendance was raised from six to nine years, so that children from the age of six were to attend six-year primary schools and then three-year junior high schools until they were fifteen. Secondary schools became co-educational. The Board of Education Law of 1948,[20] in spite of opposition from Ministry officials, provided for the election of prefectual and local school boards. They were voted in on October 5, 1948, with powers similar to those exercised by school boards in the United States. The Ministry of Education Establishment Law of May 1949 relegated the Ministry to a body which could offer advice, provide information and carry out research. At about this time, however, the process of turning over the conduct of domestic affairs to the Japanese Government and its agencies began. This decision, the Cold War with the Soviet Union and the Korean War marked the end of an era and heralded one during which American policies were designed to strengthen Japan's economy rather than to isolate her. The stage was set for the development of education under the influence of competing forces within the country rather than at the behest of foreign advisers. Almost immediately in 1950 the issue of moral education was raised

---

[18] See R. S. Anderson, U.S. Office of Education, Department of Health Education and Welfare, *Japan: Three Epochs of Modern Education*, Government Printing Office, Washington (1959).

[19] Art. 26, *The Constitution of Japan: Effective May* 3, 1947, Washington, U.S. Government Printing Office (1947).

[20] For details of legislation prior to 1959, see *op. cit.* in note 18, above.

by the Minister of Education, Mr. Amano, who stated that it should again be a separate course of study. Since then much research has gone into the problem of finding a satisfactory replacement for *Shushin*, so that the spiritual vacuum [21] left when it was proscribed after the war in 1945 could be filled.

The willingness of the Japanese to accept the principles of American democracy was due in part to their wish to fill the spiritual void created by defeat and the destruction of the Imperial way of life, and partly because the feelings of many people had been released. Nothing was exempt from criticism in the new-found freedom of speech.[22] The Constitution, war criminals, the incompetence of government, the position of women in society, the role of family enterprises, the occupying forces and indeed everything from the past were criticised. Students went on strike and responsible educators became concerned. Not all of them were prepared entirely to reject the past. They held that militarism and ultra-militarism were unfortunate deviations from the social process of modernisation set in motion during the *Meiji* period and the blooming of democracy during the *Taisho* period (1911 to 1926), and that post-war democracy should return to that tradition and the country modernised within it.[23]

Opponents of this position, many of whom had spent their youth in an atmosphere of militarism, rejected past achievements completely and accepted post-war democracy as something new, with no links with pre-war efforts. For example, they rejected, some from a Marxist viewpoint, the tradition of blind obedience to authority, the foundations of traditional Japanese democracy. They felt themselves victims

---

[21] Analyses of the conditions which gave rise to this vacuum have been made. These are relevant to any understanding, however partial, of the politics of educational development in Japan since 1945. In a report edited by the Japanese Commission for UNESCO, *The Role of Education in the Social and Economic Development of Japan* Ministry of Education, Japan, 1966, *e.g.* some analysis of the causes of rising rates of juvenile delinquency and suicides (among those attending schools) are given. T. Akabori states that child-centredness has become non-interference resulting in increased delinquency and a tendency among children to internalise " vice " rather than " morality." Against this picture should be juxtaposed one of Japanese students working hard, achieving high standards on international criteria of attainment and suffering, sometimes to the point of suicide, as a consequence of failure: see T. Akabori, *Dotoku-Kyoiku no Kenkyu* (1971).

[22] See Hall, *op. cit.* in note 8, above, at pp. 12–17 for a discussion of the disillusionment and student reaction immediately after the war.

[23] Many Japanese scholars have discussed how opinion in post-war Japan was polarised. One group of people accepted, consciously or sub-consciously, that there had been something seriously wrong before the war, were prepared to doubt the divinity of the Emperor and were relieved when SCAP tried to democratise the country. A second group held that the war had been legitimate, held themselves responsible for defeat and sympathised with the Emperor in the new situation. This group maintained that to accept Americanisation would be to destroy Japan's true and unique identity and this, they felt, should be preserved and developed under the new circumstances. See T. Wakamori, *op. cit*, in note 12, above.

of a defeat which had destroyed their value system but had also brought them into contact with new democratic values. In rejecting their past experience, and in criticising traditional values, members of this group tried to forge more progressive concepts of democracy.

(c) *Post-Occupation Reaction*

As the conservatives regained their confidence, power clashes were inevitable. Conflict between members of opposing political parties erupted in parliament. Disputes between labour unions and management became more common. Student unrest turned to vicious and prolonged violence. Of particular interest is the clash between the Ministry of Education (*Monbusho*) and the Japan Teachers' Union (*Nikkyoso*), which was formed from several unions in 1947 and embraced nearly all the 400,000 teachers [24] in the country. It has been ably described by Benjamin C. Duke in *Japan's Militant Teachers*. It was a battle for control which turned on relationships between the Ministry and school boards, which had been set up and given considerable power under SCAP. Legislation in 1956,[25] creating school boards by appointment rather than by election, tilted the balance of power back in favour of the Ministry. The newly-appointed school boards contained a higher proportion of conservative than progressive members. The Teachers' Union immediately proposed that the position of Minister of Education should be abolished and a democratically elected council should replace him. Class size should be reduced to 50 or less. Senior high school education should be made compulsory and its quality improved. Science and technological education should be promoted. Moral education should inform the whole of education and a special ethics course should not be reintroduced. Teachers should be free to select textbooks which should not have to be authorised by the Ministry.[26] These recommendations, opposed by the government, and the Teacher's Efficiency-rating Plan (*Kinmu Hyotei*), became issues over which the Union and Ministry fought for several violent years.

(d) *The Present System*

In the event, some of the hopes expressed by the American

---

[24] These figures relate to the period when the Japan Teachers' Union was being formed. In the early 1970s while the number of teachers was approaching the 1 million mark membership of the Teachers' Union, *Nikkyoso*, had not risen to many more than half a million teachers. See B. C. Duke, *Japan's Militant Teachers* (1973).

[25] See *op. cit.* in notes 18 and 24, above.

[26] The Ministry was not able to insist that textbooks should be prepared by its nominees. A complicated system of authorisation nevertheless exists. The only textbooks which do not have to be approved by the Ministry are those dealing with " moral education."

Mission and by the Teachers' Union in the early 1950s have been realised. Provision has been vastly expanded.[27] By 1975, 64 per cent. of children aged four and five were enrolled in kindergartens. By 1982 it is hoped that all such children will be admitted if their parents so wish although at present the majority of kindergartens are privately controlled. Everyone attends school for nine years—six in the elementary school from the age of six, and three in lower secondary schools. While admission to prestigious upper secondary schools is on a competitive basis, by 1975 almost 92 per cent. of pupils leaving lower secondary schools were admitted to upper secondary schools or technical colleges. The vast majority of those admitted attend full-time, but some 5·6 per cent. study either part-time or by correspondence. The content of upper secondary education is under review, but there are already general courses for those wishing to go on to a university; and technical, commercial, agricultural, fishing, domestic arts, fine arts, and science and mathematics courses among others for students choosing a vocational career. In " miscellaneous " schools, entered either after a lower secondary or an upper secondary education, courses of about a year in dressmaking, cooking, book-keeping, typing, motor car driving and repair work, and computer techniques are provided. Class size has been reduced so that now most classes are marginally smaller than comparable ones in England and Wales.

Since 1945 higher education has expanded enormously so that some 30 per cent. of the age group 18 to 21 is enrolled in public or private institutions of higher education compared with 5 per cent. in 1950. Practically all the universities and junior colleges admit candidates on the basis of competitive entrance examinations and upper secondary schools records. Fees are charged for all but the elementary and lower secondary schools. At the end of school year 1975–76, 821,000 students applied for admission to institutions of higher education of whom 73 per cent. were successful (599,000), but some 36 per cent. of these had probably failed to gain admission at the first attempt. Expansion, in short, has been associated with intense competition for places in either a prestigious upper secondary school or university. Thus, while the proportion of students in higher education is nearly three times that in England and Wales, the " zeal for education " is such that few pupils are " cooled out " and the demand for education is apparently insatiable.

Apart from the expansion of provision, several other features of Japanese educational development since 1945 are worthy of note.

---

[27] For a general account of the development and present system of education in Japan see T. Kobayashi, *Society Schools and Progress in Japan* (1976), and Ministry of Education, Science and Culture, Government of Japan, *Outline of Education in Japan* (1976).

Throughout the system the percentage of girls and young women attending school has risen to match, or even exceed (higher education in 1975), that of boys and young men. Private education has flourished. At present some 77 per cent. of the universities and colleges are private and more than 91 per cent. of students at junior colleges attend private institutions. In upper secondary schools, 30 per cent. of the pupils are in private school and 75 per cent. of the children enrolled are in private kindergartens. In 1975 a law provided for public subsidies to private institutions in order to improve the quality of provision. Fees in private institutions may be five or six times those charged in comparable public institutions. Private institutions offering science, technology, medicine and dentistry charge even higher fees. Even so, since 1967 the rise in these courses has been phenomenal.

Doubtless this expansion and the shift towards science and technology, the extension of teacher training courses and rises in the salaries of teachers, have contributed to Japan's economic growth. They have provided the country with the higher education and trained manpower it needs. The zeal for education has undoubtedly produced a social, political, and economic élite made up for the most part of university graduates.[28] Superficially this élite has, since 1945, successfully, as was the case during the first period of economic growth, developed both the economy and the educational system of Japan. The tensions which developed during the final phase of the pre-war period suggest that a more careful analysis should be made of the societal changes which have accompanied economic growth and the adequacy of the educational response.

(e) *Traditions and Economic Change*

Clearly Japanese traditions have their origins in a feudal, agricultural society. Diligence and thrift were virtues; waste and consumption vices. Social control was maintained by the strength of the traditional family (*Ie*). Human relationships within the household were regarded as more important than any others and these were dominated by the concept of filial piety. As stated this concept was built into the notion of a nation family with loyalty to the Emperor as head of the nation all important. The Sino-Japanese and Russo-Japanese Wars contributed to this unity. During the 1930s it was used by militarists and ultra-nationalists to persuade the Japanese people to engage in aggressive, international adventures which resulted in disaster.

---

[28] See Y. Ide and T. Ishida, " The Education and recruitment of governing elites in Modern Japan," in R. Wilkinson, *Governing Elites* (1969). It should be noted that the expansion of higher education has meant that some graduates must now accept what might be regarded as " menial " jobs.

The strength of the family survived economic changes. In 1872, five years after the *Meiji* Restoration, 84 per cent. of the work force worked on the land. This proportion declined steadily, so that in 1930 it stood at 49 per cent. Urbanisation accompanied industrialisation but the code of behaviour even in the modernising and urban areas of Japan continued to be based on family loyalties and relationships. A group consciousness, symbolised by the term *kaisha* (company), informed commercial and industrial activities in pre-war Japan. It did not mean that individuals were bound by contractual relationships but rather that they thought of the company as " theirs " and the community as all important in their lives.[29]

Since 1945 industrialisation and urbanisation have gained momentum. In 1972 only 15 per cent. of the labour force, a figure only slightly higher than in the United Kingdom, was engaged in agriculture. The world pre-eminence of the Japanese ship building, electronics and car industries needs only to be mentioned to explain how *per capita* disposable incomes have increased and why higher education has become so prized. Inevitably, economic changes of this kind have transformed the role of women who have been drawn out of the home into the social and economic life of the country. Commentators suggest that under these circumstances diligence and thrift have been replaced by consumer society attitudes towards personal satisfaction, consumption and leisure. On the other hand, a comparison of attitudes in 1953 with those expressed in 1973 suggests that the period when material success mattered most has passed and that health and happiness were regarded much more highly by the Japanese in the 1970s than wealth.[30] Again, it should be noted that there are regional differences. Attitudes in the more rural areas are more traditional than in the big cities and industrial areas. Attitudes in Tokyo seem to have moved farthest from those associated with the pre-war emphasis on family (*Ie*).

If the original concepts of filial piety and family as the source of morality have weakened there remains in modern industry and commerce a group consciousness and commitment to the company (*kaisha*) which are not matched elsewhere in the modern world. Human relationships are still characterised in Japanese companies by paternalism. Life employment, for example, is sufficiently honoured

---

[29] See C. Nakane, *Japanese Society* (1970), for an analysis of the influence of urbanisation, industrialisation and the expansion of education on the role of women in society and the persistence of group consciousness in modern Japanese companies.

[30] The first survey of the Japanese National Character was carried out in 1953 and since then similar questionnaires have been sent out every five years. The fifth survey was conducted in 1973 by a Research Committee of the Institute of Statistical Mathematics of the Ministry of Education and involved interviewing 4,600 people over the age of 20.

in Japan's industrial society to be one of its unique features. Employers frequently take on workers straight from school or university and retain them until they are 55.[31] This feature of industrial life and the fact that the unions, as enterprise unions, are associations of all the workers of one company rather than groups with similar skills and function give to union-management conflict the characteristics of a family row. Alliances and disagreements between middle management and union leaders make for harmony or violent dissent. Relationships between the Ministry of Education and the Japan Teachers' Union since 1945 illustrate aspects of problems arising from the persistence under vastly different conditions of codes of behaviour based upon the strength of the family. For this reason it is very important to examine in some detail an issue which has occupied the attention of educationists since 1945, namely " moral " education in Japanese schools. The issue has not yet been settled.[32] The aims of " moral " education have not yet been finally decided, nor the way in which it should be taught unanimously agreed.

(f) *Conflict over " Moral " Education*

Basically the issue turns on whether or not pre-Second World War family traditions and codes of behaviour can and should form the basis of a new morality. One school of thought is that ultra-militarism of the 1930s distorted soundly-based concepts developed in the Meiji and Taisho periods.[33] To accept American concepts of democracy and put them into practice would destroy those traditions which gave the Japanese people their identity and a unique way of life and thought. Those traditions, it was held, should be preserved and developed under the new circumstances of the post-war world. Opposed to this view were those who thought, consciously or subconsciously, that the pre-war policies pursued by military men rather than civilian politicians had been wrong. They were not prepared to accept the legitimacy of the war or their responsibility for Japan's

---

[31] See R. C. Clark, " Union-Management Conflict in a Japanese Company," in W. G. Beasley (ed.), *Modern Japan: Aspects of History, Literature and Society* (1975).

[32] Scholars in Japan including Professor Hiratsuka continue to work on the problem of finding an adequate form of " moral education." In 1968 revised guidelines for teaching moral education in the primary school were issued. Similar revisions for the lower secondary school (1969) and the upper secondary school (1970) were introduced. Between 1978 and 1983 a further complete revision of these programmes is intended.

[33] Among Japanese scholars the contribution of the *Jiyu Minken Undo* (the liberal and democratic movement) during the Meiji period is debated. Doubts have been raised about the extent to which members of the movement fully understood the real meaning of " liberty " and " democracy." The period between 1872 and 1890 was one of trial and error. See Japanese National Commission for UNESCO, *op. cit.* in note 21, above; and M. Nagai, *Kindaika to Kyoiku* (1969).

defeat.[34] They were relieved when the war ended and were willing to accept the new democracy introduced by the allied powers. Behind the two extremes are many shades of opinion.

The stage was set for a clash of opinion and a prolonged battle for power when SCAP proscribed *Shushin* in favour of social studies and dismissed teachers suspected of militarism. In 1946 many teachers gave their unqualified support to the American Mission's recommendations. Along with other workers teachers were organising unions, and among the union leaders were some prominent pre-war Communists. Others had been educated under the harsh régime of pre-war Normal schools for teachers where they had been indoctrinated with militaristic ideas and had subsequently become elementary school teachers in rural schools. They had not been members of the pre-war élite and consequently had little chance to share the more liberal ideals of the *Meiji* and *Taisho* democracies. The war and its aftermath had persuaded many such teachers that they had been wrong to support the pre-war régime. Guilt and anger drove them to the left to support either the Socialist Party or become members of the Communist Party.[35]

American reaction to the Cold War with the Soviet Union, the creation of the People's Republic of China in 1949, and Communist gains in the Teachers' Union (*Nikkyoso*) was to purge Communist teachers from the entire school system.[36] At the same time many teachers, classified as militarists during the period 1945–47, were reinstated. The result was that, while the leadership of the Teachers' Union became more moderate, and after the start of the Korean War in 1950 the Public Service Law made teachers civil servants and restricted their political freedom and right to strike, the Japan Teachers' Union moved into open and violent opposition to the Ministry of Education. The latter seemed determined after the Occupation ended in 1952 to reverse many of the reforms introduced by the allied Powers. Among the proposals most vehemently resisted by the Japan Teachers' Union was one made by the Minister of Education, Amano Teiyu, in 1951 to reintroduce moral education as a separate subject as part of a national re-assessment [37] of Japan's needs.

The reaction was sufficiently fierce to force the Ministry to postpone action and allowed the extreme left-wing faction of the Union to

---

[34] Duke quotes the appeal issued by a group of teachers (*Zenkyo*) in which the deception of the government and the wartime activities of the Ministry of Education are condemned. See *op. cit.* in note 24, above, at p. 35.

[35] See *ibid.* p. 195, where Duke describes the background of the leaders of the Japan Teachers' Union movement.

[36] *Ibid.* pp. 90–93.

[37] *Ibid.* p. 105.

regain some lost ground. The Ministry, however, laid a framework of reform within which prefectual and local school boards were appointed and not elected (1956). A Central Advisory Council on Education was appointed to advise the Minister (1953), the political activities of teachers were restricted (1954), the government proposed that textbooks should be prepared and authorised by the Ministry (1956) [38] except those used in moral education, and curricula in elementary, lower secondary and upper secondary schools were revised. The general tendency was to re-emphasise " basic " subjects like language, mathematics and science and to encourage vocational courses. Geography and history were again taught in the elementary and lower secondary schools (1956). The Teachers' Union opposed these moves.

Moral education remained one of the most controversial issues. In 1955 Minister of Education, Ichiro Kiyose, proposed that it should be incorporated into social studies. The Curriculum Council,[39] however, recommended the re-introduction of a separate subject on the grounds that the teaching of morals through social studies and other subjects had not been effective—because it was neither systematic nor consistent. The notion that it could be provided by studying " problems " (an American theory) was mistaken because present-day living is extremely complicated and teachers vary in their assessment of essential problems. Trivial everyday problems may be studied at the expense of more important issues. Consequently, it was argued, the use of social studies and other subjects as the vehicle for teaching morality placed it at risk and certainly made it difficult for less confident and knowledgeable teachers to deepen its content and internalise the values presented. While the intention was that every educational activity should contribute to moral education a separate and compulsory subject was re-introduced into the curricula of schools in 1958 with the support of many influential groups in Japan.

(g) *A New Concept of " Man "*

If the new Constitution and Fundamental Law of Education had not provided adequate guidelines, in spite of the eagerness with which people in Japan accepted that pre-war policies had been wrong and that peace and democracy should be the goals of policy,[40] a major dilemma remained. How should new courses in moral education be constructed? Should they reject Japanese family traditions or build on them? Research was immediately undertaken by Professor M.

---

[38] *Op. cit.* in note 18, above.
[39] Report by the Advisory Council for the Curriculum, Ministry of Education, Tokyo, 1958.
[40] See T. Akabori, *op. cit.* in note 21, above.

Hiratsuka, then at Kyushu University, and his colleagues in an attempt to find an answer.[41] It was a most imaginative comparative study of the attitudes developed in Japanese, English, French and German schools, and of the methods used in each of the systems to achieve stated aims.

The interdisciplinary group of educationists included a psychologist, an historian, an administrator, a sociologist and a philosopher. Attitude tests were constructed in Japan and administered to Japanese pupils. The tests were translated into the appropriate language and administered in each of the three European countries. Members of the group made a careful study of relevant documents, visited a number of schools and discussed their problems with educationists. Subsequently, the data were analysed with the greatest of care in Japan with the help of three scholars from Europe. A distinction was drawn between the attitudes of children in rural and urban areas and towards God, democracy and other " Western " ideals. The exercise pointed to a fundamental difference between Japanese and European traditions. The former ascribe authority to the individual, and particularly the head of the family. Filial piety, obligation and duty dominate. European theories emphasise that the authority for behaviour are principles rather than persons. Principles should guide behaviour and provide criteria for judging proper beliefs and behaviour.

Doubtless this research had some influence on the establishment by the Central Advisory Council on Education [42] in 1966 of a new moral code to be taught in schools. A comparison of *Shushin* based in the Imperial Rescript of 1890 and *Dotoku* (course of morals) is very instructive.[43] The aims of pre-war moral education (*Shushin*) were to inculcate nationalism and respect for persons in authority. The aims of *Dotoku* were to foster a respect for humanity, a desire to create a unique democratic society and the will to contribute to world peace. The content of courses designed to promote this ideal image were spelled out in some detail. The order in which items

---

[41] Professor Hiratsuka was joined in Europe by Professors Ushijima, Ishi, Masui and Yoshida. They were assisted in Japan by B. Holmes (England), W. F. J. Koelle (Federal Republic of Germany) and R. A. V. Mallet (France), who spent three months helping to analyse data collected in Japan and Europe.

[42] *Op. cit.* in note 24, above, at p. 228.

[43] The following comparison between the aims and content of *Shushin* and *Dokotu* reveals the extent to which changes have been made. While some Japanese authors claim that the order in which the contents are placed does not reflect the degree of emphasis to be placed on the items (see A. Naka, *Nihon Kindai Kyoiku-Shi* (1973), for the order in *Shushin*, and J. Miyata and K. Matsumura (eds.), *Shogakko: Gakushu Shido Youryo no Tenkai: Dokoka-hen* (1968), for the order in the Guidelines for Teaching Moral Education (Primary School), it is nevertheless interesting to note that the analysis made of the importance of *Ie* (family morality) is reflected in the place accorded in *Shushin* to family relationships.

appear is in sharp contrast to that established in *Shushin*. In that document filial piety and family obligations came first, followed by virtues such as thrift, trust, generosity and hard work. Finally, *Shushin* was expected to develop respect for the law and to promote a wish to contribute to society. First on the list of attitudes appropriate to the ideal human being were the values of life, health and safety. These were followed by principles relating to appearance and language, respect for property, punctuality, freedom and justice. Family relations and love of country were placed very low in the sequence of attitudes appropriate to the ideal human being.

The emphasis of the document was clearly different from that which informed pre-war moral education. It modified the latter without rejecting it. The new code gave the individual a central place and described how he should behave at home, in society and as a citizen. His freedom, strength of character, individuality and respect for others were central principles on which attitudes should be based. The model was designed to give new meaning to life by re-interpreting the great traditions of the Japanese way of life. It was criticised on several grounds. To begin with, because it was the result of government initiative,[44] and not a genuine grass roots response to the situation in which the Japanese found themselves; finally, some critics thought that in failing to emphasise the independence of individuals the new code might re-enforce family consciousness and foster some undesirable pre-war loyalties.

The problem has been the subject of much discussion in Japan. Some writers point to the sense of inferiority experienced by Japanese scholars who have come closely into contact with Western ideas.[45] Lacking is a spirit of independence and the presence of a dependency which has its roots in the family and Emperor (*Tenno*) systems.

---

[44] See *e.g.* M. Murai, *Gendai Nihon no Kyoiku* (1968). The writer maintains that whether the new moral education is nationalistic or democratic the method of its introduction was undemocratic and a reflection of how policies were introduced in pre-war Japan. He regrets that the new ideal was not established by the people themselves. See also N. Murata, *Gendai Dotoku Kyoiku-ron* (1974); the writer considers that it was unnecessary to introduce a special subject since immediately after 1945 moral education had been provided through daily activities. T. Akabori, *op. cit.* in note 21, above, argues that, " The ideal image of a human being " has not yet been established as the basis of moral behaviour. H. Kamidera, *Dotoku Shido no Honshitsu to Keito-sei* (1969), found that among lower secondary school pupils more than 60 per cent. saw no great virtue in " moral education " and that teachers, while overtly accepting the course, probably did not understand it deep down or in a practical sense. Y. Shimizu, *Kyoiku to Shakai no Aida* (1973), contrasts the support in Western societies of family, church and local organisations with the dependence on schools in Japan for the teaching of moral education.

[45] The concept and realisation in practice of " individual independence " have received considerable attention in Japan. See N. Yoshida in M. Murai (*et al.*) *Henbo-suru Kyoiku* (1970), and E. O. Reischauer, *The Japanese* (1977), and T. Doi and H. Matsubara, in T. Wakamori, *op. cit.* in note 12, above.

Social relations are still conceived in terms of parent and child. Post-war critics have pointed to the ill-effects of over-protecting children as well as to the harm done by an over-strict family régime.[46] Rapid economic development, changes in industrial society and the appearance of nuclear families with far fewer children have added to the confusion. Yet the Japanese are still prepared to subordinate their individualism to the group and place high value on duty. They have not yet, so some writers maintain, learned to depend on themselves as individuals. In the search for a better life they have worked like "economic animals," created serious problems of pollution, and caught up with and overtaken many developed countries.[47] The fact that the Japanese do not instinctively understand the principles which inform human and international relationships have made for tense relationships and economic conflicts with other countries.[48] In short, Japanese critics are conscious of the problems resulting from economic success and consider that in future education will have to contribute more to the making of a good international citizen than to the preparation of a good worker.

III—PRESENT DILEMMAS

(a) *Changing Attitudes*

There is some evidence to show how attitudes in Japan have changed since 1945. Surveys of the Japanese national character have been carried out every five years by a research committee of the Institute of Statistical Mathematics.[49] A nation-wide survey (1975) of the values held by Japanese, conducted by the Research Institute for Broadcasting and Public Opinion, confirmed the results of the fifth national survey of 1973. Both showed that in the 1970s health, home life and happiness had replaced material success and wealth in the order of priorities. Democracy and liberalism remained the favoured political ideologies. Socialism, Communism and Fascism were poor runners-up. A surprising feature of these tests of opinion was that half of those who answered took the pragmatic view that whether

---

[46] See K. Sato in K. Kihara and H. Matsubara (eds.) *Gendai Shakai no Ningen Keisei* (1976), for an analysis of the confusion created under the forces of industrialisation after 1945.

[47] For analyses by Japanese scholars of the consequences of rapid economic growth, see S. Endo, *Nihonjin o Kataru* (1974); N. Kanayama in T. Wakamori (*et al.*), *op. cit.* in note 12, above; T. Doi, *ibid.*; and Y. Shimizu, *Gendai Nihon no Kyoiku* (1968).

[48] In Pt. I of the Report issued by the Central Council on Education (1966), when " The ideal image of the human being " was spelled out, an analysis was made of the characteristics of an industrial technological society and the tensions created by Japan's successful economic development. Japanese writers are very conscious of the international tensions created by their country's enormous balance of payments surplus and foreign criticism of the low level of imports into Japan.

[49] See surveys of the Japanese National Character, referred to in note 30, above.

political systems were good or bad depended on circumstances. This represents a move away from ideological dogmatism and contrasts sharply with the willingness of many Japanese still to accept unconditionally the authority of an older, high status person.

Against these indicators of change can be placed evidence which suggests that some Japanese traditions die hard. Wakamori [50] points out that *ie* still inhibits the development of individuality. Examples are given of how members of the Japanese Red Army reacted when they were arrested. When a group of them were arrested, journalists sought out their parents and tried to blame their lack of parental discipline for the behaviour of the young radicals. Individuals may even today be considered to be less than independent agents and their families held responsible for their crimes. Another example is quoted. When a member of the Red Army was held at Tel Aviv Airport he asked an Israeli officer whether his father had committed suicide. When told that he had not done so, he expressed relief.

(b) *The Examination " Hell "*

It is against this background of change and the persistence of traditions that an assessment of Japanese schools should be made. The zeal for education is universal. Government, business and parents have all supported a quite phenomenal expansion of provision. Since 1950 the Ministry of Education has slowly regained a considerable measure of its former power and authority. The system has become highly competitive. Parents make many sacrifices to ensure that their children succeed. In crowded homes room is made for children to do their homework in peace. Mothers, in particular, urge their children to study hard. The whole family rallies round when a child is preparing to take an examination which will ensure entry into a high-status, upper secondary school, or a chosen university. The national, former Imperial universities, are most highly desired and competition to get into them is intense. The demand for special, usually privately run, " cram " schools has given rise to an " examination preparation industry." An enormous number of specially prepared textbooks are used in these schools. Entry to a prestige university is based almost entirely on examination success. Wealth buys admission to second- and third-rate institutions. The temptation facing academics to favour some rather than other candidates remains nonetheless. This kind of competition represents a marked change in the attitudes of parents and students since Jean Stoetzel [51] reported on the attitudes of youth in post-war Japan in 1955.

[50] T. Wakamori (*et al.*), *op. cit.* in note 12, above.

[51] Jean Stoetzel, *Without the Chrysanthemum and the Sword* (1955). The writer carried out a very sympathetic and careful study of the attitudes of Japan's youth in the early 1950s.

The desire of parents to ensure that their children get into " good " schools can be explained by the fact that while competition inside institutions of higher education is not pronounced the competition among university graduates for " good " jobs is very great. Many of them have to accept any one of a range of occupations such as taxi-driving. The " examination hell " [52] created by the close links between academic achievement and material success in life accounts for the stress illnesses suffered by many Japanese pupils and is probably responsible for the high and rising suicide rates among the younger generation. Traditional Japanese attitudes towards suicide cannot fully explain student deaths by their own hand since overall suicide rates in Japan are lower than in Denmark and Sweden.[53] Consequently while the " examination hell " should not be taken as the only measure it does indicate that against obvious successes including the high scores of Japanese pupils in international achievement studies, should be weighed some of the personal tragedies related to success.

(c) *Economic Growth and Political Democracy*

At another level of analysis, while the schools of Japan may have contributed to economic growth, have they ensured internal political stability and the ability of the Japanese people to cope with the tensions created by their economic achievements? How far will the preservation of a family ethic and the failure to inculcate true independence of spirit and will make the Japanese good obedient workers but not good international citizens? The history of the first period of modernisation and ultimate disaster offers some clues to the present situation in which Japan finds itself. The extent to which present attempts by concerned people in Japan to devise and make effective an appropriate system of moral education succeed will help to determine the future of Japan in a world plagued by economic,

---

[52] See E. O. Reischauer, *op. cit.* in note 45, above, for an analysis of the pressures brought to bear on young people in schools and also for discussions about some of the dilemmas which face individuals in Japan. He considers that against the willingness of the individual to subordinate his individualism to the group should be placed his deep concern for self-discipline. See also D. and E. T. Riesman, *Conversations in Japan* (1967), and T. Sofue in Akuto (*et al.*) (ed.), *Hendo-ki no Nihon Shakai* (1972) refers to Riesman's classification of types of man. Among them the Japanese belong to the " Others-orientated " group, In other words he feels uneasy if he does not belong to any one group.

[53] Recent reports of suicides in Japan arising from examination pressure suggest that traditional solutions are found for modern difficulties. Reischauer, *op. cit.* in note 45, above, suggests most suicides in Japan occur for the same kind of reasons as elsewhere. Research into suicides due to school pressures is being undertaken. In fact suicide rates are not overall noticeably greater than in some occidental countries Reischauer thinks, however, that the Japanese continue to be fascinated by suicides in the way Americans are fascinated by murders.

political and social problems. It is towards the solution of these that responsible educationists in Japan are working. Let us hope that the sincerity of their intentions finds an adequate response in the solution they formulate. History may not repeat itself but the successful economic modernisation of Japan during two recent periods of that country's history should not blind us to the fact that the first period ended in national disaster and in the 1970s many deep-seated problems remain. It is perhaps in the light of these that education today should be assessed.

THE ORGANISATION
OF AMERICAN STATES

By

BRYCE WOOD

TAKING a look at the Organisation of American States (OAS) is reminiscent of a first view of Marcel Duchamp's " Nude Descending a Staircase," except that finding the proper perspective on the OAS is even more baffling. The stairs have moved.

The OAS has clattered down a twisting, mobile flight of steps from the lofty perch it once occupied at the apex of the inter-American system. Then, in 1948, it was the pre-eminent agency for symbolising, expressing and carrying out common purposes of a revitalised association of States whose looser, more primitive " International Union of American Republics " established in 1889, had nearly broken up in 1928 when the United States maintained it had the right to intervene or " interpose " with military force in the countries of the Caribbean and Central America.

Now, however, " the OAS has been suffering from an identity crisis growing out of the frequent questioning of its utility and purpose." [1] Questions arise, for example, from a manifesto by eminent Latin American economists organised as the Foro Latino-americano, who assert that there is a " need to put an end to the so-called ' special relationship ' " between Latin America and the United States, and to terminate " those military and political agreements, systems and structures " on which it has been based. This apparently means that the Charter of the OAS should be abrogated, and such structures as the OAS itself, the Inter-American Defense Board and the Inter-American Commission on Human Rights should be demolished. In place of the OAS, the United States should deal with a new organisation, the Latin American Economic System (SELA) for the construction of a new set of inter-American relationships, hopefully to include the principles of the " new international economic order." [2]

---

[1] Alejandro Orfila, *Dynamic Latin America*, Annual Report of the Secretary General, OAS, 1975 (1976), p. 7.

[2] The manifesto, entitled " The Role of the United States in the Autonomous Development of Latin America," has been circulated in photoduplicated form as an accompaniment to a letter of June 10, 1977 from Gabriel Valdés, chairman of the group, to S. M. Linowitz. See also *The Americas in a Changing World* (1975), Report of the Commission on United States-Latin American Relations, with a preface by S. M. Linowitz; and *The United States and Latin America: Next Steps*, A Second Report by

148

Questions arise also in the United States. Representative Donald M. Fraser (D. Minn.) has publicly questioned whether the OAS is useful enough to deserve continued United States membership.[3]

A sense of crisis is not unprecedented in the OAS, but the Organisation has survived. The Charter of Bogotá was revised in 1970, principally in certain structural features, and far-reaching substantive modifications are now being officially considered in a second round of reform, a round, however, which is at a standstill, partly because of Latin American efforts to write into the Charter prohibitions against economic " intervention " by the United States.

I—ORIGINS

The OAS is, formally, a regional agency within the ambit of the United Nations Charter, established in the conviction that " juridical organization is a necessary condition for security and peace founded on moral order and on justice." [4] Its express purposes are three: (1) to strengthen the security of the hemisphere; (2) to keep peace among its members; and (3) to promote, co-operatively, the members' economic, social and cultural development (Article 4).

Informally, the OAS might be called, as was the League of Nations, the maximum of co-operation at any moment, but it is not quite so evanescent as such a definition would imply. Like other international agencies, the OAS has been founded, and continues to be funded, because its members perceive it to foster certain interests, not necessarily mutual. In addition, the OAS has an existence above and apart from its members—it embodies a set of principles, aspirations, and procedures; it reminds its constituents of their obligations to keep the peace and refrain from intervention; and it provides an impressive building, a meeting place, and a unique collection of specialised skills in its staff of some 1,500 persons. Because of its formal relationship to the United Nations as a regional arrangement, and because of its own detailed constitutional treaty structure, the OAS is a more complicated, rigid and legalistic organisation than

---

the Commission on United States-Latin American Relations (1976). The document by Foro Latinoamericano does not specifically refer to the OAS or the other bodies mentioned here.

[3] United States House of Representatives, Committee on International Relations, Subcommittee on International Organizations. " Human Rights Issues at the Sixth Regular Session of the Organization of American States General Assembly." August 10, 1976. (Washington, D.C., U.S.Govt.P.O., 1976), pp. 8–9. A suggestion that the United States withdraw from the OAS was made by William D. Rogers, shortly before he was appointed Assistant Secretary of State for Inter-American Affairs (See *Visión*, February 24, 1973). However, the proposal was influentially opposed both in Latin America and the United States, and nothing more was heard of it when Mr. Rogers took office.

[4] OAS Charter, Preamble.

two other very different international associations, the British Commonwealth and the countries of the Warsaw Pact.

The OAS forms one of the three principal elements of what is loosely termed the Inter-American System. As will be seen, it has become an agency with limited functions. In addition, the shifting relationships of the American States are also served by other organisations such as the Inter-American Development Bank, the Pan-American Health Organisation and others that are fiscally and administratively separate from, although related to, the OAS. Finally there is a broad range of matters that are dealt with mainly in bilateral negotiations between Washington and individual countries. These include nuclear energy policy with Argentina and Brazil; sales or grants of armaments; and immigration policy with Mexico. There are also unilateral actions exemplified by the failure of the United States to consult with Latin America on its recent increase in the duty on sugar. The web of policy is fascinatingly intricate, but this paper deals mainly with the OAS as one part of the system.

In the Second World War, the American States developed a measure of political and economic co-operation never before approached. Endeavouring to enhance and extend this relationship, they signed the Inter-American Treaty of Reciprocal Assistance (Rio Treaty, 1947) and the Charter of the OAS (Bogotá, 1948). These treaties formalised their responsibilities and hopes, and offered opportunities as understood in the circumstances of the post-war period. It is in the interplay of these features of the organisation, on the one hand, with the objectives of the diverse national policies of the members, on the other, that a perspective will be sought on the OAS over the ensuing three decades.

In early 1945, as the time approached for the United Nations to descend from rhetoric to constitution and administration, the prevailing view in Washington was that peace and security were worldwide issues. The Dumbarton Oaks proposals of the Great Powers made no provision for decisions on these matters by agencies other than those of the United Nations.

The Latin American governments, however, successfully insisted at the San Francisco Conference on the incorporation of ideas that gave to regional organisations broader competence than the Great Powers had originally intended. The Latin Americans were not afraid of being left alone in the Western Hemisphere with the United States. The Good Neighbour policy initiated by the Roosevelt administration in 1933 had paved the way for advantageous co-operation in the Second World War. Latin American statesmen desired both to join the United Nations and to secure a large measure of regional autonomy. In framing the OAS, they secured both a non-intervention pledge from the United States, and agreement that there would be no veto. All important decisions would be made by a two-thirds vote. They thus " did not fall naively into the jaws of the wolf." [5] but they enthusaistically urged the United States to enter a regional arrangement that would minimise the power of the United Nations in the Americas, and would also hobble the United States. Perhaps the Latin Americans were less naive than some critically influential North Americans, for Senator Warren R. Austin remarked that the United States delegation at the United Nations conference in 1945 was " ' astounded . . . that the Latin Americans, who formerly regarded the Nation up north as a sort of club over their heads, now were not only willing but eager to participate in the Monroe Doctrine.' " [6] Participating in the Monroe Doctrine, to the Latin Americans, meant trying to extirpate a noxious creed. They failed, however, and this is one major reason for what Dr. Orfila has called the present crisis of the OAS.

II—PROCESSES OF CHANGE

Changes have occurred over time in the policies of members of the OAS and, consequently, in the scope and capabilities of the organisation. Some of these changes are here described as functional secessions, and others as functional accretions. These may be viewed in the light of three broad changes in the global setting, or *ambiente*, surrounding the American States. It is in this sense, as suggested above, that " the stairs have moved." The first of these was the gradual manifestation of the capability of the Soviet Union to exert political and military influence in the Western Hemisphere, culminating in the Cuba Missile Crisis of 1962. The second was the transformation in the strategic situation of the Americas. In the Second World War, the United States depended on Latin America for such immediate aid as air bases in Brazil, and refuelling facilities in Mexico, and, over the long haul, on ready availability of oil, tin and other resources. The defence of the hemisphere after 1950, however, in view of nuclear developments, became largely the responsibility of the United States as sole possessor of the relevant weapons. Thirdly, the hopes of Latin Americans that the substantial economic assistance provided them by the United States during the war would be continued, proved illusory.

(a) *Functional Secessions*

(i) *Economic secessions*

With respect to the Charter's purpose of promoting economic

---

[5] M. Ojeda, *Alcances y límites de la política exterior de México* (1976), p. 25.

[6] R. B. Russell and J. E. Muther, *A History of the United Nations Charter: The Role of the United States, 1940–1945* (1958), p. 563.

development, serious differences developed early. The United States did not substantively respond to Latin American requests for transitional aid in the immediate post-war period, and an OAS economic conference planned for June 1945, was indefinitely postponed. The conferences in Rio de Janeiro and Bogotá did not produce any significant inter-American collaboration in the economic field. Consequently there occurred the first of several functional secessions from the OAS that have marked its descent in prestige and influence over the past three decades.

Even before the Bogotá Charter was drafted, and against disapproval in Washington, the Latin American governments unanimously turned their backs on the OAS for certain purposes, and secured authorisation and funds for the Economic Commission for Latin America from the United Nations, thus escaping inhibitory influences of the United States government. The United States was represented in ECLA, which was based in Santiago, Chile, but Latin Americans dominated its work, and the staff, directed by Raúl Prebisch, an Argentine economist, was almost wholly Latin American. ECLA produced yearly economic surveys; and elaborated theories both to explain underdevelopment in terms of restrictive policies of the advanced countries, and to justify changes in the international economic system that would aid producers of raw materials. ECLA also became a specialised research seminar that trained Latin Americn economists, many of whom became influential government officials.

The formation of ECLA was the first major step in a sustained drive towards Latin American economic integration that, by excluding the United States, could only be maintained by a functional secession from the OAS. In this drive, four Latin American agencies, among others, have been created with various aims and records of achievement. These are: The Central American Common Market (CACM); the Latin American Free Trade Association (LAFTA); the Andean Pact; and SELA, already mentioned.

A major effect of these developments is a reduction of the role of the OAS largely to that of an observer of activities of other international agencies in the field of economic policy and organisation. Evidence of a recognition of these developments is presented in the coining of a phrase by Ambassador AndrewYoung when he referred to " the countries of the ECLA region." [7]

A second form of secession from the OAS is discernible in the entry of the Latin American States into the United Nations

---

[7] "A New Unity and a New Hope in the Western Hemisphere: Economic Growth With Social Justice," Address to ECLA, Guatemala, May 3, 1977, Department of State *Bulletin*, May 30, 1977, p. 573.

Conference on Trade and Development (UNCTAD). However, this time the secession was favoured by the United States and a special conference was held under OAS auspices to enable Latin America to formulate a common position for presentation at UNCTAD's first meeting. This and related events marked a distinct orientation of Latin America towards the Third World, a disengagement from United States tutelage, and a strong tendency to pursue its major economic interests by collaboration with other developing countries in preference to negotiations within the OAS. The most spectacular examples of this tendency are the memberships by Ecuador and Venezuela in the Organisation of Petroleum Exporting Countries (OPEC); and the Latin American identification in UNCTAD with the Group of 77—the least developed countries. This group surprised the "West" by its unity, forthrightness, and a sophistication derived in part from ECLA's studies and the fact that Prebisch was Secretary-General of UNCTAD in its first five years.[8]

Linked to these developments are the current Latin American plans for reform of the Charter that concentrate on inserting the principle of " collective economic security," with the consequent provision for sanctions against " economic aggression." The kind of aggression contemplated is the United States refusal of trade preferences to Ecuador and Venezuela because of their joining OPEC. It is also desired to put articles in the Charter that would obligate members to refrain from taking measures, such as diplomatic protests or economic discrimination, to protect private corporations abroad These additions, obviously aimed at the United States, are unacceptable to it, certainly in their present form.

A unanimous Latin America presented a set of economic resolutions including some of the above ideas to the United States at the Inter-American Economic and Social Council (ECOSOC) meeting in 1972. The proposals were rejected, and it is clear that the United States desires to avoid other confrontations in the OAS. It regards issues such as trade preferences, transfer of technology and others as worldwide issues, and would prefer to consider them and others in the United Nations or in UNCTAD, where consideration may be given to moves towards a new international economic order by all States, great and small, and where the United States would have some allies from what is sometimes called " the West " in the " North-South " dialogue. In other words, since Latin American countries, on economic issues, moved quickly out of the OAS to ECLA and

---

[8] See J. S. Nye, " UNCTAD: Poor Nations' Pressure Group," in R. W. Cox, and H. K. Jacobson, *The Anatomy of Influence: Decision Making in International Organization* (1973), pp. 334 *et seq.* Nye notes: " Raúl Prebisch has been one of the most successful men in the twentieth century in the use of an international organization—first ECLA, later UNCTAD—to affect governmental policies " (p. 348).

UNCTAD, the United States wants to meet them on their chosen ground, in company with other advanced countries and, indeed, on a global stage with countries of the Eastern bloc.

Confrontation over major economic issues between the one and the 24 may be avoided, as Secretary of State Cyrus R. Vance has strongly implied, by keeping the provisions of the Charter flexible on substantive economic issues; by combining the three OAS Councils (education, science and culture; economic and social; and political) into a single body; and by replacing " much of the standing bureaucracy " by informal consultations. These consultations, in Vance's view, " should not be institutionalised in the OAS Charter," but should take the form of temporary committees or *ad hoc* meetings, preferably of ministers of finance or trade, rather than of the ambassadors to the OAS.[9] Secretary Vance is evidently trying to make a break with an old pattern. " Most inter-American economic conferences in the past have been featured by Latin American demands upon the United States, and by defensive efforts on the part of the latter to avoid unrealistic commitments and to emphasise the necessity for self-help on the part of others." [10]

On broad issues of economic policy and integration, Latin America and the United States have, for the present and near future, joined in a functional secession from the OAS. In other economic fields, however, the OAS has played a significant role. In the decade following 1948, the United States opposed Latin American moves towards economic integration; refused to offer Latin America anything like the Marshall Plan for Europe; rejected suggestions for establishment of an inter-American bank; and urged its neighbours to follow development policies that would promote investment by foreign enterprise, which in practice would be largely from the United States, since no other important sources of private capital were available at the time.

These " rather narrow economic policies," [11] however, were extensively broadened in the early 1960s, in consequence of the hostile receptions given in 1958 to Vice-President Nixon by angry crowds in Peru and Colombia; of the events following the Cuban revolution in 1959; and of intensified Latin American initiatives in the OAS.

Finally responding to repeated urgings via the OAS, the United

---

[9] Statement at the OAS General Assembly, Grenada, June 14, 1977. Dept. of State, Office of Media Services, *Speech*, p. 3.

[10] J. C. Dreier, " New Wine in Old Bottles: The Changing Inter-American System," *International Organization*, Spring 1968, p. 478. Mr. Dreier is a former ambassador of the United States to the OAS.

[11] J. Grunwald, *The Alliance for Progress* (1965), p. 78.

States agreed to provide more than half the funding for the Inter-American Development Bank (IDB) which began operating in 1960. The IDB made loans of 1·5 billion dollars in 1976, and its cumulative net lending is now over 10 billion dollars. Twelve European members, and Israel and Japan, have been admitted, and the IDB has been successful in securing financing in private capital markets. The United States does not have a veto in the IDB on "hard loans," and has on occasion found itself in a minority of one, as when it opposed an IDB loan to Chile in 1976 on the ground of violations of human rights by the Chilean government.

Similarly responding to Latin American suggestions, notably the "Operation Pan America" of former Brazilian President Juscelino Kubitschek, the 10-year Alliance for Progress was launched in 1960. This bold experiment involved economic and political reforms by Latin American governments; grants and investments of funds by the United States, international agencies such as the World Bank and IDB, and advisory, evaluative and staff services by the OAS. The fundamental decisions on the allocation and administration of grants and loans were made by the financial institutions including AID in the United States, and there was no Latin American body comparable to the Organisation for European Economic Co-operation (OEEC) that received moneys and disbursed them in its discretion during the period of the Marshall Plan. That Plan's success was not matched by the Alliance for Progress, and debate continues as to assessment of the latter's achievements. It is, however, intriguing to speculate whether, if allocation decisions had been surrendered to a Latin American OEEC, perhaps within the OAS, Latin American integration, and the Organisation itself might have been strengthened.

(ii) *Political secessions*

1. *The Dominican case.* The United States, by sending troops to the Dominican Republic in 1965, intervened, violating Articles 15 and 17 of the OAS Charter, and ignoring provisions of the Rio Treaty of 1947.[12]

This was a functional secession from the OAS, as the term is employed here, since the very act denied the applicability to the United States of its obligations in the Charter to refrain from

---

[12] The existence of a contrary view should be noted. Ambassador Ellsworth Bunker defended the action of the United States by asserting that "' This was not intervention in any sense by the United States in the affairs of the Dominican Republic. United States forces were dispatched purely and solely for humanitarian purposes for the protection of the lives not only of United States citizens but the lives of citizens of other countries as well.'" Quoted from *Américas*, May 1965, pp. 42–43, in G. Connell-Smith, *The Inter-American System* (1966), p. 337.

intervention. The definition of " intervention " is difficult, as the United Nations' long struggle testified, but if it means anything, it means the landing of troops on foreign territory for other than ceremonial purposes. The failure to consult was almost certainly due to the Johnson administration's justifiably strong doubts that the Organ of Consultation of the OAS would give prior authorisation to the action it had determined to take. The subsequent approval by the OAS for the formation of a temporary inter-American peace force consisting of the United States troops, and such additional military units as other members might supply, can hardly be regarded as support for Washington's policy. (Brazil furnished about 1,200 men and token contingents were provided by Costa Rica, El Salvador, Honduras and Nicaragua.) No vote of censure was taken against the United States. Instead, it appears that the vote of approval of a peace force in the OAS (the bare 14 required) found its source in the conviction on the part of some Latin American statesmen that participation in the peace force might give them their best opportunity for exercising some measure of beneficent constraint on the behaviour of the occupying forces of the United States.

The Dominican crisis illustrates the complexities of perception, judgment and co-operation facing American statesmen in issues affecting the security of the hemisphere. In the Cuba Missile Crisis, the Council of the OAS was informed of plans for a quarantine against Soviet ships, and the Council immediately and unanimously approved a demand, in the name of the OAS, for the removal of missiles from Cuba; and by a vote of 17 to 3, authorised the individual or collective use of force by members of the OAS in pursuance of this demand. In this instance, the threat was clear and the presence of weapons in Cuba had been confirmed. In the Dominican case, the menace was unclear, and the official allegations of communist control of the uprising were responsibly questioned both in the United States and Latin America.

2. *The policy of Mexico.* The Dominican case highlights the issue of subversion of democratic institutions, in which the thorniest and most divisive divergences among the American States have flourished. Mario Ojeda has suggested that its nearly obsessive fear of subversion, especially after the Cuban revolution but evident in the Guatemala case in 1954, induced the United States to formulate a policy of " penetration " at all levels of Latin American societies. In the judgment of the Mexican Government, this policy reduced the sovereignty of the other American States to a secondary position, and so created a conflict with the two most precious attainments of the inter-American system—the express recognition by the United States of self-determination for its neighbours, and its own obligation

to refrain from intervention.[13] In this view, the penetration of the American States was accomplished through: (1) the Alliance for Progress with its accompanying North American supervision of the administration of loans and grants; (2) negotiation of bilateral military assistance agreements; and (3) the training at centres in Panama and the United States of Latin American military officials and police officers in techniques of counter-insurgency.[14]

Mexico resisted this penetration by participating less in these programmes than any other Latin American country, and, even before the Dominican intervention, Mexico commenced its own functional secession from the OAS. Mexico rejected its clear obligation under the Rio Treaty (Articles 8 and 20) to apply economic and other sanctions against Cuba in 1964, despite their approval by the necessary two-thirds vote of the OAS Organ of Consultation. Mexico's position was that the Rio Treaty should not have been invoked at all in this case in which Cuba had supplied arms to Venezuelan guerrillas; and its offer to refer the dispute to the World Court was not taken up, although all the other American States did apply the sanctions voted. Later, after the Dominican intervention, the Mexican Government, dropping from coolness to disillusionment over the OAS, decided to refrain from making proposals to augment the sphere of action of the OAS, and to orient its multilateral engagements primarily in co-operation with the Third World, and towards the United Nations.[15]

3. *Pacific settlement*. A third secession of a rather different type was achieved by a majority of Latin American countries in 1956, when they drastically curtailed the powers of the Inter-American Peace Committee (IAPC).

With the experience of the Second World War vividly in mind, together with their own failures to prevent armed conflicts in America in the Chaco War, the Leticia conflict and the Peruvian invasion of Ecuador in the period 1933–1941, American statesmen gave first priority in their thinking about a new inter-American organisation to matters of peace and security. Even before the

[13] *Op. cit.* in note 4, above, at p. 7.
[14] On this last activity see W. F. Barber and C. N. Ronning, *Internal Security and Military Power: Counterinsurgency and Civic Action in Latin America* (1966).
[15] Ojeda, *op. cit.* in note 5, above, at pp. 52–53. The Mexican case has its special features. It is presented here because it is thought to be representative of views shared by some other American Republics, and because Ojeda's book presents a responsible and refreshingly vivid glimpse of motivations behind foreign policies of a major country of the hemisphere. *Cf.* O. Pellicer de Brody, " México en la OEA," *Foro Internacional*, October 1965–March 1966, p. 288, on Mexico's " lack of enthusiasm " towards the OAS after 1955. It should be noted, however, that Mexican disinvolvement in the OAS, which reached an extreme under President Luis Echeverría, has been reversed by President José López Portillo, who recently affirmed his government's support for the basic principles and structures of the OAS.

structure of the OAS was erected in 1948, the American States completed the Rio Treaty of 1947, which provided that an armed attack on an American State from whatever source " shall be considered as an attack against all the American States," and that the signatories would assist the attacked State. The Organ of Consultation as established in 1947, would co-ordinate measures to aid the victims of aggression.

The OAS began its career, then, primarily as an agency both for defending the hemisphere against external enemies, and for keeping the peace among its members. Its economic and social objectives were not entirely neglected, but they were regarded, in Washington at least, as distinctly subordinate to the larger tasks.

The first six years of the OAS passed serenely so far as issues affecting the security of the hemisphere were concerned. Bilateral mutual defence assistance agreements were signed in this period between the United States and a dozen Latin American countries. These were made outside the OAS, and the Cold War did not at that time pose any direct threats.

The OAS was effectively employed in this period in stifling armed conflicts among several small countries of the Caribbean and Central America. There was unity among the non-combatants in rapidly bringing pressure to bear on fiery, if feeble, forces in Costa Rica, Nicaragua, Haiti, Cuba and the Dominican Republic. The Inter-American Peace Committee, an informal and slightly irregular body unmentioned in the Charter, but created by the Council of the OAS in order to carry out certain purposes envisaged by the Rio Treaty, quickly appeared at the scenes of fighting, and by making authoritative recommendations, helped each side to find peace with dignity. The Committee, or special committees under the Rio Treaty, were dispatched by the Council without asking permission of the disputants, and their effectiveness was largely a result of an ability to act rapidly and make objective assessments of the situation on the basis of first-hand knowledge. This useful work is generally regarded as the most significant accomplishment of the OAS in the area of peace-keeping.

In 1956, however, a group of countries in which Peru took the lead, imposed the restriction on the IAPC that it could not speed to the site of hostilities in an inter-State dispute unless it were invited by both contending governments. This restriction was ratified by the Charter reform of 1970, and it remains as a potential limitation on the capability of the OAS to bring its collective weight to bear in a disturbance of peace among American States.

However, this legal limitation has not so far amounted to a practical curtailment of the influence of the OAS on quarrelling members. A truce was arranged in the fighting between El Salvador and Honduras in 1969, and, in October 1977, an OAS committee was appointed at the request of Costa Rica that settled its dispute with Nicaragua over guerrilla activities. In practice, therefore, the prestige of the OAS, and the fact that it is the unique, established source of conciliation, has enabled it to continue to operate effectively. The informal, flexible capabilities of the OAS are considerable in this area. The Secretary-General may be quietly influential, and there is wide scope for " corridor work " since the representatives of the OAS are regularly in Washington, and it may be unnecessary to attract attention by calling special sessions of a formal body. The OAS may therefore maintain an informal and valuable peace-keeping role as concerns the small States of the Caribbean, but its capabilities in case of a major struggle in South America have, happily, yet to be tested.

In summary, from the point of view of the OAS as an organisation, it has never been allowed to carry out large projects for promoting economic, social or cultural development of the members. From the point of view of the interests of Latin America, the Dominican invasion by the United States broke the shield borne by the non-intervention clauses of the Charter, and both governments and rebels may be expected to adapt their strategies accordingly. From the point of view of the United States, the OAS has not been permitted to organise and equip an inter-American peace force for defence of the hemisphere against either subversion or armed attack.

However, such shedding of important functions, in terms of expectations in 1948, does not mean that the OAS has no useful part to play in the present and future relations of the American States.

(b) *Functional Accretions*

If the members of the OAS have chosen to limit some of their activities, and shrink some of their obligations, they are also intensifying their interactions in other realms of the OAS, notably with respect to human rights and technical assistance.

(i) *Human rights*

The Inter-American Commission on Human Rights (IACHR) established in 1959 to promote the observance of human rights by OAS members, was originally regarded as a harmless body that would occasionally exhort governments to treat their citizens humanely. The Commission performed competently in the Dominican crisis of 1965 by securing fair treatment of prisoners and mitigating the plight of refugees. The work of the IACHR was, however, almost wholly ignored by the Permanent Council and General Assembly of the OAS until the latter body met in Santiago, Chile in 1976. The Commission had made a visit to Chile in 1974 and had published two reports detailing violations of human rights by the Pinochet government. The reports were denounced by the Chilean and other delegations, and resolutions were passed that, in form, requested the OAS Council to re-examine the procedures and prerogatives of the IACHR, and in intent were aimed at disabling it. The Commission's action coincided with a strong movement in the United States Congress to require the administration to refuse economic and military aid to countries that consistently violated human rights, and Secretary Henry A. Kissinger told the Chileans that their policies on human rights had adversely affected relations between the two countries.

The IACHR, which is not a political body like the United Nations Commission, but is composed of seven individuals nominated by governments and selected by the Permanent Council as private citizens, stoutly defended its procedures and prerogatives, and presented to the General Assembly in 1977 a third report on human-rights violations in Chile. About 90 per cent. of the whole discussion at this session in Grenada was taken up with the question of human rights. Two resolutions were passed, one supported by the United States, which received a bare majority, that commended the IACHR and called for an increase in its budget; and a second, sponsored by Colombia, that obtained a larger majority and requested a reconsideration by the IACHR of its procedures, " based on non-discriminatory principles." In addition, it was recommended that a " new and effective inter-American co-operation for the integral development of the American countries " be sought as " a basic means to promote full legal recognition of human rights in the juridical as well as economic, social, and cultural spheres." [16]

The IACHR has suddenly become the liveliest and most controversial organ of the OAS. The United States, with support from countries of the Caribbean area, warmly favours increasing its staff and preserving its present capabilities, and a substantial number of Latin American countries, including among others, Argentina, Brazil and Chile, strongly desire to rein it in. In 1977 and 1978, a sudden increase in ratifications of the American Convention on Human Rights of 1960 has brought the Convention into effect among 12 States and elections of judges of the Court, to be sited in Costa Rica, will take place in the near future. The role of the IACHR in a situation where Argentina, Brazil, Chile, Mexico and the United States are among the non-ratifiers, remains uncertain and the forthcoming

---

[16] Doc. OEA/Ser.P. AG/Doc. 890/77, rev. 1, June 22, 1977, pp. 103, 104.

struggle over its capabilities may provide a severe test both for the OAS and for the policy of the United States.

(ii) *Development assistance*

In the field of technical assistance, the OAS demonstrates a spectacular accretion of functions in the past two decades. The staff has increased three-fold from 488 in 1959 to some 1,500 in 1976. The annual, assessed, regular budget has increased six-fold from 5·6 million dollars to 35 million dollars in the same period, and voluntary annual funds of 40 million dollars have been contributed. The new figures are accounted for largely by new activities in a broad category called direct services to member States. Apart from the regular budget, which is expended for headquarters expenses, publications, conferences, and administration of long-established agencies such as the Inter-American Commission of Women, the Inter-American Children's Institute, and others, about three-quarters of the voluntary funds are disbursed for fellowships (15 per cent.), training (21 per cent.), and technical aid (40 per cent.). Thus, the bulk of the non-administrative activity at present is of such a character as to justify the view that the OAS is principally engaged in educational work and development assistance in the hemisphere.

A major element of the educational programme is fellowships for study abroad, which the OAS has administered for many years. About 2,000 fellowships are now awarded annually, from a competition among more than 10,000 applicants. In addition, institutes and seminars are offered in Latin America for training in teaching methods and materials, organisation of school and university libraries, and methods of adult education and educational research.

Development assistance comprises a broad range of fields, and also specific projects in science and technology. Among the latter, as a few of many examples, are the ecology of the humid, tropical forest; utilisation of sugar cane by-products; genetic control of cattle; aerial surveys of river basins; oil shale exploitation; and a planned Census of America for 1980. These activities are well regarded by the American States, and increases in their financing have been regularly forthcoming. Financing is participatory in that Latin America has provided one-third of the funds, and the United States two-thirds.

The United States has given formal notice that it intends over the next several years to reduce its share of the regular OAS budget from two-thirds to 49 per cent. This is by way of a challenge to the other members, probing the depth of their concern about allocation and size of administrative funds. However, the United States will probably maintain its 66 per cent. share of voluntary funds for development assistance, so long as these are matched by Latin American contributions. If these are increased, the United States may find itself actually providing larger absolute sums for development work. In this connection, a policy of retrenchment seems to have begun with the dismissal in 1976 of some 125 members of the OAS staff; and an additional contingent of about the same size is expected to be released in 1977–78. This action is consonant with Secretary Vance's suggestions at Grenada that the OAS should become " a balanced and healthy organisation . . . flexible and lean in formal machinery." [17] It may be noted, however, that the OAS, in terms of salary scales, is already " leaner " than the Inter-American Development Bank.

Objections have been raised in the United States to the administration of technical assistance by the OAS, on the ground that it duplicates, and is less administratively efficient than, programmes of other agencies such as the United Nations Development Program (UNDP), the IDB, the Inter-American Foundation, or the Caribbean Development Bank. Co-ordination among these agencies is not close, and the OAS programme is one of the smallest, although relatively large for development aid as contrasted to loans. However, the regular contributions of the OAS members demonstrate a conviction that the OAS desirably complements other sources of funding for technical assistance.

III—A Look Ahead

Officials in the United States and Latin America refer frequently to the desirability of " strengthening " the OAS, but they mean very different things. The former have in mind capabilities of OAS organs that would facilitate leadership by the United States; while the latter are thinking of new Charter provisions to restrain the United States from exercising its power. The trouble with strength for the OAS, from the Latin American viewpoint, is that " masked intervention " would thereby be furthered. Charges are often heard that the OAS is merely " a cloak " to conceal or justify United States policies, and the Guatemalan and Dominican cases are usually cited as evidence. If a strong OAS could quickly render a decision that one State were an aggressor, the United States, thus attired in virtue, might bring coercive pressure to uphold the OAS decision. Similarly, a strong IACHR could produce a report on atrocities in a given country that would offer the United States collective cover for refusing military or economic assistance. It is manifest that this kind of association of one Great Power and 24 lesser Powers can readily become more the instrument of the strong than the defender of the weak. Therefore,

---

[17] *Loc. cit.* in note 9, above, at p. 12.

the weak members try to prevent the association itself from authorising action or even issuing judgments about the behaviour of individual governments, so that the major Power cannot serve its own interests by a display of might in an overtly righteous cause. This seems to qe a major reason for the muzzling of the OAS Secretary-General, who is not allowed to issue a " state of the hemisphere " report, as can his counterpart in the United Nations with respect to the world.

Tension, mild or critical, has thus characterised the OAS ever since 1945, when Foreign Minister Eduardo Rodríguez Larreta of Uruguay proposed that the principle of non-intervention should not prevent the American governments from taking collective action against an anti-democratic régime in their midst. The United States welcomed the idea as the logical alternative to its own renunciation of intervention to prevent the intrusion of foreign totalitarian régimes into America. The Latin Americans, however, feared to authorise any joint intervention, because it would probably be directed by the United States, and they preferred to risk putting off any judgment until individual cases might arise. Joint pressure in the form of sanctions was in due course voted by the OAS against the Dominican Republic in 1960 and Cuba in 1964, for intervention and aggression against Venezuela.

The existence of tension does not, however, invalidate the association. To paraphrase an English economist: " The only thing worse than being defended by the United States is not being defended by the United States." While it is of paramount interest to Latin America to bell the cat as far as possible, it is also recognised that the cat may scare away more voracious predators. Indeed, some of the smaller Latin American and Caribbean countries may look to the OAS for protection even against some of the greater Latin American States, whose power is constantly increasing in relative terms.

Continued adherence to the OAS may also be expected because Latin Americans are aware that the OAS and other regional agencies offer them a stronger hold on, and readier access to, United States resources than do other international organisations. In the IDB, for example, which Latin Americans sometimes call " our institution," their control of funds is nearly complete. In the several development assistance programmes of the OAS, selection of projects and allocation of resources are very largely in their control. Further, the experience of Latin America with efforts at integration such as LAFTA has been frustrating and ineffectual. Their newest organisation, SELA, funded for 2 million dollars a year, mainly by Mexico and Venezuela, has disappointed the hopes of its patrons, and so far has accomplished little more than the formulation of co-operative projects in the field of shipping, among others. Brazil has remained uninterested in SELA, and so far SELA shows no signs of acquiring the solidarity and representative quality that would allow it to replace the OAS in dealings with the United States, as the Foro Latinoamericano has proposed.[18]

It is often said that the OAS was founded on " the myth of the mutuality of interests." For the period 1933–1948, the myth rested upon solid foundations in the Good Neighbour policy, and co-operation during the Second World War. The appearance of rifts in the myth in the past 30 years does not, however, mean that interests are now wholly antagonistic. Solidarity might suddenly reassert itself in the face of another crisis comparable to that of missiles in Cuba. In the absence of such a crisis, even if the mutuality of interests is now at a low point on economic policy, it is possible that the Organisation may receive support from all members because it serves the interests of different groups for certain purposes. For example, Ecuador and Brazil are deeply interested in studies of the management of equatorial forests in relation to their plans for promoting barge transportation on the Amazon and Putumayo rivers; although the United States may be concerned in this and other matters only because it may accept in part the notion that " It is in the interest of the strong to strengthen the unity of the weak." [19] On the other hand, the United States has become deeply interested in furthering the observance of human rights in the hemisphere, and this concern may be humoured by enough countries so that the work of the IACHR will not be impeded, because they see advantages in participating elsewhere in the arena of the OAS where the collaboration of the United States is desired, and dangers to the existence of the OAS if they frustrate Washington's thrust. A complex game of compromise and trade-offs may thus be played in the OAS, even though the opponents may agree on no more than that the Organisation itself should continue to sponsor the competitions.

In this connection, it may be noted that a new element has recently entered the political manoeuvring in the OAS. Barbados, Grenada, Jamaica, Trinidad and Tobago and Surinam now constitute one-fifth of the membership. In the OAS, where votes are of great importance, in contrast to the Commonwealth or Warsaw Pact, these non-Latin members, though small in size, may exert great electoral influence. In the Grenada meeting, voting with the United States, they provided 36 per cent. of the bare majority of 14 that

[18] See the introduction to this paper, above; and R. D. Bond, " Regionalism in Latin America: Prospects for the Latin American Economic System (SELA)," *International Organization*, Spring 1978.
[19] Foro Latinoamericano, cited in note 2, above, p. 6.

carried the resolution to give more funds to the IACHR. (The other eight States were: Costa Rica, Dominican Republic, Ecuador, Haiti, Mexico, Panama, Peru and Venezuela.) If the United States is able to secure majorities that include these States, plus others in the Caribbean and Central America, a disturbing factor will be inserted in the traditional equation. It has even been suggested by a few opponents of continued United States membership in the OAS, that consideration should be given to withdrawal, and the formation of a new association with those countries of the Caribbean region that may share more fully than others in the hemisphere, the economic, political and security orientations of Washington. Secretary Vance's proposal at Grenada that the Charter should be amended to allow all independent States of the Americas to join the OAS is probably made in the hope that Guayana and Belize might become backers of policies of the United States.[20]

In summary, the OAS has fair prospects for survival. It may still mediate in domestic quarrels. It keeps ready a skilled staff, files full of established procedures, and a venerable legal tradition that may all come into play on behalf of American States that find themselves in a dispute or conflict—if and when they both wish to terminate it with faces saved.

Secondly, the OAS offers neutral ground for consideration of members' mutual concerns as they may change over time. Keeping in touch through regular sessions in which all members participate is also essential for the proper management of the complex and variegated set of non-political relationships that the American States have created and desire to maintain. Education co-operation through scholarships, training institutes and research is one such set. Another comprises the work of specialised organisations such as the Pan-American Health Organisation, which began life as the Pan-American Sanitary Bureau, the Inter-American Children's Institute, the Inter-American Institute of Agricultural Sciences, to mention only some of them.

A third area of which we have been reminded recently is co-operation in disaster relief following hurricanes and earthquakes, as in Honduras, Guatemala, Ecuador and Nicaragua. In addition, there are other spheres of co-operation—tourism, standardisation of census statistics and protection of cultural heritages that command the interest and financial support of member States. Finally, there may be specialised types of technical assistance that the members would prefer to have administered by the OAS rather than by other organisations.

Many of the members of the British Commonwealth share a

[20] *Op. cit.* in note 9, above, at p. 3.

common language, parliamentary institutions, cricket and football. In the Americas, baseball is only circum-Caribbean; representative democracy is rare; and there is no common language, although there are more than 12 million residents of the United States whose mother tongue is Spanish. Still, the OAS symbolises common, cherished possessions of the countries of America. The escape from European domination was mutual and nearly contemporaneous. The aspiration towards democratic values, however frequently violated even as at present, is embodied in constitution after constitution. The Bolivarian hope for Latin American unity foundered on distance and parochialism at first, but the OAS, as the successor to Latin American failures, has not blocked Latin American integration, but may well have furthered it. If SELA and its sister agencies fall short, inadequacies result from Latin American disunity and mistrust, and can hardly be blamed on the OAS. As a Caribbean statesman has said, there is " a permanent partnership " with the United States that requires a continuity of a measure of faith in the United States at least by its nearer, smallest neighbours, and a reciprocal restraint and sympathy by the United States for the welfare of newly-independent entities that can hardly be other than dependencies, apart from legal status. There are even Latin Americans like the Minister of Foreign Affairs of Costa Rica, who made a stirring speech at Grenada, placing his country on the side of the United States as a powerful defender of free institutions.

It may be that one of the greatest strengths of the OAS is in its ceremonial uniqueness. Granted failures in co-operation and performance by all its members, the OAS will live because it welcomes initiatives, and promises opportunities; and because statesmen shrink from the stigma of destroying the symbol of an ideal. The principles and instruments of unity do not have to be reinvented. It may perform a fundamental civilising mission even in a primitive society by helping the weak restrain the strong and by extending to the latter acceptable condolences in the form of a sense of virtue and long-term advantage for the sacrifice of momentary interest. It holds open a hospitable door that may lead to the discovery of future mutual interest and ways of co-operation for emergencies that cannot now be foreseen. An interesting example of unusual action in a current emergency is the OAS mediatory mission in Nicaragua.

By

E. S. MILENKY

THE Andean Group, or Cartagena Agreement as it is known formally, has been facing one of three possibilities: continued, but slowed, progress towards higher levels of economic and political co-operation; progressive disintegration; or stagnation. This international organisation, composed of Bolivia, Colombia, Ecuador, Peru, Venezuela, and until October 1976, Chile, is the Third World's most sophisticated effort at collective co-operation for development and autonomy in the face of widely-perceived feelings of weakness and dependence in world affairs. Despite a serious crisis generated by disagreements among its members and compounded by the world energy and economic crisis, the Andean Group has survived. Therefore, its experience illustrates the future of international co-operation for development among Third World countries.

I—CONCEPTUAL FOUNDATIONS

Latin American countries have experimented with three generations of regional economic co-operation and integration organisations. The first included the Latin American Free Trade Association (LAFTA) and the Central American Common Market, the second the Andean Group, and the third, the Latin American Economic System (SELA). All three are responses to what Latin Americans perceive as their dependent, semi-colonial position on the periphery of a world economic and political order dominated by a centre of industrial countries.[1] Regional international organisation has been seen as a way to pool resources, improve bargaining power, and stimulate national development, or more particularly industrialisation, through co-operation and economies of scale.

The Latin American Free Trade Association (LAFTA) founded in 1960 and including all of Spanish-speaking South America, Mexico, and Brazil, was based on the ideology of integration. Some degree of regional self-sufficiency, especially in manufactured products, was to have been achieved by relying on market forces and tariff cuts among member States. In keeping with an underlying

---

[1] United Nations, Economic Commission for Latin America (ECLA), *The Economic Development of Latin America and Its Principal Problems*, E/CN.12/89 Rev 1, April 27, 1950.

167

West European model, a common market was to have been the ultimate objective.[2] However, the free-trade zone projected as a first step fell victim to economic disparities among its members and to the increasing popularity of central planning as compared to free enterprise. Despite the often substantial benefits which went to indigenous enterprises, critics disparaged the organisation for allowing multi-national corporations, long-standing symbols of political and economic dependence, to gain from an emerging regional market.[3]

The Andean Group was a response to the failings of LAFTA, the new ideological climate, and continued Latin American perceptions of dependence. In place of integration this second generation organisation was founded on developmental nationalism. Autonomous industrialisation on a strictly national, as distinct from a regional basis, would be promoted through the planned exchange of marketing opportunities and the allocation of production opportunities for new sectors among the participants. The member-States would break their dependence on the sale of primary products in unstable world markets by achieving a degree of self-sufficiency in basic, formerly imported manufactured goods in the context of a protected market. Chile's Christian Democratic Frei government and Peru's military government, both of which were inclined strongly towards State planning, control of foreign investment, and economic nationalism, were the strongest backers of the Cartagena Agreement. Venezuela, Ecuador, and Bolivia saw the pact as a way to escape from nearly exclusive dependence on primary products.

Developmental nationalism found expression in the Cartagena Agreement of 1969. Five countries, joined after 1973 by Venezuela which delayed ratification because of domestic business opposition, provided for industrial programming. A series of sectoral agreements would distribute exclusive production opportunities in basic industries. Each country would exercise a local monopoly for its assigned items within a common market established through linear, automatic tariff reductions and a full common external tariff. A sub-regional development bank, the Andean Development Corporation (CAF) would invest in national industry and locally owned multi-national enterprises. Common policies for restricting foreign investment, promoting physical integration, and harmonising national economic policies would promote autonomous industrialisation.

    [2] United Nations, ECLA, *Multilateral Economic Co-operation in Latin America* E/CN.12/621, 1962; see also E. S. Milenky, *The Politics of Regional Organization in Latin America: The Latin American Free Trade Association* (1973).

    [3] G. Margarinos, " La inversion extranjera y la integracion latinoamericana, seminario sobre Politica de Inversiones Extranjeras y Transferencias de Tecnologia en América Latina," FLACSO-ILPES (1973), p. 57.

An independent Junta of three technocrats would oversee the planning process and promote agreement in the inter-governmental Commission. As relatively least-developed countries Bolivia and Ecuador received additional, non-reciprocal opportunities to invest in new production for the sub-region and to adopt tariff cuts and the common external tariff more slowly than the other members.[4]

However, the Andean Group did not provide a means of responding to global pressures which became acute after the 1973 oil crisis. As the first truly Pan-Latin American organisation, with members from the English-speaking Caribbean and Cuba, the Latin American Economic System was designed for bloc bargaining with the industrial Powers and *ad hoc*, project-oriented economic co-operation among its members. However, by late 1978 SELA had failed to organise a true collective approach to the major Powers or significant intra-regional development projects. Therefore, the third generation approach, bloc bargaining on a broad coalition base, was not succeeding.

II—ACHIEVEMENTS

Until the 1975–76 crisis which challenged its foundations the Andean Group made steady, important gains in trade, industrial programming, the regulation of foreign investment, and the operation of its sub-regional development bank. However, if the organisation's ensuing political problems are to be understood, then each area must be evaluated in comparison to the global needs of the member-States as well as in absolute economic terms.

Absolute gains in trade volume are impressive. Member-State exports to the sub-region reached 638 million dollars in 1976 as compared to 170 million dollars in 1969. Industrial products were 48 per cent. of the total in 1969 but 67 per cent. in 1974.[5] By mid-1975 tariffs among the member States were down over 40 per cent. from the 1971 starting point for the treaty programme and a minimum common external tariff was in place. However, this trade represented only 8 per cent. of the average Andean country exports to world markets.[6]

In industrial programming the Cartagena Agreement moved from a general development strategy and reservation of 2,000 products in the dynamic basic industrial sectors to the adoption of agreements.[7] The Metal-Mechanical Agreement of August 1972 assigned exclusive

---

[4] Treaty text in 5 *Derecho de la Integracion* (1969), pp. 103–117.

[5] Comision Economica para América Latina, *Notas sobre la economia y el desarrollo de America Latina* (1977), p. 2.

[6] 25 *Comercio Exterior* (1975), p. 126.

[7] In Decision 25: autos, petrochemicals, fertilisers, machine tools, steel, pesticides, shipbuilding, chemicals, textile and printing machinery, paper; see *Grupo Andino* (1971), p. 4.

production rights for 102 industrial items, including railroad equipment, electrical generators, agricultural machinery, machine tools, and other capital goods with the ultimate goal of supplying 72 per cent. of the sub-region's needs.[8] By 1976 80 firms were expanding or being established to serve the market, often with the assistance of foreign firms or licensed technology.

Investments totalling 2·5 billion dollars in 56 product groups distributed among the six participants were projected in the August 1975 Petrochemical Agreement. This programme also left unassigned a large group of items which would move in free trade behind a common external tariff and allowed any country to produce any product for export outside of the common market. Venezuela's highly-developed industry demanded this concession. In this area the participants built on experience with a 1968 " complementarity agreement," a specialised trade arrangement concluded under LAFTA by Chile, Colombia, Peru, and Bolivia.[9]

However, the member States failed to meet the December 1975 treaty deadline for concluding substantially all of the projected sectoral industrial agreements. In September 1977 they did sign the vehicles pact after three years of tendentious negotiations over the assignment of production rights and the rationalisation of the industry through a general reduction in the number of models and makes manufactured. Draft proposals for electronics and steel were being discussed in the Commission, but the Junta was still labouring over plans for other sectors.

Each successive pact restricts the participating countries' national development plans still more, involves progressively more sensitive industries, but does not necessarily build confidence. The agreements are too new to have a performance record. Therefore, it is not surprising that the Junta's 1972 general industrial development strategy, which was to have co-ordinated all of the pacts, was quietly dropped in 1975 as too speculative and confining.[10]

Still more speculative were the benefits of regulating foreign investment under Decision 24, originally adopted in response to the threat of foreign control of the sectors designated for industrial programming.[11] Decision 24 banned new foreign investment in public services, insurance, commercial banking, the media, and internal transportation except when a government chose to grant a waiver. It forbade foreign purchases of domestic firms and limited profit

[8] *Grupo Andino* (1975), pp. 1–5.
[9] 3 *Latin America: Economic Report* (1975), p. 91.
[10] 10 *Bank of London and South America Review* (1976), p. 829.
[11] See statement to this effect in Group's official newsletter, *Grupo Andino* (1971), pp. 3–6.

remittances to 14 per cent. annually of the authorised direct investment. Above all the code provided for the transformation of all
firms into " mixed enterprises," with 51 per cent. local ownership
and management, or " national enterprises " with 80 per cent. local
control within 15 years of a June 1971 starting date in Chile,
Colombia, Peru, and Venezuela, and within 20 years in Bolivia and
Ecuador.

There have been few concrete results. Various escape clauses and
waivers have made the foreign investment rules less than uniform.
By 1975 only Colombia had adopted all of Decision 24 into national
law, and Ecuador and Peru had just ratified.[12] Foreign investment did
decline, but most probably in reaction to uncertainty and to expropriations in Peru and Chile.

Aside from the investment code the Andean Group has taken few
major steps towards harmonising national economic policy. The
Andean Reserve Fund, established with an initial capital of 300
million dollars in November, 1976, plus an additional 100 million
dollars Venezuelan contribution, is a step towards common monetary
policy. Its loans will promote balance-of-payments stabilisation.[13]
However, differing levels of development and ideological disparities
make co-ordination of other policy areas unlikely.

The Andean Development Corporation (CAF) has given aid but
has not promoted multinational investment. Bond sales of 50 million
dollars in the New York financial market, a 60 million-dollar
Venezuelan trust fund, and outside grants from the United States,
Finland, Canada, and West Germany have expanded the initial
capitalisation of 100 million dollars in shares sold in member
countries. Some grants have supported pre-investment studies for
the sectoral industrial agreements, but Bolivia and Ecuador have
received the largest share of loans, often for basic development
projects unrelated to the Cartagena Agreement. In this fashion CAF
has sought to balance the benefits of membership in the organisation
as a whole by aiding the weakest members. CAF's loans reached
174 million dollars in 1976, but the organisation has promoted no
multinational projects of its own.

III—DISINTEGRATIVE PRESSURES

Substantial economic achievements notwithstanding, the Andean
Group suffered a severe political crisis from early 1975 to late 1976.
Chile withdrew. The timetables for industrial programming and
trade liberalisation were postponed. Whatever balance is ultimately
struck among powerful disintegrative forces, the unifying potential

---

[12] AFP, Paris, November 22, 1975, and *op. cit.* in note 11, above (1976).
[13] Loan and capital figures from *op. cit.* in note 11, above, at 1971–76.

of changes made in the Cartagena programme after the crisis and the impact of global economic and political pressures will determine the future of the organisation.

Geographically the Andean Group remains partly an artificial creation. Aside from dominant trade and investment links to the major Powers the member countries have maintained important intra-Latin American affiliations. Chile's most important local trading and transportation links are with the southern cone of South America, especially Argentina, while the Gran Colombia countries of Ecuador, Colombia, and Venezuela form another unit. Although the potential for north-south maritime links among coastal population centres exists, rail and road connections are poor, especially to Bolivia.

Economic rivalries and problems divide the member States. As the most industrialised countries, Chile and Colombia compete. Venezuela has high-cost, protected industry, and special problems as the only hard-currency country. Bolivia and Ecuador are dependent, respectively, on exports of tin and bananas. In the latter case, oil is important, but has slipped behind bananas as an export because of high production costs. As a result the Andean Pact has worked against diverse, well-established national economic interests.

Ideologies of national development have also been at odds, from the beginning or because of changes of government. In Chile the Allende government's preference for central planning and economic nationalism has given way since the 1973 *coup* to the military junta's programme of export-oriented industrialisation, sell-offs of nationalised firms, low tariffs, and a Chicago-School, market-oriented approach to macro-economic policy. Peru's mounting economic problems have forced its nationalist military government to go slow on expropriations and distributive policies in favour of extensive foreign borrowing and attempts to revive a sagging balance of payments. However, the administration of Venezuelan President Carlos Andres Perez, which inherited a large, publicly owned industrial complex and several government-run development projects, has nationalised the petroleum industry, and emphasised economic independence and diversification away from exclusive reliance on oil revenues.[14] Therefore, in some respects the original consensus behind the Cartagena Agreement no longer exists.

Unresolved border disputes and political tensions also divide the Andean countries. Peru and Bolivia lost coastal provinces to Chile in the 1879 War of the Pacific. Since diplomatic relations were restored in February 1975 after a 13-year lapse Chile and Bolivia have been negotiating a Bolivian proposal for a corridor to the sea north of the

---

[14] A. Briones, " Crisis del Pacto Andino y opciones y desarrollo en América Latina," 26 *Comercio Exterior* (1976), p. 716.

Chilean port of Arica through former Peruvian territory. Under the 1929 Treaty of Ancon, Peru has a veto over the retransfer of its lost province, making it a party to the talks. By late 1978 Peru had not given its consent for the transfer, and Bolivia and Chile had not agreed to a firm plan.[15] As a result, the seacoast issue was poisoning relations among all three countries.

Peru and Chile are also ideological and military rivals. In 1974 the approach of the 100th anniversary of the War of the Pacific, in which Chile occupied Lima as well as conquered territory, reportedly caused younger, more nationalist factions in the Peruvian army to contemplate military action. Peru's purchases in 1976 of Soviet tanks and aircraft, the first to be introduced to South America, also raised tensions.[16]

Other, less intense border disputes also exist. Ecuador and Peru dispute ownership of Amazonian lands awarded to Peru by arbitration following a brief war in the 1940s. Colombia and Venezuela are attempting to settle their maritime boundary in the Gulf of Venezuela over areas which may be oil-bearing. All of these pending problems are symptomatic of deeper distrusts and ideological differences between military and civilian governments, those with a socialist and central-planning orientation *versus* those with a more capitalist bent, and weaker and stronger local powers.

Finally, bilateral problems are related to a wider Latin American balance of power. Chile and Peru are respectively Brazilian or Argentine allies out of fear of their larger neighbours. Oil, natural gas, and a buffer-State location have made Bolivia the object of competition between its larger neighbours. Venezuela has recently attempted to use its oil wealth as the basis for regional and Third-World leadership. For members of the Andean Group these rivalries often produce competitive trade and investment arrangements with outside Powers.[17]

IV—THE 1975–76 CRISIS

Economic difficulties, ideological disparities, and political frictions produced the Andean pact's 1975–76 crisis. The issues included every area of the Cartagena programme: treatment of relatively less-developed countries, trade and tariffs, industrial programming, and regulation of foreign investment. In the outcome no area was left untouched.

---

[15] E. S. Milenky, *Argentina's Foreign Policies* (1978), pp. 209–211; *La Opinion*, Buenos Aires, September 13, 1975, p. 2.

[16] J. O'Leary, " Peru Watched for Move Against Chile," *The Washington Star-News*, August 4, 1974.

[17] " Peru y Argentina intensificaron sus relaciones económicas y comerciales," *El Peruano* (1974), pp. 1 and 4.

Disparities in level of development have plagued all of Latin America's integration experiments, including the Cartagena Agreement. Under unregulated free trade or investment the danger that capital and production will flow towards the strongest economies exists. In response to this problem Bolivia and Ecuador received the right under the Cartagena Agreement to export a range of products duty-free to the other members and to implement all commitments on a stretched-out schedule. However, by late 1974, neither country was meeting its deadlines for the production of new items under the sectoral industrial development agreements. In response to growing apparent inequalities in the distribution of benefits Bolivia and Ecuador began to exert strong pressures for remedial programmes.[18]

Trade liberalisation became the focus of a growing ideological debate. By December 1975, Chile and Colombia were favouring more stress on trade liberalisation than industrial programming, while the other four members supported the reverse. Product assignment facilitated central planning and meant a guaranteed market. Free trade would favour Chilean and Colombian industry over their less-developed competitors and would be consistent with more liberal national economic policies. In practice Chile and Colombia wanted to reduce the product coverage of the sectoral industrial agreements, leaving more items subject to linear, automatic tariff cuts.

Because of its impact on national price levels in economies highly dependent on imports, the common external tariff was an even more critical issue than the place of trade liberalisation in the sub-regional programme. Local sources for vital capital goods would be more expensive and frequently less sophisticated and of lower quality until new production was firmly established. In keeping with their support of freer competition, Chile and Colombia backed the lowest possible rates for the future common external tariff. Bolivia also supported this position because of its extreme dependence on capital goods imports for incipient industries. In favour of high, protective rates were Ecuador, Peru, and Venezuela, which hoped to lower the cost of the continued substitution of industrialisation for imports through foreign sales to the region. The Andean Junta of technocrats backed intermediate rates which would have protected only labour-intensive industries. As a result the inter-governmental Commission failed to meet the treaty deadline of December 1974 for scheduling the phased introduction of a common external tariff for full effect in 1985.[19]

As noted earlier, industrial programming was also off schedule because the Commission did not meet the December 1975 deadline for adopting substantially all of the sectoral agreements. Peru,

---

18 Editorial, *Presencia*, La Paz, October 9, 1976, p. 3.
19 3 *Latin America: Economic Report* (1975), pp. 197 and 143.

Venezuela, Bolivia, and Ecuador supported adoption of pending pacts for glass, steel, pulp and paper, electronics, and fertilisers in accordance with the original developmental nationalism strategy. Towards the end of 1975, the Commission was forced to choose between continuing negotiations deadlocked over product assignments and tariff levels, or amending the Cartagena Agreement to postpone the deadlines in the hope that an extended timetable would make the required commitments easier to accept.[20]

Chile attacked Decision 24, the foreign investment code, for restricting the flow of capital it regarded as essential to its recovery from the post-Allende economic collapse and for impeding the development of global economic relationships. In late 1974, the military government precipitated the crisis by adopting a " Statute of Investment " contrary to the code. Import duties were liberalised for projects with more than 20 per cent. foreign participation, and firms held by CORFO, the State-owned development corporation, were sold to foreign investors. Chile also called for increasing allowable profit remittances and revising the fade-out formula for foreign participation in industry to increase outside investment.[21] Colombia, Bolivia, Ecuador, and the Venezuelan business community also supported some liberalisation of the rules for similar reasons. However, aside from Chile the other governments were anxious to maintain Decision 24 as a first step towards technological autonomy.[22]

Sub-regional institutions and key governments produced the eventual compromise. The Andean Junta of technocrats was designed as an independent, prestigious expert committee which would intervene in the negotiations to promote solutions which advanced the treaty programme and strengthened international institutions. In 1975 and 1976, this function was critical to the survival of the pact itself. Junta members visited all member governments offering a plan based on extending deadlines for the common external tariff and industrial programming, giving new benefits to Bolivia and Ecuador, and allowing any four countries to establish a sectoral industrial agreement binding only on the participants. The Junta's past record in drafting proposed agreements and the ability of its members to muster support from a wider Latin American transnational intellectual élite contributed to its influence.[23]

After a December 1975 meeting with the Junta, Presidents Carlos Andres Perez of Venezuela and Alfonso Lopez Michelson of

---

[20] *Op. cit.* in note 10, above, at p. 60.

[21] LATIN, Buenos Aires, May 30, 1975, and Radio Mineria, Santiago, August 18, 1976.

[22] F. Sagasti, " Intergración económica y política tecnología: el caso del Pacto Andino." 25 *Comercio Exterior* (1975), p. 49.

[23] *Op. cit.* in note 10, above, at pp. 317–319.

Colombia gave the plan decisive backing. Together they represented the two ideological wings in the Andean Group, as well as its two strongest economies. Colombia was the area's largest exporter, while Venezuela considered the organisation vital for its export diversification plans and as a group of potential supporters for other foreign-policy goals, such as preservation of the Organisation of Petroleum Exporting Countries (OPEC) against United States pressure and leadership of Latin America. Venezuela's oil wealth and its greater disposition to an active foreign policy made Perez's role the most important. A combination of threats to quit and offers of aid apparently enabled Venezuela to promote a solution through negotiations in the intergovernmental Commission.[24]

V—THE OUTCOME

The consensus reached in mid-1976 attempted to conciliate Chile, Bolivia, and Ecuador, the principal dissidents, and to readjust the Cartagena programme to suit both free traders and central planners. This balancing of interests appears in changes made in Decision 24.

Foreign investment rules were loosened, and a one-time concession made in a vain effort to keep Chile in the Andean pact. Provided that the new owners were excluded from sub-regional programmes, and the 15-year fade-out rule were maintained Chile was authorised to sell CORFO-controlled firms to foreign investors. For all countries the starting date for achieving majority local control of all business was moved to January 1974 providing an additional three-year grace period. New investment would be permitted as long as local control of the enterprises concerned were maintained. All companies exporting at least 80 per cent. of their production to third countries, or solely involved in tourism, were exempted entirely from Decision 24. The ceiling on profit remittances was raised from 14 per cent. of the original investment to 20 per cent.[25] However, the basic principle, that majority local control of all private enterprise operating within the Andean Pact programmes would be achieved, was maintained.

Bolivia and Ecuador also received concessions. Decision 98 proposed special aid in establishing production for the sectoral agreements. Decision 100 reserved a list of products from both countries which would enter the other member countries duty-free, beginning in 1978.[26]

Problems with trade and industrial programming were approached through the Protocol of Lima to the Cartagena Agreement. December

---

[24] AFP, Paris, June 2, 1976.
[25] *Grupo Andino* (1976). The acronym CORFO stands for *Corporacion de Fomento* (The Nations' Development Corporation).
[26] *Op. cit.* in note 25, above.

1977 was chosen as the new deadline for approving the remaining sectoral agreements in fertilisers, glass, electronics, pulp and paper, and pharmaceuticals. In the future any four States may establish a sectoral agreement binding only the signatories after attempts to reach unanimous consent have failed. Full free trade was delayed until 1989. Finally, a decision by the Commission redefined the common external tariff as a band of rates from 50 per cent. to 60 per cent. *ad valorem* and scheduled implementation to begin in 1979.[27]

VI—THE AFTERMATH

The crisis of 1975–76 left the Andean Group with one less member but with a potentially more viable programme capable of surmounting the ideological divisions between free traders and central planners and the political frictions which have impeded all types of co-operation. In October 1976 Chile quit after spurning the common external tariff as too high, the foreign investment rules as too restrictive, and a final offer of suspended membership until national economic conditions improved as unworkable. However, its real reasons for leaving probably also included fear of Peruvian and Bolivian territorial pressures and isolation within the organisation as a conservative military régime more akin to Brazil and Argentina than to radical Peru or democratic Colombia and Venezuela. Immediately following its departure, Chile expressed interest in joining the Plata Basin Group which included Brazil, Argentina, Paraguay, Uruguay, and Bolivia. Important bilateral trade and investment agreements have been signed with Argentina and Brazil.

Chile's departure removes one extreme of the schism between supporters of developmental nationalism and adherents of a more *laissez-faire* approach to macro-economic policy, but will impose few economic penalties on the Andean Group. Existing sectoral development agreements will have to be restructured, but most of Chile's tariffs are too low to affect trade patterns. However, some analysts project a loss of 6 million dollars in Chilean exports to pact members.[28]

Formal changes in the Cartagena Agreement are less important than the new realism which seems to pervade the Andean countries' approach to a complex, co-operative economic programme in an unstable global economic and political environment. The changes in Decision 24 are probably years away from formal adoption into national law and will only recognise existing tacit flexibility in the application of the foreign investment rules. The December 1977 deadline for the sectoral industrial development agreements appeared

---

[27] *Op. cit.* in note 25, above.
[28] *Op. cit.* in note 10, above, at p. 612.

crucial if the programme was not to lose political momentum in this area. Postponement of trade liberalisation and the common external tariff merely recognised existing, and largely uncontrollable, external pressures.

The Andean Group must contend with an international environment radically changed from its founding years. Political frictions among the member-States are not likely to be submerged as they once were in appeals to Latin American solidarity or to the higher politico-economic logic of regional co-operation. During the earlier phases of the integration movement the United Nations Economic Commission for Latin America (ECLA), which originated much of the dependency model underlying the three generations of organisations which have been established, enjoyed an ideological and technical prestige which by 1977 had declined. The failure of integration to bring dramatic changes and the emergence of a more cohesive bloc of developing countries, which for the moment seems to promise more results with less national sacrifice from bloc bargaining with the industrial Powers, are responsible. Declining United States interest and influence in the hemisphere, which once stimulated Latin American solidarity while suppressing intra-regional quarrels is also a factor.

An emerging regional international system also affects the Andean Group's future. The balance-of-power factors described above are part of emerging interdependence in Latin America. Aside from Argentina, Brazil, and Venezuela, Cuba and Mexico are also important regional Powers. Political and ideological influences travel transnationally between societies more frequently. Even geographic barriers to expanded communication are falling as Brazil pushes roads and population to its frontiers. Above all, more Latin American nations are emerging as rising middle Powers, advanced developing countries, or even, as in the case of Brazil, as nascent major influences in regional, perhaps in global politics and economic affairs.

Global pressures on the future of regional co-operation must also be considered. Unstable world markets still make attractive a protected arrangement in which Venezuela is serving as banker and backer. However, smaller countries such as those in the Andean Group also find at least the illusion of greater freedom in an increasingly multipolar world which rewards tactical flexibility and promises stability only through a multiplicity of relationships. Peru is an active member of the non-aligned group. Venezuela is a leader in OPEC and the United Nations Group of 77. Bolivia and Ecuador will cultivate global links for protection against stronger neighbours.

However, late development and industrialisation in an age of interdependence are perilous. National viability in the form of the classic, somewhat self-sufficient nation-State, the model of development for the Andeans and most of the Third World, is at best conditional.[29] Peruvian policy makers are struggling with external debt. Colombia still reacts to coffee price fluctuations. OPEC has not made Ecuador immune to the bargaining power of multinational oil companies.

Therefore, the Andean Group is best understood as an evolving response to the contradictory pressures of an interdependent world order and the drive for national autonomy and self-definition experienced by developing countries. The Cartagena Agreement is not likely to secure for its members full, national autonomous industrial bases in accordance with its original plans. Rigid timetables will erode still more under the pressures of nationalism and interdependence. However, the Andean Pact is likely to continue as a compromise between unachievable autarchy and intolerable dependence growing out of the limited resources and low power positions of its members. Therefore, of the three possibilities posed at the beginning, continued but slowed progress towards higher levels of economic co-operation and more limited political co-ordination is the most likely possibility, albeit through evolving means.

---

[29] H. Jaguaribe, *Political Development, A General Theory and a Latin American Case Study* (1973), pp. 399–402; for a more theoretical presentation, see *op. cit.* in note 15, above, at pp. 293–311.

COMMONWEALTH CARIBBEAN
REGIONALISM: LEGAL ASPECTS

By

A. R. CARNEGIE

AT least 16 separate political units in the Caribbean region and its peripheral areas participate in varying measure in the Commonwealth Caribbean regional movement, which is the current edition of the recurring historical theme of the attempt to impose the logic of centralisation on the reality of fragmentation in the British and post-British Caribbean.[1]

Bibliographical Note

Research in the area of the subject-matter of this paper faces the difficulty of the unavailability of any sufficiently up-to-date printed and indexed series containing the texts of the regional treaties. The texts to which reference has been made below are therefore taken from a miscellany of sources, as follows:

Treaty establishing the Caribbean Community Treaty, 1973 (cited as Caribbean Community Treaty), including the Caribbean Common Market Annex to the Treaty establishing the Caribbean Community Treaty (cited as Caribbean Common Market Annex): undated text published by the Government Printer, Jamaica, collected in 12 *International Legal Materials* (1973), 1033–1079;

Agreement establishing the Caribbean Development Bank, 1969 (cited as Caribbean Development Bank Agreement): text as in Final Act of the Conference of Plenipotentiaries on the Caribbean Development Bank and Agreement establishing the Caribbean Development Bank, Cmnd. 4254;

Agreement establishing the Caribbean Agricultural Research and Development Institute, 1974 (cited as Caribbean Agricultural Research and Development Institute Agreement): mimeographed text supplied by the Caribbean Community Secretariat;

Agreement establishing the Caribbean Examinations Council, 1972 (cited as Caribbean Examinations Council Agreement): mimeographed text produced by the Commonwealth Caribbean Regional Secretariat;

Agreement establishing the Caribbean Food Corporation, 1976 (cited as Caribbean Food Corporation Agreement): Schedule to the Caribbean Food Corporation Act 1977 (Guyana 1977–13);

Agreement establishing the Caribbean Investment Corporation, 1973 (cited as Caribbean Investment Corporation Agreement): Schedule to the Caribbean Investment Corporation Act 1973 (Trinidad and Tobago 1973–29);

Agreement establishing the Council of Legal Education, 1970 (cited as Council of Legal Education Agreement): Schedule to the Council of Legal Education Act 1975 (Trinidad and Tobago 1975–41);

Agreement establishing the Caribbean Meteorological Organisation, 1973 (cited as Caribbean Meteorological Organisation Agreement): mimeographed text supplied by the Caribbean Community Secretariat;

Agreement establishing the East Caribbean Common Market, 1968 (cited as East Caribbean Common Market Agreement): text published by the Attorney-General's Chambers, Castries, St. Lucia, June 9, 1968;

Agreement establishing a West Indies Shipping Corporation, 1975 (cited as West Indies Shipping Corporation Agreement): Schedule to the West Indies Shipping Corporation Act 1977 (Trinidad and Tobago 1977–17).

[1] The most ambitious and comprehensive attempt, the Federation of the West Indies, disintegrated in 1962. See the West Indies Act 1962 (U.K. 10 & 11 Eliz. 2, c. 19);

180

Six of these 16 units are sovereign States and full members of the Commonwealth: the Bahamas, Barbados, Grenada, Guyana, Jamaica, and Trinidad and Tobago. Five units are in a status of " association " with the United Kingdom, the Associated States of Antigua, Dominica, St. Kitts-Nevis-Anguilla, St. Lucia and St. Vincent.[2] The remaining five units are British colonies: Belize, British Virgin Islands, Cayman Islands, Montserrat, and the Turks and Caicos Islands. This counting ignores the separate colonial administration of Anguilla [3] because there is no formal participation by Anguilla as a unit in the regional arrangements and because the Caribbean Community, the focal point of the regional movement, seems to adhere to a policy of non-recognition of the Anguillan secession.[4]

I—The Mixed Character of the Law
of Commonwealth Caribbean Regionalism

The interrelationships of these units among themselves partake to a certain extent of international law, and to a certain extent of municipal constitutional law. A salient characteristic of the system, however, is an elaborate system of ostensibly legal relationships which are clearly not constitutional-law relationships, but which give rise to difficulties in respect of traditional statements of doctrine if they are ascribed to international law.

The relationships which are clearly those of international law, granted the demise of the *inter se* doctrine of intra-Commonwealth relationships,[5] are those which concern solely the independent States and are expressed in familiar forms of international law. Examples of

the West Indies (Dissolution and Interim Commissioner) Order in Council 1962 (S.I. 1962 Nr. 1084).

[2] See the West Indies Act 1967 (U.K. 1967, c. 4), ss. 1 and 19 (1), the West Indies Act 1967 (Appointed Days) Order 1967 (S.I. 1967 Nr. 222), the West Indies Act 1967 (Appointed Day) Order 1969 (S.I. 1969 Nr. 1499), and the following Constitution Orders made under the powers conferred by s. 5 of the Act: S.I. 1967 Nr. 225 (Antigua), S.I. 1967 Nr. 226 (Dominica), S.I. 1967 Nr. 228 (St. Christopher, Nevis and Anguilla), S.I. 1967 Nr. 229 (St. Lucia), and S.I. 1969 Nr. 1500 (St. Vincent). Although the list of Associated States is accurate at the time of going to press in October 1978, independence for Dominica is imminently expected, and negotiations relating to independence are either in progress or in the offing for the remaining Associated States.

[3] See the Anguilla Act 1971 (U.K. 1971, c. 63) and the Anguilla Constitution Order 1976 (U.K. S.I. 1976 Nr. 50).

[4] At the inaugural meeting of the Heads of Government Conference of the Caribbean Community in July 1974, the Heads of Government adopted a Resolution expressly recognising the competence of the government of St. Kitts-Nevis-Anguilla to adhere to the Caribbean Community Treaty " in a manner consistent with its constitutional status and full territorial integrity " (Caribbean Community Secretariat Press Release 32/1974, July 22, 1974, p. 1 and App. 1).

[5] J. E. S. Fawcett, *The British Commonwealth in International Law* (1963), pp. 144 *et seq.*

such relationships have sometimes been provided by agreements open to independent States and to others, but which have come into force initially only between the independent States. Thus, the Caribbean Community Treaty itself came into force on August 1, 1973, on its ratification by Barbados, Guyana, Jamaica, and Trinidad and Tobago,[6] and the Caribbean Common Market Balance-of-Payments Mutual Support Interim Facility came into force on June 22, 1976, among the same four States.[7]

International law relationships include also the sub-relationships among the independent States in the constitutional structure of the Caribbean Community and other regional organisations. Although that Community is an international organisation established by the independent States and others, the treaty creating the Community expressly limits participation in the deliberations of the Standing Committee of Ministers responsible for Foreign Affairs established by that Treaty to member States of the Community possessing the necessary competence,[8] which would in many instances restrict participation to the independent States. Even where there is no such express restriction, the general treaty obligations in their application to independent States in relation to each other would seem indisputably obligations in international law.

The position is similar to the participation of mutually non-recognising States in multilateral treaties,[9] or of States whose international personality might be challenged.[10] This could hardly be accepted as casting doubt on the binding force in international law of the engagements which such multilateral conventions produce between contracting States as between whom no difficulty of recognition or of want of full international personality presents itself.

The participation of some British colonies in the system gives rise necessarily to constitutional law relationships, since all British colonies participate in the constitutional legal system of the United Kingdom and Colonies.[11] In general, that relationship does not fall for consideration here because it is not peculiarly regional: it does

---

[6] Caribbean Community Treaty, Art. 24; the last of the four ratifications deposited was that of Jamaica on July 31, 1973 (Caribbean Community Secretariat List of Agreements in respect of which the Secretariat performs Depositary Functions, August 1976 (mimeo.), folio 1).

[7] Caribbean Community Secretariat List of Agreements, above at note 6, folio 18.

[8] Caribbean Community Treaty, Art. 17.3. *Cf.* also *ibid.*, Art. 31.4.

[9] *e.g.* the adhesion of both Germanies to the 1949 Geneva Conventions for the Protection of War Victims. See C. Parry and C. Hopkins, *An Index of British Treaties* 1101–1968 (1970), Vol. 3, p. 1039.

[10] *e.g.* the frequent participation in such treaties of the Byelorussian and Ukrainian Soviet Socialist Republics. See H.-J. Uibopuu, " International Legal Personality of Union Republics of U.S.S.R." in 24 *International and Comparative Law Quarterly* (1975), pp. 811–845, at pp. 833 *et seq.*

[11] *Madzimbamuto* v. *Lardner-Burke* [1969] 1 A.C. 645 at pp. 720–721. See generally Sir Kenneth Roberts-Wray, *Commonwealth and Colonial Law* (1966).

not apply to Montserrat and the British Virgin Islands in any way differently from its application between the British Virgin Islands and Hong Kong. There does, however, seem to be at least one instance of a purely regional constitutional law interrelationship, that constituted by the Supreme Court of Grenada and the Associated States.[12] The Supreme Court of Grenada and the Associated States is a regional institution serving, in addition to Grenada, the Associated States and the colonies of Montserrat and the British Virgin Islands. It appears, nevertheless, to be entirely an institution of constitutional law. It was created by the use of the Crown's and the United Kingdom Parliament's powers to legislate for the islands as in some measure dependent territories—a power operating *ex facie* in the context of the constitutional law of the United Kingdom and colonies. Only in respect of Grenada, moreover, does the appearance call for challenge. From the point of view of Grenada, it is the Privy Council problem at a lower level.[13] The Court can no doubt be characterised in international law as an institution of which Grenada in its sovereignty makes convenient use,[14] without providing any constitutional link binding together the States which make use of it. But from the point of view of the Associated States, Montserrat and the British Virgin Islands, it seems to be part of the residuary constitutional law, notwithstanding its historical creation in some measure by agreement.[15]

The relationships which fit less easily into either the category of constitutional law or that of international law are those created by the participation in the regional movement of the Associated States and the colonies on an equal contractual footing with the independent States. It has become the standard practice for such relationships to be dealt with in intergovernmental treaty forms following usual international law patterns, even where, as in the case of the East Caribbean Common Market at its formation, there are no participants to the agreement which are independent States.[16]

---

[12] See the West Indies Act 1967 (U.K. 1967, c. 4), s. 6, and the West Indies Associated States Supreme Court Order 1967 (S.I. 1967 Nr. 223).

[13] For the Privy Council's own views on the problem of explaining the perpetuation of its jurisdiction in relation to former colonies after they have become sovereign States, see *Ibralebbe* v. *R.* [1964] A.C. 900.

[14] Cf. *Ibralebbe* v. *R.*, in note 13, above, at pp. 924–925.

[15] See Report of the Antigua Constitutional Conference 1966, Cmnd. 2963, paras. 24–33; Report of the Windward Islands Constitutional Conference 1966, Cmnd. 3021, para. 6 and Annex B; Report of the St. Kitts/Nevis/Anguilla Constitutional Conference 1966, Cmnd. 3031, para. 11 and Annex B, paras. 26–37. See also the West Indies Associated States Supreme Court Order 1967, note 12 above, s. 15, and the West Indies Associated States Supreme Court Agreement 1967 (*Ordinances passed by the Legislative Council of the Virgin Islands during the year* 1967, pp. 214–218).

[16] The signatories were the Associated States, St. Vincent and Montserrat (St. Vincent did not become an Associated State until 1969): East Caribbean Common Market Agreement, Arts. 1 and 24.

Quite apart from the intention evinced by the choice of international law forms, relationships such as these cannot without great difficulty be treated as based on constitutional law. Agreements between different colonial governments and between such governments and that of the United Kingdom have not been at all unknown, but the usual device for settling the legal character of such agreements would seem to have been the use of an Imperial statute, as in the cases of the great federations of Canada [17] and Australia.[18] In the post-Federation practice in the Commonwealth Caribbean, no use has been made of this device: such statutory incorporation of agreements as has taken place has been used obviously as the standard pattern of treaty-implementation in the non-self-executing British treaty system,[19] and has not included legislation by the United Kingdom Parliament.

Without the use of the Imperial statute mechanism, the doctrine of the indivisibility of the Crown in the United Kingdom and its dependent territories,[20] which possessed such nuisance value in relation to treaty forms in the early period of Dominion status,[21] would seem to stand in the way of giving any justiciable character in constitutional law to agreements between different governments within the system. Recourse to intergovernmental rather than Head of State forms, as indeed is the practice in relation to the agreements presently under discussion, could hardly be expected to provoke a recognition of a concept of a " government " or " the State " as distinct from the Crown at common law,[22] and consequently in the constitutional law of the United Kingdom and colonies.

Where the regional treaty arrangements entail the participation of the Associated States and the colonies with the independent States in the same treaty, this may well constitute by implication in international law an operative recognition by the independent States of an international personality of the Associated States and colonies in question.[23] But not even the internally autonomous Associated States, let alone the colonies, can be easily accommodated in the traditional instances of non-sovereign States with treaty-making capacity, since they have only such freedom of action in matters of

---

[17] British North America Act 1867 (U.K. 30 Vict., c. 3).

[18] Commonwealth of Australia Constitution Act (U.K. 63 & 64 Vict., c. 12).

[19] See *e.g. Walker* v. *Baird* [1892] A.C. 491; Caribbean Investment Corporation Act 1974 (St. Christopher, Nevis and Anguilla, 1974–16).

[20] For a recent reference, see *Town Investments Ltd.* v. *Department of the Environment* [1977] 1 All. E.R. 813 at p. 833 (Lord Simon).

[21] See J. E. S. Fawcett, *op. cit.* in note 5, above, pp. 144–176.

[22] *Town Investments Ltd.* v. *Department of the Environment*, above at note 20.

[23] See *e.g.* the material relating to the practice of the United States collected in M. M. Whiteman, *Digest of International Law*, Vol. 2 (1963), pp. 557–567. For an instance where the recognition appears to be express, and not merely implied, see the Resolution of the Heads of Government cited in note 4, above.

external affairs as the United Kingdom allows them.[24] Forms might well, of course, have been devisable whereby the desired results might have been achieved consistently with orthodoxy by means of an expressed participation by the United Kingdom in such agreements, but this possibility has been largely ignored [25]: the participation of the United Kingdom in the treaty establishing one institution of Commonwealth Caribbean regionalism, the Caribbean Development Bank,[26] is not as representing the non-independent States in any sense but as representing the separate United Kingdom Government interest as a financial contributor to the Bank's resources.[27]

Since international law develops by practice, an attempt to achieve what international law considers impossible may lead in principle not only to the conclusion that the attempt is devoid of legal consequences, but, in other cases, to the conclusion that the law has changed. But if practice such as that in the Commonwealth Caribbean regional movement were to be regarded as establishing in international law a competence of colonies to conclude treaties, it might well become questionable whether the attribution of treaty-making capacity has retained any indicative value in determining the possessors of international legal personality. From the point of view of order in international law, the continuous erosion of the boundary lines of international personality might well be considered to call for resistance at some point, and a conclusion accepting at its face value the operation of the Associated States and the colonies on the international plane might possibly be considered to be beyond such a point.

It is suggested, nevertheless, that policy-type arguments of general relevance to international law as a whole may support this development in limited degree. International law must perforce adjust to the

---

[24] West Indies Act 1967, note 2 above, s. 2 (1) (*a*). See M. Broderick, " Associated Statehood—a New Form of Decolonisation," in 17 *International and Comparative Law Quarterly* (1968), pp. 368–403, at pp. 375 *et seq.*; H. J. Geiser, P. Alleyne and C. Garjaj, *Legal Problems of Caribbean Integration* (1976), pp. 22–26.

[25] For the view that the United Kingdom does indeed become the true legal contracting party by authorising the participation of the Associated States and colonies, in the Caribbean Community Treaty, see D. E. Pollard, " Institutional and Legal Aspects of the Caribbean Community," in 14 *Caribbean Studies* (1974), pp. 39–74, at p. 49, note 45. For an instance of orthodoxy, see the Agreement on the Rescue of Astronauts, the Return of Astronauts and the Return of Objects Launched into Outer Space, April 22, 1968, where the United Kingdom expressly contracted in respect of the then Associated States (8 *International Legal Materials* (1969), pp. 224–225). For an instance of a non-regional arrangement entered into by an Associated State, see the agreement between St. Lucia and the United States on Investment Guaranties of August 9, 1968 (7 *International Legal Materials* (1968), p. 1199); and by a colony, the similar agreement between British Honduras and the United States of February 8, 1966 (5 *International Legal Materials* (1966), p. 587).

[26] Caribbean Development Bank Agreement, Art. 3 and Annex. A.

[27] Caribbean Development Bank Agreement, Art. 6 and Annex A.

new conditions of the proliferation of members of the family of nations, and to the progress of the self-determination principle. These new conditions include the problems of the future of micro-States. It is hardly conceivable that the problems of the future of micro-States anywhere present themselves in a substantially more acute form than in the Commonwealth Caribbean. Pending the solution of the problems, tolerance may be shown to the particular *modus vivendi* between self-determination and viability which the practice of the Commonwealth Caribbean regional movement represents. It seems undesirable from the viewpoint of international order that such *ad hoc* solutions should in substantial measure be relegated to a vacuum incapable of being filled either by international law or municipal law. The filling of the vacuum should, moreover, be the responsibility of international law rather than municipal law, bearing in mind the historically colonialist-tainted character of the only readily available municipal law context, *viz.*, the constitutional law system of the United Kingdom and Colonies.

II—THE INSTITUTIONS OF COMMONWEALTH CARIBBEAN REGIONALISM

Intergovernmental co-operation in the Commonwealth Caribbean takes place on such a scale, in such a variety of forms and in such a multiplicity of areas that the task—not here being attempted—of compilation of a comprehensive list of all the institutions of Commonwealth Caribbean regionalism would be problematic.

There is no doubt that the Caribbean Community stands at the pinnacle of the structure of such co-operation. This would tend to follow in practical terms from the fact that one of its principal organs, the Heads of Government Conference, consists of Prime Ministers and Premiers.[28] This is also clear from the breadth of its concerns, as illustrated by the areas of " functional co-operation " listed in the schedule to the Caribbean Community Treaty,[29] and the fact that its competence extends as far as the co-ordination of foreign policies of members.[30] The Community's pride of place among regional institutions appears by obvious design, too, in the Article of the Treaty whereby the other major regional institutions are " recognised " as Associate Institutions of the Community.[31]

It ought not to be inferred from the name " Caribbean Community," or from the name of the other important organisation created by the Caribbean Community Treaty, the Caribbean Common Market, that the law of the Treaty of Rome is in any way an especially apt source of comparisons relating to the law of the

---

[28] Caribbean Community Treaty, Arts. 6 and 7.
[29] *Ibid*. Arts. 4 (*c*) (iii) and 18 and Schedule.
[30] *Ibid*. Arts. 4 (*b*) and 17.　　　　　　　　　　　　　[31] *Ibid*. Art. 14.

Caribbean organisations. These organisations have no parallel to the European Commission, the European Parliament, or the Court of Justice of the European Communities, nor has any attempt been made in the Commonwealth Caribbean regional movement to emulate the direct applicability law of the European Economic Community.[32]

The organisations listed in the Associate Institutions article of the Caribbean Community Treaty seem suited to being added to the Caribbean Community Treaty's two organisations, the Community and the Caribbean Common Market, as a core list of the institutions of Commonwealth Caribbean regionalism. That list would be comprised as follows:

the Organisations of the Treaty: the Caribbean Community, the Caribbean Common Market; *the Associate Institutions*: the Caribbean Development Bank, the Caribbean Investment Corporation, the West Indies Associated States Council of Ministers, the East Caribbean Common Market Council of Ministers, the Caribbean Examinations Council, the Council of Legal Education, the University of Guyana, the University of the West Indies, the Caribbean Meteorological Council, the Regional Shipping Council.

One item of inclusion in this list seems surprising enough to call for special comment. The University of Guyana is an exclusively national institution in its formal juridical character,[33] and at first sight seems not to merit consideration as a regional institution. But not only is it designated as an Associate Institution of the Community by the Caribbean Community Treaty, it has in practice acted as an international person to the extent of exercising treaty-making functions.[34] It seems, moreover, that the University of Guyana may in this connection eventually prove to have been the tip of an iceberg: a special meeting of the Heads of Government Conference in 1976 adopted as one of a number of " guidelines " the principle that " *all* national tertiary institutions [of education] would be regarded as regional institutions serving all the countries of the region." [35]

When regard is had to what the list above excludes, there is the obvious problem of keeping it up to date with developments subsequent to the conclusion of the Caribbean Community Treaty, such

[32] See *e.g.* Art. 192 of the Treaty of Rome and *Legal and Constitutional Implications of United Kingdom Membership of the European Communities,* Cmnd. 3301, collected in B. A. Wortley (ed.), *An Introduction to the Law of the European Economic Community* (1972), pp. 96–109.

[33] University of Guyana Act (*Laws of Guyana* Rev. 1973 c. 39:02), as amended by Guyana 1977—21.

[34] Council of Legal Education Agreement, Art. 10.1; Caribbean Community Secretariat List of Agreements, in note 6, above, folio 7.

[35] Caribbean Community Secretariat Press Release 12/1976, April 28, 1976, pp. 6 and 8 (emphasis supplied).

as the creation of the Caribbean Agricultural Research and Development Institute and the Caribbean Food Corporation: these institutions will no doubt be added to the Associate Institutions category in due course under the residuary designating powers conferred on the Conference of Heads of Government by the article.[36] Another issue arising out of the continuous development in regional co-operation is the fact that many institutions have only been formally established by treaty after they have been functioning for some time, such as the Heads of Government Conference and the Standing Committees of Ministers in the Community. For this reason, the total picture of regional co-operation might also be considered to include regional organisations *in statu nascendi*, such as the present regional machinery of co-operation in areas like, for example, statistics [37] and standards [38] might eventually turn out to be.

It is a commonplace that intergovernmental co-operation, even as between sovereign States, can be organised in purely municipal law forms.[39] The inclusion of the University of Guyana in the list of Associate Institutions indicates clearly enough that municipal law rather than international law character is not a disqualification from inclusion, and the same argument might have been derived from the presence of the University of the West Indies, which was, with the consent of the relevant governments, re-established in 1972 as a chartered corporation in the municipal law of 14 of the 16 component units of the regional movement. In the case of the University of the West Indies, however, unlike the University of Guyana, it does function on a regional basis, with its major policy decisions of a financial kind effectively being taken as a result of intergovernmental negotiation. There are other post-Community Treaty instances of regional co-operation being organised on a municipal law rather than an international law basis, notably the airline company LIAT (1974) Ltd.,[40] the CARICOM Corn/Soya Co. Ltd.[41] and the Caribbean Tourist Centre Ltd.[42] Whether or not such bodies are granted Associate Institution status, it would, it is suggested, be unreasonable to discount them as important organisations of the regional movement.

The Supreme Court of Grenada and the Associated States [43] is

---

[36] Caribbean Community Treaty, Art. 14.1 (*k*).

[37] See Commonwealth Caribbean Regional Secretariat Press Release 17/1973, April 27, 1973.

[38] See Caribbean Community Secretariat Press Release 24/1976, May 21, 1976.

[39] See W. G. Friedmann, O. J. Lissitzyn and R. C. Pugh, *Cases and Materials on International Law* (1969), pp. 213–215.

[40] Incorporated in Antigua September 20, 1974.

[41] Incorporated in Guyana November 6, 1975.

[42] Incorporated in Barbados September 5, 1973.

[43] *Loc. cit.* in note 12, above.

an important regional institution insofar as its existence entails an attempt to remedy by co-operation the problems of inadequacy of size of individual territorial units. Notwithstanding that its function of exercising a basically municipal law jurisdiction markedly lacks any significant flavour of international law, the fact that the same institution serves both a sovereign State and other entities may be considered to impart a sufficient element of international law interest to justify some reference in the context of a discussion of Caribbean regional institutions.

The Commonwealth Caribbean regional movement is in principle open to States other than those of the Commonwealth Caribbean,[44] although entry to some of the institutions must be *via* entry to the Community and the Common Market.[45] However, the principle still awaits translation into practice in those major institutions, notwithstanding the existence of an application from at least one other State for admission.[46] Participation by States outside of the Commonwealth Caribbean does function, nonetheless, in some institutions, especially the Caribbean Development Bank.[47] Such participation may at the borderline pose questions of difficulty as to whether or not the organisation concerned deserves to be classified as an organisation of the Commonwealth Caribbean regional movement. An example of this potential difficulty might be provided by NAMUCAR,[48] a multinational shipping enterprise of Caribbean States in the negotiations for whose establishment Jamaica, Trinidad and Tobago and Guyana were involved but were outnumbered by their Latin neighbours. Had the headquarters not been placed in Costa Rica and had Trinidad and Tobago and Guyana remained in the negotiations and signed with Jamaica, NAMUCAR might have been a less clear example than it is of a Caribbean, but not a Commonwealth Caribbean, regional organisation.

III—ASPECTS OF THE TREATY-BASED INSTITUTIONS

The final part of this discussion considers cursorily some aspects which tend to attract attention in the law of international organisations,

[44] See Caribbean Community Treaty, Art. 2.1 (*b*); Caribbean Common Market Annex, Art. 2.1 (*b*).

[45] Caribbean Agricultural Research and Development Institute Agreement, Art. 2.1 and Annex; West Indies Shipping Corporation Agreement, Art. 3.1 and Annex.

[46] An application from the Government of Haiti for membership of the Community was referred by the Heads of Government Conference to the Secretariat for further study at the meeting of the Conference in July 1974: Caribbean Community Secretariat Press Release 32/1974, July 22, 1974, p. 6.

[47] Members of the Bank include the United Kingdom, Canada, Colombia and Venezuela. *Loc. cit.* in note 26, above; *Caribbean Development Bank Annual Report 1973*, p. 16; *ibid.*, 1974, p. 27.

[48] Multinational Shipping Corporation of the Caribbean Inc.: see L. F. Manigat (ed.), *The Caribbean Yearbook of International Relations 1975*, pp. 28 and 574 *et seq.*

illustrated from a sampling of the treaties creating those of the organisations of the Commonwealth Caribbean regional movement constituted ostensibly on the plane of international law.

(a) *Membership*

The pattern of membership provisions among the treaty-based institutions is subject to variations. In the case of the Caribbean Community Treaty, the Treaty establishes two organisations with a basic difference of membership: the Bahamas are in the list of named States to which membership of the Community is open,[49] but are omitted from the similar list of States to which membership of the Common Market is open.[50] The Cayman Islands are a party to the Council of Legal Education Agreement and to the Caribbean Examinations Council Agreement, although they are not listed as a potential party to either of the creations of the Caribbean Community Treaty.[51] The Turks and Caicos Islands participate in the Caribbean Examinations Council, despite the relative rarity of their participation in regional institutions—a rarity perhaps surprising in view of their geographical position and their history of dependency on Jamaica until 1962.[52] The Caribbean Development Bank has extra-regional metropolitan members and Caribbean non-Commonwealth members as well as the regional members.[53] The East Caribbean Common Market is by the terms of its Agreement originally participated in only by non-sovereign States. The reasons for these variations seem to be political: there is no question of the differing juridical status of the various States determining the issue, since, for example, the participation of the colony of Montserrat is a commonplace while that of the Bahamas, a sovereign State, is relatively occasional by comparison.

It is common, but not universal, practice in the regional treaty-based institutions, as the cases of the Community and the Common Market illustrate, to provide for the admission of other States,[54] although there tend to be safeguards incorporated to enable the Commonwealth Caribbean States to prevent undue dilution of their special Anglophone post-British colonial interest group.[55] In such

---

[49] Caribbean Community Treaty, Art. 2 (i) (*a*) (ii).

[50] Caribbean Common Market Annex, Art. 2 (i) (*a*).

[51] Caribbean Community Treaty, Art. 2 (i) (*a*); Caribbean Common Market Annex, Art. 2 (i) (*a*).

[52] See Jamaica Independence Act 1962 (U.K. 10 & 11 Eliz. 2, c. 40), ss. 3 (4) and 4.

[53] *Loc. cit.* in note 47, above.

[54] See *loc. cit.* in note 44, above. There is no provision for participation by States outside the Commonwealth Caribbean in the Council of Legal Education: see Council of Legal Education Agreement, Art. 11 and Annex A.

[55] In the case of the Caribbean Development Bank, Art. 3.3 of the Agreement ensures that representatives of two-thirds of the members must agree to the admission of a non-regional member. On October 29, 1971, the Board of Governors decided that Commonwealth Caribbean members should always have a majority of the voting power

provisions, the problem of defining " State " could give rise to interpretative problems similar to those arising from the interpretation of the same word in Article 4.1 of the United Nations Charter.[56] Some of the instruments include provisions for associate membership as well as for full membership.[57]

In the case of the Caribbean Investment Corporation, express provision is actually made for membership of individual residents of member States.[58]

(b) *Withdrawal and termination of membership*

It is common for the instruments to provide expressly for withdrawal,[59] although not always for suspension [60] or expulsion, thus contrasting with the Charter of the United Nations, which provides for suspension or expulsion but not for withdrawal.[61] The organisations are sufficiently small, however, for concerted withdrawal to be potentially and practically capable of achieving more wide-ranging effects. The novation, for instance, of the predecessor treaty to the Caribbean Community Treaty, the Caribbean Free Trade Association Agreement, might have been assisted in its accomplishment, despite the hesitation of some eventual participants,[62] by the concerted exercise of the principal members of their right of withdrawal from that predecessor agreement.[63] This illustrates the possibility, therefore, of a *de facto* suspension and expulsion by similarly indirect means.

(c) *Organs*

There are some striking features of the organs of the Commonwealth Caribbean regional organisations. The most notable such feature, perhaps, is the level of political participation in the organs

---

(*Caribbean Development Bank Annual Report 1971*, p. 13). Where admission to the Community or Common Market is concerned (above at notes 44 and 45 and accompanying text), any Head of Government can veto membership (Caribbean Community Treaty, Arts 2.1 (*b*) and 9; Caribbean Common Market Annex, Art. 2.1 (*b*)).

[56] See L. M. Goodrich, E. Hambro and A. P. Simmons, *Charter of the United Nations* (3rd ed., 1969), pp. 88–89.

[57] Caribbean Community Treaty, Art. 30; Caribbean Common Market Annex, Art. 72. See Geiser, Alleyne and Gajraj, *op. cit.* in note 24, above, at pp. 99–103.

[58] Caribbean Investment Corporation Agreement, Art. 2.

[59] See *e.g.* Caribbean Community Treaty, Art. 27; Caribbean Common Market Annex, Art. 69; Caribbean Meteorological Organisation Agreement, Art. 31.

[60] For examples of suspension provisions, see Caribbean Development Bank Agreement, Art. 41; Caribbean Investment Corporation Agreement, Art. 26.

[61] United Nations Charter, Arts. 5 and 6.

[62] See " Public Statement by the Carifta Council of Ministers on the Legal Aspects of the Transition from CARIFTA to CARICOM," Caribbean Community Secretariat Press Release 41/1973, October 16, 1973, pp. 2 *et seq.*

[63] *Ibid.* p. 5; Caribbean Community Secretariat Press Release 52/1973, December 10, 1973; Caribbean Community Secretariat Press Release 29/1974, July 6, 1974. See the Caribbean Free Trade Association Agreement 1968 (7 *International Legal Materials* (1968), pp. 935–977), Art. 33.

of the Community. One of the Community's principal organs is the Heads of Government Conference,[64] and its policy-making Institutions, the Standing Committees, are comprised of Ministers.[65]

Another characteristic is an interlocking structure resulting from the use of organs common to more than one organisation. The Community and the Common Market are not only established by the same treaty: the Common Market Council is an organ of the Community,[66] the Community Secretariat is an organ of the Common Market,[67] and the Heads of Government Conference functions, in effect, as an organ of the Common Market as well as of the Community by virtue of its function of ratification of agreements concluded by the Common Market.[68] There are also interlocking arrangements between the Community and other organisations created by different treaties, in particular the function of the Community's Institutions, the Standing Committees, as the chief organs of other organisations: thus the Standing Committee of Ministers responsible for Agriculture is the chief policy organ of the Caribbean Agricultural Research and Development Institute.[69]

In the many organs where the functions are technical, the usual structure of decision-making is two-tiered, with a political, superior body appointing a technical Board of Directors.[70]

The interlocking nature of different organisations is likely to present problems of determining whether an organ which belongs to more than one organisation is to be treated nevertheless as a different entity for the purpose of each organisation. Even where the drafting suggests a different intention, the conceptual separation might be helpful in avoiding problems of reconciling conflicting treaty provisions: thus, the West Indies Shipping Corporation Agreement debars from participation in the Standing Committee of Ministers responsible for Transport, in relation to its functions under the Agreement, a country which has withdrawn from the Agreement,[71] but this seems in clear conflict with the provisions of the Caribbean Community Treaty which confer a right of participation on such a withdrawing member State by virtue of its membership, not of the Corporation,

[64] See *loc. cit.* in note 28, above.
[65] Caribbean Community Treaty, Art. 10.
[66] *Ibid.* Art. 6(b); Caribbean Common Market Annex, Arts. 5 and 6.
[67] Caribbean Community Treaty, Art. 15; Caribbean Common Market Annex, Arts. 9 and 10.
[68] Caribbean Common Market Annex, Art. 70.
[69] Caribbean Agricultural Research and Development Institute Agreement, Arts. 4.1 and 5.1; Caribbean Community Treaty, Art. 10(f).
[70] See *e.g.* Caribbean Development Bank Agreement, Arts. 25, 26 and 29; Caribbean Agricultural Research and Development Institute Agreement, Arts. 4.1, 5.1 and 6. This follows the pattern of *e.g.* the International Monetary Fund Agreement, 1945, Art. 12.1–3.
[71] West Indies Shipping Corporation Agreement, Art. 22.3.

but of the Community.[72] The Caribbean Food Corporation can be contrasted with this instance, since the term " Board of Governors " is used instead of " Standing Committee of Ministers responsible for Agriculture," [73] notwithstanding that both bodies could have identical membership.

(d) *Voting schemes*

The notion of the equality of the participating States seems possibly even more impractical in the regional integration movement than on the global scale,[74] owing to the lack even of juridical sovereignty on the part of most of their number, but some such equality seems nevertheless to be the norm from which departures are measured.

This equality is most prominently institutionalised in the supreme decision-making body of the Community, the Heads of Government Conference, in which the principle of unanimity governs.[75] Abstentions do not prevent unanimity, provided concurrence of a specified number of the More Developed Countries is achieved.[76] This language clearly seems to exclude, as well as to render to some extent practically unnecessary, the Security Council's interpretation in practice of the meaning of a " concurring " vote.[77]

The instruments use different devices, in addition to that mentioned relating to the requirement of concurrence of a specific sub-category of States, to adjust the equality norm to reality. In the cases of the Caribbean Development Bank and the Caribbean Food Corporation, these are voting rights weighted in part proportion to ratios of financial shareholdings.[78] In the Council of Legal Education, the specified membership of the Head of the Judiciary of each participating territory [79] cuts down the relative representation of the States who share the Supreme Court of Grenada and the Associated States. At the outset, membership of one representative of each association

---

[72] Caribbean Community Treaty, Arts. 10(h) and 13.1. The Heads of Government Conference agreed to designate to the Standing Committee of Ministers responsible for Transport an Institution of the Community under Art. 8.2 of the Treaty at the meeting of the Conference in July 1974: Caribbean Community Secretariat Press Release 32/1974, July 22, 1974, p. 7.

[73] Caribbean Food Corporation Agreement, Arts. 4.1(a) and Annex, 16, and 17.1; Caribbean Community Treaty, Arts. 2.1(a) and 10(f).

[74] As in the principle of " sovereign equality " under Art. 2.1 of the United Nations Charter.

[75] Caribbean Community Treaty, Art. 9.

[76] *Ibid.* The More Developed Countries are defined by Art. 3 of the Treaty as Barbados, Guyana, Jamaica and Trinidad and Tobago.

[77] United Nations Charter, Art. 27.3. See Goodrich, Hambro and Simmons, *op. cit.* in note 56, above, at pp. 229–231.

[78] Caribbean Development Bank Agreement, Art. 32; Caribbean Food Corporation Agreement, Art. 19.2. *Cf.* the formula in Art. 12.5 of the International Monetary Fund Agreement.

[79] Council of Legal Education Agreement, Art. 1.1(a)(iii).

of professional lawyers also had a weighting effect owing to the existence at the time of the conclusion of the Agreement of a fused profession of barristers and solicitors exclusively in the non-independent States.[80] In some other instances, the smaller territories are required to accept joint representation.[81] In the particular case of the Caribbean Investment Corporation, there is actually some counter-weighting in favour of the Less Developed Countries, by virtue of their monopoly of the Chairmanships of the Board of Governors and the Board of Directors.[82]

Weighted voting would have no effect where unanimity is required. Fortunately for the effectiveness of the regional movement, the Caribbean Community Treaty scheme is not typical of the other organisations, and its use even in that Treaty is qualified by powers of making " recommendations," but not " decisions," over negative votes,[83] some of which recommendations set the stage for a decentralised system of sanctions by reciprocal non-compliance if the recommendations are not acted on.[84] The normal mode of decision is by majority vote, qualified by some requirements of special majorities.[85] There are, too, variations between the Chairman's casting vote only [86] and original and casting vote systems,[87] extending even to the instance of a Chairman without a vote of any kind.[88]

(e) *Settlement of disputes*

The Commonwealth Caribbean regional movement has no permanent tribunal exercising an international law jurisdiction, notwithstanding the existence of a regional court with jurisdiction in municipal law questions, nor is there any incorporation of United Nations mechanisms for the settlement of disputes, such as the International Court of Justice.[89]

---

[80] *Ibid.* Art. 1.1(a)(vi).

[81] Caribbean Development Bank Agreement, Art. 29 and Annex B; Caribbean Investment Corporation Agreement, Art. 17.1(a) and (b).

[82] Caribbean Investment Corporation Agreement, Arts. 14.4 and 19.1.

[83] Caribbean Community Treaty, Art. 13.3; Caribbean Common Market Annex, Art. 11. See D. E. Pollard, *op. cit.* in note 25, above, at pp. 54–57.

[84] Caribbean Common Market Annex, Art. 11.

[85] See *e.g.* Caribbean Examinations Council Agreement, Art. 6.5, and West Indies Shipping Corporation Agreement, Art. 17.2. In relation to special majorities, see.*e.g* Caribbean Food Corporation Agreement, Art. 28.1; Caribbean Development Bank Agreement, above, at note 55.

[86] Caribbean Agricultural Research and Development Institute Agreement, Art. 8.2.

[87] Caribbean Examinations Council Agreement, Art. 6.7.

[88] Caribbean Meteorological Organisation Agreement, Art. 8.3 and 4. There is provision for the appointment by the State represented by the Chairman of another voting representative, and for the Chairman to vote if no such other representative has been appointed.

[89] There had been no declaration by any Commonwealth Caribbean State accepting as compulsory the jurisdiction of the International Court of Justice under Art. 36.2 of the Statute of the Court up to July 31, 1977 (*I.C.J. Yearbook* 1975–1976, pp. 49–79).

Many of the treaties contain provisions for compulsory settlement of disputes by reference to *ad hoc* arbitration machinery.[90] In the Common Market Annex to the Caribbean Community Treaty, the *ad hoc* arbitration machinery is used only at the option of the Council, whose primary responsibility it is under the treaty to settle the dispute.[91]

Questions of the use of force in relation to disputes within the regional system are sufficiently remote as not to be adverted to in any of the regional instruments. Thus, there are no expressed obligations to settle disputes by peaceful means, and there is no centralised machinery for the use of force in keeping the peace. Quite apart from the participation of the independent States and the colonial power in the United Nations system of peacekeeping,[92] however, most of the independent States in the regional movement may also have potential access to such a system by virtue of their participation in the Organisation of American States.[93]

(f) *Issues of legal personality*

The *Reparations for Injuries* Advisory Opinion [94] has provided a beacon for a generation of scholars to see in every international organisation a new subject of international law, and to point to certain main *indicia* of that personality. The admittedly derivative personality of such bodies from that of the traditional international persons who create them, *i.e.* States, has not hindered the growth of aspects of personality even beyond those expressly conferred by their creators.

In the case of the institutions of the Commonwealth Caribbean regional movement, the relatively short length of the period during which the organisations have existed may have limited the opportunity to establish by reference to the practice of the organisations and of their member States the extent to which their international capacities exceed those expressly conferred in the treaties.[95]

---

[90] See *e.g.* Caribbean Meteorological Organisation Agreement, Art. 23; Caribbean Food Corporation Agreement, Art. 36.

[91] Caribbean Common Market Annex, Arts. 11 and 12.

[92] United Nations Charter, Chap. 7.

[93] Charter of the Organisation of American States, Arts. 27 and 28. Barbados, Grenada, Jamaica and Trinidad and Tobago are members of the Organisation. For the participation of Trinidad and Tobago in, and the representation of Barbados and Jamaica at, the Conference of Plenipotentiaries for the Amendment of the Inter-American Treaty of Reciprocal Assistance, September 2, 1947, in July 1975, see 14 *International Legal Materials* (1975), pp. 1117–1118.

[94] *I.C.J. Reports*, 1949, pp. 174 *et seq.*

[95] F. Seyersted, " International Capacities of Intergovernmental Organisations: Do their Capacities really depend on their Constitutions?" in 4 *Indian Journal of International Law* (1964), pp. 1–74; P. Reuter, Third Report on the Question of Treaties concluded between States and International Organisations or between two or more International Organisations, *I.L.C. Yearbook* 1974, Vol. 2, Part 1, pp. 135–152, at pp. 145–152.

Where the express provisions are concerned, wide variations appear in respect of the various indicia, such as clauses expressly conferring legal personality, treaty-making capacity, and privileges and immunities.

It is standard practice in the regional instruments to include a clause clearly designed to ensure that the organisation will have legal personality in the municipal law of the contracting parties,[96] a result normally requiring implementing legislation.[97] In the Caribbean Community Treaty, the relevant clauses are not confined to the question of the effect in municipal law: the clause relating to the status of the Community speaks of " full juridical personality," [98] and that relating to the status of the Common Market speaks of " international juridical personality." [99] Since the Community is clearly superior to the Common Market, " full juridical personality " must have been intended to encompass at least the international legal capacity expressly bestowed on the Common Market. The consequential further inference that the " full juridical personality " conferred on the Community must have been intended to mean full international juridical personality has understandably evoked the criticism that such a result is beyond the reach of any entity other than a State.[1]

Where treaty-making capacity is concerned, the extensive activity seemingly contemplated by the Caribbean Community Treaty and the Caribbean Development Bank Agreement is not characteristic of other organisations.[2] Even in the case of the Caribbean Community, it would sometimes appear that its wider treaty-making activity has been concerned as much with centralised assistance to negotiation by its member States as with the process of contracting international rights and obligations on its own behalf.[3]

---

[96] Caribbean Community Treaty, Art. 20; Caribbean Common Market Annex, Art. 63.2 and 3; Caribbean Investment Corporation Agreement, Art. 30; Caribbean Examinations Council Agreement, Art. 8.

[97] For instances of such legislation, see Council of Legal Education Act 1973 (Barbados 1973—16), s. 3; West Indies Shipping Corporation Act 1977 (Trinidad and Tobago 1977—17), ss. 2(2) and 3.   [98] Caribbean Community Treaty, Art. 20.1.

[99] Caribbean Common Market Annex, Art. 63.1.

[1] Geiser, Alleyne and Gajraj, *op. cit.* in note 24, above, at p. 89. The view there expressed that this was an unintentional drafting error is contrary to that of Pollard, *op. cit.* in note 25, above, at p. 51, note 52.

[2] Caribbean Community Treaty, Arts. 20.3 and 28; Caribbean Common Market Annex, Art. 70; Caribbean Development Bank Agreement, Art. 48.2. But for an express power to negotiate headquarters-type Agreements, outside of these treaties, see Caribbean Examinations Council Agreement, Art. 3.3.

[3] Thus, the Community has contributed to some extent in respect to the negotiations for the Lomé Convention (Caribbean Community Secretariat Press Release 52/1974, December 6, 1974, p. 1), the GATT Multilateral Trade Negotiations (*ibid.* 14/1975, June 18, 1975, p. 1), and the International Sugar Agreement (*ibid.* 1/1977, January 15, 1977, p. 1), as well as negotiating as a Community with Mexico (Caribbean Community-Mexico Joint Commission Agreement, July 30, 1974: Caribbean Community Secretariat

Interestingly, parties to the Council of Legal Education Agreement include the two Universities,[4] neither of which is a treaty-based organisation and one of which has no international character. If the effect of this entails recognition of either as an international person, this might have the further consequence that a provision of an instrument to which the Universities are not parties, calling for negotiation of agreements between the organisation constituted by the instrument and a University, might be considered to be a treaty-making power by virtue of being a Power to conclude agreements with another international person.[5]

Where privileges and immunities are concerned, the spectrum of approaches ranges from the relatively high level of immunities specified in the Caribbean Development Bank Agreement [6] to the total silence of the Council of Legal Education Agreement. There are instances of specific denial or qualification of immunities relating to taxation of members of organisations and of their payees,[7] relating to liability for motor vehicle accidents [8] and relating to freedom from exchange control restrictions.[9] In the instances of the Caribbean Development Bank and the Caribbean Investment Corporation, there are clauses which appear to amount to a treaty submission to municipal jurisdiction,[10] going beyond the issue of capacity to sue and be sued, which would arise from the clauses dealing with the legal status of the organisations.

Other instances of clauses relevant to the issue of the international legal personality of regional organisations include clauses following the model of Article 100.2 of the United Nations Charter, requiring member States to respect the exclusively international character of the organisation.[11] As an instance of an opposed tendency to such a clause, there is the provision requiring ships of the West Indies Shipping Corporation to sail under the flag of a member State,[12]

Press Release 35/1974, August 2, 1974) and the European Economic Community (Caribbean Community Secretariat Press Release 36/1977, September 16, 1977, p. 1).

[4] See *loc. cit.* in note 34, above.

[5] See Caribbean Agricultural Research and Development Institute Agreement, Arts. 13.2 and 14.

[6] Arts. 49–55.

[7] Caribbean Development Bank Agreement, Art. 55.5; Caribbean Investment Corporation Agreement, Art. 34.3 and 4.

[8] West Indies Shipping Corporation Agreement, Art. 34.2.

[9] *Ibid.* Art. 34.1(b); Caribbean Development Bank Agreement, Art. 54(b).

[10] Caribbean Development Bank Agreement, Art. 49.1; Caribbean Investment Corporation Agreement, Art. 31.

[11] Caribbean Community Treaty, Art. 15.5; Caribbean Development Bank Agreement, Art. 35.3.

[12] West Indies Shipping Corporation Agreement, Art. 21: it is assumed in the text accompanying this note that the Standing Committee would restrict the exercise of its discretion to select the country of registration to the selection of a member State. See note 72, above.

stifling at birth any aspiration which the organisation might develop to follow the pattern of claims by the United Nations Organisation in this respect.[13] Nor is this the only instance of the express adoption of the law of a member State as governing activities of a regional organisation.[14]

(g) *State succession*

The factor of the participation of Associated States and colonies together with independent States in the instruments of Commonwealth Caribbean regionalism is in some way linked to a general political assumption that any condition falling short of independence is a transitional stage to independence.[15] The achievement of independence notoriously sets the stage for controversies concerning succession to treaty obligations, and the queue of Associated States waiting to follow the Grenada example [16] means that a repeating number of instances giving rise to these issues imminently faces the regional movement.

In this connection, the theoretical difficulties involved in categorising the level of participation of the not-yet-independent States in regional instruments will be counterbalanced by facility in identifying the status of those States in relation to the regional instruments on independence, as having succeeded automatically to the rights and obligations they incurred before independence. In contrast, a reflection of the difficulties which arose on the partition of India and Pakistan in relation to India's membership of the United Nations [17] might be expected as likely to appear in the near future in relation to the Associated State of St. Kitts-Nevis-Anguilla.[18]

The general understanding that the transition to independence is to result in such automatic State succession is to some extent internally derivable from the terms of the instruments of regionalism themselves. Article 17.4 of the Caribbean Community Treaty, for example, provides that the applicability of the obligation to co-ordinate foreign policies shall be a matter of election by a member State on its achievement of sovereign status, and this express exception to an automatic succession result clearly presupposes the

---

[13] *Cf.* Geneva Convention on the High Seas, 1958, Art. 7.

[14] See Caribbean Investment Corporation Agreement, Art. 22.2 (duty of corporation to keep registers required by the law of the host State).

[15] The Heads of Government Conference passed a resolution in support of another resolution by the Governments of the Associated States to this effect at its meeting in December 1975; see Caribbean Community Secretariat Press Release 33/1975, December 16, 1975, pp. 11–13.

[16] Grenada, formerly an Associated State, became a sovereign State in 1974: see West Indies Act (U.K. 1967, c. 4), s. 5 and S.I. 1973 Nr. 2155.

[17] See D. P. O'Connell, *State Succession in Municipal Law and International Law*, Vol. 2 (1967), pp. 184–187.

[18] See notes 3 and 4, above at the beginning of this paper.

generality of such automatic succession in relation to the remainder of the treaty. Again, elaborate provisions governing withdrawal from membership are a recurring feature in the instruments, without any reference to a possibility of an effective withdrawal by operation of law on attaining independence such as a general optional succession régime would constitute,[19] and it may fairly be inferred that the draftsmen of these instruments did not consider such an optional régime a possibility.

(h) *Novation and amendment*

The primacy of *pacta sunt servanda* and the absence of a legislature from the international system combine to pose formidable obstacles to revision and updating of multilateral instruments, since, in the absence of initially contracted provisions in such instruments, the logically impeccable, but practically unworkable, reciprocal consent régime has to rule.[20] In this light, it is to the credit of the Commonwealth Caribbean regional movement that it has already been able to achieve, not merely amendment, but complete novation of a major instrument of regional co-operation in the replacement of the Caribbean Free Trade Association by the Caribbean Community and the Common Market.

It is hardly possible, moreover, to attribute this success to technical legal considerations, although the use of the withdrawal provisions in the Caribbean Free Trade Association Agreement may materially have assisted the universal acceptance of the Caribbean Community Treaty.[21] The amendment provisions of the treaties are, moreover, still being drafted to require unanimity for their amendment,[22] with the result that the legal forms are likely to hinder rather than to help the process.

It seems very likely that one political factor contributing to the effectiveness of the updating and amendment process, as illustrated by the substitution of the Caribbean Community and Common Market for the Caribbean Free Trade Association, and also to the successful conclusion of so many agreements in a relatively short space of time, has been the inequality of the parties institutionalised in the Caribbean Community Treaty by the categorisations of More Developed Countries and Less Developed Countries.[23] The relative

---

[19] See Caribbean Community Treaty, Art. 27; Caribbean Development Bank Agreement, Art. 40; West Indies Shipping Corporation Agreement, Art. 22.

[20] *Cf.* the Vienna Convention on the Law of Treaties 1969, Arts. 39–41 and 57–59.

[21] *Loc. cit.* in notes 62 and 63, above.

[22] Caribbean Community Treaty, Art. 26; Caribbean Examinations Council Agreement, Art. 15; Caribbean Meteorological Organisation Agreement, Art. 30; West Indies Shipping Corporation Agreement, Art. 37. In the case of the Caribbean Development Bank Agreement, Art. 58 provides a power of partial amendment in the absence of unanimity.　　　　[23] Caribbean Community Treaty, Art. 3.

strength and influence of the M.D.C.s of Barbados, Guyana, Jamaica and Trinidad and Tobago in relation to the other participants in the regional movement has meant that their agreement among themselves has often appeared sufficient to spur general agreement, with the result that the effective negotiation required may have been merely quadripartite, and not in political reality as multipartite as the list of participating units and the unanimity principle might suggest. But it yet remains to be seen how far this and other political factors promoting the cause of Commonwealth Caribbean regional co-operation will be able to maintain the impetus of the regional movement in the face of the inherently disintegrative effects of the State sovereignty base of the international legal system.

SMALL DEVELOPING STATES
AND THE
EXTERNAL OPERATIONAL ENVIRONMENT

By

AGRIPPAH T. MUGOMBA

" All things being equal, the State with great economic resources and a large population has more influence on events outside its frontiers, greater security from pressure and attack, more prestige, and a larger element of choice in respect of the national policy it pursues. A small State is more vulnerable to pressure, more likely to give way under stress, more limited in respect of the political options open to it and subject to a tighter connection between domestic and external affairs." David Vital, *The Inequality of States* (1967).

THE study of the foreign-policy behaviour of " small States " is still somewhat an underdeveloped and neglected area of international relations. The vast body of literature existing which is devoted to comparative foreign-policy analysis focuses mainly on the large and powerful States (and, to a lesser extent, the middle Powers) which, traditionally, have always been assumed to have a much greater impact on international politics than small States, whether developed or underdeveloped. Where regional studies do exist in substantial numbers, they often dwell on the domestic politics of small States (and in particular the underdeveloped ones) which are assumed to explain, in the majority of cases, their external behaviour.[1] More precisely, an assumption appears to be manifest that most, or probably all, small States which pursue comparatively active international policies do so quite consciously in the belief that attention can be shifted away from salient issues pertaining to the domestic arena to those in the wider external environment. This paper will attempt to argue that this is often an erroneous interpretation of small-State international politics. It offers the view that displacement is a strategy available to and employed by most States in the international system. Furthermore, it contends that except for those very small States which are categorised as mini-States or micro-States, a fairly large

---

[1] See *e.g.* R. L. Rothstein, " Foreign Policy and Development Policy: From Non-alignment to International Class War," 52 *International Affairs*, Nr. 4 (October 1976), especially pp. 598–603. See also R. Butwell (ed.), *Foreign Policy and the Developing Nations* (1969) and M. K. O'Leary, " Linkages between Domestic and International Politics in Underdeveloped Nations," in J. N. Rosenau (ed.), *Linkage Politics* (1969), pp. 324–346.

number of small States pursue genuinely active foreign policies, although this is likely to depend on which issue-areas they perceive to be most salient in the external, operational environment and the interests they value most, often to the extent of ignoring the limitations on the range of means available to them.

Although a number of general theoretical studies have appeared since the late 1960s focusing more directly on the foreign policies of small States,[2] there is a definite need for more critical ones. Even more important is the need to give adequate attention to the problems of defining " foreign policy " in an operationally meaningful sense; for without that the concept " small State " itself is troublesome to deal with. It is not necessarily an exaggeration to say that there is no broad consensus among international-relations scholars on what is or constitutes a foreign policy. It is a fact, however, that most writers employ the *instrumental* definition of foreign policy, which suggests that policy is goal-oriented behaviour aiming at producing certain intended effects.[3] Such a definition limits itself almost exclusively to the foreign policies pursued by the greater States, which are assumed to possess the capabilities needed to initiate actions which will tend to have significantly more powerful impact on other units in the international system. The power model of foreign-policy analysis thus adopts the perspective that the lesser States, and

---

[2] Among them are the following: B. Benedict (ed.), *Problems of Smaller Territories* (1967); D. Vital, *The Inequality of States* (1967); R. L. Rothstein, *Alliances and Small Powers* (1968); R. O. Keohane, " Lilliputians' Dilemmas: Small States in International Politics," 23 *International Organization*, Nr. 2 (Spring 1969), pp. 291–310; W. E. Patterson, " Small States in International Politics," IV *Co-operation and Conflict*, Nr. 2 (1969), pp. 119–123; A. Baker Fox, " The Small States in the International System 1916–1969," 24 *International Journal*, Nr. 4 (Autumn 1969), pp. 751–764; D. Vital, *The Survival of Small States* (1971); J. Rapoport (*et al.*), *Small States and Territories: Status and Problems* (1971); A. Shou and A. O. Brundtland (eds.), *Small States in International Relations* (1971); T. Mathisen, *The Functions of Small States in the Strategies of the Great Powers* (1971); R. Vayrynen, " On the Measurement and Definition of Small Power Status," VI *Co-operation and Conflict*, Nr. 2 (1971), pp. 91–102; M. R. Singer, *Weak States in a World of Powers* (1972); R. P. Barston (ed.), *The Other Powers: Studies in the Foreign Policies of Small States* (1973); M. A. East, " Size and Foreign Policy Behaviour: A Test of Two Models," 25 *World Politics*, Nr. 4 (July 1973), pp. 556–576; G. L. Reid, *The Impact of Very Small Size on the International Behaviour of Microstates*, Sage Professional Papers in International Studies, Vol. 2, Nr. 02–027 (1974); P. J. McGowan and K.-P. Gottwald, " Small State Foreign Policies: A Comparative Study of Participation, Conflict, and Political and Economic Dependence in Black Africa," 19 *International Studies Quarterly*, Nr. 4 (December 1975), pp. 469–500; M. A. East and J. D. Hagan, " Approaches to Small State Foreign Policy: An Analysis of the Literature and Some Empirical Observations," paper presented at the 17th Annual Convention of the International Studies Association, Toronto, February 25–29, 1976; M. Hirsch, " Influence Without Power: Small States in European Politics," 32 *The World Today*, Nr. 3 (March 1976), pp. 112–118; and N. Amstrup, " The Perennial Problem of Small States: A Survey of Research Efforts," XI *Co-operation and Conflict*, Nr. 3 (1976), pp. 163–182.

[3] See *e.g.* E. J. Meehan, " The Concept ' Foreign Policy '," in W. F. Hanrieder (ed.), *Comparative Foreign Policy* (1971), p. 268.

especially the largest group composed of small developing States, are essentially on the terminal or receiving end of the actions of the great (and middle) Powers. Consequently, their own policies consist mainly of reactions displayed in the form of declarations relating to external "events," [4] implying a dependence approach to international issues.

If, on the other hand, foreign policy is conceptualised in terms of *responses* (whether calculated or not) to *situations* that represent *challenges* and demand *attention*,[5] then it becomes clear that all States in the international system not only have the capacity but do actually act and react in their interactions, even if the behaviour of some States (for example Uganda under Idi Amin) will be viewed by others as irrelevant relative to their own. More important is the fact that in an increasingly interdependent world, a world characterised, in part, by the emergence of transnational class interests, the pursuit of either active or passive (or some other) foreign policies is no longer determined by " objective conditions " alone but, rather, by the interplay of both national and transnational élite perceptions of these factors along with the particular circumstances of given States and the element of choice leaders view as well as exercise in their decision-making processes.

Although there are countless definitions of foreign policy in existence,[6] almost all of them converge on certain themes deemed central to the conceptual idea itself. One of these is the general notion of treating foreign policies as being the purposive actions of governments, *i.e.*, the legitimate pursuit or otherwise of external values associated with the elusive term " national interest " or of " goals " thought to be in the national interest. Yet not all such policies ever have specific aims; foreign policy can also be conceived of as merely adaptive behaviour, *i.e.*, the need to adjust and to cope with the salient issues of the external environment rather than the desire to actually change it entirely or to alter certain aspects of it.[7]

---

[4] C. F. Hermann, " What is a Foreign Policy Event? " in Hanrieder (ed.), *Comparative Foreign Policy*, p. 303.

[5] D. O. Wilkinson, *Comparative Foreign Relations: Framework and Methods* (1969), p. xiv.

[6] A quick glance through the contents of the annual volume *Sage International Yearbook of Foreign Policy Studies* would be enough to illustrate the point. For a variety of other definitional concoctions, see especially Hanrieder, *op. cit.* in note 4, above; W. Wallace, *Foreign Policy and the Political Process* (1971); P. J. McGowan and M. B. Shapiro, *The Comparative Study of Foerign Policy: A Survey of Scientific Findings* (1973); J. N. Rosenau (ed.), *Comparing Foreign Policies: Theories, Findings and Methods* (1974); and C. W. Kegley, Jr. (*et al.*), *International Events and the Comparative Analysis of Foreign Policy* (1975).

[7] J. N. Rosenau, " Foreign Policy as Adaptive Behaviour," 2 *Comparative Politics*, Nr. 3 (April 1970), pp. 365–387, and " The External Environment as a Variable in Foreign Policy Analysis," in J. N. Rosenau, V. Davis and M. A. East (eds.), *The Analysis of International Politics* (1972), pp. 145–165.

No doubt there are different types and strategies of adaptation involved.

Most definitions tell little, however, about whether foreign policy should be viewed as either a dependent variable for analysis (although this is the more common usage), or an independent variable (*i.e.*, a determinant of other policies, especially future ones), or indeed an intermediate variable with elements of both the independent and dependent variables. Furthermore, it is not wholly possible to establish clear-cut analytical boundaries between the purely " external " and the more " internal " or " domestic " aspects of foreign policy, principally because of the linkages that operate between the issues pertaining to each domain.

While there is a lack of consensus on the specific definition of foreign policy, what that policy is all about is more generally accepted. Essentially, foreign policy deals with the " courses of action " initiated by " actors " who employ certain " strategies " or " means " by which to " influence " or " promote " the achievement of " goals " or " objectives " in an " external environmental setting." These policies may also be characterised in terms of diplomatic " styles." It is further assumed that policies differ between and among States according to their scope, the nature of the goals, values and interests articulated, capabilities (material and psychological) and even the determination or vigour with which they are pursued, as well as the relative weight or impact that some variables have in the policy-making processes which others do not.[8] Meaningful discussions of foreign policy cannot, however, be conducted without bringing in the dominant actors or agents involved in the interactional relationships.

I—DEFINITION OF A SMALL STATE

The concept of small State on its own has no relevant operational meaning at all. This is because (1) " small " is a relative term (which refers to an even more vague one, that of " size ") and the concept itself is really shorthand for " a State in its relationships with greater States " [9]; (2) an attempt at an objective (as distinguished from a subjective) definition of a small State leads to circularity revolving around the lack/possession of resources and ability/inability to

---

[8] *E.g.* Rosenau discusses the relative influence of idiosyncratic, role, governmental, societal and systemic variables in decision-making processes and the impact they have on operational policies. See his " Pre-Theories and Theories of Foreign Policy," in R. B. Farrell (ed.), *Approaches to Comparative and International Politics* (1966), pp. 27–92. See also P. J. McGowan and M. B. Shapiro, *The Comparative Study of Foreign Policy, op. cit.* in note 6, above.

[9] E. Bjøl, " The Small State in International Politics," in Schou and Brundtland (eds)., *op. cit.* in note 2, above, at p. 29.

maintain an independent international role [10]; (3) the terms " State," " nation," " territory," " Power " and " country " are often used interchangeably, which further confuses any positive definition; and (4) the impact of size on small-State foreign policy behaviour depends on how the State sees itself in relation to others and the position which other States see it as occupying in the international system.[11] The definition of a small State does not in itself obviate the analytical utility of the concept as such, as " the problems, possibilities and behaviour of small States vary according to the types of international systems in which they operate—hegemonial systems, confrontation systems, integration systems, security communities—according to the geographic parameters which condition their foreign policy, and according to their domestic structures. It is questionable whether even . . . States which undoubtedly belong to the same category of domestic political systems can also be put into the same small State category internationally." [12]

Most attempts at establishing some kind of international stratification of States take size and status as important variables. In particular, they consider a wide range of indicative factors covering geographic area, gross national product, population, armed forces, level of international involvement, *etc.* On the basis of these and other criteria, loose distinctions are made between colonies, micro-/mini-States, small/regional States, small/minor Powers, medium/middle Powers, secondary/great Powers and primary/super-Powers. A broadly-perceived or " conventional " model of small-State behaviour would thus assume that such States are characterised by (a) small land area, (b) small total population (10–15 million being the upper limit), (c) small GNP, and (d) small level of military capabilities.[13]

The literature on small-State behaviour identifies several approaches that have been used to depict the foreign policies of these States. One recent study [14] identifies four main ones: it characterises the first as the " Great Powers writ small " approach, which focuses on the lack of significant material resources and military capabilities and the relative impact of these factors on a small State's perception of its security position. The second approach, identified as the " Capacity

---

[10] D. Vital, *The Inequality of Small States* (1971), p. 7; K. J. Holsti, " National Role Conceptions in the Study of Foreign Policy," 14 *International Studies Quarterly*, Nr. 3 (September 1970), pp. 233–309; and H. Hveem, " Foreign Policy as a Function of International Position," VII *Co-operation and Conflict*, Nr. 2 (1972), pp. 65–86.

[11] R. L. Rothstein, *Alliances and Small Powers* (1968), p. 7.

[12] *Cf.* Bjøl, *op. cit.* in note 9, above, at p. 29. See also Hirsch, *op. cit.* in note 2, above, at pp. 112–113 and Amstrup, *op. cit.* in note 2, above, at p. 165.

[13] East, *op. cit.* in note 2, above, at p. 557. See also Reid, *op. cit.* in note 2, above, at p. 11; and L. J. Cantori and S. L. Spiegel, *The International Politics of Regions: A Conceptual Approach* (1970), chap. 1.

[14] East and Hagan, *op. cit.* in note 2, above, at p. 2.

to Act " approach, emphasises the concern that a small State may have in respect of its ability to act in a positive manner in foreign affairs, not merely on military and security issues but in the economic and diplomatic spheres too.[15] The third approach, called the " Demands and Needs " approach, refers to the effects on a State's foreign policy of the factors of size and the level of modernisation. The fourth is the " Uses of Foreign Policy " approach, whose major distinguishing feature is the domestic uses and functions of foreign policy. In general, however, the existing studies on small States range between those that ignore definitions entirely because such attempts are viewed as unnecessary or even irrelevant, and those calling for integrative schemes linking together approaches focusing on rank/status, external systemic penetration, and the degree of specificity in behaviour, identification of interests and role conception and role playing.[16]

The broad characteristics that identify small States and the approaches that may be employed in analysing their foreign policies point to a number of behaviour patterns that appear to bear a marked difference compared to those of large States. These include (a) lower levels of overall participation in world affairs; (b) higher levels of activity in intergovernmental organisations; (c) higher levels of support for international legal norms; (d) a general tendency to avoid the use of force as a technique of statecraft; (e) general avoidance of behaviour and policies which tend to alienate the more powerful States in the system; (f) a narrower functional and geographic range of concern in foreign-policy activities; and (g) more frequent utilisation of moral and normative positions in international issues.[17] The dominant assumption implicit in these behaviour patterns that are attributed to small States is that the extent or scope of involvement in international affairs is very limited and confined mainly to those issues that attract the interest of most of these countries. They also suggest that there are major differences in the international roles played by large and small States.

II—DIFFERENCES BETWEEN LARGE AND SMALL STATE FOREIGN POLICIES

It has been argued in recent theoretical studies on small-State foreign policy that the concept of élite perception of systemic role is of major significance. That view maintains that a small State is one whose leaders believe or acknowledge that the State is incapable

---

[15] See also Barston, " The External Relations of Small States," in Schou and Brundtland (eds.), *op. cit.* in note 2, above, at p. 40.

[16] See Amstrup, *op. cit.* in note 2, above, at pp. 165–167.

[17] East, *op. cit.* in note 2, above, at p. 557; and McGowan and Gottwald, *op. cit.* in note 2, above, at pp. 165–167.

of making a significant impact on the external international environment. Consequently, a small State's foreign policy is either one that is essentially passive or one that is influenced greatly by the centrifugal forces of passive withdrawal on the one hand and active involvement on the other. This foreign-policy élite orientation thus inclines to the view that " a great (or primary) Power is a State whose leaders consider that it can, alone, exercise a large, perhaps decisive, impact on the international system; a secondary Power is a State whose leaders consider that alone it can exercise some impact, although never in itself decisive, on that system; a middle Power is a State whose leaders consider that it cannot act alone effectively but may be able to have a systemic impact on a small group or through an international institution; a small Power is a State whose leaders consider that it can never, acting alone or in a small group make a significant impact on the system." [18]

It is doubtful, however, whether most leaders of " small " States actually consider their countries to be so utterly powerless or that they are merely pawns to be captured or traded off in global power politics. This uncertainty is compounded by the more serious problems of (a) sorting out " small States " from the broad category of States that are not included among the primary, secondary and middle Powers; (b) distinguishing between " developed " and " underdeveloped " small States; and (c) defining small States separately from other types of lesser States (*e.g.*, " weak "/" strong " States and " micro-States "). The available literature has not yet advanced far enough in that direction; consequently, the process of identification remains arbitrary and heavily subjective.

The implicit view that international politics is almost the exclusive preserve of the greater States does not appear to be vindicated by contemporary realities. For example, the actions of States such as Uganda, Cuba and Israel in recent times are clearly at variance with such an assumption. On a global scale, the trend towards the adoption of a confrontational position by Third-World countries in relations with the major industrialised States is indicative of the now prevailing attitude among them that they should no longer be expected to continue to tolerate " Northern injustice " and to accept a subordinate position in the political economy of international relations.[19] Increasingly vocal demands for the establishment of a " new international order," particularly in the all-important economic sphere, are no longer being ignored by the major Powers, which now

---

[18] Keohane, *op. cit.* in note 2, above, at p. 296. See also Vital, *op. cit.* in note 10, above, at p. 5; and " The Analysis of Small Power Politics," in Schou and Brundtland (eds.), *op. cit.* in note 2, above, at pp. 19, 25–26.

[19] See R. D. Hansen, " The Political Economy of North-South Relations: How much Change? " 29 *International Organization*, Nr. 4 (Autumn 1975), p. 926.

acknowledge (albeit grudgingly) their legitimacy and are gradually inclining to the view that the continuation of gross material inequalities among States threatens " world order "and may lead to international anarchy. Those incessant demands appear to represent a new and more vigorous type of involvement in international politics, while the process of readjustment that the major Powers seem to be going through may reflect an acknowledgement of the growing impact of Third-World countries on the international system.

The prevailing assumptions about the general international behaviour of small States have led to a number of hypotheses which emphasise some of the major differences between States in the style and techniques employed in handling foreign policy issues.[20] First, the observation has been made that in small States, resource limitations are almost inevitably reflected in the size and the organisation of the foreign affairs establishment: " With fewer resources available for allocation to the foreign affairs sector, the size and capacity of the organization charged with the primary responsibility for foreign policy are likely to be small. This means that there will be fewer persons involved in monitoring international events and executing foreign policy decisions. One consequence of this is their inability to cope adequately with the total range of international issues facing the small State. Certain functional and geographic areas must be emphasized, while others are ignored. Moreover, this reduced organizational capacity in foreign affairs means that small States will be less active overall, and differentially active in various areas of policy." [21]

Secondly, small States are much more prone to slow perception of events and developments in the international environment than larger ones. Lack of an intelligence-gathering agency or an adequately staffed research unit in the foreign ministry often means that important foreign-policy decisions have to be made with the minimum of background information. Quite often, the persons responsible for making the decisions are also the ones that must prepare the briefs. Because of their involvement in multiple role-playing activities, the competing salience of issues to be coped with usually leads to distortions in perceptions of external events. The very limited capacity to monitor effectively events and developments in the international system means that small-State foreign policy élites are less likely to " perceive various early warning signals indicating new developments and important policy shifts by other international actors. This, in turn, can have a profound effect on their foreign policy behaviour. . . . [Often] by the time the signals are perceived

---

[20] See *e.g.* the inventory on micro-State foreign policy behaviour proposed by Reid *op. cit.* in note 2, above, at pp. 45–49.

[21] East, *op. cit.* in note 2, above, at p. 559; Reid, *op. cit.* in note 2, above, at p. 22; and Barston, *op. cit.* in note 15, above, at p. 43.

by the small State, the situation may have reached a stage of development where definite, unambiguous, high risk behaviour must be taken. A small State does not enjoy the luxury of engaging in early, low-level, ambiguous behaviour when trying to take effective action in such situations." [22]

Thirdly, cost-effectiveness is a paramount concern in small-State conduct of foreign policy: because of the severe limitation imposed on resources that may be made available to foreign affairs, small States must as a matter of priority seek methods of interaction that are least expensive and most economical. Thus, in attempting to achieve the maximum possible impact at a minimum cost, small States employ a variety of techniques of statecraft which include multilateral diplomacy, international conferences, regional organisations and multiple diplomatic representation.[23] Special leadership qualities and the skilful use of diplomacy can add to the relative weight of the small State in international affairs.

Fourthly and finally, a major difference in the foreign policies of large and small States is found in the perception of the salient issues in international politics. Since the foreign affairs establishment of a small State is unable to cope with the entire range of international phenomena, it must be selective in the issues to which it will attach emphasis. In particular, sensitivity to economic vulnerability means that the State will tend to focus attention on economic issues in its foreign policy. To many small States, with the exception of those located in areas where regional security issues predominate, the economic threat posed by the unrestrained activities of multinational corporations is the dominant factor in their perception of matters pertaining to " national security." Perceptions of threat depend on which policy is adopted between confrontation and collaboration. The point, however, is that " because of the primacy of internal demands on political decision-making (a situation even more acute in small States because of their lack of economic surplus and their small total resource base),certain traditional issues in international politics are generally of little interest to the small States. These are issues such as the Cold War, global prestige and influence, acquiring or maintaining alliances or spheres of influence, and territorial expansion. On the other hand, those international issues which are directly related to their economic growth and development will be most salient for small States." [24]

---

[22] *Ibid.*

[23] East, *op. cit.* in note 2, above, at p. 560; Reid, *op. cit.* in note 2, above, at p. 23; and Barston, *op. cit.* in note 15, above, at p. 44.

[24] East, *op. cit.* in note 2, above, at pp. 560 and 573; Reid, *op. cit.* in note 2, above, at pp. 22 and 33; Barston, *op. cit.* in note 15, above, at pp. 44, 47–48; and Vital, *op. cit.* in note 10, above, chap. 5.

It is one thing to theorise about the foreign-policy behaviour of small States; it is quite another, however, to measure their actual power and influence in the world. Although lacking in the variety of political and military resources Great Powers have, some small States can command greater influence than their rank and status in the global hierarchy of power would suggest. This could derive from a number of sources, *e.g.*, by participation in alliances, location in a region marked by conflict attracting the interest of major Powers, possession of strategically important resources, or simply by supporting certain " punitive " actions taken by other resource-rich small States against a selected group of industrialised consumer nations.

III—THE " POWER " OF SMALL STATES
IN THE THIRD WORLD

It has been suggested that there are two distinct kinds of power in Third-World politics, which may be described very loosely as " regional influence " and which is exercised in " limited neighbourhoods " (regional environments) by " local leviathans " (regional middle States) such as Iran, India, Brazil, Nigeria and South Africa, and " extra-regional influence," which is global in scope and " is brought into play in world forums or is made to infringe directly on the industrial centre of the international economic order." [25] In the latter case, Algeria, for example, has in recent years successfully used forums in the United Nations to harass the industrialised rich nations before world public opinion. Similarly Saudi Arabia, taking full advantage of its enormous oil reserves, has influenced substantially American, West European and Japanese perceptions of the vital significance of the energy issue-area in their foreign policies. Indeed, the cartelisation of the oil resource by the member States of the Organisation of Petroleum Exporting Countries (OPEC) has brought to them the potent " power of intimidation," which they have applied with considerable effectiveness to wring out political and other concessions from the major consumer nations.

Although most analyses of small-State foreign policy behaviour continue to lay stress on what are often seen as the futile attempts by these States to project power and extend influence beyond the regional environment, it seems certain that the recent development of Third-World global power will cease to be viewed as an abnormality and perhaps only a temporary phenomenon in world politics today. It is becoming increasingly evident that new challenges (particularly in the economic issue-area) are being pressed on the industrialised

---

[25] J. W. Howe, " Power in the Third World," 29 *Journal of International Affairs*, Nr. 2 Autumn 1975), p. 113.

nations of the North by the underdeveloped nations of the South [26]; that one of these challenges—that of the OPEC group—has actually altered certain objective power relationships in favour of the South [27]; and that although there has not been, nor is there ever likely to be, any overall change in the distribution of power, except perhaps in respect of the unusual position of the oil exporters, there has been, nevertheless, a subjective change in the perception of power—both in the South and in the North—" which has made the South more assertive in its relationship with the North and made the North take Southern demands more seriously." [28]

This is not to suggest there is any uniform perception of power in the Third World. Rather, it means that all Third-World States are affected by and share perceptions on the issue of international inequality but only a few of them have ascended to the position of challenging the hegemony of the rich States. The less fortunate have nevertheless been prepared to demonstrate their solidarity with the OPEC group regardless of the enormous cost of confrontation to their own vulnerable economies, perhaps in the belief that this is just the beginning of a concerted effort by the Third World to redress the long history of economic " acts of aggression " committed by Northern industrialised States. The long-established practice of watching from the sidelines is being abandoned by even the Fourth World category of underdeveloped States.[29] The capacity shown by emergent regional powers in the Third World to project power beyond the contiguous and regional environments has thus enhanced perceptions of the power of the Southern States.

In much of the literature on small-State foreign policy behaviour, size is viewed as a major determinant, though not the only one, of the parameters within which external goals are pursued, the difficulties that have to be overcome, and the extent to which such States can be treated as viable and genuinely independent members of the international community.[30] Hence the perspective that " material

---

[26] *Ibid.* See also I. W. Zartman, " Europe and Africa: Decolonization or Dependency? " in 54 *Foreign Affairs*, Nr. 2 (January 1976), pp. 325–343, and " Africa " in J. N. Rosenau, K. W. Thompson and G. Boyd (eds.), *World Politics* (1976), pp. 569–594.

[27] See *e.g.* C. F. Diaz-Alejandro, " North-South Relations: The Economic Component," in C. F. Bergsten and L. B. Krause (eds.), *World Politics and International Economics* (1975), pp. 213–241.

[28] Howe, *op. cit.* in note 25, above, at p. 113. See also Hansen, *op. cit.* in note 19, above, at pp. 932–933.

[29] For a discussion of some possible motives for expressions of solidarity, see Hansen *ibid.* at pp. 926–927. See also R. O. Matthews, " The Third World: Powerful or Powerless? " in A. Kontos (ed.), *Domination* (1975), pp. 69–87; G. F. Erb and V. Kallab (eds.), *Beyond Dependency* (1975), and Mahbub ul Haq, *The Poverty Curtain* (1976).

[30] In addition to the studies cited in note 2, above, see also S. A. Salmore and C. F. Hermann, " The Effects of Size, Development and Accountability on Foreign Policy," *Peace Research Society* (*International*) Papers, Vol. 14 (1969), pp. 15–30; and J. S. Nye,

size is the factor which is least of all given to modification through the deliberate efforts of governments. It sets the limit to what can be attained and fixes the international role and status of the nation more securely than any other." [31]

However, if too much importance is attached to size and the limitations it imposes, then one would have little choice but to accept that the overwhelming majority of small States are only passive actors in international politics. Yet there are other factors which generally appear to enhance (although they can sometimes inhibit) the pursuit of active foreign policies. These include: (a) the state's level of economic and social development (*i.e.* degree of " modernisation "); (b) geographical proximity to or location in areas marked by conflict, especially that of an ideological type; (c) strategic importance to or active competition for influence among Great Powers; (d) the existence of major international forums; (e) the state of interplay between domestic (sub-systemic) and external (systemic) factors, especially the level of population cohesion and the degree of internal support for the régime's external operations; (f) the overall nature of the environment in which the State is placed; (g) a strong ideology and the skilful use of diplomacy; (h) the quality and motivational drive of the leadership as well as the degree to which policies are personalised; and (i) a precarious economic (and military) situation, which may have the desirable effect of attracting active external sympathy and support and, consequently, affording the opportunity for exercising greater influence.

These and a variety of other circumstances and systemic conditions [32] often enable small States to exercise influence totally disproportionate to the rank and status accorded by the " objective " elements of power.

It may be presumptuous, or perhaps premature, to conclude that there is now positive perception in the international community of the rising power of Third-World countries. One reason for counselling the need to adopt a cautious attitude is obviously the fact that broad influence remains focused on what is essentially a tiny " leadership " element composed of a new class of middle-range Powers, especially those that produce and export oil in large quantities and have played the leading role in " hiking " the market prices for this essential commodity. Many of these States are strongly oriented towards capitalism (except Cuba and Vietnam), and collaborate actively with

" Nationalism, Statesmen and the Size of African States," in M. Kilson (ed.), *New States in the Modern World* (1975), chap. 8.

[31] Vital, *op. cit.* in note 10, above, at pp. 3–4 and Reid, *op. cit.* in note 2, above, at p. 9

[32] *Ibid.* See also East, *op. cit.* in note 2, above, at p. 564, and with Hagan, *op. cit.* in note 2, above; Barston, *op. cit.* in note 15, above, at p. 46; and McGowan and Gottwald, *op. cit.* in note 2, above, at pp. 473–481.

international business enterprises in making their influence felt. It seems evident enough, however, that the overwhelming majority of States located to the South of the industrialised nations are beginning not only to believe that they have power but are also acting as though they actually had such power, and—in forums in the United Nations and related agencies—the North is beginning to treat parts of the South with more of the consideration that normally is conferred on the powerful.[33] The growing polarisation of States in international politics on a North-South axis is a definite pointer to the changes now rapidly taking place in the international system. This by no means ignores the differences between States in the Third World. However, frictions in these horizontal relationships still fall below those now characterising vertical North-South ones.

The real point is that after decades of suffering in relative silence the " poor " nations have begun to " rock the boat " and the rich nations are paying attention, for a number of reasons.

(a) The underdeveloped countries are gradually cementing their ties to form a more solid bloc, the so-called Group of 77 (although its membership now exceeds 100), and are beginning to share similar ideas on issues affecting their economic interests, even though they do not as yet speak with one voice in their negotiations with the rich States.[34]

(b) The poor countries are offering proposals and making demands that go far beyond existing aid programmes; they are seeking agreement on new rules for the establishment of a " new international economic order," which would cover such topics as trade, monetary relations, private investment and credit, public loans and grants, and even the utilisation of ocean resources.[35]

(c) The exemplary behaviour of the OPEC States, especially their solidarity in setting prices and quantities of oil exported, is an important guide. Oil and the results it can produce in international relationships have decisively brought new confidence and a militant mood to the Third World, which are clearly reflected in opinions such as the following: " Now we can impose the rules of the game. . . . The only thing that has made the developed countries listen to us developing countries is energy. It's energy that has given us political clout." [36]

---

[33] Howe, *op. cit.* in note 25, above, at p. 115. See also S. Brown, *New Forces in World Politics* (1974), pp. 103–108.

[34] For a discussion of " cleavages " within the Group of 77, see Hansen, *op. cit.* in note 19, above, at pp. 930–932.

[35] See also C. F. Bergsten, *The Future of the International Economic Order: An Agenda for Research* (1973), chap. 7, and *Toward a New International Economic Order: Selected Papers of C. Fred Bergsten*, 1972–1974 (1975), especially chap. 27.

[36] Statements attributed to Algerian President Houari Boumedienne and Jamaican Foreign Minister P. J. Patterson. *Cf.* The Montreal *Gazette*, March 22, 1976, p. 9. See also M. J. Williams, " The Aid Programs of the OPEC Countries," 54 *Foreign Affairs*, Nr. 2 (January 1976), especially pp. 314–317.

(d) The underdeveloped nations realise that they are in a position to frustrate numerous international programmes—on environmental pollution (including lakes and seas/oceans), against air piracy and other acts of politically motivated terrorism, or in satellite tracking, to name just a few—simply by withholding co-operation.

The nations of the Third World are attempting to reform or possibly to restructure an international economic system that has given them only 25 per cent. of its wealth and 7 per cent. of its industrial output, despite the fact that they have 70 per cent. of the world's population and are the producers of most of the world's raw materials. The demands they are making on the rich States are as follows.

(i) Control over their own raw materials, on which most of them base their economies. These include higher and more stable markets, less subject to free-market whims or manipulations. The debate—as indicated by some of the deliberations at the fourth United Nations Conference on Trade and Development (UNCTAD IV) in Nairobi in May 1976—is increasingly over whether this will be achieved by OPEC-style cartels and price indexation, which the rich Western States object to strongly, or through jointly reached commodity agreements or price-support programmes.[37]

(ii) Control over multinational corporations (MNCs) based or with large-scale operations in Third World countries, to keep them from evading taxes or repatriating all profits and to force them to contribute to local development. There are increasingly visible signs of a trend towards the adoption of aggressive bargaining approaches by Third-World nations, including threats of expropriation without adequate compensation (though not very credible) designed to induce more meaningful concessions from the immensely powerful and often well-entrenched multinationals. The clearest and by far the most successful case up to now is that of the OPEC States, which have begun to move in the direction of assuming partial ownership and, to some extent, controlling or regulating the operations of the international oil conglomerates. There is no doubt that other producers of important raw materials, such as copper, tin, bauxite, phosphates and even bananas and sugar cane, will be tempted to emulate the OPEC group by forming their own cartels, although the success or failure of such efforts would depend on a number of factors including world demand and supply of these raw materials: " In times of recession, it has not been possible even to maintain prices of raw materials. But as the industrialized economies recover, and if they resume vigorous growth trends, it will again become easier for producers of raw materials to seek increases in prices of their

---

[37] For discussion of these issues, see Bergsten, *The Future of the International Economic Order*, chap. 7 and *Toward a New International Economic Order*, chaps. 27–28.

commodities by forming cartels. In addition to the rate of growth in demand, other factors that will help to determine the success of cartels include how many raw material producers are involved, how dependent they are on current earnings, how perishable the commodity in question is, and how easily it can be replaced by substitutes." [38] And even in cases involving low-demand raw materials, those producer States that are clear enough about what they want from MNCs and have the will to pursue their goals unrelentingly, can succeed in their persuasive efforts provided, not unexpectedly, compromises are struck which allow the MNCs to make satisfactory profit margins. [39]

(iii) A " transfer of technology " from rich to poor nations so that the Third World can also have large factories, mines and plantations and, most important of all, grow more food; such a transfer means not only " gifts " and technical aid in building and installing the factories but also the training of local personnel, establishment of local scientific and research facilities, and perhaps the development of joint ventures, particularly in the overly neglected area of rural development. [40]

(iv) More money, through aid and through a reform of the world monetary system, to give the poor States more access to hard currency and credits. In addition, the Third-World States are demanding active assistance in creating Western markets for their goods and broad-scale tariff cuts to give them an advantage on these markets.

The pros and cons of these North-South issues fall outside the scope of the present discussion. What is significant, however, is that the Third-World nations are playing for high stakes in their negotiations with the Northern countries. In specific international forums, they are using their voting power to achieve positive gains. Although they remain weak in such bodies as the International Monetary Fund and the World Bank, they have nevertheless been making demands that more of international economic decision-making should take place in the United Nations, where they will be better-placed to challenge the continuing economic hegemony of a small group of rich States. Some of the negotiating tactics adopted by the

---

[38] Howe, *op. cit.* in note 25, above, at p. 116. See also P. Connelly and R. Perlman, *The Politics of Scarcity: Resource Conflicts in International Relations* (1975), chap. 5 and T. H. Moran, *Multinational Corporations and the Politics of Dependence: Copper in Chile* (1974), chaps. 6–8.

[39] See also N. A. Hussein, " Corporate Social Responsibilities: The Future of Multi-national Corporations," paper presented at the Annual Conference of the Canadian Association of African Studies, Victoria, B.C., February 18–21, 1976; R. L. Sklar, *Corporate Power in an African State: The Political Impact of Multinational Mining Companies in Zambia* (1975); and C. G. Widstrand (ed.), *Multinational Firms in Africa* (1975).

[40] See also W. R. Kinter and H. Sicherman, *Technology and International Politics: The Crisis of Wishing* (1975), chaps. 6–7; and E. Rothschild, " Food Politics," 54 *Foreign Affairs*, Nr. 2 (January 1976), pp. 285–307.

Third-World States have understandably led to accusations by some rich Western countries that the former are seeking to overthrow the free-market systems and mixed economies on which Western wealth is built. The Third World response to this charge is, however, that the new economic order they are demanding would increase the size of the international economic pie, with bigger slices for everyone (although, admittedly, this amounts to side-stepping the real issue, *i.e.*, how to replace an international system characterised by the overdevelopment of a few States and the underdevelopment of the majority of other States).

These unfolding developments indicate a new and formidable ability on the part of the nations of the South to stick together on North-South economic issues. They are also manifestations of a rapid change in the sense of power felt by small States and their growing perception of their importance and influence in world politics. It has to be acknowledged, however, that the idea will die hard that " *no objective change has occurred which centrally challenges or threatens the dominance of the international economic order by the countries of North America, Europe and Japan.*" [41] Be that as it may, it now seems imperative that many current theories of the foreign-policy behaviour of small States should be substantially modified or revised to accommodate the altering power distribution in the international system as a consequence of the ascending position and enhanced influence of some of its more " subordinate " actors.

---

[41] Howe, *op. cit.* in note 25, above, at p. 117. (Emphasis original.)

REGIONAL SECURITY COMMUNITIES
AND WORLD ORDER

By

RONALD J. YALEM

THE concept of security-community was first articulated by Richard Van Wagenen who defined it as a " group which has become integrated, where integration is defined as the attainment of a sense of community, accompanied by formal or informal institutions and practices, sufficiently strong and widespread to assure peaceful change among members of a group with ' reasonable ' certainty over a ' long ' period of time." [1] Karl Deutsch later considered the integrative processes necessary to produce a security-community which he identified as the acquisition of similar patterns of thought among individuals comprising a security-community; assimilation through " a process in which participating individuals or political units become . . . similar . . . to one another in language, culture, political and economic habits and institutions . . ."; mutual interdependence of diverse political units; mutual responsiveness of political units; and simple pacification or the abandonment of the use of force among political units. [2]

Whereas Van Wagenen limited security-communities to the type formed by the amalgamation or merger of formerly independent political units into one entity, Deutsch added the pluralistic type which could exist with few or no common institutions. [3]

The concept was further refined in 1957 by Deutsch and associates in connection with a well-known study that illustrated historically the attainment of security-communities, especially those of the amalgamated type. [4] Van Wagenen's original elements of integration, sense of community, and peaceful change were retained, but with a redefinition of peaceful change. Van Wagenen had argued that the use of authorised force did not violate the concept of peaceful change; in the Deutsch study peaceful change was defined as " the resolution of social problems, normally by institutionalised procedures, without resort to large-scale physical force." [5] Since 1957 security-communities

---

[1] R. W. Van Wagenen, *Research in the International Organization Field* (1952). pp. 10–11.

[2] K. W. Deutsch, *Political Community at the International Level* (1954), pp. 36–38

[3] *Op. cit.* in note 1, above, at p. 11; and *op. cit.* in note 2, above, at p. 41.

[4] K. W. Deutsch *et al.*, *Political Community and the North Atlantic Area* (1957).

[5] *Op. cit.* in note 1, above, at p. 11; and *op. cit.* in note 4, above, at p. 5.

have largely been identified on the basis of peaceful change proposed by Deutsch.

In the 1957 study the character of a pluralistic security-community was further clarified as an entity in which the independence of separate governments is retained as, for example, the United States-Canada pluralistic security-community.[6]

J. S. Nye has described the concept of security-community as one of the first manifestations of interest in the theory of international integration, but is dubious about empirical verification because of the difficulty of adequate measurement.[7]

Despite the problems of measurement described by Nye, I believe that it would be useful to examine the concept of security-community in a context that has not been previously applied, namely, the regional *milieu*. The historical case studies of security-community presented by Deutsch and his associates were confined to bilateral relationships. Theoretically, it may be argued that a security-community could be multilateral as well as bilateral. Regional security-communities may be defined as regional groupings (in the sense of geographic proximity) that have renounced the use of force as a means of resolving intra-regional conflicts. In all likelihood such communities will have attained a high degree of political and economic integration as a necessary precondition of peaceful relationships, though not necessarily on the basis of common institutions.

At a time when there is increasing academic interest and research on world order models, the concept of regional security-communities may offer an approach to world peace that has not been considered.[8] World order is defined as an empirical condition of the global system in which the level of international violence is low in proportion to the level of non-violence. Violence may be defined as acts of force perpetrated by a State or States against another State or States. It may also include the coercive response of States to direct attacks in the form of international war. Of primary interest here is foreign conflict as opposed to internal conflict. To the extent that the concept of security-community is regionalised, the stability of the international community as a whole may be enhanced through the diminution of violent international conflict.

---

[6] *Op. cit.* in note 4, above, at p. 6.

[7] J. S. Nye, *Peace in Parts* (1971), p. 25. The difficulty of measurement arises out of uncertainty as to whether States are planning war against each other (see p. 47). According to Deutsch, the concept of security-community may be tested " in terms of the absence or presence of significant organized preparation for war or large-scale violence among its members." *Op. cit.* in note 2, above, at p. 34. Thus, the difficulty arises out of testing the first indicator but not the second.

[8] On world order models, see S. Mendlovitz (ed.), *On the Creation of a Just World Order* (1974), and R. A. Falk, *A Study of Future Worlds* (1975).

The discussion that follows stresses the condition of security-community rather than the requisite background factors or the complex process of community formation at the regional level. While a voluminous literature exists with regard to the process of regional integration especially in Western Europe, it is not clear that the factors which operate among nation-States to produce such integration are identical with the factors that produce a regional security-community. In fact there has been no historical case study of a security-community wider than two States. Security-community implies a certain solidarity among States sufficient to assure that disputes will be resolved peacefully, though formal institutional integration may be unnecessary. For example, Western Europe may be classified as a pluralistic regional security-community even though it lacks political integration. In the absence of empirical research on the process of building a regional security-community, it seems logical to concentrate on the theoretical aspects of the concept especially with regard to the hypothetical relationships that could result from the existence of a series of regional security-communities.

In theory it might be argued that a security-community at the regional level could be amalgamated as well as pluralistic. An amalgamated security-community could be formed by the merger of a number of separate sovereignties into a single political unit. This would approximate a form of world government at the regional level. Since the practical prospects for the attainability of an amalgamated regional security-community seem much less than for the pluralistic type, I have decided to concentrate on the latter rather than the former.

The concept of security-community has been criticised because it implies such a solidarity among nation-States that armed conflict is academic so that the concept becomes a tautology.[9] But as K. J. Holsti points out, " this criticism fails to acknowledge that some very serious differences have arisen among States in security communities, and that some special characteristics of these relationships have prevented the quarrelling governments from adopting forms of behavior typical in conflicts involving threat or use of force." [10] For example, the United States has had some serious differences with France regarding the proper relationship between American and European roles in defending Western Europe. The United States and Canada have been in conflict over American tariff policies toward Canadian goods. Yet in neither case was armed conflict considered an acceptable mode of behaviour.

If the international system could be transformed into a series of

[9] K. J. Holsti, *International Politics* (2nd ed.—1972), p. 498.
[10] *Ibid.*

pluralistic regional security-communities, would the problem of world peace be resolved? By world peace is meant a condition characterised by the absence of international violence rather than in the more positive sense of social justice described by Johan Galtung.[11] The case for the regional security-communities approach to world order rests on the assumption that a safer alternative to the present international system is both necessary and desirable. Despite the optimism generated by Soviet-American and American-Chinese détente, the system is changing only with regard to the structure of power (from bipolarity to tripolarity) and not in terms of the fundamental attributes of that structure.[12] So long as national military power is decentralised, the capacity of the system to restrain or curtail the unauthorised use of force by nation-States will remain limited. The formation of regional security-communities would theoretically reduce the sources of conflict from 150 units to less than 10.[13] While this would not necessarily resolve the problem of world peace, it would considerably lower the number of friction points in the international system.

As long as nuclear deterrent relationships are stabilised among the most powerful States, a precarious peace by fear is possible. It might even be argued that the Soviet Union and the United States have achieved a virtual no-war community if not a security-community.[14] But the risk of war emanates not so much from the most powerful as from the least powerful States that are considered the most probable sources of international conflict in the decades ahead.[15]

Some might reason that the formation of bilateral security-communities is preferable to the establishment of multilateral communities since it is easier to get two friendly States to co-operate than five or 20. Yet the establishment of a worldwide network of bilateral security-communities would still make it possible for war to occur between innumerable dyadic combinations across regions.

A better means for establishing peace would be a series of pluralistic regional security-communities on a global basis. This would not

[11] J. Galtung, " Peace Thinking," in A. Lepawsky, E. H. Buehrig, and H. Lasswell (eds.), *The Search for World Order* (1971), p. 120.

[12] Ronald J. Yalem, " Tripolarity and World Politics," in this *Year Book*, Vol. 28 (1974), pp. 23–42.

[13] While analysts disagree as to the number of regional sub-systems, most writers limit their attention to the major geographical regions of the world which would probably be less than 10.

[14] Deutsch defines a no-war community as " a limited political community within which . . . the only command expected and backed by formal or informal sanctions is the command not to resort to war in the settlement of disputes. In contrast to a security-community, however, the possibility of war is still expected and to some extent preparations are made for it." *Op. cit.* in note 2, above, at p. 41.

[15] O. Young argues that major conflict sources are shifting towards Africa and Asia. " The United Nations and the International System," XXII *International Organization* (1970), p. 908.

be the ideal solution to the problem of world order, however. Regional peace does not necessarily guarantee inter-regional peace.[16] There are also serious obstacles to the achievement of such communities in a world marked by intra-regional rivalries and diversities. This is an important problem. For if the regional security-community idea has no practical means of being achieved, the case for this approach to world order may be as utopian as the case for world government.

Bruce Russett has made a study of dyadic conflict from 1946 to 1965 involving 41 pairs of States in which each conflict involved more than 100 fatalities.[17] When these conflicts are analysed regionally, Western Europe was the only region free from violence.[18] Only Western Europe therefore constitutes a pluralistic regional security-community. On the basis of a number of factors such as volume of trade, cultural and social homogeneity, common participation in international organisations, and geographic proximity, Russett concluded that the probability of violent conflict in Western Europe is extremely low, moderately unlikely in Eastern Europe and Latin America, and much more probable in Africa, Asia, and the Middle East.[19] Russett's findings clearly suggest that the security-community concept needs to be extended to Asia, Africa, and the Middle East and strengthened in Latin America and Eastern Europe.

If we assume that in the distant future the number of pluralistic regional security-communities could be expanded, the fundamental problem of regionalism is whether the probability of conflict is increased between regions when its probability is reduced within a region. Many scholars would subscribe to this assumption, but we have no conclusive evidence that a set of regional security-communities would operate in this fashion. I have argued elsewhere that regional groups could function on a basis of peaceful co-existence comparable to the pattern of peaceful co-existence between the Soviet Union and the United States; if such groups possessed nuclear weapons, a process of inter-regional nuclear deterrence might be possible.[20] In the absence of regional security-communities, it is not possible to test the validity of the positive or negative consequences that could result. Nevertheless, it may be useful to

[16] According to E. B. Haas, while the regional integration process " may create a relatively small number of integrated political communities the growth of fewer and larger political communities will contribute to regional, but not to universal peace." " International Integration: The European and the Universal Process," reprinted from XV *International Organization* (1961), in *International Political Communities* (1966), p. 129.

[17] B. Russett, *International Regions and the International System* (1967), p. 196.

[18] *Ibid*. p. 202.

[19] *Ibid*. p. 203.

[20] R. J. Yalem, " Fusing the International System: Notes on Regional and Global Integration Processes," *International Interactions* (1977).

consider the possibility that regional groups could function peacefully with each other as well as discordantly.

The problem of expanding the number of regional security-communities is a formidable one given the minimal integration of Latin America, the Middle East, Africa, and Asia. It is unlikely that the United Nations can play a positive role in this regard despite Richard Van Wagenen's claim that the organisation has promoted a greater sense of world solidarity that will lead eventually towards a broader security-community than now exists.[21] He presents no evidence to support this generalisation. It is, therefore, difficult to agree with his conclusion that " the work of the United Nations system . . . will help to grow more of what we have been calling pluralistic security communities where they do not yet exist." [22] No doubt the United Nations has played an important role in sponsoring economic and social co-operation during the past generation, but unless evidence is presented that its efforts have contributed directly or indirectly to the attainment of the non-use of force to resolve international conflicts, the assumption that the United Nations can be an effective catalyst for stimulating future security-communities must be questioned.

As was suggested earlier, there is a lack of research on the building of regional security-communities. How do regional groupings acquire the broad consensus that assures the peaceful resolution of intra-regional conflict? Until we have some answers to this question and possibly to others as well, it will be difficult to specify the practical possibilities for expanding the number of regional security-communities.

The conception of a network of regional security-communities proposed here has been vigorously criticised by Johan Galtung as an example of a " harmony of interests " model leading to world government.[23] Galtung contends that the enlargement of security-communities on a global basis ". . . overlooks the simple circumstance that all along, in this process of extending the concentric circles, there remain pockets which are tied to the center in associative, but highly inegalitarian relationships. And where these pockets are geographically defined . . . disintegration or fission or secessionist movements are bound to take place sooner or later." [24]

It should be emphasised that the " harmony of interests " model described by Galtung is not presumed here because the emphasis has been placed on pluralistic regional security-communities in which the

---

[21] R. Van Wagenen, " The Concept of Community and the Future of the United Nations," XIX *International Organization*, Summer 1965, p. 826.
[22] *Ibid.*
[23] Johan Galtung, *op. cit.* in note 11, above, at p. 152.
[24] *Ibid.*

independence of co-operating States is taken for granted and not on the establishment of an amalgamated security-community on a global basis in the form of world government. Whether such a group of security-communities will operate harmoniously or discordantly is unknown. Further, it is theoretically possible for the world to be arranged on a regional basis without any regional community transferring political power to a powerful centre structure as Galtung implies. A centre structure may exist in the form of an international organisation like the United Nations only loosely associated with various regional security-communities. In such a system the notion of fission or secession by such communities away from the centre appears to be irrelevant.

The regional security-communities approach to world order which I have outlined offers an alternative path to peace that deserves additional critical discussion. In theory the formation of a number of such communities in the future would reduce the incidence of inter-State conflict by assuring the peaceful settlement of intra-regional disputes. But there is also the possibility that the scope of international conflict could be enlarged if regional security-communities became pitted against each other in inter-regional war. In the absence of a group of such communities we cannot ascertain whether their formation would contribute to or detract from a more peaceful world order. Nevertheless, without a universal amalgamated security-community or world government likely in the years ahead, a regionalised security-community structure represents a desirable if somewhat distant alternative. In an era in which there is widespread condemnation of both conventional and nuclear war, this approach deserves further theoretical and empirical analysis.

BEHAVIOURAL SCIENCES
IN INTERNATIONAL RELATIONS

By

CAREY B. JOYNT

THE great scientist and mathematician Poincaré once remarked scornfully on the study of sociology, " the most methods; least results." The comment, while perhaps unduly patronising, does represent a commonly-held view of scientific attempts to produce sound explanations in human affairs. It must also be admitted that the seemingly endless and inconclusive debates over the proper approach to the subject of international relations have fortified this general viewpoint. Worse, they have tended to polarise opinion and to divide people into warring camps.

This is a pity since there are unsolved problems enough and to spare. Indeed our lack of understanding should impel us to seize every opportunity to contract the area of our ignorance, since the issues in the field do involve, after all, questions of human survival. Yet the human problems—the complex jargon in which concepts are all too often expressed, exaggerated claims for behavioural approaches, a too-facile denigration of traditional models—combine to set very strict limits to an advance in understanding. In short, ordinary human weakness sets up constraints which need to be overcome if progress is to be made on a broad front.

Other limitations appear when we consider the extreme disparities which exist in our preparation for the subject. The profession resembles the navy of Charles II, of which Macaulay wrote that " it contained both seamen and gentlemen; but the gentlemen were not seamen and the seamen were not gentlemen." The result is a dichotomy between those converts to behavioural studies who project vistas of a new heaven and a new earth (which often turn out on closer examination to be much like the old world after all), and those whose distrust, suspicion and disdain for the whole enterprise leave them content with more traditional approaches to the subject. The painful process of dialogue is thus avoided and advances to a better understanding are blocked.

Even if these very real difficulties could be removed, formidable obstacles to progress would remain. The most obdurate of all is probably the sheer volume of the material to be handled. One example must suffice: between 1960 and 1974 over 1,000 articles and books were published in the area of the social psychology of bargaining alone. Only recently has an attempt been made to summarise the results.[1] Once completed, however, such a study can, if properly used, provide valuable insights for our understanding of how bargaining proceeds and, in particular, the nature of the key variables and their interaction. The catch lies in the qualification: if properly used.

I—MODELS AND THEIR USES

Proper use involves a basic understanding of the nature and uses of models and their limitations. Unfortunately, such understanding is not widespread, judging by utterances like the following, an example which could be multiplied many times over: " A strange conviction dictates that a pattern becomes the more intellectually respectable the more it is expressed in abstract language." [2] Here the criticism confuses a proper dislike for mere verbal mystification with quite another point, namely: the utility of an abstraction to deal with a range of facts and to point to relationships hitherto unrecognised or perhaps too lightly disregarded.

The truth of the matter lies in recognising that even the most abundant narrative is selective and that it contains within it explicit, or implicit, models of the nature of man, the processes of change, and a host of other often unacknowledged assumptions. The virtue of the behavioural sciences is that they force us to make our assumptions more explicit. They also compel us to realise that any model is always a partial representation of reality and that the test of any model is its adequacy for a given purpose. There is no such thing as the *only* model of a given situation. We cannot give a general answer, therefore, to the question, " How useful are behavioural models," as distinct from, say, the models utilised by historians. Each case would have to be examined in detail, which means in effect that the utility of a model is bound to be case-specific. All models leave out certain aspects of reality and therefore may very well not address certain important issues. It is, therefore, quite mistaken to assert that " in order to increase understanding . . . a theory must take account of all factors." [3] No single theory or conceivable set of theories can do any such thing.

A related error is to denigrate a particular model in oversweeping terms as when the power-politics approach is consigned to oblivion by the use of pejorative terms such as the " billiard ball " model.[4]

---

[1] J. Z. Rubin and B. R. Brown, *The Social Psychology of Bargaining and Negotiation* (1975).

[2] G. R. Elton, *The Practice of History* (1969), p. 129.

[3] E. Luard, *Types of International Society* (1976), p. 23.

[4] J. W. Burton, " The Relevance of Behavioral Theories of the International System," in J. N. Moore (ed.), *Law and Civil War in the Modern World* (1974), pp 92–93.

By so doing, important distinctions are blurred. In the case in point, it is one thing to argue that State-centred models cannot explain *all* international behaviour. It is quite another to show that such models do not provide us with the most important and central concept available, as I believe the evidence indicates.

Other important issues are involved here. Those who use State-oriented, power politics models are surprised to learn that such models ignore a range of variables such as perception, motivation, values, assessment of conflict costs, and so on. They are even told such a model must be zero-sum and not positive-sum.[5] The result is a stereotype achieved by the simple process of arbitrary exclusion on the part of the analyst.

The truth is surely otherwise. Models which are not State- or power-oriented do point to processes which ought to be analysed. The danger is that such a change of perspective can lead to a blurring of focus in such a manner as to produce a grave distortion of the processes at work. The major foundations of the subject must remain State-oriented if we are to remain true to the weight of the evidence. Moreover, we must not be led astray by our sense of the dangers involved for mankind and ignore the unpleasant fact that nearly every aspect of these relationships involves the dilemmas and uses of power. Driven out at the front door by the newer conflict studies, power comes in at the back door, bolder and more demanding than ever. New approaches can refine and enrich our understanding, but they cannot displace power models as effective analytical devices. Perhaps we would not all agree with Raymond Aron when he argues that the chief contribution of sociology and anthropology has been to establish power,[6] and the facts relating to it, as the central concept of history, but in the end I am convinced that the protagonists of the new school will find that they have been unwilling participants in the writing of a new grammar of power.

Part of the dilemma involves drawing lines which are to some extent arbitrary. Time, diminishing utility and lack of knowledge, no doubt all play their part in this process. There may, in fact, be a serious loss in effective analysis if one proceeds to deeper and deeper levels of description, going beyond basic motivations to intricate investigation of perceptions, images and goals of the participants. This can be described as " the basement level," [7] but those who prefer reducing the problems still further would argue for a floor below even the basement, to wit: a plunge into the murky depths of

---

[5] Burton, *op. cit.* in note 4, above, pp. 97–98.

[6] R. Aron, " Thucydide et le récit historique," *History and Theory*, Vol. 1 (1960),' pp. 103–128.

[7] J. W. Burton (*et al.*), *The Study of World Society: A London Perspective* (1974) p. 13.

psychoanalysis. Witness the recent study of Hitler which reduces his entire career and all his decisions to a nauseatingly detailed account based on a Freudian syndrome.[8] One can only reply, " Interesting no doubt, but it is not politics." In other words, the level at which behavioural studies are done does reflect back upon the subject. The result can be to dissolve it unless great care is used.

Other dangers abound, as when too much emphasis is placed on the sheer power of a model to mould the minds and actions of men.[9] No doubt all models do this—certainly we have ample evidence that Burton's does so—but men do have the ability to free themselves from their conceptions and recognise the limitations of their outlook. Even statesmen have this capacity, on occasion. Indeed, one can argue with some persuasiveness that it is the capacity of the State to adapt itself in all manner of subtle and devious means to changes in its environment, that constitutes one of its chief characteristics and that, by so doing, it can, and does, manage to protect or even extend its existing power, authority and claims.[10] Thus, we can argue, as Burton does, that " a concept of systems interacting is more realistic than a concept of States interacting " and that a model describing " the map of world society [as] one cobweb of transactions imposed on another " would be " nearer contemporary reality." [11] Such transactions exist, no doubt, but are they in no way controlled by the State? The persistent and costly efforts of tyrannies to control communications, and movements of people, impediments to free migration, the use of propaganda and the limitations imposed on functional institutions argue otherwise. As for the control of multi-nationals, the issue is complex but States have nationalised many of these to the obvious discomfort of their stockholders. Even the trans-national forces of science and technology, so essential to the Burton-ian model, have not by any means always restricted the domain of State power. A good example is the extent to which such develop-ments have accelerated the process by which the boundaries of the State are being pushed out to take in new, previously shared inter-national areas. State frontiers are in fact growing substantially through the expansion and solidification of national control over new territories. The process goes on apace.[12] In sum, one can argue that

[8] R. Binion, *Hitler Among the Germans* (1976).
[9] Burton, *op. cit.* in note 4, above, at p. 93.
[10] For a recent analysis of how power is being transformed, see K. Knorr, *The Power of Nations* (1975).
[11] *Op. cit.* in note 7, above, at p. 6. The evidence cited in support of the utility of this model is described as " communications, movements of people, the epidemic spread of ideas and ideologies, transnational corporations, functional institutions that are universal, tourism, migration, sympathies and support across boundaries. . . ."
[12] See Z. J. Slouka, " Technological Change and the Hardening of International Boundaries." Paper delivered at the International Political Science Association meetings, Edinburgh (August 21–26, 1976).

the evidence indicates the shortcomings and deficiencies of Burtonian models and the advantages of State-oriented concepts. Systems interactions can and will be put to State uses.

II—DEFINITIONS OF THE FIELD
AND THE ISSUES

Needless to say, the utility of behavioural models as one approach to problems in the field often runs aground on the problem of definition. For example, there are enormous differences of opinion about exactly what the term " behavioural " means, with the result that supporters and opponents of the movement all too often are engaged in a dispute about the meaning of words with the end product consisting largely of a sophisticated muddle in which key issues are blurred, or even lost altogether. Excessive claims are made—" all segments of political science can be treated behaviourally " [13]— which in turn call forth sharp rebuttals and denials.[14] It is all great fun for the participants but when the smoke of battle has cleared away, exactly what has been learned?

The answer one gives to this question will depend almost entirely on how broadly or narrowly the issues are defined. If, for example, one begins by defining behavioural explanations as involving individuals rather than groups as the proper units for analysis, as excluding normative approaches and including regularities but never particular occurrences,[15] it is easy to show that the approach leaves out significant aspects of politics which interest most students of the subject. If, on the other hand, one lists the assumptions of the behavioural approach as involving " empirical observations " which are " systematic, visible, explicit, and reproducible," [16] then any attack must, in effect, challenge the validity of scientific method, a difficult task indeed. A careful perusal of a recent summary of research findings reveals the interesting fact that analysts have studied groups as well as individuals (and at many levels from individual statesmen to the global system), have described individual events as well as observed regularities and included value studies among their concerns.[17] Hence one set of objections is revealed as nothing more than an arbitrary use of definitions for polemical purposes. It is true, and will always remain true, that if we define an approach so as to

[13] R. A. Dahl, " The Behavioral Approach in Political Science: Epitaph for a Monument to a Successful Protest," 55 *American Political Science Review* (1961), pp. 763–772.

[14] K. W. Kim, " The Limits of Behavioral Explanation in Politics," 31 *The Canadian Journal of Economics and Political Science* (1965), pp. 315–327.

[15] *Ibid.* p. 316.

[16] S. D. Jones and J. D. Singer, *Beyond Conjecture in International Politics* (1972).

[17] *Ibid.* pp. 48, 84, 142, 146, 220.

exclude important subjects germane to an enquiry, that approach will be (by definition) deficient. If, however, we include all pertinent matters, the question of whether an approach is valid or fruitful tends to become a function of the adequacy of the data available and the ingenuity of the theorist. Nor is it necessary to demand, as Easton seems to do,[18] a genuine synthesis of social science disciplines bringing together generalisations concerning fundamental units of analysis. This demand is premature and too ambitious for our present state of knowledge. Rather, the demand should be that sources are specified and that the data used be explicit, systematic and reproducible. No more is required and surely no less.

If this modest proposal is taken as a starting point we can ask a more specific question: " In what ways can the behavioural sciences contribute to a study of international politics?" First, it is vital to make clear what they *cannot* do. They cannot provide a total approach to the subject. They can never *be* the study of international politics which occurs within particular structures under particular conditions.[19] They can, however, " contribute once relevant points of application have been identified." [20] The key questions then are posed, not in terms of absolutes, but rather in terms of what kinds of relevance such subjects have, and what the limits of relevance are for the study of international politics. In short, what can we learn from them, and how do they help us explain the phenomena?[21] A specific answer for social psychology is that it can contribute directly to the study of public opinion in the foreign-policy process, it can aid in studying individual decision-makers, it can provide concepts for the study of the processes of negotiation and decision-making, and it can aid in an examination of the assumptions of theory building and policy recommendations.[22]

If we look at some of the issues raised by social psychologists who have tried to apply their knowledge to international politics, we find the following: aware that public opinion on foreign policy is a compound of ignorance and apathy, scholars go on to discriminate among *effective* public opinion, attempts to manipulate opinion,

---

[18] D. Easton, " The Current Meaning of ' Behavioralism '," in J. E. Charlesworth (ed.), *Contemporary Political Analysis* (1967). See also H. Elau (ed.), *Behavioralism in Political Science* (1969).
    The key methodological points are that (1) units of study (decisions, systems, etc.) do not define a field of study since they are selected by the theory which postulates them, and (2) since all theories from the social sciences are partial and incomplete, they are eclectic when approaching empirical problems out of sheer necessity. (See S. Greer, " Sociology and Political Science," in J. M. Litsit (ed.), *Politics and the Social Sciences* (1969), pp. 54–55. Greer argues that there are only two basic analytical schemes for the study of human behaviour—the psychological and the sociological.
[19] This point is made with clarity and force by H. Kelman (ed.), *International Behavior, a Social-Psychological Analysis* (1965), p. 31.
[20] *Ibid.* p. 31.   [21] *Ibid.* p. 579.   [22] *Ibid.* p. 580.

constraints perceived by the decision-makers and so on. In short, they move to delimit the study of opinion formation and its impact on decision-making. In the study of individuals, they do not fall into the trap of equating decision-making with the idiosyncratic behaviour of individuals, but rather they place such persons in the context of the roles which they play in the machinery of State, the images and motives which are national, or élitist, or personal in character and, in the process, throw light on the context and processes within which decisions are made.[23] Thus, the analysis is as much concerned with behaviour in terms of roles as it is with the behaviour of persons and eliminates the superficial critique that such studies either reify the State or deal only with unique individuals. In fact they deal both with the structured nature of behaviour (and hence the constraints on freedom of action) as well as with the distinctive type of behaviour that occurs in the special circumstances which provide freedom of action in cases of vital national interest.[24]

III—EXPERIMENTAL FINDINGS
AND THEIR PROBLEMS

A good deal of legitimate criticism of the uses to which behavioural studies are often put relates to the indiscriminate employment of experimental findings. These criticisms apply not only to experiments on inter-personal and inter-group relations but also to efforts to reproduce in the laboratory some of the basic conditions of inter-national relations.[25] It is pointed out that a sharp difference exists between laboratory conditions and real-life situations, that participants in simulated studies are often students with no experience of actual decision-making dealing with make-believe stakes, and that the results, therefore, are useless.[26]

Like much of life, these criticisms tend to be valid in what they affirm but less reliable in what they deny. The key issues in evaluating the experimental approach would seem to be the following: Has the experimenter isolated the crucial variables which govern the relation-ship in question? If so, does the experiment incorporate the important conditions of the situation which affect the factors being studied?[27] No general answer can be given to these two questions. Each experi-ment has to be evaluated in light of them and this means, among

---

[23] *Ibid.* Chaps. 2–8; see particularly pp. 586–594 for a concise summary of the approaches used. For an imaginative and suggestive use of the concept of "images" placed in the full context of international politics, see R. Jervis, *The Logic of Images in International Relations* (1970).   [24] *Ibid.* p. 591.

[25] Some of the best experiments have been done by M. Sherif (*et al.*), *Intergroup Conflict and Cooperation* (1961); on simulation experiments see H. Guetzkow (*et al.*), *Simulation in International Relations* (1963).

[26] Kelman, *op. cit.* in note 19, above, at pp. 596–597.   [27] *Ibid.* p. 597.

other things, that *only co-operative work is likely to prove fruitful in this area of research* since the evaluation and testing of experiments requires expert knowledge of both international relations and social psychology. More important, no laboratory results can have universal validity, but rather each generalisation must be " re-examined for each specific problem." [28] This means, in effect, that experimental results can be used to generate hypotheses in a given area of research if and only if significant variables are identified, if crucial conditions are reproduced and if results are tested in the real world and results are integrated with more general research. Needless to say, very few studies meet these demanding conditions. Every article describing experiments designed for application in international relations should bear the inscription " use with care and caution."

These admonitions, however, are not meant to disparage or discourage the application of theories and hypotheses generated in behavioural studies to international relations. They are intended to warn against direct application in cases which presumably pose dangers of sharply different conditions. Nor should advocates of more traditional approaches rejoice concerning the difficulties described herein, since their own work is subject to exactly the same limitations. They, too, must make assumptions about psychological processes, whether about individuals or about policies. All too often they put forward mere analogies as if they were general models, and generalise airily across decades of time in a manner which ignores radically changed conditions.[29] In short, no matter what approach is used, the same problems of constructing demonstrable knowledge remain.

It will be realised at once that the issues posed by the application of behavioural science findings to international relations go to the very foundations of philosophy—to the nature of truth itself. The methods of the behavioural sciences must ultimately stand or fall by a basically pragmatic test: Do they attain their intended purposes of explaining, predicting or controlling the world? [30] In evaluating their claims to do so we must remember that their propositions are only *plausible*, not certain, *tentatively* acceptable in the light of the evidence, and ultimately *defeasible*.[31] If these criteria are kept in mind

---

[28] *Ibid.* p. 599.

[29] A classic book which contains all of these methodological errors is H. J. Morgenthau, *Politics Among Nations* (5th ed., 1973).

[30] For a short but brilliant analysis of the logical issues involved, see N. Rescher, *The Primacy of Practice* (1973), especially pp. 3, 14–16, 42–43 and 66–67.

[31] *Ibid.* pp. 14–15. This view of truth does not require us to deny that human values are involved in either the derivation or application of theories. Clearly the very notions of " control," " survival " and so on are derived from man's view of himself. See M. Hesse, " In Defence of Objectivity," 58 *Proceedings of the British Academy* (1972), pp. 275–292. Objective knowledge demands neither the total separation of man from nature nor the converse.

we can offer a modest " yes, they can help us to some degree, particularly since they remind us that much of what passes for knowledge is mere speculation and therefore should be treated with caution, especially since such speculations form the basis for decisions which seriously affect the lives of ordinary citizens."

It is vital to grasp the fact that evaluation of empirical studies in behavioural science requires an intimate knowledge and study of the materials discussed in the literature. General collections of pro- positions are not likely to prove of much use, consisting as they do of a bewildering variety of hypotheses at different levels of analysis with little or no effeort being made to clarify the behavioural assumptions on which the hypotheses rest.[32]

Some idea of the very real difficulties which lie in the path of applying empirical studies to problems in international relations will be revealed if we examine in detail work which has been done in the area of decision-making under conditions of uncertainty. This is an area of great potential interest to students of international politics, particularly that part of it which deals with risk-taking behaviour since it is obvious that statesmen do take decisions which involve risks. Hence if studies revealed any patterns of risk-taking behaviour in typical situations, a good deal of light might be thrown on a variety of important political activities.[33]

In this general area pioneer work was done by Ward Edwards,[34] who conducted experiments on preferences among choices which differed in the probability of winning. His models assumed that a gambler will choose a bet with the maximum value and that this alternative can be calculated by multiplying the value of each out- come by the probability that the outcome will occur and summing these products over all outcomes. Among his findings was the fact that subjects had definite preferences for betting at some probability levels rather than others. Thus, at first blush, there appeared to be a certain measure of stability in what might be called a psychological

[32] See *e.g.* H. R. Alker and P. G. Bock," Propositions About International Relations," *Political Science Annual* 1972, pp. 385–495. B. Berelson and G. A. Steiner, *Human Behavior, an Inventory of Scientific Findings* (1964), is more easily used since the scientific assumptions on which the propositions rest are clearly indicated. However, very few hypotheses relate directly to international situations.

[33] It should be pointed out that the following section does *not* deal with mathematical theories of decision-making. These attempt to arrive at methods of reaching optimum decisions by eliminating subjective elements through the use of formal rules. For a short, incisive treatment of some of the main theories, see D. J. White, *Decision Theory* (1964).

[34] W. Edwards, " Probability-Preferences in Gambling," 66 *American Journal of Psychology* (1953), pp. 349–364 and that same *Journal*, Vol. 67 (1954), pp. 441–452; also his " The Prediction of Decisions Among Bets," 51 *Journal of Experimental Psychology* (1955), pp. 201–214, and " Subjective Probabilities Inferred from Decisions," 69 *Psychological Review* (1962), pp. 109–135.

scale of probabilities, a scale which did not correspond to a strict mathematical concept of probability. Other experiments showed that psychological probability exceeded mathematical (*i.e.* statistical) probability at low values, and is exceeded by the latter at high values. The findings applied to sophisticated people familiar with the mathematical theory of probability as well as naïve subjects.[35] Hence, subjects did not maximise utility since, no matter what the size of the prize, they paid for prizes with small probabilities too generously and took prizes with large probabilities as bargains.

If additional experiments repeating Edwards' tests had confirmed his findings, the hopeful student of international politics could have gone happily away to see if he could discover similar patterns in international decisions. Unfortunately, the waters were muddied by other persons who tested Edwards' models for successful prediction with only moderate success.[36] Other scholars argued that, in addition to probability preferences, people's attitudes to risk involved what are called variance preferences—that is the amount of deviation in outcomes from the average amount obtained by betting. For example, an even money bet of 5 dollars and one at 1 dollar both have an expected value of zero but the potential losses are different in the two cases. In a series of tests Edwards [37] found shifts in preferences among bets which could be attributed to the variance factor. Once again a potentially clarifying result was blurred when the experiments were repeated with very different results. Slovic found that, while some persons had shifts in preferences which corresponded to Edwards' findings, others had preferences which were stable at different probability levels, while still others had probability preferences which shifted systematically as the variance of the bets changed.[38] Results, therefore, were inconsistent with no clear-cut hypothesis explaining the relation between probability preferences and high-risk taking. In short, observations of choices did not distinguish the extent to which risk taking was determined by individual differences in the *perception* of risk or by differences in the *reaction* to that perceived risk.[39] A similar problem confronts anyone trying to explain the reactions of Kennedy and Khrushchev in the Cuba Missile Crisis and much the same conclusion emerges. The evidence does not permit us to specify unequivocally whether the decisions taken turned on the perception of, or the reaction to,

[35] M. G. Preston and P. Baratta, " An Experimental Study of the Auction-Value of an Uncertain Outcome," 61 *American Journal of Psychology* (1948), pp. 183–193.

[36] Dean G. Pruitt, " Pattern and Level of Risk in Gambling Decisions," 69 *Psychological Review* (1962), pp. 187–201.

[37] Edwards, *op. cit.* in note 34 above (1954), at pp. 441 *et seq.*

[38] Paul Slovic, " Assessment of Risk Taking Behavior," 61 *Psychological Bulletin* (1964), pp. 220–233.　　　　　　　　　　　　　　[39] *Ibid.* p. 229.

perceived risks, let alone in exactly what manner and proportion. The truth is that risk is a concept with many dimensions. No one has fully explored that part of it which deals with preferences involving expected value, variance and probability in the precise sense that all three variables have been manipulated in a systematic manner.[40] Results are inconsistent, at least in part because the measures used tap different dimensions of the behaviour, and because the experiments tried are often too crude to cope with the facts. If this applies to the relatively simple experiments surveyed, how much more difficult it would be to structure into the laboratory situation the kind of fear which must be present when decisions are taken in a great crisis involving the potential use of nuclear weapons. Clearly one's estimate of risk must be affected by the level of fear involved and this latter in turn must be related in some fashion to the probabilities of miscalculation and the magnitude of the disaster which would occur if such weapons were ever used.[41]

Some conception of the distance between the experimental results obtained in the above literature and the real world of international politics can be glimpsed if we now examine a theory of risk-taking derived from an actual study of several major crises.[42]

Let us now turn to the actual course of history and ask whether various crises show similar or different patterns in particular periods of history, what precisely the similarities or differences are, and, whether, for convenience, they can be ordered into a useful typology.

It should be said at once that the choice of crisis periods and of the factors selected as crucial will be decisive for the fruitfulness of the analysis. Bell, for example, regards the inter-war and post-war periods as comparable on the ground that the essential factors—the nature of the decision-makers, the communication between them, and the means available to make decisions effective—were not widely different in the two periods.[43] On the very face of it, this comparison seems odd, since one would have thought significant differences existed between the two eras in terms of two of the criteria she selects.

[40] For additional material, see J. Cohen and I. Christensen, *Information and Choice* (1970); and J. Cohen, *Psychological Probability* (1972). These studies add a great deal to our understanding of risk but, because they show clearly the complexity of risk-taking behaviour, they need to be used with great caution. See *e.g.* Cohen and Christensen, pp. 74 *et seq.* for an evaluation of some experiments. They show that among the variables ignored are: the degree of interest in the gambling situation, belief in luck, the extent to which skill can be used, all of which may significantly affect psychological probability or utility significantly. A model based solely on the latter two factors (probability and utility) could therefore be of little value. Hence experimental evidence teaches us to be wary in our use of common-sense concepts.
[41] J. Cohen and M. Hansel, *Risk and Gambling* (1956). The authors suggest that the estimate of risk is directly proportionate to the level of fear.
[42] C. B. Joynt, " The Anatomy of Crisis," in this *Year Book*, Vol. 28 (1974), pp. 15–22.   [43] C. Bell, *The Conventions of Crisis* (1971), p. 17.

Certainly no risk-taker comparable to Hitler has emerged on the international scene as yet, and although communications may not differ all that much, the variation in means available do differ enormously. Bell attempts to get around this discrepancy by drawing a strained analogy between the present fear of nuclear war and the inter-war concern about the potential devastation available through conventional bombing.

Her analysis thus slides over some of the key differences in the two periods. The differences centre around the speed, scale and certainty of the destruction available to decision-makers and amount to a radical change in the nature of deterrence. It was possible to argue, in the inter-war period, that while the costs of war would be very great indeed, the gains from war would produce a balance of advantage. Hence, everything turned on whether a significant lead in military capabilities could be exploited, first diplomatically, and then in the crucible of battle itself. In the conduct of crises, this meant that deterrence was ineffective relative to the superior side, and crisis management was virtually a synonym for surrender. In short, superior capabilities could be translated into political gains; whereas, in the nuclear era, the strength of deterrent forces tends to produce conditions of stalemate. Nuclear deterrence cannot, except under special conditions, be used as a compellent.

Further, when Bell argues that identical weight has been given by decision-makers to the penalties of war throughout the post-1945 period, one feels that important distinctions between crises have been blurred. I would argue, on the contrary, that symmetrical expectations on penalties existed only in the period from the Cuba Missile Crisis to the present. In the 1945–53 period, the United States had a monopoly of both the nuclear bomb and the means of its delivery, and hence American decision-makers could and did feel that, in a grave crisis, they held the high cards. This effect operated throughout the 1953–62 period and may even have played a critical role in the Cuba Missile Crisis itself. Symmetrical expectations do become important in the age of mutual deterrence but only as between parties with substantial second-strike capabilities.

All this indicates that we are unlikely to discover general patterns and regularities which can be applied to crises regardless of the time frame in which they occur. Rather, we must look for limited patterns, transitory regularities, which are temporarily restricted within definite bounds.[44] The most fruitful approach will be to regard risk-taking as the central focus with military capability as the key factor in

---

[44] For an extended analysis of this general problem, see C. B. Joynt and N. Rescher, " On Explanation in History," 68 *Mind* 383–388, and by the same authors, " The Problem of Uniqueness in History," *History and Theory*, Vol. 1, pp. 156–157.

deterrence. Hence, the major time division for purposes of comparison should be between pre-nuclear and nuclear crises, with a further subdivision based on the relative capabilities of the parties.

This comparison between behavioural studies of risk-taking and an inductive approach based on the studies of actual cases has several important lessons of which the following are of interest: (1) the variables in the process are complex and experiments reveal this to us with clarity; (2) experimental results cannot be transferred directly to international politics without dangerous over-simplification; (3) behavioural studies tend not to be time-specific, whereas the political realm is embarrassingly so. One conclusion, therefore, is that we must be our own theorists.

This does *not* mean, however, that helpful insights might not be gained in theory-building by using behavioural techniques as a supplement to, and a check on, the empirically derived crisis model. For example, it would be most interesting and enlightening if a group of simulation experiments were devised to test the validity of the model both in terms of its own internal consistency and in terms of modifications suggested by the response of subjects. It is evident that any such experiment would gain in reality if participants in the first instance were experienced decision-makers familiar with the uses and effects of weapons. Their responses could be checked over the whole range of the model and then compared with results based on the responses of naïve subjects whose expertise was minimal. One suspects that a reasonably good test of the model's general accuracy would be obtained and some more or less severe changes indicated by the pattern of replies. Conflicts between the theory and the simulation could then be dealt with by reviewing the basic historical data for new evidence in the light of discrepancies, refining the model accordingly or, perhaps, abandoning it completely for a better model suggested to the experimenters in the light of the simulation. It is in some such interplay between real world models and laboratory tests that many of the contributions of the behavioural sciences can best be realised.[45]

An equally interesting source for the generation of hypotheses and their testing would be to compare State behaviour with the behaviour of gangs in a field situation. Even a tentative look at one major study of gangs reveals some startling similarities in the two sets of behaviour.[46] A gang, like a nation State, is a conflict group which develops through strife and thrives on warfare; its status is maintained through fighting; it defends or attacks territory, endures crisis escalation;

[45] An excellent example of a fruitful interplay between behavioural studies and case histories is R. Little, *Intervention. External Involvement in Civil War* (1975).

[46] F. M. Thrasher, *The Gang* (1927). See especially pp. 54–56, 173–175 and 183–184. Also H. A. Block and A. Niederhoffer, *The Gang* (1958).

fears intervention by third parties; engages in cycles of conflict and accommodation; forms alliances and federations; enters into treaties of peace, and so on. Both groups are engaged in a struggle for survival in a hostile world and are caught up in the quest for power with a drive to dominate and manipulate others. It is difficult to believe that a co-operative study comparing and contrasting the behaviour of these two groups would not reveal a great deal of interest, particularly in how crises develop, subside or escalate into open war, the specific conditions which lead to negotiations and settlement, the part played in conflict by considerations of prestige and status and, finally, as a test of differing theories of conflict resolution.

Behavioural studies can make a contribution at a different level entirely than any mentioned thus far. We refer to a host of studies on the nature of aggression [47] dealt with by ethnologists, psychologists, sociologists and anthropologists. These are attempts to get at the roots of behaviour, to understand and analyse those aspects of experience which trigger, increase or diminish aggression.

These findings are of peculiar relevance because they go to the heart of the question whether human aggression is somehow a part of our animal ancestry and therefore in some sense inevitable. Lorenz argues that aggression is a product of natural selection, that it is spontaneous in the sense that it results from internal drives which must find expression. As such, it is virtually unmodifiable. His critics [48] accuse Lorenz of using biased examples, of misinterpreting the evidence, of drawing false parallels between animals and man and of using a false dichotomy between behaviour which is genetically determined and behaviour which is derived from experience. The latter point is of great importance for it poses the issue as to the extent to which genetic endowment or the environment is responsible for differences which exist between individuals or between species. [49]

The present state of our knowledge does not apparently permit a clear, unequivocal answer to this last question. For one thing ethnologists keep telling us that no two species behave alike. [50] For another, it is very difficult to distinguish between variables within the

---

[47] The following will be found extremely useful: K. Lorenz, *On Aggression* (1966); D. Morris, *The Naked Ape* (1967); N. Tinbergen, " On War and Peace in Animals and Man," 160 *Science*, Nr. 3835 (June 28, 1968), pp. 1411–1418; E. B. McNeil, *The Nature of Human Conflict* (1965); R. A. Hinde, " The Nature of Aggression," *New Society*, Vol. 9 (March 2, 1967), pp. 302–304; R. A. Hinde, " Aggression Again," *New Society*, Vol. 11 (February 20, 1969), pp. 291–292; J. H. Masserman (ed.), *Violence and War*, *Science and Psychoanalysis*, Vol. 6 (1963).

[48] L. M. F. Ashley Montagu (ed.), *Man and Aggression* (1968).

[49] R. A. Hinde, *op. cit.* in note 47, above, at p. 291.

[50] N. Tinbergen, *op. cit.* in note 47, above, at p. 1414.

animal and variables in the environment. No generally accepted conclusions are available for basic questions such as: Is readiness to attack constant or variable? Could fighting be reduced by reducing population density or provocative stimuli? Tinbergen points out that animals do avoid bloodshed. Aggression rarely occurs in a pure form but is one of two aspects of adaptive behaviour. For example, members of a territorial species divide available living space after which they attack intruders but outside its home range the species withdraws when it meets an established owner.[51] Tinbergen is inclined to believe that man still carries within him the animal heritage of group territoriality, which cannot be eliminated by different ways of up-bringing. If this is so, it is obvious that our historical experience has reinforced this behaviour since all living space is divided on national and tribal lines. The issue then comes down to whether the behaviour associated with group territoriality can be modified sufficiently to permit human survival in an age when " attack " involves the potential use of weapons of mass destruction. The question is of transcendent importance in that, if man's ability to adjust his behaviour is completely outpaced by historically determined changes in his environment (particularly the population explosion and the development of weapons), the chances for human survival are extremely small.

Anthropologists, while not denying the survival value of aggression in terms of the functions of spacing out populations, selection of the fittest mates for propagation and protection against predators, argue that we should begin with the patterns of violent behaviour formed by culture.[52] In this view man is a domesticated caged animal in the sense that he is confined by nature and culture. He does have bio-logically learned propensities towards aggression, but he differs in important ways from other animals. For example, he is not protected by instinctive responses which terminate ritual battles. More im-portant, he has a choice of viewing other men as being of the same species or as predators or prey. While it is true that no wild species displays the savagery of man in feuds, blood vengeance or torture, it remains the case that man can alter his cultural cage and regard other men as brothers entitled to protection. In short, man can restructure his culturally-elaborated categories including the concept of war.

For the anthropologist war is a cultural invention which involves the social sanctioning of killing members of an opposing group. It does not have a specific biological base independent of culture. Rather, it is a functional response to a variety of identifiable condi-tions. All the evidence from anthropology suggests that a functioning

⁵¹ *Ibid.* p. 1413.

⁵² For a short summary see M . Mead, " Violence in the Perspective of Culture History," in J. H. Masserman (ed) ,*Violence and War* (1963).

invention will be used until rendered obsolete by another invention, by the disappearance of the function it performed, or by becoming itself disfunctional. The question whether war has reached this latter point or not becomes at this juncture a matter for statesmen and peoples to decide. If the answer is " yes "—as it surely must be on any objective analysis of the evidence—we are left with the problems of how best to modify violence in the short-run and finally how to eliminate it from inter-group relations.

Once again we will find that the behavioural sciences can be of considerable assistance in approaching these tasks. Only a few examples will be cited but they will indicate the usefulness of a multi-disciplinary approach both in terms of a division of labour and the advantages to be gained from cross-fertilisation through new ideas and concepts. Promiscuous eclecticism is the most preferable orientation in these areas as in the studies previously referred to.

IV—CONTROLLED COMMUNICATION AND CONFLICT RESOLUTION

One of the most provocative and interesting developments in recent work has been an emphasis on controlled communication as a technique of conflict resolution.[53] The argument is that there has been a progression in the modern world from direct judgment and enforcement to methods which draw on the points of view of the parties by techniques which inject new information concerning perception, escalation, interpretation, assessment of values and costs in a manner designed to assist in conflict settlement.[54] This view challenges the traditional realist view of international politics as based on State relations—the so-called " billiard ball " model—and the assumptions about conflict on which it rests. In particular it challenges the view which holds international society to be in a state of anarchy in which conflicts can only be settled or contained within a framework of threats and violence.[55] Hence legal rules as a restraint on aggression and intervention, sanctions enforced by law, arbitration, the control of conflicts by Great Powers or by supra-national institutions, are described as deficient methods or even as contributing to conflict. Instead, this view argues that conflict is a subjective condition and that resolution of conflict is possible by non-coercive means.

The assumption which underlies controlled communication is that conflict is a subjective phenomenon which occurs when accurate assessment of costs and values is prevented rather than a process

---

[53] J. W. Burton, Conflict and Communication (1969). Also *op. cit.* in note 4, above.
[54] Burton, *op. cit.* in note 53, above, at p. 174.
[55] *Ibid.* pp. 177–178.

produced by aggressive tendencies determined by power relations.[56] Aggressive behaviour is the result of a faulty appraisal of the total situation based on misperception by the parties in which distortion, negative feedback, reinforcement and so on rigidify the conflict. What is required is to transform a power relationship into a problem-solving one. To do this the following procedures are crucial: each step must be fully under control of the parties with no obligation to accept settlement in advance; the role of third parties is to explain conflict in terms of origins, to expose the misperceptions which exist and to provide an accurate assessment of the costs of conflict relative to the goals sought. The conflict should be broken down into sub-disputes and, if necessary, as to the various factions involved. A key principle, therefore, is to resolve the conflict at local levels. Felt needs of the parties provide the framework for the exploration of possible solutions.

Basically, the aim is to move towards areas of functional co-operation which then provides the conditions for negotiations between the parties. Thus structural and institutional changes proceed from the level of the greatest transactions and are not imposed from the top.

At a world level the argument is that the " billiard ball " model promotes the status of authorities at the price of inhibiting political and social change by means of restrictive intervention through a threat system. Controlled communication, on the other hand, is based on the trends in world society which emphasise interdependence, smaller, non-aligned political units and the growth of functional institutions. In sum, the new approach looks towards the transformation of conflict into problem-solving based on the need to assist and adjust to change.

How are we to evaluate the basic validity of this contribution to conflict resolution? A number of ideas suggest themselves at the outset. Undoubtedly our perceptions of reality do tend to create the reality which they attempt to describe. If we perceive a world of hostile and aggressive States we tend to behave accordingly, finding it necessary to create threat structures in the shape of weapons and alliances to deal with these evils. But it does seem to be playing with words to assert that such perceptions are entirely misconceived. Studies of perception do show that people treat inputs from the environment in ways which involve the application of concepts to the data and the way the mind conceptualises is determined in part by what has resulted from past interaction. This is then modified by failures in pay-off when interacting with the world.[57] Who is to decide whether a particular model, which has been developed on the

---

[56] Burton, *op. cit.* in note 4, above, at p. 13.
[57] *Knowledge and Necessity: Royal Institute of Philosophy Lectures* (1970), p. 64.

basis of such a process is a more rational inference from the data of experience than another? From a strictly scientific standpoint Burton's model of perception is no more, and no less, subjective than the billiard-ball model which he rejects. Where, then, can we turn for analytical help? While it is true that no political facts exist independently of our perception of them, the achievement of independent criteria to determine the *extent* of our misperception is no easy task. Earlier in this chapter we suggested that the practical test should be the success of theory in the effective guidance of action in the light of a governing purpose. That is to say, the test will be which model is more conducive to the achievement of the practical objective—in this case conflict resolution. By this test, Burton's model would seem to provide many helpful hints and insights. There is a great deal of empirical evidence to support his major contention that intense conflict impairs perception and communication, that it limits the capacities of the parties for profound creative solutions, that competent and trustworthy third parties are necessary to illuminate the conflict, establish ground rules and suggest alternative solutions.[58]

If, however, the practical objective is not simply to resolve conflict but to resolve it on one's own terms, or, if one's objective is to expand one's position of power and influence through coercive techniques, then Burton's model fails lamentably. Indeed, he is to be found in the company of Woodrow Wilson who argued the Burtonian thesis a long time ago. " Peace," Wilson said, " could be secured if issues were settled not by diplomats or politicians eager to serve their own interests but by dispassionate scientists—geographers, ethnologists, economists—who had made studies of the problems involved." [59] The world has really made very little progress towards Wilson's goal in the intervening period. Some of this lack of progress can no doubt be attributed directly to misperceptions of the sort which Burton describes. A good deal of it, however, is no doubt due to other causes altogether, particularly the insistence of men and groups that power and favourable circumstances should be used for selfish purposes and to gain maximum advantages. This is, no doubt, wrong-headed and, in today's world, extremely short-sighted. It is also a fact about the nature of reality, and as long as it is so there will be room for diplomacy based on pressure and threats, and men will continue to rely at least in part on the uses of violence.

Both theory and reality, however, combine in the study of conflict to warn us that the old ways are becoming increasingly outmoded.

[58] B. R. Brown, " Reflections on Missing the Broadside of a Barn," 9 *The Journal of Applied Behavioral Science*, Nr. 4 (1973), pp. 450–458; B. Brown and J. Rubin, *The Social Psychology of Bargaining and Negotiation* (1973); Roger Fisher (ed.), *International Conflict and Behavioral Science* (1964), pp. 91–109.

[59] R. S. Baker, *Woodrow Wilson and World Settlement*, Vol. 1, p 112.

Science, technology and nuclear weapons all point in the direction of functional obsolescence for the organised violence we call war. Burton and the behavioural sciences point us towards the future to a world as yet unborn when the arts of conflict resolution and problem-solving are taken more seriously by men and nations.[60]

[60] The most thorough and careful analysis of conflict resolution I have yet found is M. Deutsch, *The Resolution of Conflict* (1973). The overall results support the basic approach of the power-politics school on a number of counts: harmful and dangerous elements drive out those which tend to keep conflicts within bounds, a heavy reliance on threats, coercion and deception, the importance of enhancing one's own power and minimising the power of an opponent and so on. It does support several of Burton's theses concerning the role of communication but in a much more restricted fashion than Burton's model asserts. General statements concerning the futility of coercion or deterrence are simply not in accord with the evidence. Specific conditions are all important. Empirical case studies of deterrence confirm this latter point. See A. L. George and R. Smoke, *Deterrence in American Foreign Policy: Theory and Practice* (1974).

WHY OUGHT TREATIES TO BE KEPT?

By

HIDEMI SUGANAMI

THE argument of this paper is based on a number of assumptions of which the following two are most crucial. In the first place, treaties are assumed to be a sub-species of promise. A treaty is thus regarded as a promise made between States, not distinguishable logically from promises made between individuals, or groups of individuals other than States. Secondly, promise-making is regarded as an institution, constituted by a conventional principle that the use of certain words, such as, " I hereby promise to do x," creates an obligation, within that institution, for the speaker to do x. Thus, in the following discussion the obligation to do x within that institution is treated as distinguishable from a less well-defined obligation of similar type: *e.g.*, the obligation not to betray the expectation which one may be said to have induced in the minds of the hearers when one has unilaterally declared one's intention to do x, or when one has hinted at the possibility that one might do x in future.

These assumptions may in themselves be mistaken. However, it is the contention of this paper that, to the extent that these assumptions are accepted, the normative foundation of the principle of *pacta sunt servanda* at the international level can be found in the combination of two factors: (i) the "natural necessity" of the *intra-societal* institution of promise-making for the fulfilment of basic human needs; (ii) the logical rules governing the use of moral concepts, which compels us to regard as morally right only a certain type of principle, and not others. The logic of moral concepts cannot by itself establish why the institution of promise-making, and the very notion of promise, need ever to have been invented. On the other hand, the thesis of " natural necessity " (i) cannot be applied well to international relations, and (ii) needs to be complemented by the consideration of the logic of moral concepts in order to show why it is morally wrong to take a parasitic advantage of that institution.

In the following, I shall first examine the applicability to international relations of the thesis of " natural necessity " with reference to the idea of the "minimum content of Natural Law," developed by H. L. A. Hart from the writings of Hobbes and Hume. I shall then go on to show how the logic of moral concepts, as systematically exposed by R. M. Hare, forces us to acknowledge that the demands of national interest cannot override a statesman's moral obligation to observe treaties. This will be followed by a critical examination of the various versions of the " realist " thesis on the question of international morality, to which this paper is diametrically opposed.

The present paper has grown out of dissatisfaction with the idea, predominant among International Relations specialists, that their subject-matter can be studied satisfactorily within the narrow confine of " ethically neutral " empirical observations. It also stems from disagreement with the view that normative questions are beyond the reach of rational argument, or that they would best be left to moral philosophers. The possibility of rational argument in normative questions, I hope, will become apparent in the following. As regards the second point about the academic division of labour, it must be admitted that it is dangerous for a specialist in one field to ignore his own jurisdiction, so to speak, and to interfere with a problem in another sphere. However, the cumulative effect of inter-disciplinary non-interference is potentially even more disastrous, for once the legitimacy of a disciplinary jurisdiction is established, a whole generation of students may remain unaware of the vitally relevant questions outside of it.

I—THE MINIMUM CONTENT OF NATURAL LAW

Hart, who characterises his book on the concept of law as " an essay in descriptive sociology," first draws attention to a set of contingent facts about man's nature, and the nature of his environment.[1] Thus, it is said that men are neither angels nor devils, are mutually vulnerable, roughly equal in their power, and have a desire to live in an environment in which resources are limited. These are contingent factual conditions which make social norms, such as positive law and conventional morality, both necessary and possible.

Under such circumstances, Hart argues, it is rational for men wishing to live together to adopt a certain set of principles regarding their relationships. This set of basic principles will prohibit killing, prescribe mutual forbearance and compromises, establish the institution of property (though not necessarily individual property), regulate the transfer, exchange or sale of goods, recognise promises as a source of obligation, and authorise sanctions for the enforcement of such rules.

This line of argument, however, does not apply well to international relations, and can even be used to highlight the contrast between the domestic and international conditions. In international relations, the vital factors of the mutual vulnerability of the units, and the rough equality of their power, have been lacking to a large extent,

---

[1] The following is based on H. L. A. Hart, *The Concept of Law* (1961), pp. 189 *et seq.*

and so the sovereign States have not had the rationale for developing international law along the lines of Hart's Natural Law. Most significantly, international society has been unable to develop a system of law based on organised sanctions. Moreover, Hart's line of argument cannot be applied convincingly to international relations even where his Natural Law principle *does* find its counterpart in positive international law, as in the case of *pacta sunt servanda*.

In the case of individuals, it can be conceded that their need for food, clothes and shelter, in an environment of limited resources, would make it rational for men to adhere to some scheme for the division of labour among them, and that this in turn would make it rational for them to adopt the institution of promise-making, as a method of creating obligations as circumstances require. Moreover, it may even be conceded that, given human nature and the nature of man's environment, the status of " natural necessity," or some such title, must be accorded to the rationality involved in setting up the institution of promise-making.[2]

By contrast, it seems difficult to argue conclusively that an international division of labour, and the international adoption of the principle of *pacta sunt servanda*, are as essential for the fulfilment of the basic human needs as are the division of labour, and the institution of promise-making, within a domestic society. If the principle of *pacta sunt servanda* at the international level is helpful for the fulfilment of the basic human needs, it is nevertheless uncertain whether this principle is required with the same degree of urgency as is the institution of promise-making within the domestic sphere. Thus, it seems doubtful whether the international adoption of the principle of *pacta sunt servanda* can be said to be dictated by the same *" minimum content* of Natural Law."

To this it may be objected that some domestic societies, especially underdeveloped ones, are unable to fulfil the basic human needs of their citizens without relying on aid, and hence on international intercourse based on the principle of *pacta sunt servanda*. It may also be argued that the growing interdependence of domestic economies has, even for the developed countries, rendered obsolete the idea, traditionally associated with Hobbes and Spinoza, that States are less vulnerable, and more self-sufficient, than individuals.

Such assertions, if accepted fully, will force us to acknowledge the conclusion that, given the present conditions of the world, international intercourse, based on the principle of *pacta sunt servanda*,

---

[2] It is important to note that by " natural necessity " is not meant " casual necessity." The " necessity " to include Hart's " minimum content of Natural Law " in a system of positive social norms is " natural," not in the sense that human beings are pre-determined, neurophysiologically or otherwise, to do so, but in the sense that, in their habit of teleological thinking, it appears to them " natural " to fulfil this necessity.

among others, has become more decisively vital for the fulfilment of basic human needs than ever before.

Two points still remain unclear, however. First, given the growing interdependence between domestic economies, it still is not clear whether, in the fulfilment of basic human needs, the principle of *pacta sunt servanda* is as essential at the international level as it is at the domestic. Secondly, the present global conditions are themselves, arguably, the result of international intercourse. Thus, to claim that such a situation is vitally dependent on international intercourse, and therefore, on various international institutions such as the principle of *pacta sunt servanda*, is to beg the question as to the initial necessity, for the fulfilment of basic human needs, of international intercourse.

It may, finally, be argued that the international adoption of the principle under consideration is urgently required, not by the basic *human* needs perhaps, but clearly by the basic needs of *sovereign* States. To this it may be added that among the various needs of sovereign States, territorial integrity and political independence are of utmost importance, and that even a relatively strong military Power may sometimes have to rely on its allies for its security and independence. From this it may be argued that the principle of *pacta sunt servanda*, without which an alliance cannot be formed, is absolutely essential for the basic needs of sovereign States.

This argument is deceptive. A State is not a natural entity in the sense in which man is, and cannot logically be said to have basic needs in the same sense as can man. Nor can it be said to have basic needs independently of the basic needs of human beings. Thus what, in this context, we can safely say along Hart's thesis seems to be this: that the principle of *pacta sunt servanda* helps to satisfy what sovereign States themselves claim to be their " basic needs." To this it might be added that the system of sovereign States, despite its many shortcomings, helps in its turn to fulfil, at least to a tolerable degree, the basic needs of human beings. The degree to which the present system of sovereign States can help fulfil their basic needs is, however, a matter of controversy.[3]

In seeking to establish the normative foundation of the principle of *pacta sunt servanda*, one would be committing a methodological error if one were merely to examine the applicability of Hart's line of argument to international relations. The fundamental weakness of such an approach is that it presupposes the validity of a rule of promise-keeping and then tries to see whether the argument that establishes its validity holds true at the international level. However, we are not yet certain as to whether a *moral* validity can be accorded to the rule of promise-keeping as established by H. L. A. Hart. Thus,

---

[3] See, for instance, H. Bull, *The Anarchical Society* (1977), esp. Part 3.

even if the arguments, so far advanced, as regards the inapplicability of Hart's thesis to the international sphere are all mistaken, it will still not follow that his thesis as applied to international relations, can establish the moral nature of the principle in question.

II—THE LOGIC OF MORAL CONCEPTS

The procedure ought in fact to be reversed. As will become clearer presently, we have a reason to doubt the moral validity of Hart's Natural Law precepts *unless* they are formulated in such a way that would not exclude their international application. This point requires further classification and elaboration.

As we have seen, Hart's contention is that there is a natural necessity for a group of people living together to incorporate in their social norms a " minimum content of Natural Law," such as not to kill or not to break a promise. Insofar as these rules are said to have natural necessity only in relation to each particular group of persons living together, they must be regarded as implicitly containing a proviso, " within this society." Thus, Hart's Natural Law may in fact state: " Do not kill anyone in your society "; " Do not break a promise you make with other members of your society "; *etc*. These rules may in turn be taken to imply, " You are free to do whatever you like to those who do not belong to your society "; " You need to establish the institution of promise-making only within your own society, and within your society, you must keep your promises, but if you happen to have made a promise with a foreigner, you may break it whenever it is in your interest to do so." There is nothing in Hart's thesis, as such, to exclude such an interpretation of his Natural Law.

It may be objected that such chauvinistic principles are bound to incite retaliations from abroad. This, it may be argued, could result in the conquest, and enslavement or annihilation, of the upholders of those principles, on the grounds, perhaps, that they are barbarians. Under such circumstances, the basic human needs of the society, evidently, could not be said to have been fulfilled.

This, however, would be the worst possible contingency that could arise out of the adoption of the chauvinistic version of Hart's Natural Law. Such a contingency might be alleviated by incorporating in the minimum content of Natural Law provisions for military strength. In other words, there is nothing in Hart's thesis, as such, to stop a society from adopting internally a policy of cohesion, and externally an imperialistic, or at least Machiavellian, policy. To this extent, Hart's Natural Law cannot be said to satisfy moral criteria. This requires further clarification.

As has been systematically exposed by R. M. Hare, it is logically not permissible to say that x is right for me, but not for you, unless it is possible to show a morally relevant difference between us. This is the case because of a logical rule governing the use of the word, " right." According to this rule, if I state that x is right for someone, I am logically committing myself to a universal thesis such as the following: x is right for *anyone*, provided that he shares those characteristics of the first person, and of his circumstances, which I had taken into consideration when I said that x was right for him. The same point can be made with regard to the use of the word " ought." If I state that someone ought to do x, I am logically committed to a universal thesis such as the following: x ought to be done by anyone provided that he shares those characteristics of the first person, and of his circumstances, which have made me say that he ought to do x.[4]

Once such a logical character of the specifically moral use of words, such as " right " and " ought," has been noted, we are one step nearer to establishing the chauvinistic version of Hart's Natural Law to be lacking in moral quality. Let us examine the case of killing first.

The chauvinistic version of the prohibition of killing states: " Do not kill anyone in your society; but you can do whatever you like to those who do not belong to your society." Suppose I adhered to such a position, and felt like doing something nasty to a foreigner who happened to be passing through my society's (*de facto*) territory. According to my position, I can do whatever I like to him, including killing him: it is " right " for me to kill this outsider because he is an outsider and because I feel like killing him. It is important to note that here I am maintaining that *it is right for me to do this*, and not simply, *I feel like doing it*. Because of this, I am committing myself logically to a universal thesis such as the following: it is right for *anyone* in a society to kill *an outsider* if he feels like it. This, however, will put me in trouble, for I cannot seriously commit myself to saying that if *I* were a foreigner, it would be right for any indigenous member of a society to kill *me*. This, however, is one the logical implications of the universal thesis to which I am logically committed. And because I cannot *seriously* commit myself to saying this, I am prohibited from adhering to the position that it is right for me to kill this foreigner.

Precisely the same line of reasoning applies to the chauvinistic version of promise-keeping. I cannot adhere to the view that it is right for me to break a promise with a foreigner whenever it is in my interest to do so, merely because he is a foreigner, for I cannot *seriously* commit myself to saying that if I were a foreigner, it would

---

[4] See R. M. Hare, *Freedom and Reason* (1963).

be right for any member of the society to break a promise with me, when it is in his interest so to do.[5]

III—Pacta Sunt Servanda in International Relations

We can thus show the binding nature of promises made between individuals belonging to two different societies. The situation envisaged here assumes that the institution of promise-making has already been introduced to each society, and that two individuals from the different societies have come into contact with each other, and made an extended use of their respective institutions of promise-making. It is also assumed that the individuals in questions can communicate with each other, at least to the extent of being able to share an understanding as to what it is to make a promise. The logic of moral concepts compels us to argue that such a trans-societal promise, while not based on an established trans-societal institution, nor dictated by the basic human needs, is nevertheless binding in the same way as an intra-societal one.

It should at this stage be noted that, while the thesis of " natural necessity " explains why the intra-societal institution of promise-making, and the very notion of promise, need ever to have been introduced to each society, it does not explain why, given this institution, one ought not to be its parasite. The explanation is to be found in the following line of reasoning. One cannot seriously commit oneself to saying that it would be right for anyone to take a parasitic advantage of this institution against oneself, and thus one is prohibited from taking a parasitic advantage oneself against others. This is the case because of the logical rules governing the use of moral concepts such as " right " and " ought." Thus, similarly, if trans-societal promise-making ceases to be undertaken on an *ad hoc* basis, but becomes institutionalised, it is also clear that one ought not to take a parasitic advantage of that institution.

The normative foundation of the principle of *pacta sunt servanda* at the international level can be found in the logical extension of such an argument. Two societies can make an extended use, either of their respective intra-societal institution, or of their common trans-societal institution, and come to make a promise between themselves. If they do so, it is, from the viewpoint of morality, binding, in the same way either as an intra-societal promise, or as a trans-societal one. Moreover, once an inter-societal institution of promise-making has been introduced, a society ought not to take a parasitic advantage of it.

---

[5] The word " seriously " is emphasised, for, obviously, it is not difficult to *say* anything, if it is merely a matter of moving one's mouth and producing relevant sounds in the right order.

This reasoning must apply to the case of *pacta sunt servanda* at the international level, where the societies in question are sovereign States.

The principle of *pacta sunt servanda* is now well-established in international society. Thus, when two States conclude a treaty, they need neither make an extended use of their respective domestic institution of contract-making, nor resort to an analogy from a trans-societal system of law like the *jus gentium* of the Roman Empire.[6] Taking a parasitic advantage of this principle is morally unacceptable, not because it is wrong to disobey a well-established principle, but because we cannot seriously commit ourselves to saying that it would be right for the leader of a country, with which our country has concluded a treaty, to take a decision involving its violation against us whenever his country's interest demands it. Thus, a statesman, in taking a political decision, has a moral obligation to avoid violating a treaty to which his country is a party, and this moral obligation cannot be overridden by the demand of his country's national interest.[7]

IV—COUNTER-ARGUMENTS

To such a line of argument a number of counter-arguments can be anticipated, of which the following two may be dealt with here: (i) the morality of the institution of treaty-making, as such, has not been shown, and, until this is done, we cannot be certain that it is morally wrong to be a parasite of that institution; and, (ii) whether a treaty ought to be kept depends on the content of the treaty and the circumstances in question, and cases are conceivable where it is morally permissible to break a treaty. These counter-arguments are not in fact against the argument so far advanced, and, when accommodated, help to qualify and strengthen the thesis of this paper.

As regards the first point, it can readily be conceded that there are social institutions that are, as such, morally unacceptable. For example, the present system of ownership in international society, under which a sovereign State has an exclusive right to the natural resources available within its jurisdiction, may be shown to be unjust. It can also be admitted that there have existed morally dubious

---

[6] For the relationship between *jus gentium* and international law, see this author, " A Note on the Origin of the Word ' International,'" 4 *British Journal of International Studies*, Nr. 3 (October 1978).

[7] It is conceivable that a leader of a country A, contemplating breaking a treaty between A and another country, B, argues as follows: it is right for me to take a decision involving the breach of this treaty, not because the people of B are foreigners, but because they are black, they have hooked noses, etc. This kind of assertion can be countered as before. We may ask this leader whether he can seriously adhere to the view that such features of the people of B are morally relevant, if he realises that it is logically possible for him and his compatriots to have these features themselves. For a full discussion of this issue, see *op. cit.* in note 4, above, pp. 93 *et seq.*

elements in the traditional institution of treaty-making. Most notably, the traditional principle of positive international law, according to which a treaty concluded under duress, unlike a private contract made under threat, is nevertheless legally to be treated as valid, may be shown to be unjust.[8]

Thus, there may be one or more subsidiary principles, belonging to the positive law institution of treaty-making, that may be shown to be morally unacceptable. However, a set of principles, determining what is to count as a valid *pactum*, can logically be separated from the principle of *pacta sunt servanda* as such. The argument that there are morally unacceptable elements in the traditional positive law institution of treaty-making, can be countered by pointing out that the principle of *pacta sunt servanda* is to be supplemented and qualified by other moral considerations case by case.

It may conceivably be objected that by becoming a party to the principle of *pacta sunt servanda* at the international level, we are contributing indirectly to the perpetuation of the sovereign States system, which is, it may be held, a morally unacceptable way of organising mankind as a whole.

Supposing, for the sake of argument, that the system of sovereign States has been shown conclusively to be morally objectionable, it follows that any principle that contributes to the maintenance of the system is similarly condemned. However, the principle of *pacta sunt servanda* contributes to the maintenance of any system, regardless of whether its units are sovereign. Thus, even if the sovereign-States system were to be abolished, and the world reorganised, say, on the federal model, there still would remain some necessity for this principle. Moreover, were the sovereign-State system to be abolished, the institution of promise-making would be applied freely across the " border " and former sovereign entities would be bound by this, just as would be any individuals or groups of individuals existing on the globe.

As regards the second counter-argument we have noted, it must be pointed out that, when a statesman is said to have a moral duty to keep a treaty, it is not meant that he is absolutely unconditionally bound morally not to violate it. No moral prescriptions are of this form. It is even contrary to the very idea of morality to formulate a substantive moral rule and act on it stubbornly as a matter of

---

[8] Note, however, that Art. 52 of the Vienna Convention of the Law of Treaties of 1969 provides as follows: " A treaty is void if its conclusion has been procured by the threat or use of force in violation of the principles of international law embodied in the Charter of the United Nations." Although this Convention has not entered into force, this rule was approved by the International Court of Justice in the *Fisheries Jurisdiction* case. See M. Akehurst, *A Modern Introduction to International Law* (3rd ed., 1977), p. 131.

principle. Such an attitude will involve closing one's eyes entirely to morally relevant aspects of particular circumstances.

Therefore, it can readily be admitted that circumstances are conceivable in which it is morally permissible to break a treaty. Thus, for instance, if the effect of keeping a treaty would be to assist a State in outright aggression against another, this would make us say that in these circumstances it would be our moral duty to break the treaty. As has been pointed out, the principle of *pacta sunt servanda* must be supplemented and qualified by such moral considerations.

V—International Morality
and the Realist Critique

The argument so far advanced on the normative foundation of the principle of *pacta sunt servanda* is in direct opposition to the general view of morality in international relations, held in accordance with the " realist " mode of thought about international politics. Some further discussion on this point is necessary as the " realist " view of international morality is fairly commonly accepted, even among those who do not whole-heartedly adhere to the " realist " school of thought.

Three major types of argument are conceivable as being advanced by a " realist," or a thinker sympathetic to the " realist " outlook, on the question of morality in international relations in general, and on the principle of *pacta sunt servanda* in particular. In the first place, he may make a factual generalisation that statesmen rarely, if ever, sacrifice what they conceive to be their national interests for the sake of treaty-observance. Secondly, he may argue that, internationally, statesmen act " in a moral vacuum," and that their actions are, internationally, not subject to moral obligations at all. From this initial assumption, he may deduce that there can be no such thing as an obligation to observe a treaty. Thirdly, he may advance a moral argument and maintain that statesmen have moral obligations, attached to their offices, to serve their respective countries, and that those " public " obligations ought to override their personal moral views as well as international obligations. We shall examine these arguments in turn.

It is clear that the first of these arguments is not opposed logically to the argument of this paper. A factual generalisation as to what statesmen tend to do, even if correct, is of no logical consequence to the validity of our moral reasoning. The force of such factual generalisation lies not in its ability logically to refute our normative reasoning (for it is unable to do so), but in its tendency to show the practical limit to which moral reasoning, advanced by an academic thinker, is likely to affect statesmen's actual decision-making.

It can readily be conceded that academic writing, whether or not it advances moral reasoning, cannot by itself do much to influence government policy. However, the specific role of an academic writer *is* to advance a cogent argument, and as an academic writer he cannot hope to do anything else. Moreover, the extent to which thought influences action should not be underestimated. A policy is adopted and supported on the belief, however mistaken, that it is a right thing to do, and therefore the existence of a theoretical foundation that enables a critical examination of such a belief cannot be without some practical consequences.

The second type of argument, according to which statesmen are said to act, internationally, " in a moral vacuum," is highly ambiguous, and can be interpreted to mean a number of things.

When a " realist " formulates his argument in such a way, he may mean to point out that sovereign States, unlike the individuals within a domestic society, have not developed a set of norms worthy of the title of international morality. This, however, is a factual assertion as to the non-existence of a set of " positive " social norms in the international sphere. The existence or otherwise of " positive " social norms can be established by an empirical investigation as to what in fact is thought by the members of a society to be right. Normative reasoning is logically independent of the result of such an empirical enquiry. The reasoning which has led us to say that a statesman has a moral duty to observe a treaty, even against his perception of the national interest, is logically independent of whether, as a matter of fact, there can be said to exist a corresponding " positive " social norm in the practice of States.

Moreover, so far as the principle of *pacta sunt servanda* is concerned, its existence as a positive social norm in international relations is not doubted. A technical question may remain as to whether this principle, apart from being a customary principle of international law, can be said to belong to positive international morality. However, it is a common characteristic of such basic principles of social life that their prescriptions are contained simultaneously in logically separable systems of norms, such as conventional morality, custom, positive law and religious precepts.

The " realist " may, however, mean to say that, due to certain specific conditions of the international environment, moral questions cannot arise for foreign policy decision-makers, and that it is impossible to pass moral judgments on their international actions. Among such specific conditions, the absence of political authority, the lack of unity in value-preferences and the " nasty and brutish " nature of international life are commonly pointed out.

This type of argument is not a factual generalisation as to what statesmen tend to do, or what criteria tend to be used in judging their actions. On the other hand, it is not a normative argument as to what statesmen ought to do, either. The upholders of this position appear to be concerned with sociological conditions that must be satisfied before it becomes possible to introduce normative questions. However, none of these "specific conditions" can create a "moral vacuum" in the international environment.

To begin with, when we are asking whether an act is right, we are debating whether to subscribe to the view that it is right, and, accordingly, to all the logical consequences of that view. If we find ourselves unable to subscribe to the consequences, we cannot subscribe to the view itself. The absence in the international environment of political authority makes no difference to this argument, which is one to which statesmen acting in that environment are subject whether or not there is any such political authority. Therefore a "realist" cannot justifiably maintain that statesmen are internationally free from moral obligations, such as the obligation to keep treaties, merely because there is no political authority above States.

The realist, however, may further argue as follows. Granted that the principle of *pacta sunt servanda* is morally valid among States, it must be regarded as impicitly containing the proviso of *rebus sic stantibus*, for, unlike in a domestic society, there is no legislature in international society to take account of changed circumstances.

To this we can reply again by advancing moral reasoning. Can we seriously commit ourselves to saying that it is right for any State to regard a treaty as abandoned whenever, in its view, the circumstances under which the treaty was concluded have changed, given that there is no international legislature to take such a change into consideration and modify the treaty? The answer seems clearly to be in the negative. While a State can invoke changed circumstances as a reason for opening negotiations to modify or abrogate the treaty, it is unlikely that anyone can adhere to the view that it is right for any State unilaterally to abandon a treaty on the ground of changed circumstances against his country.

The "realist" may also point out the lack of cultural unity in international society. He may say that the deep disagreements in value-preferences that exist in the world in effect create a "moral vacuum." Such a possibility cannot be discounted. Supposing that the elementary logic necessary for moral reasoning is universally accepted, it may still be that the question of whether one can seriously subscribe to all the logical consequences of saying that x is right, which is an essential part of moral reasoning, is answered differently according to one's cultural bias.

However, this is a point that can be worked out only by trying moral reasoning ourselves. We cannot reject the possibility of moral reasoning, as such, in an *a priori* manner, merely because we might in the end find ourselves disagreeing with each other. The " realist " cannot justifiably assert that there exists a " moral vacuum " in the international environment, in the sense that moral questions cannot logically be asked about statesmen's international actions, merely on the ground that there is no cultural unity, nor agreement in value-preferences, at the international level. Thus, he cannot reject our reasoning, establishing that treaties ought to be kept, by alleging the existence of a " moral vacuum " in international relations by reference to the lack of cultural unity.

The " realist " may, however, go on to claim that morality is possible only if there exists a fair expectation within a society that its members live in accordance with moral principles, and that in international relations, life is so " nasty and brutish " that there is no such expectation shared by the participants.

Such a position may be criticised for its excessively pessimistic and deterministic outlook. While from time to time " nasty and brutish " scenes occur they certainly are not the permanent, nor even the most predominant feature of international relations. Treaties are negotiated and concluded day by day on the assumption, and with the fair expectation, that they will be honoured, and while outright violations of some relatively demanding treaty-obligations may be noticed, the rest continue to be observed as a matter of course.

While we cannot establish the extent to which such a degree of order as exists in international relations is attributable to the moral considerations of the statesmen, we need not accept the " realist " dogma that mutual distrust among the sovereign States is so deep as to render utterly impossible their practising of morality. More-over, granted that the moral questions facing statesmen in foreign policy decision-making are immensely more complex than those facing private individuals, this by no means shows that moral con-siderations are either logically impossible or unnecessary in the international sphere.

The third type of argument which a " realist " may advance as regards international morality is that statesmen have overriding moral obligations, attached to their offices, to serve their respective countries. According to this view, this " public " moral duty of statesmen precludes the application of their personal moral principles, such as " keep your promises," which they would be able to follow if they were acting as private individuals. Furthermore, according to this view, the overriding domestic duty of statesmen morally entitles them to disregard any international obligations, such as the principle of *pacta sunt servanda*.

This third position is a special case of a more general assertion according to which everyone ought to do whatever is best for his country. It is absolutely essential to see the difference between such an assertion and an egoistic nationalism. The difference between the two is easy to overlook because a selfish nationalistic desire is often expressed as if it were a realisation of a universal principle.

What matters to an egoistic nationalist is *his* country's interest, and not that of any other country. Therefore, a patriotic Briton will advocate that the British national interest be enhanced at the cost of that of other nations. If he is an ordinary selfish nationalist, he will not say that, for instance, the Icelanders, in a case of conflict with the British, are just as much morally entitled to frustrate the British policy as are the British to implement it. Thus his determination to serve the United Kingdom cannot be a realisation of a universal principle, such as " one ought to do what is best for one's country."

When a " realist " claims that a statesman ought to do whatever he can to serve his country, it must clearly be understood that he, the " realist," is not making a nationalistic assertion. On the other hand, in advancing this third type of argument, the " realist " is not making a psychological statement as to what statesmen generally feel constrained to do: he is making a normative statement. He is arguing that statesmen ought to do whatever they can to serve their respective national interests, and that, for instance, if they break treaties for the preservation of their national interests, they are acting commendably.

Because of the nature of this claim, the " realist " must be regarded as logically committing himself to the position that it is right for any national leader to take such an attitude against other countries, including his (the realist's) own, and, in the final analysis, against his own personal interest.

It is important to note that, however ardently he may wish to be an " ethically neutral " observer, the " realist " cannot secure for himself the privileged position of a detached commentator on international relations. He is himself participating in world affairs either as a citizen or a national leader. Therefore, unless he claims to be a fanatic who gets satisfaction out of watching the " nasty and brutish " spectacle of international relations even at the cost of becoming the victim himself, he cannot seriously commit himself to the view he is advancing.

COUNTER-NATIONALISATION

By

I. SEIDL-HOHENVELDERN

IN his work *Foreign Investments and International Law*, Georg Schwarzenberger has proposed counter-nationalisation by capital-exporting States as a possible means of protection of private property from foreign nationalisation. " This pattern involves the substitution of the home State as the creditor of loans or owner of property abroad by legislation or agreement with the nationals concerned." [1]

The effectiveness of this proposal has not yet been proved by the crucial test, *i.e.* that the capital-importing country concerned, under such circumstances, would indeed refrain from taking such private foreign property, previously " nationalised " by the capital-exporting State concerned.

In a somewhat different way, decrees by the Netherlands Government-in-exile " vesting " the property held outside the Netherlands by Netherlands nationals and residents [2] could also be considered as counter-nationalisation. These decrees in practice protected residents in the occupied Netherlands who owned such assets, from being forced by the German occupation authorities to cede them to these authorities. The Netherlands decrees in question, as well as the requests by the German occupation authorities, could in both instances be qualified as nationalisation—in spite of the vast difference between these measures, as far as their compatibility with international law is concerned. Had the owners of such assets been able to express themselves freely, they certainly would have agreed to this protective vesting. Thus, these decrees would meet two of the criteria figuring in Schwarzenberger's proposal, but not the third. If we consider these vesting decrees as counter-nationalisation, the " vesting " protected such property only in third countries [3] against the relatively small risk that such countries would recognise the German taking measures; however, the " vesting " did not produce any protective effect inside the country where these measures had been enacted.

---

[1] G. Schwarzenberger, *Foreign Investments and International Law* (1969), pp. 193–194.

[2] Decree of May 24, 1940. See M. Domke, *Trading with the Enemy in World War II* (1943) pp. 346–348.

[3] *Anderson* v. *N.V. Transandine Handelsmaatschappij*, Ann. Dig. 10 (1941–42), pp. 10 *et seq.*

I—NETHERLANDS VESTING ORDERS
AS PRECEDENT?

The protective vesting by the Netherlands Government-in-exile, in turn, may be compared with a little known Austrian case concerning counter-nationalisation by Pope Pius XII in respect of Austrian assets belonging to the Hungarian diocese of Györ (Raab).[4]

II—AUSTRIA'S GENERAL REJECTION
OF FOREIGN NATIONALISATION

Following the end of the Second World War, Austria was confronted with the efforts of the neighbouring Socialist countries which were seeking to obtain control of assets in Austria belonging to citizens of the countries concerned. Such claims were often based on an alleged extra-territorial effect of nationalisation laws enacted by these countries. Austrain courts constantly rejected these claims as incompatible with the sovereignty of Austria.[5]

The countries concerned thereupon tried to obtain control of at least parts of such assets by another tactic. They brought pressure on those of their residents holding assets in Austria, who either had remained unaffected by the nationalisation or who, but for this nationalisation, would have been the owners of such assets or would have been authorised to dispose of such assets for other reasons, *e.g.* as directors of a company. The persons concerned were obliged to sign powers of attorney to an Austrian lawyer enjoying the confidence of the State concerned. This lawyer then sold their Austrian assets and transferred the proceeds to the State concerned. In some cases the signatories of such powers of attorney received the countervalue of the proceeds of the sale in local currency at completely unrealistic rates of exchange; in other cases they received not even that.

Such a " repatriation " of foreign-held assets, as such, is compatible

---

[4] Austrian Supreme Court, September 19, 1956, *Österreichische Richterzeitung* (1957), p. 28, discussed in F. Schwind, *Handbuch des österreichischen Internationalen Privatrechts* (1975), pp. 137–138.

[5] Austrian Supreme Court, April 19, 1961, 40 *I.L.R.* (1970), p. 16; Austrian Administrative Court, October 1, 1959, *Nationalisation of Czechoslovak Enterprise (Austrian Assets) Case*, 28 I.L.R. (1963), pp. 14 *et seq.*; Austrian Supreme Court, June 2, 1958, *Koh-I-Noor L. & C. Hardtmuth v. Koh-I-Noor, Tuzkarna*, 26 I.L.R. (1958 II), p. 40; Austrian Supreme Court, December 18, 1957, *Carl Zeiss Foundation Case*, 24 I.L.R. (1957), p. 42; Austrian Supreme Court, January 5, 1955, *Nationalisation of Czechoslovak Savings Bank Case*, 24 I.L.R. (1957), p. 40; Austrian Supreme Court, February 3, 1954, *Danuvia Feinmechanische und Werkzeugfabrik Nationalunternehmen v. Seiberth*, 21 I.L.R. (1954), pp. 38 *et seq.*; Austrian Supreme Court, October 30, 1951, *Re Erste Znaimer Brauerei u. Malzfabrik AG*, 18 I.L.R. (1951), p. 201; Austrian Supreme Court, May 31, 1951, *Lederer-Ponzer v. Rautenstrauch*, *ibid.* p. 204.

with international law.[6] It is a feature common to many foreign exchange control laws, yet the country *rei sitae* is not bound to enforce such foreign repatriation orders, not even within the framework of the Bretton Woods Agreements.[7]

Two conflicting motives prompted Austria to reject not only any attempt of direct enforcement of such orders, but also any such " repatriation by powers of attorney."

In a reply to a question in the Austrian Parliament on September 26, 1963, the Austrian Federal Chancellor, Dr. Gorbach, still put the accent on the protection of private property.[8] In cases where it appeared doubtful whether the consent of the owner granting the power of attorney had been given freely, Austrian courts could appoint a " curator of conflicting interests " (*Kollisionskurator*),[9] who in this type of case could plead such lack of consent before Austrian courts.[10] Moreover, in such cases, Austrian administrative authorities also could appoint an Austrian public administrator, as the absent owner was " incapable to return or to defend his rights." [11]

However, simultaneously, Austria had another more partial reason for objecting to such repatriation. In paragraph 1 of Article 27 of the Austrian State Treaty [12] the Allied and Associated Powers declared " their intention to return Austrian property, rights and interests as they now exist in their territories or the proceeds arising out of the liquidation, disposal or realisation of such property, rights or interests." [13] When negotiating lump-sum compensation agreements

---

[6] *Cf.* separate opinion of Judge Gros in the *Barcelona Traction* case, International Court of Justice, February 5, 1970, *I.C.J. Reports* 1970, p. 270.

[7] Court of Appeals Amsterdam, April 9, 1959, *Lembaga and Republic of Indonesia* v. *Brummer*, 30 I.L.R. (1966), p. 25; see Seidl-Hohenveldern, " Probleme der Anerkennung ausländischer Devisenbewirtschaftungsmassnahmen," 8 *Österr. Zeitschrift für öffentliches Recht* (1957), p. 101.

[8] II–168 of the Annexes to the Stenographic Records of the Austrian Parliament (Beilagen zu den Stenographischen Protokollen des Nationalrats), X. Legislative Period, *Österr. Neue Tageszeitung* (Vienna newspaper) October 3, 1963, p. 2.

[9] Art. 271 of the Austrian General Civil Code, P. Baeck, *The Austrian General Civil Code* (1972) p. 47.

[10] English courts had refused to recognise the validity of a cession made under duress in a foreign State to that State (*Republica de Guatemala* v. *Nuñez* [1927] 1 K.B. 669 (C.A.) 2 Rabels Z. (1928) p. 253. Austrian courts, too, would have refused to recognise the validity of powers-of-attorney given under such circumstances.

[11] Art. 2, sub-para. 1 lit. c of the Austrian Law on Public Administrators, Austrian *Bundesgesetzblatt* (BGBl.) Nr. 100/1953.

[12] 49 Am.J. of Int. Law, Off. Doc (1955), p.184.

[13] An Expert Opinion rendered to the Austrian Federal Ministry of Foreign Affairs (27 *Österr. Zeitschrift für öffentliches Recht* (1976), p. 342) interpreted this passage to the effect that it does not refer to general nationalisation measures taken *inter alia* also against Austrian property. Art. 27 prevents merely a taking of Austrian property in Czechoslovakia as *enemy property*, but not in virtue of Czechoslovakia's right to nationalise pursuant to international law. However, it may not be easy to distinguish such a nationalisation from the " liquidation, disposal or realisation of property " on behalf of Czechoslovakia.

concerning compensation for Austrian property nationalised in East European countries, Austria could use assets in Austria owned by citizens of such countries as leverage.[14] These assets might have constituted a legitimate object of reprisals, if the nationalising countries had persisted in their refusal to indemnify Austrian citizens. The above-quoted passage [15] of the Austrian Law on Public Administrators was held " inappropriate " to the appointment of public administrators for *this* purpose.[16] Hence an amendment adopted in 1964 authorised the appointment of such administrators in all cases where absent owners were nationals of a State having nationalised Austrian property without compensation.[17] The Austrian Constitutional Court held this amendment compatible with the Austrian Constitution and with international law.[18] These measures, in any case, produced the desired effect. Austria concluded lump-sum compensation agreements with the States concerned.[19] In some cases, in part payment of the stipulated compensation, these States assigned to Austria property held by their nationals in Austria.[20]

III—THE AUSTRIAN ASSETS
OF THE DIOCESE OF GYÖR

The case of the Austrian assets of the diocese of Györ (Raab) could

---

[14] Seidl-Hohenveldern, " Austrian Practice on Lump Sum Compensation by Treaty," 70 Am.J. of Int. Law (1976), p. 765.

[15] See note 11 above.

[16] Annex No. 430 to the Stenographic Records of the Austrian Parliament, 10 Legislative Period.

[17] Art. 2, sub-para. 1, lit. f of Austrian Law on Public Administrators, Austrian *Bundesgesetzblatt* Nr. 151/1964.

[18] Austrian Constitutional Court, October 15, 1966, Official Collection No. 5378, 97 *Clunet* (1970), p. 356; Austrian Constitutional Court, October 15, 1966, Official Collection No. 5382, 97 *Clunet* (1970) p. 356, 47 I.L.R. (1974), p. 412 and Austrian Constitutional Court, September 27, 1967, Official Collection Nr. 5565, 97 *Clunet* (1970), p. 340.

[19] Seidl-Hohenveldern, *op. cit.* in note 14, above.

[20] For this aspect of the Austrian–Hungarian Lump Sum Compensation Agreement of October 31, 1964 (Austrian *Bundesgesetzblatt* Nr. 263/1967, 605 U.N.T.S., 77, Lillich-Weston, *International Claims: Their Settlement by Lump Sum Agreements*, Vol. II (1975), p. 307), see Seidl-Hohenveldern, " The Impact of Public International Law on Conflict of Law Rules on Corporations," 123 Hague Academy *Recueil des Cours* (1968 I), pp. 39–40. A similar provision in the Austrian–Czechoslovak Lump Sum Compensation Agreement of December 19, 1974, Austrian *Bundesgesetzblatt* Nr. 451/1975, led to the enactment of an Austrian Law of December 13, 1976, Austrian *Bundesgesetzblatt* Nr. 713/1976, authorising the Republic of Austria to take such assigned property of foreign corporations in Austria, as has not been claimed by the owners concerned and use the proceeds of such takings as a partial contribution to the lump-sum compensation to be distributed by the Austrian State to Austrian citizens affected by nationalisation in the assigning State. This assignment by Czechoslovakia, reminiscent of the Roosevelt-Litvinov Agreement of 1933 (Schwarzenberger, *op. cit.* in note 1, above, at p. 193), has been accepted as valid by the Austrian Supreme Court, June 29, 1976, 27 *Österr. Zeitschrift für öffentliches Recht* (1976), p. 336.

have been solved by either of the two methods indicated above, but for the intervention of the Pope. These assets were situated in the eastern most part of Austria, the Burgenland. Prior to 1919 this area had belonged to Hungary. For a long time the Vatican had been reluctant to recognise *de jure* changes in frontiers brought about as a result of the First World War. Yet, in *de facto* recognition of such change, the parishes in the Burgenland were put under the authority of an "Apostolic Administrator," *i.e.*, an Austrian titular bishop *in partibus infidelium*. This state of affairs continued beyond 1956, the time of the decision to be discussed. Only since 1960 has the Burgenland formed the Austrian diocese of Eisenstadt.

Property which did not belong to the individual Austrian parishes, but to the diocese of Györ as such, had remained unaffected by the appointment of the Apostolic Administrator. Thus, after 1945, the diocese of Györ had remained the owner of real estate in Austria. In 1952, this diocese represented by the Bishop of Györ, who, in turn, was represented by a Vienna lawyer, holder of the Bishop's power of attorney, instituted eviction proceedings against the Austrian tenant of this estate, in preparation for the sale of the estate concerned. Doubts as to the freedom of consent of the bishop when giving this power of attorney would have permitted a reaction by Austrian courts or administrative authorities, as indicated above.[21] However, Pope Pius XII chose another way to protect what he held to be the real interests of the Church and presumably also those of the Bishop of Györ. By a Papal decree rendered in 1953 he transferred the administration of all Austrian assets held by the diocese of Györ to the Apostolic Administrator of the Burgenland. The latter thereupon sought to cancel the eviction proceedings. In the ensuing lawsuit the court of first instance gave effect to the Papal Decree as, under ecclesiastical law, the Pope is the Supreme Administrator of all Church property. The Court of Appeal reversed this decision. According to Austrian Conflict of Law rules, the personal law of a juridical person determines who may act on behalf of such person. According to an international principle recognised also by Austria, a bishop is authorised to dispose of Church property belonging to his diocese. Therefore, only Hungarian law could decide which organs could act on behalf of the diocese of Györ. The Austrian tenant had not proved that Hungarian law, too, would recognise the Pope as a sovereign organ authorised to dispose of all Church property. Rather unrealistically, the Court of Appeals added that Hungarian law (in 1953!) quite possibly might recognise such a right of the Pope.

On September 19, 1956, the Austrian Supreme Court found in

---

[21] See text at note 11 above.

favour of the Austrian tenant and the Apostolic Administrator.
The general Austrian rules determining the power to represent a
foreign juridical person according to the latter's personal law are
subject to special rules to the contrary, *e.g.*, if an Austrian public
administrator has been appointed for the Austrian assets of such a
person, only this administrator may administer such assets.

Such special rules exist in respect to Church property in virtue of
the Austrian Concordat of 1933.[22] At the time of this decision of the
Supreme Court, there was a heated controversy in Austria concerning
the international validity of this Concordat.[23] This controversy
was reflected in a difference of opinion as to whether Austria—
between 1938 and 1945—was occupied or annexed by Germany.[24]
The first alternative would have admitted no doubt concerning the
international validity of the Concordat. This dispute was settled
only in 1960, when Federal Chancellor Raab publicly recognised the
validity of the Concordat under international law.[25] The Supreme
Court has been criticised for having avoided taking sides in such
cases,[26] by holding the relevant provisions applicable at least as
Austrian domestic law [27] as they had not been repealed by any
subsequent Austrian law.

According to paragraph 2 of Article XIII of the Austrian Concordat,
the assets of persons established under ecclesiastical law shall be
administered by organs authorised to do so under canon law. This
reference to canon law does not distinguish between the assets of
Austrian or foreign persons under ecclesiastical law, thus giving due
regard to the universal character of the Catholic Church. Therefore,
canon law as *lex loci* shall have precedence over the personal law of
such foreign persons under ecclesiastical law.

Now according to Canon 1518 of the *Codex Juris Canonici*, the
Pope holds supreme power to administer and dispose of the entire
property of the Church.[28] Thus, the Pope is the legal representative

---

[22] Concordat of June 5, 1933, Austrian *Bundesgesetzblatt* No. 2/1934 II, Commentary
by Klecatsky–Weiler, *Österreichisches Staatskirchenrecht* (1958), pp. 230 *et seq.*
[23] H. F. Köck *Die völkerrechtliche Stellung des Hl. Stuhles* (1975), pp. 376–380.
[24] St. Verosta, *Die internationale Stellung Österreichs, 1938 bis 1947* (1947), pp. 8–9.
[25] H. F. Köck, *op. cit.* in note 23 above, at p. 380.
[26] Verdross, "Jura novit curia?" 86 *Juristische Blätter* (1964), p. 235, referring to
an earlier controversial declaration of the Austrian Federal Government of December 21,
1957, admitting the validity of at least parts of the Concordat.
[27] Seidl-Hohenveldern, " Relation of International Law to Internal Law in Austria,"
49 Am. J. of Int. Law (1955), p. 460; 7 *ibid.*, " Transformation or Adoption of International Law into Municipal Law," 12 I.C.L.Q. (1963), pp. 116–117. Th. Öhlinger, *Der
völkerrechtliche Vertrag im staatlichen Recht* (1973), p. 323, deems that a treaty no longer
valid under international law can no longer be valid as domestic law.
[28] Can. 1518: " *Romanus pontificus est omnium bonorum ecclesiasticorum supremus
administrator et dispensator.*"
Cf. also Can. 218: " § 1 *Romanus Pontifex, Beati Petri in primatu successor, habet non
solum primatum honoris, sed supremam et plenam potestatem jurisdictionis in universam*

of any juridical person of the Roman Catholic Church. As such, he could deprive the Bishop of Györ of the latter's power to administer the Austrian assets of the diocese of Györ and appoint validly another administrator for these assets. According to Austrian ecclesiastical law the measures to this effect taken by the Pope produce full legal effects in Austria.

IV—EVALUATION

Was this act of counter-nationalisation necessary and effective? At the time when the Austrian Supreme Court rendered this decision, Austrian courts and administrative authorities used other means at their disposal to protect what they presumed to be the real interest of foreign owners affected by repatriation orders of their home States. Thus, *at that time*, the presumed real interests of the diocese of Györ would have been protected in Austria, even without this Papal decree. At that time, the decisive motive for issuing this decree may have been the hope of forcing the Austrian Supreme Court to take sides in the dispute concerning the validity of the Austrian Concordat under international law. However, in the long run, this Papal counter-nationalisation decree proved to afford a better protection of the interests concerned than the measures offered by Austrian juridical or administrative practice. Had an Austrian public administrator been appointed, the latter—pursuant to the 1964 Amendment of the Public Administrator law—would have had to preserve these assets as a pawn in the Austrian–Hungarian compensation negotiations. A curator of conflicting interests would have been able to invalidate the power of attorney signed by the bishop, and would thus have prevented the eviction proceedings and the contemplated sale of these assets. The assets would have remained in the ownership of the diocese of Györ, thus of an Hungarian national absent from Austria. Hence, pursuant to the 1964 Amendment, they could have been put under Austrian public administration. The Austrian–Hungarian Lump-Sum Compensation Agreement could have assigned Hungarian assets under such Austrian public administration to Austria as part of the Hungarian compensation payments to be distributed by the Republic of Austria under the pertinent Austrian Distribution Law [29] to individual Austrians affected by Hungarian nationalisation. The Austrian courts would have found such assignments

---

Ecclesiam tum in rebus quae ad fidem et mores, tum in iis quae ad disciplinam et regimen Ecclesiae per totum orbem diffusae pertinent.

§ 2 *Haec potestas est vere episcopalis, ordinaria et immediata tum in omnes et singulos pastores et fideles, a quavis humana autoritate independens.*"

[29] Austrian *Bundesgesetzblatt* Nr. 294/1967, see Seidl-Hohenveldern, " The Valuation of Nationalized Property in Austria," in Lillich (ed. and contrib.), *The Valuation of Nationalized Property in International Law*, Vol. I (1972), pp. 83 *et seq.*

unobjectionable, recognising the title of the Republic of Austria in preference to that of the former owners.[30] Thanks to the Papal Decree, the assets having belonged to the diocese of Györ could have been used for this purpose, neither by Hungary nor by Austria.

---

[30] See note 20 above, However, by contrast to the Austrian–Czechoslovak Lump-Sum Agreement, the agreement with Hungary contained no formal assignment. Yet, it was understood by both sides that Hungary would pay the stipulated lump sum in part out of the proceeds of the sale of Hungarian assets in Austria, after Austria, pursuant to the Agreement, had discontinued the Austrian public administration of such assets.

THE NEW GENEVA PROTOCOLS:

A STEP FORWARD OR BACKWARD?

By

YORAM DINSTEIN

IN 1977, after four years of travail, the Diplomatic Conference on the Reaffirmation and Development of International Humanitarian Law Applicable in Armed Conflicts produced two Protocols Additional to the Geneva Conventions of August 12, 1949: one relating to the Protection of Victims of International Armed Conflicts (Protocol I),[1] and the other relating to the Protection of Victims of Non-International Armed Conflicts (Protocol II).[2] It took the Geneva Conference of 1949 only one session to formulate some 400 clauses, which will remain in force even after the Additional Protocols become law for the Contracting Parties. But four long and occasionally stormy sessions were required to draft less than 150 new clauses. Evidently, it is not always the first step which is the hardest.

The strenuous efforts exerted by the Diplomatic Conference deserve an accolade. However, the final product raises serious doubts as to the overall success of the exercise. After all, the real test of international conventions lies not in their formulation or even ratification, but in their implementation. We live in an era in which at least one astute observer detects a trend towards a relapse into unlimited violence and neo-barbarism in the conduct of warfare.[3] It remains to be seen if the Additional Protocols will prove a step forward (in the sense of stimulating a more civilised behaviour in time of armed conflict) or a step backward (in the sense of widening the existing gap between law and reality, the normative " ought " and the actual " is ").

The legal technique underlying the Additional Protocols, and several of the issues that had come to light even before the Diplomatic Conference was convened, have already been discussed in a previous article published in this *Year Book*.[4] It is proposed to examine here the most conspicuous aspects of the Additional Protocols without covering the same ground again.

---

[1] [197–198] *International Review of the Red Cross* (1977), p. 3.

[2] [197–198] *International Review of the Red Cross* (1977), p. 89.

[3] See G. Schwarzenberger, " The Law of Armed Conflict: A Civilised Interlude? " in this *Year Book*, Vol. 28 (1974), pp. 293–309 at pp. 302–307.

[4] Y. Dinstein, " Another Step in Codifying the Laws of War," in this *Year Book*, Vol. 28 (1974), pp. 278–292.

I—" WARS OF LIBERATION "

The most controversial clause in the Additional Protocols is Article 1 (4) of Protocol I. Paragraphs 3 and 4 of Article 1 provide as follows: " 3. This Protocol, which supplements the Geneva Conventions of 12 August, 1949 for the protection of war victims, shall apply in the situations referred to in Article 2 common to those Conventions.

" 4. The situations referred to in the preceding paragraph include armed conflicts in which peoples are fighting against colonial domination and alien occupation and against racist régimes in the exercise of their right of self-determination, as enshrined in the Charter of the United Nations and the Declaration on Principles of International Law concerning Friendly Relations and Co-operation among States in accordance with the Charter of the United Nations." [5]

Article 2 common to the four Geneva Conventions of 1949 [6] restricts their scope of application to armed conflicts between two or more States, *i.e.*, inter-State wars. Hence, what Article 1 (4) of Protocol I purports to do is to lay down an authoritative interpretation—which is as arbitrary as it is obligatory (for Contracting Parties of the Protocol)—according to which all " wars of liberation " must be regarded as inter-State wars. This was the main bone of contention in the first session of the Diplomatic Conference (in 1974).[7] The issue dominated the proceedings that year and endangered the ultimate success of the Conference. Article 1 (4) was introduced as an amendment, which was carried by Committee I, against Western opposition, by 70 votes to 22 with 12 abstentions.[8] In 1977 the Plenary approved Article 1, in the form adopted by Committee I, by 87 votes to 1 with 11 abstentions.[9] In the interval, after much soul-searching, the Western countries had reached the conclusion that they must acquiesce with this stipulation—which virtually became an article of faith for the Third World and Eastern bloc countries—if they did not wish the Conference to be abortive.

The objections to Article 1 (4) are manifold. For one thing, the formulation is curious, to say the least. Eyebrows can be raised at the reference to a General Assembly Declaration, which is not *stricto sensu* juridically binding *per se*, as a source of law. But that is an aesthetic question of phraseology. What is less comprehensible is the allusion to fighting against " alien occupation." If what is meant is

[5] *Op. cit.* in note 1, above, at p. 4.
[6] 1 *Kitvei Amana* (Israel Treaty Series) (Nr. 30), pp. 387, 423, 453, 559 at pp. 387–388, 423–424, 453–544, 559–560.
[7] See D. P. Forsythe, " The 1974 Diplomatic Conference on Humanitarian Law: Some Observations," 69 *American Journal of International Law* (1975), pp. 77–91 at pp. 78–84.
[8] [158] *International Review of the Red Cross* (1974), pp. 231–232.
[9] [196] *International Review of the Red Cross* (1977), p. 359.

alien occupation in the context of international peace, there is a terminological redundancy involved. In such circumstances, the situation is already covered by the broad term " colonial domination ": the colonial Power is alien by definition and occupation signifies domination. On the other hand, if (as one is inclined to think) the occupation envisaged is belligerent occupation, the superfluity in Article 1 (4) is a matter of substance. Belligerent occupation can anyhow take place only in the course of an inter-State war. The occupation itself is ancillary to that war, and so is any fighting against the occupant which may take place. While fighting continues, and, even in the absence of fighting, as long as the occupation is belligerent, war lasts. With or without Article 1 (4), the Geneva Conventions would therefore be applicable. Those fighting against the occupant may not be lawful combatants entitled to all of the privileges of the Conventions, but that is a separate issue discussed below.

The crux of the matter, however, is the reference in Article 1 (4) to fighting against colonial domination and racist régimes. The idea is that a rebellion by a people fighting for self-determination (a so-called war of liberation) is to be automatically viewed as an inter-State war. Yet, as long as the rebels have not managed to establish a new State and no other State intervenes in the conflict—so that only one single State is affected by the fighting—the clash of arms can only be regarded as a civil war. The fact that the goal of the rebels is laudable (namely, liberation from foreign yoke) does not change the nature of the conflict. A civil war is a civil war irrespective of the merits of the case.

A civil war does not come within the ambit of common Article 2 of the Geneva Conventions, and should not be covered by Protocol I: Protocol II is the germane instrument. Under general international law, a civil war is governed by the rules operating in an international armed conflict only when the rebels are recognised as a belligerent party, such recognition being contingent not on the justice of their cause but on the magnitude of the rebellion (in terms of the area subject to the rebels' control, the degree of their organisation and the extent of the hostilities).[10] What Article 1 (4) professes to do, is to confer *a priori* a belligerent status on all liberation movements despite the absence of recognition and heedless of the actual dimensions of the rebellion. This is palpably absurd. When all is said and done, if the rebels have failed to gain effective control over a significant portion of the territory, if they are not led by a responsible quasi-governmental authority, and if hostilities are limited to

---

[10] See Y. Dinstein, " The International Law of Civil Wars and Human Rights," 6 *Israel Yearbook on Human Rights* (1976), pp. 62–80 at pp. 75–77.

episodic hit-and-run incidents, there is simply no point in pretending that the laws of inter-State warfare can be implemented by them. How will they observe the rules in regard to the safekeeping of prisoners of war? How will they treat the wounded and sick? And if they ignore these niceties, how can the government troops be expected unilaterally to observe the rules *vis-à-vis* the rebels? [11]

In practical terms, the import of Article 1 (4) is dubious. Inasmuch as there is no objective machinery to determine authoritatively whether a particular rebellion is in reality a war of liberation, it is a safe assumption that the central government of a State beset by a civil war will always deny that such is the case. Can any statesman be seriously expected to confess in public that he represents a " racist régime " and that consequently Article 1 (4) comes into operation? This pragmatic inconceivability lies at the root of the reluctant Western acquiescence with the clause. As the head of the American delegation stated in a news conference, " No State is ever going to admit it is a racist régime or exercising alien or colonial domination." [12] He therefore pointed out that Article 1 (4) would be harmless because he was " quite confident it will never be applied." [13]

The trouble, however, is that Article 1 (4) is complemented by Article 96 (3), which stipulates: " 3. The authority representing a people engaged against a High Contracting Party in an armed conflict of the type referred to in Article 1, paragraph 4, may undertake to apply the Conventions and this Protocol in relation to that conflict by means of a unilateral declaration addressed to the depositary. Such declaration shall, upon its receipt by the depositary, have in relation to that conflict the following effects: (a) the Conventions and this Protocol are brought into force for the said authority as a Party to the conflict with immediate effect; (b) the said authority assumes the same rights and obligations as those which have been assumed by a High Contracting Party to the Conventions and this Protocol; and (c) the Conventions and this Protocol are equally binding upon all Parties to the conflict." [14]

The implication is that the unilateral declaration of the liberation movement binds not merely itself but also the adversary. In other words, notwithstanding the express desire of the central government to treat the conflict as a civil war regulated by the rules of internal (intra-State) wars, the rebels are apparently entitled to force its hand by opting for the application of the rules operating in inter-State wars. What happens if the central government still objects by denying that

[11] See R. R. Baxter, " Humanitarian Law or Humanitarian Politics? The 1974 Diplomatic Conference on Humanitarian Law," 16 *Harvard International Law Journal* (1975), pp. 1–26 at p. 16.   [12] *New York Times*, June 11, 1977, p. 5.   [13] *Ibid.*   [14] *Op. cit.* in note 1, above, at pp. 70–71.

the rebels represent a people engaged in a war of liberation? In the absence of machinery for amicable settlements of such disputes, the central government may probably thwart the purpose of Article 96 (3) by steadfastly refusing to concede the applicability of Article 1 (4) to the conflict in question. Nevertheless, the Protocol has to be interpreted and applied in good faith. A State which does not wish to find itself in a false position in this context should either decline to ratify the Protocol or ratify it subject to an explicit reservation excluding the application of Articles 1 (4) and 96 (3). We shall revert to the topic of reservations below.

II—THE STATUS OF PRISONERS OF WAR

The *jus in bello* is based on the fundamental distinction between combatants and civilians. The distinction is conducive to the protection of civilians from the rigours of war. Civilians may be put under a protective aegis only if and when they can be told apart from combatants. Blurring the lines of division between combatants and civilians is bound to result in indiscriminate warfare. This is the primary reason for another basic distinction in the *jus in bello*, between lawful (or privileged) combatants who are entitled to the status of prisoners of war when captured by the enemy, and unlawful (unprivileged) combatants who expose themselves to prosecution and punishment for their acts.[15] The rationale is the imposition of penal sanctions on those combatants who masquerade as civilians so as to mislead the enemy and avoid detection. Such tactics are not a legitimate ruse of war because of the potential menace to all civilians, who run the risk of being suspected as combatants under disguise.

Under existing international law, a combatant is entitled to the privileged status of a prisoner of war only when several (cumulative) conditions are met. These conditions are specified in the 1899 and 1907 Hague Regulations respecting the Laws and Customs of War,[16] as well as the 1949 Geneva Conventions.[17] *Inter alia*, lawful combatants must comply with the laws of war, carry their arms openly and have a fixed distinctive sign. Admittedly, due to their cumulative effect, the conditions are onerous and they may present insurmountable obstacles for irregular forces.[18] For that reason it was expected from the very beginning that Protocol I would rectify the legal position and make the conditions more palatable to *guerrilleros*.[19] The question was debated at length in the Diplomatic Conference.

---

[15] *Ex p. Quirin et al.* (1942), 317 U.S. 1 at pp. 30–31.

[16] J. B. Scott (ed.), *The Hague Conventions and Declarations of* 1899 *and* 1907 (1915), p. 107.

[17] Art. 13 of the First and Second Geneva Conventions and Art. 4 of the Third. *Op. cit.* in note 6, above, at pp. 393, 429, 455.

[18] See Y. Dinstein, *op. cit.* in note 4, above, at p. 283.   [19] *Ibid*, at p. 284.

The text ultimately adopted is allegedly " the best possible compromise " on a crucial point.[20] The overwhelming margin by which it was carried indicates that it was indeed viewed as a compromise which could not be opposed.[21] Whether the " compromise " was irresistible or merely unresisted is a somewhat moot point. What counts in the final analysis is that the text now forms an integral part of Protocol I.

Article 44 of Protocol I states: " 1. Any combatant, as defined in Article 43, who falls into the power of an adverse Party shall be a prisoner of war,

" 2. While all combatants are obliged to comply with the rules of international law applicable in armed conflict, violations of these rules shall not deprive a combatant of his right to be a combatant or, if he falls into the power of an adverse Party, of his right to be a prisoner of war, except as provided in paragraphs 3 and 4.

" 3. In order to promote the protection of the civilian population from the effects of hostilities, combatants are obliged to distinguish themselves from the civilian population while they are engaged in an attack or in a military operation preparatory to an attack. Recognizing, however, that there are situations in armed conflicts where, owing to the nature of the hostilities an armed combatant cannot so distinguish himself, he shall retain his status as a combatant, provided that, in such situations, he carries his arms openly: (a) during each military engagement, and (b) during such time as he is visible to the adversary while he is engaged in a military deployment preceding the launching of an attack in which he is to participate. Acts which comply with the requirements of this paragraph shall not be considered as perfidious within the meaning of Article 37, paragraph 1 (c).

" 4. A combatant who falls into the power of an adverse Party while failing to meet the requirements set forth in the second sentence of paragraph 3 shall forfeit his right to be a prisoner of war, but he shall, nevertheless, be given protections equivalent in all respects to those accorded to prisoners of war by the Third Convention and by this Protocol. This protection includes protections equivalent to those accorded to prisoners of war by the Third Convention in the case where such a person is tried and punished for any offences he has committed.

" 5. Any combatant who falls into the power of an adverse Party while not engaged in an attack or in a military operation preparatory to an attack shall not forfeit his rights to be a combatant and a prisoner of war by virtue of his prior activities.

---

[20] See comments *op. cit.* in note 9, above, at p. 342.
[21] The results of the votes were 66:2:18 in Committee III and 73:1:21 in the Plenary. *Ibid.* at pp. 342, 360.

" 6. This Article is without prejudice to the right of any person to be a prisoner of war pursuant to Article 4 of the Third Convention.

" 7. This Article is not intended to change the generally accepted practice of States with respect to the wearing of the uniform by combatants assigned to the regular, uniformed armed units of a Party to the conflict.

" 8. In addition to the categories of persons mentioned in Article 13 of the First and Second Conventions, all members of the armed forces of a Party to the conflict, as defined in Article 43 of this Protocol, shall be entitled to protection under those Conventions if they are wounded or sick or, in the case of the Second Convention, shipwrecked at sea or in other waters." [22]

The language of Article 44 is so convoluted that it may have been left unopposed on the ground that, in any event, it is obscure to the point of incomprehensibility and therefore irrelevance. However, if a singular effort is made to reconcile its disparate paragraphs with one another, a distressing picture emerges. Some lip-service is paid to the time-honoured distinction between combatants and civilians. Yet, when the chips are down, combatants are only required to carry arms openly during military engagements and while visibly deploying preceding to the launching of attacks. It follows that *guerrilleros* are permitted, under Article 44, to camouflage themselves as civilians when setting an ambush (which, by definition, is a concealed position that precludes their being " visible to the adversary "). Furthermore, whereas combatants are still exhorted to comply with the rules of warfare, non-compliance no longer deprives them of their prisoners-of-war status (*i.e.*, it does not turn them into unlawful combatants) unless they fail to carry their arms openly in the circumstances stated, and even then they must be accorded protection equivalent to that of prisoners of war. Which is to say that only he who manages to conceal his weapons during a military engagement, or immediately preceding it, will be stigmatised as an unlawful combatant (and the practical effect of the stigma remains unclear). But the possibility that a person will carry arms clandestinely in the course of a military engagement (assuming that he does not refrain from fighting, thereby betraying his own comrades when the moment of truth arrives, and that he does not confine his activities to the planting of mines) simply boggles the mind. Why anyone who accomplishes this acrobatic feat should be signalled out for harsh treatment is a matter of conjecture. At all events, ordinary mortals—who are not up to such sleight-of-hand—must be viewed as lawful combatants, under Article 44, notwithstanding their total repudiation of the rules of warfare. The net result of the Article is that a *guerrillero* may lose himself in a

---

[22] *Op. cit.* in note 1, above, at pp. 31–32.

crowd of civilians, keep his weapons concealed until the last conceivable moment, and then violate with impunity all the rules of warfare: he may slaughter the enemy wounded and sick, use " dumdum " bullets, and so forth. Nevertheless, he does not forfeit his right to be a prisoner of war: having defied the most fundamental tenets of the *jus in bello*, he will enjoy the benefits of that law. This is a preposterous conclusion, which may undermine the whole structure of the rules of warfare. It will certainly prove unacceptable to quite a few States. Some may wish to ratify Protocol I subject to a reservation excluding the application of Article 44. Others may construe the Article in practice in ingenious, albeit artificial, ways that will blunt its edge. But, as it stands, Article 44 is a dangerous retrogressive step in the evolution of the *jus in bello*.

The whole thrust of Article 44 is to expand the status of prisoners of war and make it widely available to persons who, under existing international law, are to be classified as unlawful combatants. Yet Protocol I explicitly denies that status to two categories of persons. One category, under Article 46,[23] is that of spies. This exception is in conformity with general international law,[24] and there is no need to belabour the point. The other category, however, is new. Article 47 proclaims: " 1. A mercenary shall not have the right to be a combatant or a prisoner of war.

" 2. A mercenary is any person who: (a) is specially recruited locally or abroad in order to fight in an armed conflict; (b) does, in fact, take a direct part in the hostilities; (c) is motivated to take part in the hostilities essentially by the desire for private gain and, in fact, is promised, by or on behalf of a Party to the conflict, material compensation substantially in excess of that promised or paid to combatants of similar ranks and functions in the armed forces of that Party; (d) is neither a national of a Party to the conflict nor a resident of territory controlled by a Party to the conflict; (e) is not a member of the armed forces of a Party to the conflict; and (f) has not been sent by a State which is not a Party to the conflict on official duty as a member of its armed forces." [25]

This is a departure from existing international law, and it is obviously impelled by political and non-humanitarian motives. Article 46 was adopted owing to African pressure to put an end to the phenomenon of European adventurers fighting for the highest bidder in wars which are none of their concern. However, the contrast between villains (mercenaries) and saints (foreign volunteers like those who shed their blood for liberty and justice, as members

---

[23] *Ibid.* at p. 33.
[24] See R. R. Baxter, " So-called 'Unprivileged Belligerency': Spies, Guerrillas, and Saboteurs," 28 *British Year Book of International Law* (1951), pp. 323–345 at pp. 330–331.
[25] *Op. cit.* in note 1, above, at p. 34.

of the International Brigades, in the Spanish Civil War) is chiefly in the mind of the beholder. Article 46 almost invites abuses and concomitant disputes. Admittedly, the definition of mercenaries is drawn up quite restrictively. Thus, foreign technicians and military advisers, who do not " take a direct part in the hostilities," are excluded from its scope. So are members of a standing " Foreign Legion," who are not recruited to fight in a specific war. Still, the definition hinges on the venal motivation of other foreign volunteers. This subjective element can rarely be established objectively: who knows what keeps an adventurer on the go? In the final analysis, mercenaries will be placed beyond the pale not because of their frame of mind, but because of that of their judges.

III—PROTECTION OF THE CIVILIAN POPULATION

The protection of the civilian population against the danger of indiscriminate warfare has been hailed as the main accomplishment of Protocol I.[26] However, the advance made is not equal across the board. Significant strides were taken in the novel sphere of civil defence.[27] An as yet unknown international distinctive sign of civil defence will soon become familiar: it consists of an equilateral blue triangle on an orange ground.[28] In other fields, such as relief and conditions of internment, existing rules have been tightened. But in several important respects the protection of civilians is as elusive as ever. At times this is due to the fact that the Diplomatic Conference did not go far enough. In other instances it overshot the mark by going too far.

Thus, Article 52 of Protocol I [29] prohibits attack against civilian objects, and properly delineates them as all objects which are not military objectives. Unfortunately, the latter are defined as follows: " military objectives are limited to those objects which by their nature, location, purpose or use make an effective contribution to military action and whose total or partial destruction, capture or neutralization, in the circumstances ruling at the time, offers a definite military advantage." [30]

Such abstract definitions are the hallmark of brilliant draftsmanship. But they are not of much help to the victims of war. As long as a detailed and clear-cut list of military targets is not set out, civilian objects will continue to be exposed to strategic bombing. After all, " in the circumstances ruling at the time," virtually any object may

---

[26] See International Committee of the Red Cross, *Report on the Diplomatic Conference on the Reaffirmation and Development of International Humanitarian Law Applicable in Armed Forces*, submitted to the XXIII International Conference of the Red Cross (Bucharest, 1977), p. 7.

[27] Art. 61 *et seq.*, *op. cit.* in note 1, above, at pp. 45 *et seq.*

[28] Annex I, Art. 15, *ibid.* at p. 83.   [29] *Ibid.* at p. 37.   [30] *Ibid.*

be assessed as offering a definite military advantage due to its " nature, location, purpose or use," so as to invite " total or partial destruction, capture or neutralization." Some specific objects (which, in part, will be mentioned momentarily) are expressly protected from attack. Still, the problem pertains to the vast ocean of doubt which surrounds the few islands of clarity. Surely Protocol I does not go far enough in resolving this central question.

The reverse seems to have happened with Article 54,[31] which forbids starvation of civilians as a method of warfare. The Article proscribes attack against foodstuffs, crops, livestock, water installations and irrigation works for the specific purpose of denying them to the civilian population. The prohibition does not apply when these objects are used as sustenance solely for the members of the armed forces of the adversary, and when a party to the conflict implements a " scorched earth " policy while defending its national territory from invasion. The specific interdictions and exceptions are balanced and should be widely accepted. Yet the sweeping ban of starvation of civilians as a method of warfare, if taken literally, is not realistic. One of the most common modes of operation in armed conflict, since time immemorial, has been laying siege to a fortified town. Siege means an attempt to take a fortified place through starvation and thirst, by cutting off its channels of supply. " The propriety of attempting to reduce a besieged place by starvation is not questioned." [32] Indeed, under existing law, if the place is inhabited, civilians may be prevented by the besieging force from evacuating it, so that they will drain the meagre resources available to the besieged.[33] Protocol I could (and, it is submitted, should) have modified the legal position in regard to evacuation of civilians. But what is to be done if no evacuation is contemplated by the besieged? Does the general prohibition of starvation of civilians imply that siege is no longer permissible in such circumstances? If that is the case, the Protocol is plainly utopian. It should be added that Article 54 may also have a far-reaching impact on the law of maritime blockade, but this is at least doubtful in the light of a somewhat ambiguous provision in Article 49 (3),[34] under which the rules of international law applicable in armed conflict at sea are partly left unaffected.

Other innovations relating to the protection of the civilian population, which can only be praised, deal with dangerous forces and the

---

[31] *Ibid.* at pp. 38–39.

[32] L. Nurick, " The Distinction between Combatant and Noncombatant in the Law of War," 39 *American Journal of International Law* (1945), pp. 680–697, at p. 686.

[33] See L. Oppenheim, *International Law*, Vol. 2 (7th ed. by H. Lauterpacht, 1952), p. 419.

[34] *Op. cit.* in note 1, above, at p. 35.

environment. Article 55 [35] forbids the use of means of warfare expected to cause damage to the natural environment, thereby prejudicing the health or survival of the civilian population. According to Article 56,[36] dams, dykes and nuclear electrical generating stations—or other military objectives located in their vicinity—must not be attacked, if the attack may cause the release of dangerous forces and consequent severe losses among the civilian population. A special international sign for works and installations containing dangerous forces is introduced. It consists of a group of three bright orange circles of equal size.[37]

IV—OTHER SALIENT PROVISIONS OF PROTOCOL I

This is not the opportune place to examine in detail every specific clause in Protocol I. Yet a number of its more significant provisions deserve special mention.

(a) *Protecting Powers and Substitutes*

Article 5 of the Protocol [38] addresses itself to the problem of Protecting Powers and their substitutes. The modern institution of Protecting Powers (originating in the Franco-Prussian War of 1870–71) seems, paradoxically enough, to have thrived in international custom only as long as it was not the subject of international legislation.[39] By contrast, since the regulation of the subject in the four Geneva Conventions of 1949,[40] Protecting Powers have been appointed in only three situations of conflict (Suez, Goa and Bangladesh).[41] The designation of a Protecting Power is contingent on the triple consent of all concerned (both belligerents plus the selected neutral country), and such consent has become hard to come by in recent conflicts. The Diplomatic Conference did not propose to eliminate the requirement of triple consent. Hence, the big question was whether the Protocol would enable a substitute (such as the International Committee of the Red Cross) to " assume that role automatically." [42] The text, as finally approved, creates an " *appearance* of automaticity," yet the operation of a substitute is " explicitly made dependent on specific State consent." [43] Neutral supervision of the implementation of international humanitarian law can

---

[35] *Ibid.* at pp. 38–39.   [36] *Ibid.* at pp. 39–40.
[37] Annex I, Art. 16, *ibid.* at p. 84.   [38] *Ibid.* at pp. 6–7.
[39] See H. S. Levie, " Prisoners of War and the Protecting Power," 55 *American Journal of International Law* (1961), pp. 374–397 at p. 377.
[40] Art. 8 of the first three Conventions and Art. 9 of the Fourth. *Op. cit.* in note 6, above, at pp. 290, 426, 458, 563.
[41] See D. P. Forsythe, " Who Guards the Guardians: Third Parties and the Law of Armed Conflict," 70 *American Journal of International Law* (1976), pp. 41–61 at pp. 64–48.
[42] *Ibid.* at p. 48.   [43] *Ibid.* at p. 56.

therefore still be frustrated. This is one of the most disappointing aspects of the Protocol.

(b) " *Grave Breaches* "

The four Geneva Conventions furnish lists of acts committed against protected persons and property, which are considered " grave breaches " of the Conventions.[44] Protocol I supplements these lists with a lengthy enumeration all its own; it also declares that " grave breaches " of the Conventions as well as the Protocol shall be regarded as war crimes.[45] Whereas the original " grave breaches " of the Conventions in effect constitute war crimes or crimes against humanity,[46] the new list presents a number of difficulties. For instance, under Article 85 (4) (c), practices of *apartheid* shall be regarded as " grave breaches " (and consequently also as war crimes), " when committed wilfully and in violation of the Conventions or the Protocol." [47] *Apartheid* has already been branded as a crime against humanity in the controversial 1973 International Convention on the Suppression and Punishment of the Crime of Apartheid.[48] The double condemnation as a crime against humanity and a war crime demonstrates the sense of revulsion of the overwhelming majority of States from this practice. Still, legally speaking, *apartheid*—reprehensible as it is—cannot possibly be viewed as a war crime without making a mockery of the whole concept couched in this term of art.

(c) *Reprisals*

Numerous prohibitions of reprisals are interspersed in Protocol I. Reprisals are forbidden against the persons and objects protected by the whole of Part II (dealing with wounded, sick and shipwrecked); the civilian population in general; civilian objects; cultural objects; objects indispensable to the survival of the civilian population; the natural environment; and works or installations containing dangerous forces.[49] These specific exclusions of reprisals do not cover the entire spectrum of the *jus in bello*, but—particularly when superimposed on similar prohibitions contained in the four Conventions [50]—they are comprehensive enough. Some reprisals, which

---

[44] Art. 50 of the First Convention, Art. 51 of the Second, Art. 130 of the Third and Art. 147 of the Fourth. *Op. cit.* in note 6 above, at pp. 409, 443, 519, 622.

[45] Art. 11 (4) and 85, *op. cit.* in note 1, above, at pp. 12, 63–65. The reference to war crimes appears in Art. 85 (5), *ibid.* at p. 65.

[46] See Y. Dinstein, " International Criminal Law," 5 *Israel Yearbook on Human Rights* (1975), pp. 55–87, at p. 63.

[47] *Op. cit.* in note 1, above, at p. 64.

[48] 13 *International Legal Materials* (1974), p. 51, at p. 52.

[49] Art. 20, 51 (6), 52 (1), 53 (c), 54 (4), 55 (2) and 56 (4), *op. cit.* in note 1, above, at pp. 17, 36–40.

[50] Art. 46 of the First Convention, Art. 47 of the Second, Art. 13 of the Third and Art. 33 of the Fourth. *Op. cit.* in note 6, above, at pp. 408, 442, 461, 573.

do not come within the prescribed ambit, are still permissible. But they are few and far between. The upshot is an unrealistic expectation from a belligerent State, whose civilian population is deliberately decimated, whose prisoners of war are systematically executed, whose crops are devastated and whose dams are busted, not to retaliate in kind but to turn the other cheek. Needless to say, in actuality no belligerent country will sit idly by when atrocities are committed by the enemy. There are clear dangers in " jettisoning reprisals before securing other and more effective methods of law observance and enforcement." [51] Not the least danger is that officers and soldiers will get used to the idea that the stipulations of the Protocol are merely hortatory and need not be taken seriously.

(d) *Parachutists*

Article 42 of the Protocol [52] prohibits attack against a person parachuting from an aircraft in distress (except in the case of airborne troops). Here, in the last session of the Diplomatic Conference, Committee III reversed a position which it had taken the previous year. Initially, the Committee had refused to grant protection to persons parachuting from an aircraft in distress when it was evident that they would avoid capture by landing on friendly soil, but ultimately it was decided to afford protection in all instances irrespective of who controls the point of landing.[53] This is an important provision, which (in its final form) confirms the formulation of Article 20 of the non-binding Hague Rules of Aerial Warfare of 1923,[54] and reflects customary international law. The exception relating to airborne troops is also in keeping with existing practice.[55]

(e) *Medical Aircraft*

A whole section of the Protocol [56] is devoted to the theme of medical transportation. Article 22 [57] expands the application of the Second Geneva Convention to the case when hospital ships (and similar vessels) carry civilian wounded, sick and shipwrecked. The thrust of the section pertains to medical aircraft.[58] This is a matter of immense practical importance in view of the increasing use of helicopters to evacuate casualties from the battlefield. For some time now, the principal problem has been the proper identification of

---

[51] G. I. A. D. Draper, " The Implementation of the Modern Law of Armed Conflicts,', 8 *Israel Law Review* (1973), pp. 1–22, at p. 9.

[52] *Op. cit.* in note 1, above, at p. 30.

[53] *Op. cit.* in note 9, above, at pp. 341–342.

[54] Commission of Jurists to Consider and Report upon the Revision of the Rules of Warfare, " Rules of Aerial Warfare: 1923," 32 *American Journal of International Law* (1938), Supp., pp. 1–56 at p. 21.

[55] See M. Greenspan, *The Modern Law of Land Warfare* (1959), p. 318.

[56] Art. 21 *et seq.*, *op. cit.* in note 1, above, at pp. 17 *et seq.*

[57] *Ibid.* at pp. 17–18.   [58] Art. 24–31, *ibid.* at pp. 19–25.

medical air transports. The speed of air warfare is such that the ordinary marking of a distinctive emblem on medical aircraft has proved insufficient. With the advent of sophisticated radar systems, it has become possible to detect enemy aircraft in flight from a distance, and long-range anti-aircraft weapons are activated against them a considerable time before they become visible. Thus, a distinctive emblem painted on the fuselage fails to protect the medical aircraft simply because it is not noticeable when the trigger is pressed. The Protocol introduces the use of more effective means for identifying medical aircraft. These consist of flashing blue lights, radio signals and electronic codes (all of which are exclusively reserved for the use of medical aircraft).[59]

(f) *Civilian Medical Personnel*

The protection of medical and religious personnel and medical units—guaranteed in the First Geneva Convention only to permanent or auxiliary personnel of the armed forces—is broadened in the Protocol to civilian personnel, provided that they belong to a Party to the conflict and are recognised by its competent authorities.[60] From now on civilian medical personnel will enjoy protection without being subject to military laws and regulations.[61]

(g) *Weapons*

The last point that should be stressed is that, after much debate, the Diplomatic Conference decided to drop the subject of weapons. Article 35 (2)[62] reiterates the basic prohibition of weapons which cause superfluous injury or unnecessary suffering. But the Protocol does not tackle the specific issues (discussed at length by an *ad hoc* Committee as well as by special Conferences of Government Experts in 1974 and 1976), *e.g.*, incendiary weapons, small-calibre weapons, mines and booby traps.[63] Instead, a resolution was adopted, recommending that another diplomatic conference be convened before 1979 with a view to prohibiting or restricting the use of excessively injurious weapons.[64] In the meantime the question remains open.

V—PROTOCOL II

The legislative history of Protocol II, relating to non-international armed conflicts, is extraordinary.[65] From 1974 to 1977 the Diplomatic

[59] Annex I, Art. 5 *et seq.*, *ibid.* at pp. 78 *et seq.*
[60] Art. 12 *et seq.*, *ibid.* at pp. 12. *et seq.*
[61] *Cf.* the condition set by Art. 26 of the First Geneva Convention. *Op. cit.* in note 6, above, at p. 399.   [62] *Op. cit.* in note 1, above, at p. 27.
[63] See *op. cit.* in note 9, above, at pp. 357–358, 370–371.
[64] Resolution 22, [197–198] *International Review of the Red Cross* (1977), p 117 at p. 118.
[65] The evolution of Protocol II is described in careful language *op. cit.* in note 9, above, at p. 363.

Conference was seized with a given text which was debated, fought out and finally adopted (in one formulation or another) by the three Committees. 49 Articles emerged from the crucible of the Committees, and were officially submitted to the Plenary. However, in the course of the last session (in 1977) concurrently with the open deliberations taking place in the Committees, extensive behind-the-scenes negotiations were held with a view to reaching a shorter and simpler version that would stand a better chance of acceptance. When the Plenary convened, a simplified text, generated by the informal consultations, was presented by Pakistan. The Plenary addressed the Pakistani proposal as an amendment and took it as a working basis for discussion. The Plenary thus completely ignored the formal draft produced by the Committees and, with some modifications, gave its seal of approval to the parallel informal text. The latter became Protocol II, comprising only 28 Articles (of which approximately half are of technical or procedural nature).

As stated in Article 1 (1),[66] Protocol II develops and supplements Article 3 common to the four Geneva Conventions of 1949.[67] But, whereas common Article 3 applies to every " case of an armed conflict not of an international character occurring in the territory of one of the High Contracting Parties," [68] Protocol II applies to all instances not covered by Protocol I which: " take place in the territory of a High Contracting Party between its armed forces and dissident armed forces or other organized armed groups which, under responsible command, exercise such control over a part of its territory as to enable them to carry out sustained and concerted military operations and to implement this Protocol." [69]

Article 1 (2) of Protocol II proceeds to lay down: " This Protocol shall not apply to situations of internal disturbances and tensions, such as riots, isolated and sporadic acts of violence and other acts of a similar nature, as not being armed conflicts." [70] Common Article 3, too, is not brought into operation when mere riots or demonstrations take place.[71] Yet Protocol II has a narrower scope of application, as compared to common Article 3, in the three following respects:

(a) " Wars of liberation " come within the bounds of common Article 3, but are excluded from the parameter of Protocol II because of the express provision of Article 1 (4) of Protocol I (*supra*, section 11).

(b) Protocol II applies only to an armed conflict between the central

---

[66] *Op. cit.* in note 2, above, at p. 90.
[67] *Op. cit.* in note 6, above, at pp. 388–389, 424–425, 454–455, 560–561.
[68] *Ibid.* at pp. 388, 424, 454, 560.
[69] *Op. cit.* in note 2, above, at p. 90.　　　　　　　　　　　　　[70] *Ibid.*
[71] See A. P. Rubin, " The Status of Rebels under the Geneva Conventions of 1949," 21 *International and Comparative Law Quarterly* (1972), pp. 472–496, at p. 484.

government and rebel forces. Common Article 3 has a larger sphere of application since it also encompasses clashes between two or more competing rebel forces,[72] and it regulates the relations between rebels and expeditionary forces sent by a foreign country to assist the central government.[73]

(c) The requirement of control over a part of the territory by the rebels appears in Protocol II, but not in common Article 3. Considering that such control is typical of a fairly advanced phase in a civil war, rebellions in a nascent stage will usually be debarred from crossing the threshold of Protocol II.

The foremost aim of Protocol II is not to limit the scope of application of international humanitarian law, but to augment the protection accorded to the victims of civil wars. The Protocol includes a number of innovative provisions in this vein: (i) acts of terrorism, collective punishments and pillage are forbidden [74]; (ii) minimal humanitarian treatment is assured to internees and detainees [75]; (iii) basic human rights are guaranteed to defendants in criminal trials [76]; (iv) starvation of civilians as a method of warfare is prohibited [77]; (v) attack against works and installations containing dangerous forces is interdicted [78]; (vi) protection is bestowed on medical and religious personnel.[79] In these as in other clauses—which have their counterparts in common Article 3, but are now elaborated in greater detail—civil wars are subjected to more stringent international regulation than ever before.

Evidently, there is still no equation between the *jus in bello* and the *jus in bello interno*.[80] In particular, the status of prisoners of war is not granted to captured combatants in civil wars; though it is " prohibited to order that there shall be no survivors." [81] Nevertheless, a potential for mitigating the horrors of civil wars has been made available to States. Only the future will show what portion of the international community will consent to be bound by the Protocol and will carry out its commandments in actuality.

VI—Entry into Force and Reservations

The entry into force of each Additional Protocol requires the deposit

[72] See G. I. A. D. Draper, " The Geneva Conventions of 1949," 114 *Recueil des Cours* (1965), pp. 63–162, at pp. 86–87.

[73] See R. Pinto, " Les Regles du Droit International concernant la Guerre Civile," 114 *Recueil des Cours* (1965), pp. 455–548, at p. 529.

[74] Art. 4 (2) (b), (d), (g), *op. cit.* in note 2 above, at pp. 91–92.

[75] Art. 5, *ibid.* at pp. 92–94.   [76] Art. 6, *ibid.* at pp. 94–95.

[77] Art. 14, *ibid.* at p. 97.   [78] Art. 15, *ibid.* at pp. 97–98.

[79] Art. 9 and 11, *ibid.* at p. 96.

[80] On the problems emanating from the comparison, see R. R. Baxter, " Ius in Bello Interno: The Present and Future Law," in J. N. Moore (ed.), *Law and Civil War in the Modern World* (1974), pp. 518–536.

[81] Art. 4 (1), *op. cit.* in note 2, above, at p. 91.

of two ratifications or accessions.[82] In this matter the Protocols follow in the footsteps of the four Geneva Conventions.[83] Two ratifications patently represent an irreducible minimum, inasmuch as no agreement can be in force with less than two contracting parties.

It is too early to endeavour to predict the pace of ratifications and accessions. But it is important to emphasise that, for the most part, the two Protocols are constitutive rather than declaratory in nature. That is to say, they do not reflect existing (customary) international law, but, to the contrary, they revise and modify that law. Employing the phraseology of Article 13 (1) (a) of the Charter of the United Nations, [84] the Protocols are not a " codification" pure and simple; in general they are to be subsumed under the heading of " progressive development of international law " (some clauses, as submitted above, may indeed be viewed more as retrogressive than progressive). Consequently, those States which will exercise their prerogative not to be bound by either Protocol, may regard it as *res inter alios acta.*

The Protocols do not incorporate any specific provision in regard to the vital question of reservations.[85] As a result, the rules of general international law will be applicable. These rules are now authoritatively codified in Articles 19 to 23 of the 1969 Vienna Convention on the Law of Treaties.[86] At the time of writing the Vienna Convention is not yet in force,[87] but the International Court of Justice has already treated a number of its provisions as declaratory of customary international law, *e.g.,* Article 60 [88] regarding material breach of treaties,[89] and Article 62 [90] governing change of circumstances.[91] It is at least plausible that the stipulations pertaining to reservations equally reflect general international law.

A reservation is defined as follows in Article 2 (1) (d) of the Vienna Convention: " ' reservation ' means a unilateral statement, however phrased or named, made by a State, when signing, ratifying, accepting, approving or acceding to a treaty, whereby it purports to exclude or

---

[82] Protocol I, Art. 95, *op. cit.* in note 1, above, at p. 70; Protocol II, Art. 23, *op. cit.* in note 2, above, at p. 99.

[83] Art. 58 of the First Convention, Art. 57 of the Second, Art. 138 of the Third and Art. 153 of the Fourth. *Op. cit.* in note 6, above, at pp. 412, 444, 520–521, 523.

[84] 1 *Kitvei Amana* (Nr. 19), p. 203, at p. 209.

[85] Proposed articles relating to the subject were rejected both by Committee I and by the Plenary. *Op. cit.* in note 9, above, at pp. 351, 362.

[86] (1969) *United Nations Juridical Yearbook*, p. 140 at pp. 145–147.

[87] Under Article 84, the Convention shall enter into force following the deposit of 35 ratifications or accessions. *Ibid.* at p. 162.   [88] *Ibid.* at pp. 155–156.

[89] *Legal Consequences for States of the Continued Presence of South Africa in Namibia (South West Africa) notwithstanding Security Council Resolution* 276 (1970), [1971] *I.C.J. Reports* 16 at p. 46; *Appeal relating to the Jurisdiction of the ICAO Council* [1972] *I.C.J. Reports* 46, at p. 67.   [90] *Op. cit.* in note 86, above, at p. 156.

[91] *Fisheries Jurisdiction Case (Jurisdiction of the Court)* [1973] *I.C.J. Reports* 4 at p. 18.

to modify the legal effect of certain provisions of the treaty in their application to that State." [92]

Both Protocols are manifestly treaties in the meaning of Article 2 (1) (a) of the Vienna Convention.[93] Under Article 19 of the Convention, when a treaty neither prohibits a given reservation nor permits only specific reservations which do not include the one in question, that reservation is permissible, provided that it is not " incompatible with the object and purpose of the treaty." [94] It is not always easy to determine whether or not a given reservation is compatible with the object and purpose of a multilateral treaty. The same reservation may indeed be met with acceptance on the part of some contracting parties, while encountering objections from others. The classical doctrine held that a reservation requires acceptance by consensus. However, since the landmark Advisory Opinion, delivered by the International Court of Justice in 1951, in regard to *Reservations to the Convention on the Prevention and Punishment of the Crime of Genocide*,[95] it has gradually become clear that a reserving State may be looked upon as a contracting party *vis-à-vis* other contracting parties which have accepted the reservation, notwithstanding objections by others. In other words, an objection to a reservation on the ground that it is incompatible with the object and purpose of a multilateral treaty is no longer tantamount to veto: it is only decisive in the relations between the reserving and objecting States. Articles 20 and 21 of the Vienna Convention [96] fully endorse this new approach and even carry it a step further. Acceptance of a reservation is now presumed if no objection is raised within one year, and an objection does not necessarily preclude the entry into force of the treaty as between the objecting and reserving States. One single acceptance suffices to establish that the reserving State is bound by the treaty.

Had the Protocols been declaratory of customary international law, the power of reservation would have been severely curtailed. The International Court of Justice ruled in 1969, in the *North Sea Continental Shelf* cases, that when a treaty embodies general or customary norms—which, by their very nature, must have equal force for all members of the international community—they cannot be the subject of any right of unilateral exclusion through reservations.[97] Yet, as the Court expressly pointed out, it is characteristic of purely conventional rules that they are usually subject to reservations.[98] Since the Protocols primarily consist of non-declaratory clauses, which are purely

---

[92] *Op. cit.* in note 86, above, at p. 141. [93] *Ibid.* at p. 141.
[94] *Ibid.* at p. 145. [95] [1951] *I.C.J. Reports* 15, at p. 20.
[96] *Op. cit.* in note 86, above, at pp. 145–146.
[97] [1969] *I.C.J. Reports* 3, at pp. 38–39. [98] *Ibid.* at p. 38.

conventional in the sense that they are binding on contracting parties only, reservations should in principle be allowed.

Inasmuch as quite a few of the Protocols' provisions may be expected to arouse objections, numerous reservations excluding or modifying the effect of these provisions are likely to be formulated. The compatibility of some reservations with the object and purpose of the Protocols may be a matter of controversy. All the more so in view of the inherent difficulty in precisely defining what this object and purpose is. Plainly the Protocols (as attested by their titles) are designed to protect the victims of armed conflicts. What is the quint-essential core of that protection? More particularly, can it be argued that objectionable stipulations (such as Article 1 (4) or 44) form an integral part of the object and purpose of the Protocols? It is sub-mitted that the core of the Protocols must be firmly restricted to a *sine qua non* minimum. Clauses relating to specific issues (ranging from " wars of liberation " to mercenaries and reprisals) are not crucial to the attainment of the fundamental goal of international humanitarian law. Their exclusion or modification, in the application of the Protocols to a reserving State, would not necessarily diminish from that State's overall undertaking to extend protection to the victims of armed conflicts. A strict approach to reservations would actually prove counter-productive: imposing an all-or-nothing option on States may end in fewer ratifications and accessions. Flexibility will enable the maximal number of countries to adhere at least to a minimal number of basic obligations. On balance, the safety valve of reservations will assure more protection to the victims of war.

THE FUTURE OF THE INTERNATIONAL COURT OF JUSTICE

By

LYNDEL V. PROTT

DURING the last decade the International Court of Justice (ICJ) has been subjected to intense scrutiny. It had not received so much attention since the discussions relating to the reconstruction of the international jurisdiction at the end of the Permanent Court's life.

The reasons for this wave of interest seem to be basically two: the landmark *South West Africa* decision of 1966 which raised many issues about the role and acceptability of the Court, and the fiftieth anniversary of the founding of the Permanent Court of International Justice in 1972, which was an appropriate time for stock-taking.

Amid a plethora of learned articles and some ill-considered criticism, three major initiatives emerged which have to be considered by any serious student of the Court. These were the comments of States and debates on an item in the United Nations General Assembly on a review of the role of the International Court of Justice,[1] and two major collective works on the Court by international legal experts: one the proceedings of a Symposium on international adjudication held in Heidelberg in 1972,[2] and the other a collection of essays on the Court by a special panel of the American Society of International Law published in 1976.[3]

The current mood of all discussions is reflected in certain truisms about the Court: that it is under-used and that its business should be increased. The expert legal studies in particular carefully considered a number of proposals to this end. It is my aim here to look at the more important of these proposals, the likely prospect of their adoption, and the probable future of the Court.

All are agreed that the major reason for the under-use of the Court is the States' lack of confidence in it. Various reasons have been assigned for this: doubts as to the impartialty of the Bench (relating

---

[1] The item first appeared on the Agenda of the General Assembly at its 25th session in 1970. The 1971 Session had before it a Report of the Secretary-General based on replies from 26 governments. Action was postponed on the item at the 1971, 1972 and 1973 sessions. The Resolution finally adopted (Nr. 3232 (XXIX) on November 12 1974) did no more than recite the existence of the Court and recommend its use. No further action was to be taken. (The text of the Resolution is set out in the *ICJ Yearbook 1974–75*, pp. 124–127.)

[2] Mosler and Bernhardt (eds.), *Judicial Settlement of International Disputes* (1974).

[3] Gross (ed.), *The Future of the International Court of Justice* (1976).

to composition), deficiencies in procedure and working methods, too limited access and too limited jurisdiction, and so on. Proposals to remedy these problems have been made and are now to be examined. Yet we may even here foreshadow that there are other more fundamental issues which will not be resolved even if these proposals are adopted—which is not very likely.

I—PROCEDURE AND WORKING METHODS OF THE COURT

Some of the recent discussions have concerned the procedure of the Court; its method of conducting cases, and so on. While various improvements have been suggested and while the Court has itself amended its regulations in some important respects,[4] the consensus of learned opinion is that these improvements will not lead to States having greater confidence in the Court or using it more often.[5]

A different issue arises in relation to the Court's own working methods. There is some evidence that certain aspects of the internal functioning of the Bench may hinder its performance. Professor Gross has claimed that this aspect of the Court's functioning has not received sufficient attention in academic and governmental circles.[6] Several recent studies have begun to remedy this.[7]

To illustrate this kind of issue let us consider the form of the Court's judgments. Numerous critics have referred to the laconic or aphoristic quality of many of the Court's judgments [8] which conceal rather than expose the preliminary steps of reasoning. Furthermore even judges concurring in the majority decision may disagree with the

---

[4] The Rules of Court were amended in 1972, *ICJ Yearbook 1971–72*, p. 3, and the Committee on the Revision of the Rules has continued to sit, *ICJ Yearbook 1975–76*, p. 118.

[5] Steinberger concludes that deficiencies in the procedure or working methods of the Court are of secondary importance, " The International Court of Justice," in *op. cit.* in note 2, above, at p. 230. *Cf.* also Fitzmaurice, " The Future of Public International Law," Special Report in the *Livre du Centenaire* 1873–1973 (Institut de Droit International), at pp. 277–278; Weissberg, "The Role of the International Court of Justice in the United Nations System: The First Quarter Century," in *op. cit.* in note 3, above, at p. 176.

[6] *Op. cit.* in note 3, above, at p. 738.

[7] *Der internationale Richter im Spannungsfeld der Rechtskulturen*, 1975 (forthcoming in English as *The Latent Power of Culture and the International Judge*), esp. Chaps. II, V and VI; Lillich and White, " The Deliberative Process of the International Court of Justice: a Preliminary Critique and Some Possible Reforms," 70 *American Journal of International Law* (1976) p. 28; Petrén, " Forms of Expression of Judicial Activity," in *op. cit.* in note 3, above, at p. 445; Gros, " Observations sur la Mode de Délibération de la Cour internationale de Justice," 14 *Communicazioni e Studi* (Istituto di Diritto Internazionale a Straniero della Università di Milano) (1975) p. 337.

[8] Hambro, " The Reasons behind the decisions of the International Court of Justice," 7 *Current Legal Problems* (1954) 212 at pp. 222–225; Mann, *Studies in International Law* (1973), pp. 158–159; Kearney, " Sources of Law and the International Court of Justice," in *op. cit.* in note 3, above, at pp. 696–708.

reasoning on which it is based, so that there may in fact be no majority supporting that reasoning (as happened in the *Nuclear Tests* cases where only six of the 15 judges supported the reasoning of the majority judgment [9]). These unsatisfactory circumstances are largely due to the Court's methods of work: of discussion, drafting, and voting. [10] Yet further analysis of the latter techniques will not resolve the Court's problems. All the evidence indicates that no real progress will be made until the Bench is a better integrated group and that will not happen unless its composition becomes more homogeneous, or a greatly increased workload builds up its group personality.

Unfortunately the Court is here caught up in a vicious circle. There is no doubt that many problems relating to the way the Bench functions as a group would be resolved satisfactorily sooner or later if it had to work much more intensely: *i.e.*, if the members of the group had to interact more often: this would lead to better knowledge of the members of the group and hence to a wider range of tactics for resolving working problems. [11] Certainly a heavier workload is one reason for the better internal functioning of some other international courts, such as the European Court of Human Rights at Strasbourg and the Court of the European Communities in Luxembourg. The result is that, however much further research is done on the internal functioning of the Court, it is doubtful whether the problems exposed will be solved until the Court has more business. The difficulties and dangers of this kind of research [12] have also been noted by the writers concerned, and in the absence of prospects that their research can be fruitfully used, there may be some reluctance to take it any further.

II—Obtaining More Work
for the Court

Numerous proposals have been made for increasing the Court's workload. One would be to widen access to the Court by permitting other parties to use it. Chief among these proposals are to allow international organisations, [13] non-governmental organisations

---

[9] *ICJ Reports* (1974) p. 253. For a detailed discussion of this aspect, see this writer, " Avoiding a Decision on the Merits in the International Court of Justice," 7 *Sydney Law Review*, p. 433 esp. pp. 441–444.

[10] The Court has itself been aware of the problem and in 1976 adopted a new Resolution concerning the Internal Judicial Practice of the Court, *ICJ Yearbook 1975–76* p. 119.

[11] *Cf.* this writer, *op. cit.* in note 7, above, Chap. II.

[12] *Ibid.* Introduction: Lillich and White, *op. cit.* in note 7, above, at p. 28.

[13] Steinberger, *op. cit.* in note 5, above at pp. 243–246; Gross, " The International Court of Justice: Consideration of Requirements for Enhancing its Role in the International Legal Order " in *op. cit.* in note 3, above, at pp. 68–71; Fitzmaurice, " Enlargement of the Contentious Jurisdiction of the Court," in note 3, above, p. 461 at pp. 478–481.

(NGOs) and corporate bodies, and finally individuals to use the Court.[14] If these parties were allowed access, then clearly work would increase. The Court replies to 600 applicants per year that it has no jurisdiction to hear the claims which they wish to make before it.[15] A number of cases which did get to the Court *via* inter-State contentious proceedings were directly based on the claims of individuals or corporate bodies.[16] There is no lack of willingness therefore on the part of these potential clients of the Court. International organisations would no doubt also find such access to the contentious jurisdiction of great importance, for they have already made substantial use of the advisory jurisdiction of the Court.

What are the prospects for this kind of proposal? For the present they would appear to have no chance of success. The Court is bound by its Statute which provides in Article 34 that only States may be parties in cases before the Court. Its initiative, despite the clear development in international law since this clause of the Statute was originally drafted at the foundation of the Permanent Court,[17] is thus precluded. The States, who are capable of having this Part of the Statute amended, are most unlikely to do so, since it requires a two-thirds majority of the members of the General Assembly including all the permanent members of the Security Council. The uncompromising stand of the Eastern-bloc States on parties to international law is well-known and the one amendment to the Statute which the Court itself proposed in 1969 on the seat of the Court, came to nothing, although that proposed amendment would not have raised theoretical objections of the same kind.

Could the potential parties themselves take any action? International organisations are basically groups of States, so they would be unlikely to get a consensus on this issue, as the same problem arises for any initiative they might take as arises for amending the Statute. This consideration seems to seal the fate of some ingenious proposals, such as out-flanking Article 34 by setting up a special organ of the United Nations to request advisory opinions [18]; although the procedure has in the past resulted in one or two cases for the Court, it could not be the source of any large new influx of work for the Court without a change in the attitude of States.

The other prospective litigants (individuals and non-governmental

---

[14] Gross, *op. cit.* in note 12, above, at pp. 36–37; Fitzmaurice, *op. cit.* in note 13, above, at pp. 478–484.

[15] Buergenthal in *op. cit.* in note 2, above, at p. 68–69; Steinberger *op. cit.* in note 5, above, at pp. 264–265; *ICJ Yearbook 1975–76*, p. 123 and preceding *Yearbooks*.

[16] *e.g.* the *Asylum* case (1950), *ICJ Reports* (1950), p. 266; *Anglo-Iranian Oil* case (1952), *ICJ Reports* (1952), p. 93; *Nottebohm* case (1953), *ICJ Reports* (1953), p. 111; *Interhandel* case (1959), *ICJ Reports* (1959), p. 6 and the *Barcelona Traction* case (1970), *ICJ Reports* (1970), p. 3, to mention but a few.

[17] Gross, *op. cit.* in note 12, above, at p. 67.   [18] *Ibid.* pp. 42–43.

organisations) cannot directly change the Statute and while they could in some countries put pressure on their governments to initiate appropriate international moves, in respect of others such a programme needs only to be stated to be seen as quite unrealistic. They could unite *internationally* to form their own judicial body: numerous economic, academic and other interest groups have formed international unions, which may have no status on the inter-State plane, but are important and recognised at the international level, and some also have achieved a certain status in inter-State matters (*e.g.*, the International Committee of the Red Cross (ICRC) and other human rights non-governmental organisations which have consultative status under Art. 71 of the Charter). But even this development presupposes a degree of co-ordination, interest and planning which does not appear to be present. It would also not enable the parties concerned to sue States without the State's consent: yet this is probably their main requirement.

Does it make sense even to mention the prospect of an international court set up by non-States when talking about the International Court of Justice? This writer thinks it does because she believes that the more international cases occur, even for the most dull and routine matters, the more habituated the world will become to international judicial settlement. This could slowly provide a better climate of opinion for the International Court of Justice. Yet from the above remarks it can be seen that even this development, at least as a result of non-State juridical initiatives, must at present be seen as a very slight chance.

More indirect methods of getting the interests of legal persons other than States before the Court have been suggested. The most interesting of these are access by way of case stated and evocation.[19] These would provide a means of referring matters of international law from domestic or other tribunals to the International Court of Justice: the case stated at the instance of the tribunal, the evocation procedure at the instance of one of the parties to the case. Fitzmaurice takes the view that these would require amendments to the Court's Statute: and if this is so, their adoption is remote. But even if this were not so, the development of these procedures depends on the goodwill of States, and returns us to the vicious circle of issues centred on " confidence in the Court."

Apart from enlarging the number of possible litigants, commentators have also suggested widening the jurisdiction of the Court in respect of the issues which may be submitted to it. In respect of the

---

[19] These are dealt with by Fitzmaurice *op. cit.* in note 13, above, at pp. 484–485. He also deals with other suggested procedures such as *recours en annulation*, Mandamus and proceedings *in rem* which are subject to the same problems.

contentious jurisdiction clearly the problem here is the acceptance of the compulsory jurisdiction of the Court. It has been suggested that compulsory jurisdiction should apply to all parties to the Statute unless they make a declaration that they reject compulsory jurisdiction. It is thought that the "contracting out" principle may put more psychological pressure on States to conform than the present "contracting in" system.[20] This does not seem likely to this writer, although it may be that some smaller new States, taking up their international responsibilities, may happen to put the necessary declaration of non-acceptance fairly low on their list of priorities and so be "caught"—at least for a time—by the compulsory jurisdiction. It is hard to imagine it making any difference whatever to States with adequate expertise at hand, especially if they have a fixed philosophy against the Court.

Along with this go proposals to restrict the use of reservations which have largely emasculated the purported acceptance of the existing compulsory jurisdiction.[21] There is no provision for reservations in the Statute (other than the condition of reciprocity) and it seems that there are two possible ways of dealing with this issue: by holding that the reservations have no effect (*i.e.* that the State making the "reservation" is fully bound), or by holding that the reservation goes to the heart of acceptance and renders it a nullity.[22] Once again only those States unaware of the new policy or unable to change quickly enough would appear likely to be caught in the first case: the second would not appear to improve the present situation.

A further suggestion has been to make a list of topics from which States could choose what they thought to be "safe" topics and omit others—a kind of "*smorgasbord*" approach to jurisdiction.[23] There are some serious problems about this. Obviously some problems are going to have aspects of several issues in them or be for other reasons difficult to classify.[24] More seriously still, a State is unlikely to know, until the problem arises, just how inappropriate it may find judicial settlement of that problem. Until the commercial use of Arctic waters was feasible, and modern ecological knowledge so extensive, Canada could hardly have foreseen that it would need to reserve from its acceptance of the Court's jurisdiction, measures relating to the protection of its Arctic areas.

---

[20] *Ibid.* p. 473; Gross, *op. cit.* in note 12, above, at p. 78.

[21] Fitzmaurice, *op. cit.* in note 13, above, at pp. 474–475.

[22] Lauterpacht, *Interhandel* case (1959), *ICJ Reports*, p. 6, Separate Opinion, pp. 95 *et seq.*

[23] Steinberger, *op. cit.* in note 5, above, at pp. 239–240; Sohn, *op. cit.* in note 2, above, at p. 71.

[24] Steinberger, *op. cit.* in note 5, above, at p. 240; also *cf.* discussion by Jennings in *op. cit.* in note 2, above, at p. 41 and by Scheuner, *ibid.* at pp. 60–61.

Another suggestion has been to list not the areas where adjudication would be appropriate, but where it is clearly thought to be inappropriate—at any rate at the present time.[25] Defining certain " no-go " areas for international adjudication would seem to be a ticklish operation. What would the States agree on? Perhaps the complex related to control of foreign investment, nationalisation, etc., looking at the history of cases dealing with such issues in the ICJ (*Anglo-Iranian Oil* case, *Barcelona Traction* case), should not go to the Court. The appropriate procedure would now appear to be a specialised one, such an as arbitration under the Convention on the Settlement of Investment Disputes between States and Nationals of Other States 1965. Issues relating to conservation are unlikely to be solved in the ICJ forum either: the fate of the *Icelandic Fisheries* case, the Canadian reservation concerning control of Arctic pollution and the legislative activity concerning the deep seabed are all pointers in this direction.

But equally well one could foresee many new States refusing to submit any case which contained issues (at least in their minds) relating to " colonialism " to the Court,[26] at least during the period while it felt the Bench to be dominated by Western European judges. Now that they are far more strongly represented, it is easy to imagine Western States not wanting to submit these cases to the new Bench. In fact making up a list of this kind would, it seems to this writer, arouse all sorts of issues about impartiality and the composition of the Bench which are both basic and extraordinarily hard to resolve. These will be discussed in the next section.

Finally it has been suggested that the Court can itself assist by making the broadest interpretation possible of compromissory clauses.[27] To some extent the Court has already done so: it has upheld its jurisdiction in numerous cases where a party has denied the applicability of the instrument to the case at hand (*e.g.*, *Corfu Channel* case,[28] the mandate for South West Africa,[29] the Anglo-Icelandic Agreement on Fisheries[30]). The Court can hardly be accused of unduly narrow construction of jurisdictional instruments. Indeed, any far greater width would probably shake confidence in the Court even further and States might well decide to limit the Court's freedom of interpretation by rejecting general acceptances of jurisdiction altogether in favour of the special *compromis* for each case.

---

25 Report by Jennings, *ibid*. at pp. 40–42.
26 Anand, in *op. cit.* in note 2, above, at p. 70.
27 *Cf.* discussion in *op. cit.* in note 2, above, at pp. 759–763.
28 *Corfu Channel* case (1948), *ICJ Reports* (1948), p. 27.
29 *South West Africa* case (1962), *ICJ Reports* (1962), p. 319.
30 *Fisheries Jurisdiction (Jurisdiction)* case (1973), *ICJ Reports* (1973), p. 3.

III—CONFIDENCE IN THE COURT:
COMPOSITION AND IMPARTIALITY
OF THE BENCH

Much of the discussion about confidence in the Court has been centred on the composition of the Bench. This circles around an issue on which some comments have been made but little has been done by way of serious detailed analysis [31]: the impartiality of the judges.

What does " impartiality " mean? It includes the basic requirement of a judge's personal integrity; on the very simplest level, that he cannot be bribed. Yet this does not appear to be an allegation made by States against the Court.

A much more obvious concern for the International Court is the question of national or regional bias on the part of judges. Judge Elias, speaking before his appointment to the Bench, regarded the decisions of certain judges in the *Advisory Opinion of Certain Expenses of the United Nations* and the *South West Africa* cases as dictated by the national or regional bias of the States from which they came.[32] This view is far too simple: to begin with, he notes only Judge Jessup as consistent in his approach—teleological—in both cases, though Judge Gros, who is the target of some of his criticism, was also consistent in his adoption of a severely restricted interpretation in both cases. Indeed, this kind of accusation has been firmly rejected by Professor Anand who states that " despite the *South West Africa* case the Court's inherent impartiality was not in question." [33]

There is, though, still another aspect of impartiality to consider: that is the unconscious attitudes and cultural moulding of the judges which may clearly affect the whole train of thought and determine the solution of the case.[34] The judge, like every other human being, absorbs and adopts certain values from the human society in which he grows up. This includes values about law: its importance in human society, its priority among other values, how it is derived. Judge Mosler has said that " in order to ensure that certain tendencies are represented, a campaign is sometimes waged . . . over the filling of judicial offices. Where such efforts succeed, the process of finding the law more closely resembles a balancing of opinions than the subsuming of the facts under the objective law." [35] Yet this very comment is

[31] Franck, *The Structure of Impartiality* (1968); Prott, *op. cit.* in note 7, above, esp. at Chap. VI.

[32] Report by Elias, in *op. cit.* in note 2, above, at pp. 24–25.

[33] Anand in *op. cit.* in note 2, above, at p. 53.

[34] Examples from the jurisprudence of the International Court are given in the first work cited note 7, Chap. VI.

[35] Mosler, *op. cit.* in note 2, above, at p. 10.

itself the result of a certain attitude towards law: the vision of the judicial process as the subsuming of facts under an objective law is very much an attitude of a specific legal culture favoured in some, culturally alien in other social systems.

Hambro felt that there was not any evidence of lack of independence of the judges. " It had happened fairly often that a judge had acted and judged as a man of his legal and national background might be expected to act and judge. But the fact that the judge gave judgment in accordance with the legal opinions prevalent in his country was no proof at all of lack of independence." [36] Yet, though Hambro and Anand [37] both admit the importance of social moulding, they deny that it affected States' attitudes to the Court. This seems unduly sanguine, for in the same discussion Baxter made the comment that: " Up to now it had been difficult for a Foreign Ministry lawyer to persuade his government colleagues and the general public of the need to take treaty disputes to the ICJ, because a number of the judges would be products of a legal culture which would not have given them an appropriate background for dealing with the questions at issue. For example, it was hard to imagine the purely hypothetical case of a bilateral agreement on multinational companies between Canada and the USA being brought before a Soviet Judge." [38]

It seems to this writer that two results follow from this analysis: that a judge gives opinions consistent with the legal traditions of his own country is to be expected and it should not be regarded as an allegation of partiality against a judge to point out a particular instance of it; but that, secondly, the fact that there is a wide divergence of legal philosophies on the Court may be a very relevant criticism of its present organisation. Baxter's comment is a relevant one and suggests that too much is expected of the Court in its present shape. States would feel more comfortable with, and possibly have more confidence in, a court whose judges shared the value system of its own national society. This may well mean that there would be an advantage in setting up regional courts to do a great deal of routine work—a pattern that has proved fruitful in Europe, but perhaps because of the special place accorded to courts in European social philosophy. This is a very important issue which will be taken up again in another section of this article.

One related issue is that of competence. Indeed, Elias has said that " qualification in international law was a greater safeguard for independence than any conceivable method of selection." [39] The statutory requirements are somewhat notorious in this regard, since

---

[36] Hambro in *ibid.*, at p. 57.
[37] Anand in *ibid.* at p. 53.
[38] Baxter in *ibid.* at pp. 53–54.
[39] Report by Elias, in *ibid.* at p. 32.

they do not demand competence in international law.[40] Indeed, Fitzmaurice has suggested that on occasions two-thirds of the Bench have had to learn their international law after their appointment to the Bench.[41] There are various considerations of relevance here. First, legal expertise clearly relates to those social systems which separate out the legal system from other normative systems and have developed a distinct legal profession with high standards of technical training. This is not necessarily true of other social systems where law is less clearly differentiated. Secondly, on a quite different level, there is no kind of formal internationally recognised training in international law. Thirdly, whatever the merits of training in law generally,[42] or in international law specifically, some small and new States would find it very difficult to spare, if not to find, persons among their own nationals of the high degree of professional training thought necessary for the ICJ Bench. Finally, though the States of Western Europe have sufficient highly qualified lawyers, with considerable experience in international law, they have frequently not been proof against the temptation to nominate and vote for persons selected on quite other criteria such as being too able in domestic politics for the government of the moment to keep at home, or as deserving a highly-paid overseas job as a reward for faithful service.

These factors affect the competence of the Court and the States' confidence in it. States of the Western European tradition are certainly aware of the last-named factor and because the criteria of professional competence are hallowed in their own legal traditions, can hardly regard the result as warranting full confidence in the Court. Small new States feel disadvantaged in two ways: sparing their pre-eminent international legal expert to the Court may disadvantage them in negotiations with States who have plenty of experts to call on with the concomitant disadvantage of seeing little result for the sacrifice, since their legal system may as yet not have the distinctive features of the separate normative structure characteristic of Western legal systems and may not be seen to contribute anything distinctive to the work of the Court.

What prospect is there for changing this highly unsatisfactory state of affairs? High professional competence in the judicial office being an article of faith in most States of the Western European legal tradition, they could hardly vote against a move to revise the Statute in this regard, but the cynicism of many about the Court, revealed in their practice as to nomination, would probably prevent their

---

[40] *Cf.* the comments by Elias, *ibid.* p. 22, and in discussion at pp. 31–32.

[41] Fitzmaurice, *op. cit.* in note 5, above, at p. 288.

[42] There has been one judge of the International Court who had no training as a professional lawyer: see the Biographical Note on Judge Wellington Koo in the *ICJ Yearbook 1956–57*, at pp. 16–17.

actively promoting such a move. The Eastern-bloc States are clearly against any move to improve the Court in any way. The Third-World States are unlikely to attempt it, since higher qualifications may limit even further their pool of possible nominees. The current unsatisfactory provisions do not seem likely to be changed.

There is a sentiment, well attested by public statements by politicians and judges, that judges are expected to act and vote in a way that lawyers of their own nationality act and vote [43]; indeed, it is to some extent inevitable that this should be so. Recently some States have adverted to the fact that nationals of countries who do not accept the adjudicatory process at all can comment on the most delicate problems of States which do, knowing that their own State will never put itself in this situation. Do judges from States which do not intend ever to appear as parties before the Court's jurisdiction exercise their judicial function in exactly the same spirit and manner as judges from States which may and do thus appear before the Court? [44] On the present Court, nine of the 15 judges come from States which do not accept the Court's compulsory jurisdiction. [45] Three come from countries whose acceptance of the compulsory jurisdiction is subject to reservations [46] and three from States which although they have accepted the compulsory jurisdiction of the Court without substantial reservations, have never in fact been involved in litigation before the Court. [47] An institution lacks credibility if its members themselves are seen to doubt its worth. But once again, this is not a situation likely to be remedied; States who do accept the adjudicatory process are likely to become less and less happy about the Court the higher the percentage of judges from non-accepting States as opposed to accepting States rises, and States who do not believe in the adjudicatory principle want the Court to fail, so are not going to change things. [48]

There have been suggestions that the composition of the Bench might be improved by changing the timing of elections [49]—this seems an unrealistic hope, since horse-trading will not thereby be eliminated, merely stretched over a longer time-span. Proposals have also been made to improve the operation of the National Panel which acts as the nominating committee [50] but it seems unlikely that

---

[43] *Cf.* the statement by Judge Caneiro in the *Anglo-Iranian Oil* case (1952), *ICJ Reports* (1952), p. 93, Separate Opinion, at p. 161, and text relating to notes 26 and 32, above.   [44] Gross, *op. cit.* in note 6, above, at pp. 745–746.

[45] France, Poland, Benin, Spain, the Soviet Union, Argentina, Federal Republic of Germany, Senegal and Syria.   [46] India, the United States and United Kingdom.

[47] Uruguay, Nigeria and Japan.   [48] Gross, *op. cit.* in note 6, above, at pp. 764–765.

[49] Gross, *op. cit.* in note 12, above, at pp. 55–58.

[50] Petrén " Forms of Expression of Judicial Activity," in *op. cit.* in note 3, above, at p. 470; and Golden, " National Groups and the Nomination of Judges of the International Court of Justice: A Preliminary Report," 9 *International Lawyer* (1975), p. 333.

governments will agree to reverse the trend of increasing governmental influence over these bodies.

IV—CONFIDENCE IN THE COURT:
ATTITUDE OF STATES

From what has been said, there clearly are deep-seated reasons why most States approach the Court with some distrust. These problems relating to composition and impartiality are not easily resolved, and the background to them needs far more research, along lines to be sketched in the last section of this paper.

Among the reasons other than composition and partiality which have been given are the Court's unpredictability [51] and the uncertainty as to the law applicable.[52] The first of these objections seems a little strange, for even in a domestic court, if the result were always predictable, the prospective loser would settle unless of a particularly litigious nature or badly advised. Litigants generally calculate that they have at least a good chance of success and prefer to run it than to settle for less. Why should the International Court's decisions be any more predictable than any other court's? Sometimes this question merges into the second: the Court is said to be unpredictable because it is not known what law it will apply.[53] This is a more substantial problem. In a closely detailed analysis of some early Permanent Court cases, Kearney remarked on the notable contrast between the Reports of International Arbitral awards, showing " a reasonably consistent pattern of buttressing pivotal legal positions with references to State practice, apposite treaties, doctrinal disquisition, pertinent arbitral decisions, and private law analogies " and judgments of the Court which often consisted principally of *ex cathedra* pronouncements and a pronounced aversion to citing either the specific origin of a legal rule or the general source of that rule.[54] In more recent cases the Court appears to buttress its decisions by reference only to its own decisions. These practices raise issues which go to the very heart of the Court and which will be discussed in the next section.

Finally, there is one other act of the Court itself which has been seen to engender distrust or litigation before it: that is its recent disposition to dodge difficult questions. In the *Icelandic Fisheries* case the United Kingdom submitted that Iceland's claim to an exclusive fisheries jurisdiction of 50 miles was without foundation in

---

[51] See, *e.g.* Hambro's comment in *op. cit.* in note 2, above, at p. 57.

[52] See, *e.g.*, Kearney's discussion of the practice of the Permanent Court in *op. cit.* in note 8 above, at pp. 649–653.

[53] Report by Steinberger, cited note 15, above, at pp. 266–269.

[54] *Op. cit.* in note 8, above, at pp. 649–653; Bindschedler-Robert in *op. cit.* in note 2, above, at pp. 58–59.

international law and was invalid. The Court refused to make a
finding on that claim: its finding was restricted to Iceland's claim
vis-à-vis the United Kingdom which had historic rights in the area.
Gross surmises that "... this judgment may well come to be regarded
as the first one in which the Court without pronouncing a *non liquet*
actually declined to exercise its judicial function in disregard of its
Statute and of the compromissory clause and in which it transformed
itself from an organ of international law into an *amiable compositeur*." [55]

In another recent case the Court avoided answering the submission
put to it that the carrying out of nuclear tests in the South Pacific
Ocean was not consistent with the rules of international law. The
Court avoided answering this question by holding that the dispute
no longer existed, although this seems not to be true as a matter of
fact, and although the opinion of the strong group of dissenting
judges was very much against this dismissal *in limine*, pointing out
that the Court " has not the discretionary power of choosing those
contentious cases it will decide and those it will not." [56]

If these reasons for lack of confidence are internal to the Court
itself, there has been no lack of other suggestions about the unwillingness of States to litigate before the Court on other grounds, and
as to how this frame of mind might be changed. Fitzmaurice, for
example, suggests the submission of more politically unimportant
disputes with important legal issues,[57] the opening of the advisory
jurisdiction to States, the setting up of an international system of
appeals, and so on. These may provide avenues for more cases of
less importance to come to the Court and thus minimise the political
stake for a State in losing a case.

In gauging the attitude of States, the attitudes of the legal adviser
is of the first importance. There are plenty of indications that his
enthusiasm for the Court is generally very moderate.[58]

What part can the Court itself play to increase its authority?
Gordon has suggested that the Court should seek to promote support for its authority by seeking, both through its judgments and
outside the judicial process, to convince lay people, whom governments only sometimes represent, of its value in international
affairs.[59] This he says may entail the disenchantment of its traditional

---

[55] Gross, *op. cit.* in note 12, above, at p. 752. *Cf.* also the discussion of this case by
Kearney, *op. cit.* in note 8, above, at pp. 690–696.
[56] *Nuclear Tests* case (*Australia* v. *France*) (1974), *ICJ Reports* (1974), p. 253, Joint
Dissenting Opinion (Onyeama, Dillard, Jimenez de Aréchaga and Waldock), p. 322.
[57] *Op. cit.* in note 12, above, at p. 48.
[58] See Fitzmaurice, *op. cit.* in note 5, above, at pp. 278–280 and 358–360.
[59] Gordon, " Changing Attitudes towards Courts and their Possession of Social
Decision Prerogatives " in *op. cit.* in note 3, above, at p. 336, esp. pp. 356–357.

supporters, foreign offices, inter-governmental organisations and the Western legal élite. It is difficult to see how the Court can create a constituency for itself, for except in the literate, alert, and legally attuned societies of Europe, its degree of penetration into public awareness must be small. The degree of international contact and awareness of international affairs in most Third-World countries, largely preoccupied with questions of economics, is much lower than in the interlocked societies of the Western industrialised nations. Nor, if it alienates Foreign Offices, legal advisers and the Western legal élite, will the Court have much as a vehicle, for it needs their support to have cases in which it can write judgments. Once again there is a circle which it would seem impossible to break.

V—THE CULTURAL CONTEXT
OF " COURT," " LAW " AND " JUDGE "

It is impossible to deal adequately with the problem of State attitudes without giving some consideration to those concepts basic to the Court's operation such as *court, law* and *judge*.[60] When the Statute of the Permanent Court was drawn up in 1920, the draftsmen came from States of the Western European tradition which placed a similar value on " law " and had developed legal institutions within their own societies to a high degree. There were some differences between them, but there were at any rate certain shared elements. The ICJ has in certain cases simply assumed that everyone understood what was meant by the term " court " and did not define it in detail.[61] Mosler has spoken of certain essential elements " unanimously " agreed on for an international court [62] and Tomuschat has listed criteria for international tribunals.[63] Both lists represent a meaning of " court " familiar to Western European lawyers.

But, although these are undeniably important elements of courts, there appear to be others, equally important which are rarely

[60] In developing this section I am indebted to Professor Jacob Sundberg of Stockholm for a stimulating discussion of these issues.

[61] *Continental Shelf* case (1969), *ICJ Reports* (1969) at p. 48; *Advisory Opinion on the Administrative Tribunal of the I.L.O.* (1956), *ICJ Reports* (1956) at p. 97; *Northern Cameroons* case (Preliminary Objections) (1963), *ICJ Reports* (1963), at pp. 29–30, 33–34, 38; *Advisory Opinion on Namibia* (1971), *ICJ Reports* (1971), at pp. 22–23; *Nuclear Tests* case (*Australia* v. *France*), (1974), *ICJ Reports* (1974), at pp. 259–260 and 270–271. Some important separate opinions have also dealt with the nature of the judicial function, *e.g.* the Joint Dissenting Opinion of Spender and Fitzmaurice in the *South West Africa* case (1962), *ICJ Reports* (1962), at pp. 465–468; Separate Opinion of Fitzmaurice in the *Northern Cameroons* case (1963), *ICJ Reports* (1963), at pp. 97–108, and the Joint Dissenting Opinion of Onyeama, Dillard, Jimenez de Aréchaga and Waldock in the *Nuclear Tests* case (cited in this note) at p. 314, 321–326 and *passim*.

[62] Mosler, *op. cit.* in note 51, p. 9.

[63] Tomuschat, Preparatory Report on " International Courts and Tribunals with Regionally Restricted and/or Specialised Jurisdiction," in *op. cit.* in note 2, above, at pp. 290–312 (summarised at p. 285).

articulated and of which we are, therefore, far less conscious, *e.g.* that the impartiality concerned is only a *relative* impartiality, there being a substantial factual, though no formal, connection between members of the various élites in the social structure; that the judges to a substantial extent are drawn from the élite; that there is a substantial (but not perfect) concordance of values within the society, and so on. These aspects though they appear less lofty on the plane of idealism may be essential for courts to function properly. Are equivalent features apparent in the International Court and its environment? If not, this could be usefully explored as a possible reason for its more insecure place.

These issues are complex and cannot be dealt within the confines of one paper, but one extended example may be given: the relationship of the theory of judicial method to the Western concept of a " court."

It was for a long time a tradition of the Western legal system that judges do not make law. This fiction was so strong that it took over half a century of sustained analysis to prove that judges did make law—a truth which has only just now begun to be accepted in France[64] and appears to be still denied in Soviet theory.[65] This was because judges supported their pronouncements with a range of arguments which drew on existing legal tradition and made the result appear to be the inevitable culmination of a line of development, even though other elements were probably available which could have been used to support the opposite conclusion. The choice was often made (usually intuitively) on policy grounds.

The difficulty for an international court was that this very basic feature of courts in the Western European tradition could hardly exist: the Court itself, having no predecessors, had no previous tradition, but emerged directly from an act of will of the States. International law itself was not a unified tradition: in many important respects it did, and still does, draw on the various national legal traditions.

Various commentators have remarked on the unsatisfactory nature of the " *ex cathedra* " pronouncements of the Court on important issues without supporting reasoning, thus causing confusion about the sources of law relied on by the Court.[66] Though judges giving individual opinions have often given justification in the traditional way, majority opinions have done so far more seldom, because even when judges can agree on the result, they cannot agree on the lines of argument which justify it.

---

[64] *Cf.* Dawson, *The Oracles of the Law* (1968), esp. pp. 415 *et seq.*; Belaïd, *Essai sur le pouvoir Créateur et Normatif des Juges* (1974), still has to argue for recognition of the law-creating power of the judges.

[65] Terebilov, *The Soviet Court* (1973), p. 47.   [66] See notes 8 and 47, above.

The destruction of the myth that judges do not make law has probably had a most serious result for the ICJ.[67] The ICJ is aware of its law-creating power, but does not bother to exercise it by bolstering with principle and argument in the traditional Western way. This may have serious repercussions, for if it fails to persuade litigants that the law it pronounces can be somehow seen as a restatement or at most a development of the existing law, it lacks one of the most important features of a " court " in the Western tradition.

Closely related to the issue of judge-made law is the theory of legal reasoning. The tradition that legal reasoning is intra-systemic (*i.e.* that all the elements necessary for the judge to develop the solution of the case already exist in the legal system) has been a very strong one in the Western legal tradition. Comparatively recently, and more in the United States than in any other State of the group being discussed, a frank recognition of policy choices open to a judge in some cases has been accepted. In other countries, particularly in France, for example, the attachment to the theory of intra-systemic or " legalistic " reasoning is still very strong. Once again this creates problems for the International Court of Justice. The Court has been accused of an excess of legalistic reasoning.[68] But these writers have for the most part failed to develop an alternative theory of legal reasoning appropriate for the International Court. Arkadyev and Jakovlev, in their well-known article, claimed that the legalistic reasoning of the *South West Africa* case was " against international law." But in what way was it *against* it? For the draftsmen of the Permanent Court's Statute (taken over by the ICJ) it was a hallowed technique probably inseparable from the concept of a " court." Even today, when the legalistic theory is meeting strong competition, it remains an important and favoured technique in some of the world's major legal systems. Its use can only be *contrary* to international law if international law has completely diverged from municipal law in respect of its theory of judicial method.

This discussion gives rise to some interesting implications. The draftsman in 1920 had sufficient confidence in the mutuality of their concepts " court," " law," " judge," *etc.*, as not to feel it necessary to give any definition. Though there were some not insignificant divergences (*e.g.* on the question of written and unwritten sources of

---

[67] *Cf.* the comment of Jennings, *op. cit.* in note 2, above, at p. 37.

[68] This was the basis of most articles criticising the decision in the *South West Africa* case (1966), *e.g. Report of the Eighth Session of the Asian-African Legal Consultative Committee 1966*, pp. 433–451; Fisher, " Les Réactions devant l'arrêt de la Cour internationale de Justice concernant le Sud-Ouest Africain," 12 *Annuaire français de Droit international* (1966). pp. 144 *et seq.*; Arkadyev and Jakovlev, " International Court of Justice against International Law," *International Affairs* (Moscow) (1966), pp. 67 *et seq.*; Green, " United Nations, South-West Africa and the World Court," 7 *Indian Journal of International Law* (1967) p. 471.

law between common and code law systems) it was somehow felt that the judges could resolve these issues, and by and large they did. Their training in the various Western European legal traditions opened to them a wealth of resources from which to develop a Court new in its functions. But many of the basic ideas are not only not shared, but also are completely alien to other societies. It is the attitude of these societies which is now of importance to the International Court.

Let us examine, for example, Soviet views on " law," " courts " and "judges." The Marxist view is that law is the expression of will of the ruling class. The adaptation of that theory to international law has been difficult and led to controversies between Soviet theorists such as Korovin and Pashukanis.[69] There is little doubt that there is great difficulty in relating basic principles of Marxist theory of law, which speak of the "withering away" of State and law, first to the increasing strength of the State and law in the Soviet Union, and, secondly, to the special nature of international law.[70] Nonetheless, despite all the discussion and doctrinal changes the ultimate " withering away " of law is not doubted. It is not surprising that the legal profession does not attract the keenest students.[71] There is a definite correlation between a strong and esteemed domestic legal system and the will to create an effective international judicature. This ultimate withering away of law as the ambition of Marxist societies must be contrasted with the central position of law in others.

The needs of the Soviet Union in its external policy to make use of some of the principles of international law has led to the acceptance and invocation of some of its norms. It has not, however, modified the theoretical dislike of adjudication, courts being seen as instruments of class oppression from which derives the view cited in Soviet textbooks, that ICJ decisions have represented the interests of the capitalist States and not been impartial.[72] Despite the fact that the Soviet Union has had a judge on the ICJ Bench since 1945 this attitude has not changed. But the attitude so expressed is not just a claim that the composition of the Bench is weighted in favour of the " capitalist " States: it is much more fundamental. The Soviet Union has no tradition of a court as ultimate arbiter between power-wielders. In the recent United Nations Debate it voted against any move even to set up a committee to study the Court. It would not have been committed to accept proposals made by the Committee, or to use the

---

[69] Lapenna, " The Legal Aspects and Political Significance of the Soviet Concept of Co-existence," 12 *International and Comparative Law Quarterly* (1963), p. 756.
[70] *Ibid.*, p. 753.
[71] Lapenna, " The Bar in the Soviet Union and Yugoslavia," 12 *International and Comparative Law Quarterly* (1963), at pp. 645–648.
[72] Lewin and Kaljushnaja, *Völkerrecht* (1963), p. 390.

Court any more than it does now. This can only be seen as a fixed hostility to improvement of the International Court. Yet the idea of a court as the supreme arbiter between major power-groupings is an important part of the Western legal tradition, seen at its highest in federal systems where a court sometimes holds the power between executive and legislature, for example the United States Supreme Court, which since *Marbury* v. *Madison* has been the watchdog over the constitutional division of powers. This kind of view of a court is alien to the Soviet lawyer's mind and will never receive his support on the international level. Thus, Soviet representatives have consistently opposed giving the Court the power to interpret the Charter.[73]

In the *Northern Cameroons* case the Court discussed the " judicial function " and the " inherent limitations " of it.[74] From where did it draw its understanding of those terms? It drew them from theorists on the separation of powers such as Montesquieu (" *L'Esprit des Lois* ") and on " checks and balances " such as Dicey, and from long lines of case law in Western European courts which have gradually delimited the judicial function from other aspects of social structure. This tradition and these sources are not accepted by other societies and their implications, stated so self-evidently by the International Court, may well seem quite strange to them.

In developing the procedure, style of reasoning, form of judgment, methods of interpretation and concept of the judicial role the judges of the International Court have used, consciously or unconsciously, cultural patterns internalised by them from the legal systems and social groups in which they had been socialised. These are well-accepted processes in sociology and significant learning patterns for the bearers of important social roles.[75] No reproach should now be made against the judges of the International Court and its predecessor because of this process, which was both natural and inevitable and indeed gave us a rich jurisprudence and a developed institution. The problem is now where to go from here.

The Court's audience has widened and includes lawyers, politicians and bureaucrats from many other societies who do not share our esteem for courts, legal rules and judges. How can their support be enlisted? If they do not accept our views as to "proper judicial function," "the normal bounds of judicial activity," and so on, it

---

[73] *Cf.* the opposition of Vyshinsky to this view during a General Assembly Debate in 1947, quoted by Steinberger, Report cited in note 12, p. 198 and note 8. Similar views of Shurshalov and Morozov are set out in Grzybowski, " Socialist Judges in the International Court of Justice," 1964 *Duke Law Journal*, at pp. 548–549.

[74] *Northern Cameroons* case (1963), *ICJ Reports* (1963), p. 30; *cf.* also Fitzmaurice, Separate Opinion, pp. 97 *et seq.*

[75] An extended analysis of these concepts has been applied to judges of the International Court in first work cited note 7, above, at Chap. I.

302   *The Year Book of World Affairs 1979*

may be better for them to create other bodies which represent social structures which they do esteem. What might such structures be? The "High Command" (in a bureaucratic society), the consensus of the Elders (in a traditional society) or perhaps the "Great High Priest" (in a theocratic society)? We need more information about what structures are most valued in other societies. We should not be misled by linguistic tags; the fact that the discussion has to date always been conducted in the terms of the Western legal tradition should not be allowed to obscure the fact that we may have been talking about different things.

For example, there has been a clear trend on the part of some writers on the Court and even some judges to broaden the Court's sphere of action. Gross noted the Court's conversion to the role of *amiable compositeur* [76] and Gordon has stressed the current questioning of the allocation of decisions to either a " political " or a " judicial " body.[77] And it may well be that the third-party adjudicative process which was modelled on Western European institutions is not the best way to solve international disputes. A Polish commentator, Morawiecki, for example, has seen the judicial process as even playing a " disfunctional " role.[78] This position was hotly contested by Western European observers of the Court.[79] But the problem remains: if we call the Court a *legal* institution and insist on it performing a *judicial* function in the narrow sense of those terms, are we in fact preventing useful developments in international society? If we extend these terms to cover such other functions of an international body for dispute settlement as would be convenient in international affairs, we may obscure concepts which at present have a settled useful core of meaning and have been of great significance in the early history of international dispute settlement. We should at any rate try to work our way out of the present confusion, in which the Court has become a subject for experiment between these different views, and its function and role thrown into doubt.

VI—CONCLUSIONS

Out of all the current soul-searching about the role and future of the International Court two main conclusions seem to emerge.

---

[76] See note 48, above, and text referring to that note.

[77] Gordon, " Old Orthodoxies amid new Experiences: the South West Africa (Namibia) Litigation and the Uncertain Jurisprudence of the International Court of Justice," 1 *Denver Journal of International Law and Policy* (1971), p. 65, esp. pp. 65–72. Conversely another commentator sees this division as one of the most crucial areas to be developed in international adjudication; Report by Jennings, in *op. cit.* in note 2, above, at pp. 39–40.

[78] Morawiecki in *op. cit.* in note 2, above, at p. 49.

[79] Hambro, *op. cit.* in note 2, above, at p. 51; Golsong, *ibid.* at p. 52.

The first is that for all the technical proposals for amending the statute, widening access and jurisdiction, changing election procedure, etc. there is little chance of success. Indeed, Fitzmaurice's comment is entirely apposite, that if the will to pursue these proposals existed on the part of States, there would be will to exploit the present facilities of the Court and therefore the proposals would be unnecessary.[80]

The second is that the sources of the States' " lack of confidence " in or distrust of the Court are far deeper than have been generally considered. Tinkering with the Court's Statute or regulations will not change deep-seated attitudes deriving from cultural patterning.

If present moves for reform of the Court have reached a dead-end, it is time to consider whether more basic research into the social structure of other cultures may provide alternative paths: by suggesting other institutions which might, on a regional basis, be not only acceptable, but inspiring to certain other groups of States, thus leaving the ICJ in its traditional form as a court of Western European style with its own substantial juridical tradition. Another possibility is to adapt from these other cultures ideas for dispute settlement which might be developed for the International Court, thus substantially changing its character.

To a lawyer of the common law and Western legal tradition, the latter alternative will probably not appeal, but it would have the virtue of at least making clear what is being done. The present situation, where new ideas inimical to the traditional concept of " court " are being grafted almost surreptitiously on to the ICJ simply leads to confusion and to heated debates about the " proper " role of courts, the nature of law, the function of the judge, and so on, such as the recent bitter differences of opinion among the judges of the ICJ in the *Nuclear Tests* cases. If, nonetheless, this alternative is adopted, leading to the development of a new international body only partly wedded to traditional judicial methods, then the Western European nations may well wish to establish for themselves a " court " of the kind they know best.

[80] Fitzmaurice, *op. cit.* in note 12, above, at p. 464.

THE ANGLO-FRENCH
CONTINENTAL SHELF CASE

By

E. D. BROWN

IT seems more than likely that the Decision of the Court of Arbitration in the *Anglo-French Continental Shelf* case (1977) [1] will come to be regarded as an important landmark in the development of the rules of international law relating to delimitation of the continental shelf. On the global level, the case is important as having provided the first opportunity for an international tribunal to interpret the rules on the delimitation of the continental shelf between neighbouring States both of which are parties to the Geneva Convention on the Continental Shelf (1958). Inevitably, the Judgment of the International Court of Justice (ICJ) in the *North Sea Continental Shelf* cases (1969) [2] was heavily relied upon in the pleadings and extensively commented upon by the Court of Arbitration. The case has thus also provided a valuable opportunity for a re-examination of the earlier Judgment, given on the basis of international customary law. At a time when the Third United Nations Conference on the Law of the Sea (UNCLOS III) is still struggling to reach agreement on the rules for the delimitation of the continental shelf and the exclusive economic zone (EEZ), it may be hoped that the weary draftsmen will derive new insights from the Court's timely clarification of the law. [2a]

It seems likely that the Court's Decision will also be of considerable significance in the more local context. The United Kingdom has still to settle its continental shelf boundary with Ireland [3] in the Celtic Sea area as well as in the Rockall sector further north, [4] and many of the Court's dicta are clearly relevant to the problems dividing the parties in these other areas.

---

[1] The Decision of June 30, 1977, together with an interpretative Decision of March 14, 1978 will be published by H.M.S.O.

[2] *ICJ Reports 1969*, p. 3.

[2a] Where the abbreviated form "Court" is used in this paper the reference is to the Court of Arbitration. The abbreviated form "ICJ" is used to refer to the International Court of Justice.

[3] Ireland and the U.K. have agreed to refer the question to "some form of third party settlement of a judicial nature" (*Anglo-French Continental Shelf* case, 1977, *Decision of Court of Arbitration*—hereafter referred to as "*Decision*"—para. 26).

[4] On the Rockall sector, see E. D. Brown, "Rockall and the Limits of the National Jurisdiction of the United Kingdom," 2 *Marine Policy* (1978), pp. 181–211 and 275–303.

A comprehensive treatment of the Court's Decision would embrace, *inter alia*, a detailed analysis of the Court's dicta relating to (i) the applicable law; (ii) the " natural prolongation " rule; (iii) " macrogeographical perspectives " and the Court's competence; (iv) the status of the UNCLOS III Negotiating Texts; and (v) the law relating to reservations to treaties. Limitations of space require that such a comprehensive analysis should be presented elsewhere [5] and in this paper attention will be concentrated primarily upon what is perhaps the most important part of the Decision—the Court's dicta relating to the meaning of and relationship between " special circumstances " under Article 6 of the Geneva Convention and the corresponding rules of international customary law identified by the ICJ in the *North Sea Continental Shelf* cases. First, however, it is necessary to describe " the arbitration area " and to present the problem as it was put to the Court by the parties.

I—THE REFERENCE TO ARBITRATION

Following unsuccessful negotiations, which continued until the beginning of 1974, the two Governments agreed to submit their dispute to an arbitral tribunal.[6] As is made clear in the Preamble of the Arbitration Agreement of July 10, 1975, agreement in principle had already been reached on the delimitation of the continental shelf in the English Channel eastward of 30 minutes west of the Greenwich Meridian and the question put to the Court in Article 2 (1) of the Agreement was as follows: " What is the course of the boundary (or boundaries) between the portion of the continental shelf appertaining to the United Kingdom and the Channel Islands and to the French Republic, respectively, westward of 30 minutes west of the Greenwich Meridian as far as the 1,000 metre isobath? " [7]

Under Article 2 (1) of the Arbitration Agreement, the Court was asked to decide the question put to it " in accordance with the rules of international law applicable in the matter as between the Parties." Both States were parties to the Geneva Convention on the Continental Shelf, but France contended that the Convention had never entered into force between France and the United Kingdom because of the latter's refusal to accept certain reservations made by France when acceding to the Convention.[8] The Court found that Article 6 of the Convention was applicable in principle to all of the arbitration area, with the exception of the Channel Islands region where the

---

[5] See further E. D. Brown, *Sea-bed Energy and Mineral Resources and the Law of the Sea* (in preparation).

[6] *Decision,* p. 4.   [7] *Ibid.* p. 5.

[8] *Decision,* pp. 11 and 19. For text of French reservations and U.K. response to them, see *Decision,* para. 33–34.

delimitation had to be determined by reference to the rules of international customary law.[9]

II—" SPECIAL CIRCUMSTANCES "
AND " EQUITABLE PRINCIPLES "

In the *North Sea Continental Shelf* cases (1969), the ICJ found that the application of the equidistance rule, as incorporated in Article 6 of the Geneva Convention, was not obligatory as between the parties.[10] It was, therefore, unnecessary for the Court to consider whether " special circumstances " existed in that case or to concern itself with the scope of the concept of special circumstances. In its exposition of the corresponding rules of international customary law, however, it was apparent that the role of equity, as conceived by the Court, was similar to that of the concept of special circumstances. Since the Court's Judgment was delivered in 1969, it has frequently been assumed that the equitable factors which would justify a boundary other than an equidistant boundary under international customary law are the same as the factors which would constitute special circumstances under Article 6 of the Geneva Convention. As will be seen, the Court of Arbitration in the *Anglo-French Continental Shelf* case seems to sympathise with this view. The purpose of Part II of this paper is to reconsider in the light of the Decision of the Court of Arbitration, (i) the meaning of special circumstances in the sense of Article 6 and of the corresponding rules of international customary law as laid down by the ICJ in the *North Sea* cases; and (ii) the relationship between the two.

To place the views of the Court of Arbitration in proper perspective, it is necessary first to review the Judgment of the ICJ in the *North Sea* cases and to examine the meaning of " special circumstances " in the Geneva Convention.

(a) *The North Sea Continental Shelf cases* (1969)

The ICJ held that: " delimitation is to be effected by agreement in accordance with equitable principles, and taking account of all the relevant circumstances, in such a way as to leave as much as possible to each Party all those parts of the continental shelf that constitute a natural prolongation of its land territory into and under the sea, without encroachment on the natural prolongation of the land territory of the other." [11] The ICJ dealt with the nature of these " equitable principles " and " relevant circumstances " at some length. First, it said, " There is no legal limit to the considerations which States may take account of for the purpose of making sure

---

[9] *Ibid.* para. 74–75. [10] *ICJ Reports* (1969), para. 101.
[11] *Ibid.* p. 53.

that they apply equitable procedures, and more often than not it is the balancing-up of all such considerations that will produce this result rather than reliance on one to the exclusion of all others. The problem of the relative weight to be accorded to different considerations naturally varies with the circumstances of the case." [12] The ICJ went on to add that: " In balancing the factors in question it would appear that various aspects must be taken into account. Some are related to the geological, others to the geographical aspect of the situation, others again to the idea of the unity of any deposits. These criteria, though not entirely precise, can provide adequate bases for decision adapted to the factual situation." [13]

Subsequently, the Court specified these various " factors " which were to be taken into account in the course of the negotiations in more detail. The negotiations were to take account of: (1) the general configuration of the coasts of the Parties, as well as the presence of any special or unusual features [14]; (2) so far as known or readily ascertainable, the physical and geological structure, and natural resources, of the continental shelf areas involved [15]; (3) the element of a reasonable degree of proportionality, which a delimitation carried out in accordance with equitable principles ought to bring about between the extent of the continental shelf areas appertaining to the coastal State and the length of its coastline, account being taken for this purpose of the effects, actual or prospective, of any other continental shelf delimitations between adjacent States in the same region.[16]

The writer has subjected this Judgment to detailed criticism elsewhere and it must suffice here to re-state the conclusions arrived at as a result of that analysis: " In the writer's view, the record surveyed above amply verifies that in the course of a development over nearly a quarter of a century, the rules expressed in Article 6 (2) of the Geneva Convention on the Continental Shelf have attained the status of international customary law. Two points must be emphasised. First, in view of the fact that both the German pleadings and the Court's Judgment concentrated on the question whether the evidence sufficed to prove the existence of the equidistance rule, it is necessary to emphasis that Article 6 (2) contains three elements—agreement, equidistance and special circumstances. It is submitted that the latter two elements have now been accepted in State practice as being the rules the application of which will ensure that, failing agreement between the parties, a delimitation will be carried out in accordance with the ' equitable principles ' referred to in the Truman Proclamation.

[12] *Ibid.* p. 50.
[15] *Ibid.*
[13] *Ibid.* pp. 50–51.
[16] *Ibid.*
[14] *Ibid.* p. 54.

" Secondly, the assertion is not that State practice since 1958 (or 1964, when the Convention entered into force) has transformed the conventional rules into rules of international customary law but rather that, as a result of a process of refinement and consolidation of which the conclusion of the Convention was a part, the fundamental but vague notions of agreement and equity expressed in the Truman Proclamation were transformed into at least relatively more precise rules.

" Prima facie, the difference between this conclusion and the Court's Judgment may seem slight. It is submitted, however, that the concept of special circumstances is much more limited in scope and less open to arbitrary concretisation than the general principle of equity as interpreted by the Court. In order to develop this point, the following section is devoted to an analysis of the concept of special circumstances." [17]

The analysis of the notion of special circumstances which followed led to the conclusion that, " while it would clearly be wrong to attempt to draw up a closed list of cases of special circumstances, it would be equally unjustifiable to ignore the evidence, analysed above, which offers guidelines for a reasonably restrictive interpretation of this difficult concept." [18] The overall conclusions to which this earlier analysis seemed to point included the following:

" (1) It is submitted that the Court's Judgment suffers from an excess of deductive reasoning from vague premises and a failure to give due weight to the evidence pointing to the establishment in customary law of the three-point rule expressed in Article 6 of the Geneva Convention. Like the German pleadings, the Court seemed to be unduly concerned with the equidistance rule in isolation from the other two elements in Article 6.

" (2) The Court's interpretation of equity would seem to deprive the law on delimitation of the Continental Shelf between adjacent States of a reasonable measure of certainty, and to open the door to abusive and vexatious litigation in other parts of the world. It is moreover less than clear that reference to the ' factors ' enumerated by the Court will guarantee a fair delimitation." [19]

(b) *Anglo-French Continental Shelf case (1977)*

(i) *Relationship between Article 6 and international customary law.* In its Decision in the *Anglo-French Continental Shelf* case, the Court of Arbitration referred extensively to both the rules of international customary law as interpreted by the ICJ in the *North Sea Continental Shelf* cases (1969) and to the provisions of Article 6 of

---

[17] E. D. Brown, *The Legal Régime of Hydrospace* (1971), at pp. 61–62.
[18] *Ibid.* p. 70.   [19] *Ibid.* pp. 70–71.

the Geneva Convention; and, in several passages, the Court of Arbitration indicated its view on the relationship between the two.

It had been argued by France that the Geneva Convention was now obsolete. The Court rejected this contention but, having declared that the Convention was in force between the parties, went on to say that this finding: ". . . does not mean that it regards itself as debarred from taking any account in these proceedings of recent developments in customary law. On the contrary, the Court has no doubt that it should take due account of the evolution of the law of the sea in so far as this may be relevant in the context of the present case." [20]

The implications of this statement were spelled out in more detail in a later passage: ". . . the Court considers that Article 6 is applicable in principle, to the delimitation of the continental shelf as between the Parties under the Arbitration Agreement. This does not, however, mean that the Court considers the rules of customary law discussed in the judgment in the *North Sea Continental Shelf* cases to be inapplicable in the present case. As already pointed out, the provisions of Article 6 do not define the conditions for the application of the equidistance-special circumstances rule; moreover, the equidistance-special circumstances rule and the rules of customary law have the same object—the delimitation of the boundary in accordance with equitable principles. In the view of this Court, therefore, the rules of customary law are a relevant and even essential means both for interpreting and completing the provisions of Article 6." [21]

It is true that circumstances which would constitute " special circumstances " in accordance with the guidelines referred to above, would also constitute " factors creative of inequity " under international customary law. It is submitted, however, that the converse is not true. Factors which might be held to be creative of inequity in accordance with the rules expounded by the ICJ would not *necessarily* fall within the narrower guidelines relating to special circumstances under Article 6. Thus, the fact that the Court of Arbitration could truly say that the effect of applying or of not applying Article 6 would make very little, if any, practical difference to the boundary line *in the circumstances of this case* [22] proves nothing about the relationship between the rules of Article 6 and those of international customary law.

In another passage, the Court said that: " The double basis on which both Parties put their case regarding the Channel Islands confirms the Court's conclusion that the different ways in which the requirements of ' equitable principles ' or the effects of ' special

---

[20] *Decision*, para. 48. [21] *Ibid.* para. 75. [22] *Ibid.* para. 65.

circumstances' are put reflect differences of approach and terminology rather than of substance." [23]

Once again, this may be an acceptable statement in the circumstances of this case. If it was intended to be of general validity,
however, it goes too far. There are grounds for believing that the
Court did intend it to be of general application. Thus, not only did
it regard the rules of international customary law as " essential
means both for interpreting and completing the provisions of
Article 6 " [24]; it also referred, in connection with the special circumstances rule, to considerations which quite clearly do not fall
within the guidelines identified above.

The Court had come to the prima facie view that the existence
of the Channel Islands close to the French coast, if permitted to
divert the course of the mid-Channel median line, would effect a
radical distortion of the boundary, creative of inequity. It went on
to test this prima facie conclusion by applying the equidistance-
special circumstances rule of Article 6. It was concerned, in this
connection, to see whether a departure from the median line was
" justified " in relation to both parties and in the light of all the
" relevant circumstances." [25] Among the " relevant circumstances "
invoked by the United Kingdom and accepted by the Court " as
carrying a certain weight " were the following: (1) the particular
character of the Channel Islands as populous islands of a certain
political and economic importance; (2) the close ties between the
islands and the United Kingdom; (3) the latter's responsibility for
their defence and security; and (4) the impossibility of the islands
having any appreciable area of continental shelf except in the open
waters to their west and north.[26]

While it is true that these circumstances were allowed to have only
a very minor effect on the boundary line in this case, the Court's
reasoning does indicate just how wide it considered the category of
factors relevant to special circumstances to be. In the writer's
opinion, Professor Briggs was right to express his concern—in his
separate declaration—that the Court's interpretation of Article 6
" constitutes some threat that the rule of positive law expressed in
Article 6 will be eroded by its identification with subjective equitable
principles, permitting attempts by the Court to redress the inequities
of geography." [27]

The approach of the Court of Arbitration is particularly well
illustrated by its treatment of defence and security interests. The
French Government had argued that the application of the equidistance method in the Channel Islands region would be inequitable,

---

[23] *Ibid.* para. 148.   [24] *Ibid.* para. 75.   [25] *Ibid.* para. 197.
[26] *Ibid.*   [27] *Ibid.* p. 236.

inter alia, because it would involve severing the continental shelf of France into two zones separated by a United Kingdom zone. This, in turn, would be prejudicial to the vital interests of France in the security and defence of its territory. France referred in particular to the fact that it would be deprived of any right to control activities in the whole Hurd Deep Zone and that this would involve serious inconveniences and risks for French submarines stationed at Cherbourg, as well as affecting the French Republic's military supervision of the approaches to its territory.[28]

The United Kingdom, though as a matter of advocacy invoking similar defence and navigational interests for itself and seeking to refute the factual basis of the French claim, argued that France's security, defence, and navigational interests were not entitled to be given weight. The United Kingdom pointed out that the French argument did not take account of the legal protection given to those interests by the régime of the continental shelf itself, especially Articles 3–5 of the Geneva Convention.[29]

The Court of Arbitration took an intermediate position. In its view, ". . . the weight of such considerations in this region is, in any event, somewhat diminished by the very particular character of the English Channel as a major route of international maritime navigation serving ports outside the territories of either of the Parties. Consequently, they cannot be regarded by the Court as exercising a decisive influence on the delimitation of the boundary in the present case. They may support and strengthen, but they cannot negative, any conclusions that are already indicated by the geographical, political and legal circumstances of the region which the Court has identified." [30]

In other words, the Court was prepared in principle to regard such matters as relevant to the question of equity or special circumstances, though in the context of this case it allowed very little weight to be attributed to them.

In the writer's opinion, the analysis of the meaning of special circumstances referred to above suggests that such matters do not come within the scope of this concept.

(ii) *Status of the principle of equidistance under Article 6 and the question of the burden of proof of special circumstances.* The Court of Arbitration was obliged to consider this question because of the United Kingdom's contention that the onus of proof lay upon France to show that special circumstances existed. Before examining the Court's opinion, it is enlightening first to refer to the *travaux préparatoires* of Article 6.

(1) THE TRAVAUX PRÉPARATOIRES OF ARTICLE 6 of the Geneva

---

[28] *Ibid.* paras. 161–163.   [29] *Ibid.* paras. 175–176.   [30] *Ibid.* para. 188.

Convention throw some light on the proper characterisation of the principle of equidistance as incorporated in Article 6. The relevant records are principally those relating to the debate which took place in the 1953 and 1956 Sessions of the International Law Commission (ILC). They include the Report of a Committee of Experts convened by the ILC Rapporteur, Professor François, prior to the 1953 Session, to advise on technical questions.

A detailed review of this record, presented elsewhere, suggests that it would be fair to say that: (1) the Committee of Experts regarded the principle of equidistance as the general rule, while noting that it would have to admit of exceptions where there were " special reasons " or where its application would " not lead to an equitable solution "; (2) the International Law Commission, in its crucial 1953 Session, conducted its debate on the assumption that the principle of equidistance was " the general rule " and referred to it also as " the major principle of equidistance." " Modifications necessitated by the special circumstances of the case " were very clearly regarded as exceptions to the major principle; (3) although the shorter commentary in the ILC 1956 Report omits reference to " the major principle of equidistance " and does note that the case for a departure from the equidistance principle " may arise fairly often," there is nothing in the record of the ILC debate to suggest that the ILC had ceased to regard the equidistance principle as " the general rule " or " the major principle "; (4) the Geneva Conference (1958), having made no relevant change to the ILC's draft article, may be taken to have endorsed the Commission's view as to the status of the equidistance principle.[31]

The conclusion must be, therefore, that the *travaux préparatoires* provide strong evidence that the intention of the parties to the Geneva Convention was that the equidistance principle of Article 6 should be regarded as " the general rule " or " the major principle " and that the special circumstances rule was regarded as being an exception to the general rule.

It is submitted that the classification of the equidistance principle as " the general rule " or " the major principle " means that there is a presumption in favour of the rule; that it is the residual rule; that the onus lies on those pleading exceptions to it to prove the presence of special circumstances. Nor need this conclusion be disturbed if, following the Court of Arbitration, one regards Article 6 as having formulated a combined equidistance-special circumstances rule rather than two separate rules.

(2) THE DECISION OF THE COURT OF ARBITRATION. The Court of Arbitration adopted a different view of the status of the principle of

---

[31] See further *op. cit.* in note 17, above, at pp. 52 *et seq.*

equidistance. The United Kingdom had argued that Article 6 (1) placed an onus of proof upon France to show the existence of any special circumstances on which it relied and to show that these circumstances justified a boundary other than the median line as defined by that paragraph.[32] The Court of Arbitration considered, however, that this view did not place the equidistance principle in its true perspective and went on as follows: " Article 6, as both the United Kingdom and the French Republic stress in the pleadings, does not formulate the equidistance principle and ' special circumstances ' as two separate rules. The rule there stated in each of the two cases is a single one, a combined equidistance-special circumstances rule. This being so, it may be doubted whether, strictly speaking, there is any legal burden of proof in regard to the existence of special circumstances. The fact that the rule is a single rule means that the question whether ' another boundary is justified by special circumstances ' is an integral part of the rule providing for application of the equidistance principle. As such, although involving matters of fact, that question is always one of law of which, in case of submission to arbitration, the tribunal must itself, *proprio motu*, take cognisance when applying Article 6." [33]

For the reasons stated above, it is believed that the Court of Arbitration's view on the legal burden of proof is not in accordance with the intention of the parties to the Geneva Convention. Nor does the Court appear to be certain of its own view. They say only that " it may be doubted whether, strictly speaking, there is any legal burden of proof. . . ."

Professor Briggs also refers briefly to this point in the declaration which he appended to the Decision of the Court of Arbitration. Professor Briggs stated that: " The view that Article 6 is expressive of customary international law—a view already held by some Judges of the International Court of Justice in 1969 in the *North Sea Continental Shelf* cases—has been substantially strengthened by the subsequent practice of States, which has been elaborately analyzed by counsel in this Arbitration." [34]

Professor Briggs agreed with the Court that whether it applied the principles of international customary law or those set forth in Article 6 of the Convention would make little practical difference " *in the circumstances of this case* " [35] (emphasis added). He went on to say, however, that: " My principal concern in this respect is that the Court's interpretation of Article 6 seems, in effect, to shift ' the burden of proof ' of ' special circumstances ' from the State which invokes them to the Court itself, and constitutes some threat that

---

[32] *Decision*, para. 67.
[34] *Ibid.* at p. 236.
[33] *Ibid.* para. 68.
[35] *Ibid.*

the rule of positive law expressed in Article 6 will be eroded by its identification with subjective equitable principles, permitting attempts by the Court to redress the inequities of geography." [36] That the writer shares this opinion will be evident from the passage reproduced in the text above, at note 17.

That the Court of Arbitration was aware of the greater latitude it would enjoy as a result of equating the rules of Article 6 with those of international customary law is evident from its observation that: " Clearly, this feature of Article 6 [the right to claim the existence of special circumstances whether or not a reservation with regard to such special circumstances had been made on ratification of the Convention] further underlines the full liberty of the Court in appreciating the geographical and other circumstances relevant to the determination of the continental shelf boundary, and at the same time reduces the possibility of any difference in the appreciation of these circumstances under Article 6 and customary law." [37]

(iii) *No legal limit to considerations which may be taken into account to ensure the application of equitable principles.* As was noted above, the ICJ said in its Judgment in the *North Sea* cases that " There is no legal limit to the considerations which States may take account of for the purpose of making sure that they apply equitable procedures. . . .[38] Clearly, if this passage is read in isolation and understood literally, it might be taken as authority for the invocation of a limitless variety of considerations as constituting factors productive of inequity. It is, therefore, fortunate that the Court of Arbitration had an opportunity in the *Anglo-French* case to interpret this ambiguous and somewhat misleading passage.

Having decided that the position of the Scilly Isles constituted a " special circumstance " justifying a boundary other than the strict median line, the Court went on to say that: " It does not, however, consider that the existence of this ' special circumstance ' in the Atlantic region gives it *carte blanche* to employ any method that it chooses in order to effect an equitable delimitation of the continental shelf. The French Republic, it is true, has impressed upon this Court certain observations in the Judgment in the *North Sea Continental Shelf* cases to the effect that, in order to achieve an equitable solution, ' it is necessary to seek, not one method of delimitation but one goal ' (paragraph 92), and that ' there is no legal limit to the considerations which States may take account of for the purpose of making sure that they apply equitable procedures ' (paragraph 93). But in those cases the Parties had retained the actual delimitation of the boundary in their own hands for further negotiation in the light of the principles and rules to be stated by

---

[36] *Ibid.*   [37] *Ibid.* para. 69.   [38] *Loc. cit.* in note 12.

the International Court of Justice; and in any event the observations invoked by the French Republic have to be read in the light of certain other observations of the International Court in the same Judgment. In these other observations, it was stressed that any recourse to equitable considerations must be to considerations ' lying not outside but within the rules ' of law, and that there is no question of any decision *ex aequo et bono* (paragraph 88); and, as already noted, it was also stressed that ' there can never be any question of completely refashioning nature ' (paragraph 91)." [39]

(iv) *The proportionality factor.* As has been seen, the ICJ held, in its Judgment in the *North Sea* cases, that, to ensure the application of equitable principles to the delimitation of the continental shelf, account had to be taken of " the element of a reasonable degree of proportionality which a delimitation effected according to equidistance principles ought to bring about between the extent of the continental shelf appertaining to the States concerned and the length of their respective coastlines—these being measured according to their general direction in order to establish the necessary balance between States with straight and those with markedly concave or convex coasts or to reduce very irregular coastlines to their truer proportions." [40]

Earlier in the Judgment, the ICJ held that " given a geographical situation of quasi-equality—in the length of the coastal frontages of the three States—one must abate the effects of an incidental special feature from which an unjustifiable difference of treatment could result." [41] In an earlier work, the writer suggested that this proposition seemed to rest on three assumptions, all of which were questionable: " First, the Court isolates one factor—length of coast—and uses this as the criterion of equitable apportionment. Why not use population, *per capita* income, land area, dependence of industry on the natural resources of the shelf, relative poverty of land resources? Secondly, the shape of the German coast is described as ' an incidental special feature,' though one might well think that the characteristic shape of the whole of the German North Sea coast is less incidental than the ratio between the lengths of the coasts of the three States. Thirdly, strict application of the equidistance principle would, it is said, cause an ' unjustifiable difference in treatment.' But, of course, the treatment would only be unjustifiable in terms of the results to be expected from application of the quasi-equality doctrine, which would demand reasonable proportionality between coastal frontage and area of shelf—another assumption.

[39] *Decision*, para. 245.
[41] *Ibid*. paras. 89–91.

[40] *ICJ Reports 1969*, para. 98.

" It will be noted, furthermore, that adoption of the quasi-equality/proportionality test involves acceptance of the so-called macrogeographical perspective advocated by German counsel. The calculation of reasonable proportionality of the continental shelves of States A and B by reference to coastal frontage, may—and in this case does—require a consideration of the shelf of State C, for it is only by reference to State B's boundary with State C that the area of State B's continental shelf may be calculated. But, what justification is there for asserting the relevance of the boundary between States B and C to delimitation of the boundary between A and B? The Court certainly provides none other than its *ex cathedra* deduction from equitable principles. In a case before the Court between A and B, is State C to be bound by the frontier between it and B which the Court uses as a basis for application of the proportionality rule? " [42]

Fortunately, the Court of Arbitration has now reconsidered the significance of the proportionality factor and has placed it in its proper perspective. Having recognised that the concept of proportionality was " clearly inherent in the notion of a delimitation in accordance with equitable principles " and that it thus formed " an element in the appreciation of the appropriateness of the equidistance or any other method of delimitation," [43] the Court went on to deny that this concept had the character of a specific principle or rule of delimitation as had been contended by France. It went on to say that: " In particular, this Court does not consider that the adoption in the *North Sea Continental Shelf* cases of the criterion of a reasonable degree of proportionality between the areas of continental shelf and the lengths of the coastlines means that this criterion is one for application in all cases. On the contrary, it was the particular geographical situation of three adjoining States situated on a concave coast which gave relevance to that criterion in those cases. In the present case, the role of proportionality in the delimitation of the continental shelf is, in the view of this Court, a broader one, not linked to any specific geographical feature. It is rather a factor to be taken into account in appreciating the effects of geographical features on the equitable or inequitable character of a delimitation, and in particular of a delimitation by application of the equidistance method." [44]

The role of the proportionality factor was further specified in this passage: ". . . particular configurations of the coast or individual geographical features may, under certain conditions, distort the course of the boundary, and thus affect the attribution of

---

[42] *Op. cit.* in note 17, above, at p. 50.
[43] *Decision*, para. 98.   [44] *Ibid.* para. 99.

continental shelf to each State, which would otherwise be indicated by the general configuration of their coasts. The concept of ' proportionality ' merely expresses the criterion or factor by which it may be determined whether such a distortion results in an inequitable delimitation of the continental shelf as between the coastal States concerned. The factor of proportionality may appear in the form of the ratio between the areas of continental shelf to [*sic*] the lengths of the respective coastlines, as in the *North Sea Continental Shelf* cases. But it may also appear, and more usually does, as a factor for determining the reasonable or unreasonable—the equitable or inequitable—effects of particular geographical features or configurations upon the course of an equidistance-line boundary. . . .[45] In short, it is disproportion rather than any general principle of proportionality which is the relevant criterion or factor. . . . Proportionality, therefore is to be used as a criterion or factor relevant in evaluating the equities of certain geographical situations, not as a general principle providing an independent source of rights to areas of continental shelf." [46]

A practical example of the application of the proportionality factor is furnished by the Court of Arbitration's treatment of the Scilly Isles. In relation to these islands, the Court explained that: ". . . ' proportionality ' comes into account only in appreciating whether the Scilly Isles are to be considered a ' special circumstance ' having distorting effects on the equidistance boundary as between the French Republic and the United Kingdom and, if so, the extent of the adjustment appropriate to abate the inequity. These questions do not therefore require nice calculations of the areas of continental shelf appertaining to the United Kingdom in the north under a prospective delimitation of its continental shelf boundary with the Irish Republic. The point here at issue is simply whether the geographical situation of the Scilly Isles in relation to the French coast has a distorting effect and is a cause of inequity as between the United Kingdom and the French Republic." [47] There was thus no question of elaborate calculations of length of coasts and areas of shelf or of choosing between macro-geographical and micro-geographical perspectives.[48] Instead, the Court, having regard to the fact that the Scillies extended the United Kingdom coastline into the Atlantic twice as far as Ushant extended the French coastline, decided that application of the " half-effect " method [49] would serve to achieve the necessary abatement of the inequity so caused.[50]

It seems right to conclude that what has survived the Court's reconsideration of the " proportionality factor " is simply the

[45] *Ibid*. para. 100. [46] *Ibid*. para. 101. [47] *Ibid*. para. 250.
[48] *Ibid*. para. 166. [49] Explained in para. 251. [50] *Ibid*.

unexceptionable proposition that the broad notion of proportionality is one which may be called in aid to help in establishing whether a particular feature does constitute special circumstances because of its unjust distorting effects.

(v) *Opposite-State and adjacent-State situations distinguished.* Unlike Article 12 of the Geneva Convention on the Territorial Sea, Article 6 of the Geneva Convention on the Continental Shelf deals with opposite-State and adjacent-State situations in separate paragraphs. To the ICJ, the reason for this was plain. In an opposite-States situation, " ignoring the presence of islets, rocks and minor coastal projections, the disproportionally distorting effect of which can be eliminated by other means," [51] a median line " must effect an equal division of " [52] the continental shelf areas concerned. In the case of " laterally adjacent States on the same coast with no immediately opposite coast in front of it," [53] however, " in certain geographical circumstances . . . the equidistance method . . . leads unquestionably to inequity. . . . Thus, it has been seen that in the case of concave or convex coastlines that if the equidistance method is employed, then the greater the irregularity and the further from the coastline the area to be delimited, the more unreasonable are the results produced." [54] Obviously, such distortions are comparatively small within the narrow limits of the territorial sea,[55]—hence the difference between the delimitation rules in the two Conventions.

The ICJ's somewhat rigid differentiation between the two types of situation was again apparent in its finding—admittedly *obiter*—that Article 6 could not apply to a delimitation between Denmark and the Netherlands since they were neither " adjacent " nor " opposite " to each other.[56]

The Court of Arbitration, in its review of this question, has adopted a much broader approach to the interpretation of Article 6 which seems to this writer to be much more in accordance with the intention of the parties to the Geneva Convention.

The Court divided the " arbitration area " into an " English Channel region " and an " Atlantic region."

In relation to the English Channel region, the Court agreed with the view of the parties that it had to deal with an opposite-States situation and that the appropriate method of delimitation was, in principle, that of equidistance.[57]

With regard to the Atlantic region, the parties were not at all in agreement. France argued that, since the United Kingdom and France were separated by the Channel, the Atlantic region could not be

---

[51] *ICJ Reports 1969*, para. 57. [52] *Ibid.*
[53] *Ibid.* [54] *Ibid.* para. 89. [55] *Ibid.* para. 59.
[56] *Ibid.* para. 36. [57] *Decision*, para. 87.

considered to be an adjacent-States situation; and, since the Atlantic region lay *off* the two coasts rather than *between* them, it was not an opposite-States situation. It concluded that it was a situation *sui generis* and a *casus omissus* falling completely outside Article 6 of the Geneva Convention.[58] The United Kingdom on the other hand, contended that Article 6 was intended to deal comprehensively with the delimitation of the continental shelf and there could be no question of *casus omissus*. Moreover, even though the Atlantic region lay off the coasts of the two countries, it was still essentially an opposite-States situation.[59]

The Court endorsed the United Kingdom view that Article 6 was to be regarded as comprehensive and that all situations must, therefore, in principle, fall under either paragraph 1 or paragraph 2 of that Article.[60] It next went on to interpret the passage in the Judgment in the *North Sea Continental Shelf* cases, where the ICJ had noted that: " In certain geographical configurations of which the Parties furnished examples, a given equidistance line may partake in varying degree of the nature both of a median and of a lateral line." [61] What this meant, the Court of Arbitration held, was that "in determining whether two States are to be considered as ' opposite' or ' adjacent,' for the purpose of delimiting a continental shelf on which each of them abuts, the Court must have regard to their actual geographical relation to each other and to the continental shelf at any given place along the boundary." [62]

The Court of Arbitration cited two further passages from the Judgment in the *North Sea* cases, where, as was noted above, the ICJ had said that: " whereas a median line divides equally between the two opposite countries areas that can be regarded as being the natural prolongation of the territory of each of them, a lateral equidistance line often leaves to one of the States concerned areas that are a natural prolongation of the territory of the other." [63] It had also pointed out that: " if the equidistance method is employed, then the greater the irregularity and the further from the coastline the area to be delimited, the more unreasonable are the results produced. So great an exaggeration of the consequences of a natural geographical feature must be remedied or compensated for as far as possible, being of itself creative of inequity." [64]

Commenting on these passages, the Court of Arbitration said that: " It is also clear that the distinction drawn by the Court between the two geographical situations is one derived not from any legal theory but from the very substance of the difference between the

---

[58] *Ibid.* paras. 89–90.   [59] *Ibid.* paras. 91–93.   [60] *Ibid.* para. 94.
[61] *ICJ Reports 1969*, para. 17.   [62] *Decision*, para. 94.
[63] *ICJ Reports 1969*, para. 58.   [64] *Ibid.* at para. 89 (a).

two situations. Whereas in the case of 'opposite' States a median line will normally effect a broadly equitable delimitation, a lateral equidistance line extending outward from the coasts of adjacent States for long distances may not infrequently result in an inequitable delimitation by reason of the distorting effect of individual geographical features. In short, it is the combined effect of the side-by-side relationship of the two States and the prolongation of the lateral boundary for great distances to seawards which may be productive of inequity and is the essence of the distinction between ' adjacent ' and ' opposite ' coasts situations." [65]

Reverting to this point in a later passage, the Court of Arbitration was of the view that " the precise system of toponomy adopted for these various areas is without any legal relevance in the present proceedings; it is the physical facts of geography, not nomenclature, with which this Court is concerned." [66]

The Court developed this thinking at greater length in paragraphs 239–240 of its Decision.

" 239. As this Court of Arbitration has already pointed out in paragraphs 81–94, the appropriateness of the equidistance or any other method for the purpose of effecting an equitable delimitation in any given case is always a function or reflection of the geographical and other relevant circumstances of the particular case. In a situation where the coasts of the two States are opposite each other, the median line will normally effect a broadly equal and equitable delimitation. But this is simply because of the geometrical effects of applying the equidistance principle to an area of continental shelf which, in fact, lies between coasts that, in fact, face each other across that continental shelf. In short, the equitable character of the delimitation results not from the *legal* designation of the situation as one of ' opposite ' States *but from its actual geographical character as such*. Similarly, in the case of ' adjacent ' States, it is the lateral geographical relation of the two coasts when combined with a large extension of the continental shelf seawards from those coasts, which makes individual geographical features on either coast more prone to render the geometrical effects of applying the equidistance principle inequitable than in the case of ' opposite ' States. The greater risk in these cases that the equidistance method may produce an inequitable delimitation thus also results not from the *legal* designation of the situation as one of ' adjacent ' States but *from its actual geographical character as one involving laterally related coasts*.

" 240. What is, moreover, evident is that the relevance of the distinction between opposite and adjacent coasts is in regard to the operation of the 'special circumstances' element in the 'equidistance-special

---

[65] *Decision*, para. 95.   [66] *Ibid*. para. 204.

circumstances' rule laid down in Article 6 for both situations. What is also evident in the view of the Court, is that the answer to the question whether the effect of individual geographical features is to render an equidistance delimitation 'unjustified' or 'inequitable' cannot depend on whether the case is *legally* to be considered a delimitation between 'opposite' or between 'adjacent' States. The appreciation of the effect of individual geographical features on the course of an equidistance line has necessarily to be made by reference to the actual geographical conditions of the particular area of continental shelf to be delimited and to the actual relation of the two coasts to that particular area."

The Court was "inclined to the opinion" [67] that the Atlantic region was an opposite-States situation rather than an adjacent-States situation. More important, however, was its view that: "to fix the precise legal classification of the Atlantic region appears to this Court to be of little importance. The rules of delimitation prescribed in paragraph 1 and paragraph 2 are the same, and it is the actual geographical relation of the coasts of the two States which determines their application. What is important is that, in appreciating the appropriateness of the equidistance method as a means of effecting a 'just' or 'equitable' delimitation in the Atlantic region, the Court must have regard both to the lateral relation of the two coasts as they abut upon the continental shelf of the region and to the great distance seawards that this shelf extends from those coasts." [68]

This eminently sensible and practicable interpretation of Article 6 will be of considerable assistance to States in negotiating continental shelf boundaries with neighbouring States where nature has been untidy enough to present a situation which is not obviously either an opposite-States or an adjacent-States situation.

(vi) *Islands and archipelagos.* The Court of Arbitration had to consider whether the following features constituted special circumstances or factors creative of inequity: (1) the Channel Islands and (2) Ushant and the Scilly Isles.

(1) THE CHANNEL ISLANDS. The Court's treatment of the Channel Islands in relation to the delimitation of the continental shelf is of considerable interest, this being the first time that an international tribunal has had to consider the significance for delimitational purposes of an archipelago situated close to the mainland of one State but under the sovereignty of a neighbouring State. The Greek and Turkish Governments will certainly wish to scrutinise the Decision closely for its possible bearing upon the delimitation of the

---

[67] *Ibid.* para. 242.   [68] *Ibid.*

continental shelf in the Aegean, where the Turkish coast is fringed by a number of substantial Greek islands.

As was seen above, the Court held that Article 6 of the Geneva Convention was not applicable in this area and that this part of the boundary had to be constructed in accordance with international customary law.[69] The significance of this finding was reduced almost to nil, however when the Court reached the conclusion that " the different ways in which the requirements of ' equitable principles ' or the effects of ' special circumstances ' are put reflect differences of approach and terminology rather than of substance." [70] The Court went on to say that: ". . . the substantial point at issue is whether the presence of the British archipelago of the Channel Islands close to the French coast is a ' special circumstance ' or a circumstance creative of inequity that calls for a departure from or variation of the equidistance method of delimitation which the Parties agree to be in principle the applicable method." [71]

It would seem, therefore, that the Court would have reached the same result by way of the same arguments even if it had found Article 6 to be directly applicable.

The somewhat circuitous route by which the Court arrived at the conclusion that the Channel Islands did constitute special circumstances is reviewed elsewhere.[72] The object of this section is to examine the Court's finding only as it bears upon the question of what S. W. Boggs called islands " on the wrong side of the median line." [73]

France had argued before the Court that the opposite coasts to be taken into account were those of the two mainlands and that the boundary should consist of (1) a median line between the mainlands, and (2) a six-mile line around the islands, creating a Channel Islands enclave.[74]

The United Kingdom, on the other hand, would have had the Court treat the Channel Islands as the coast of the United Kingdom opposite to France in that part of the Channel. Accordingly, the median line should have described a deep loop south round the Channel Islands, close to the French coast.[75]

In fact, however, the Court decided to draw two boundary lines, the first being a median line drawn by reference to the two mainlands and the second a 12-mile line to the north and west of the Channel Islands archipelago. This seems to be a rather extraordinary finding and, as it will doubtless be much cited in the future, the reasoning behind it deserves close scrutiny.

---

[69] See note 9, above.
[71] *Ibid.*
[73] Quoted in *Decision*, para. 159.
[75] *Ibid.* para. 154.

[70] *Decision*, para. 148.
[72] *Op. cit.* in note 5, above.
[74] *Decision*, paras. 146–150.

The main steps in the Court's argument are as follows: (i) The region forms an integral part of the English Channel and must be viewed in its context as part of that whole maritime area.[76]

" Along the whole 300 miles of the south coast of the Channel runs the mainland coast of the French Republic; along the whole 300 miles of the north coast of the Channel runs the mainland coast of the United Kingdom. Each country has some promontories on its coast and the general result is that the coastlines of their mainlands face each other across the Channel in a relation of approximate equality." [77]

(ii) Having thus established the macrogeographical perspective in which to consider the Channel Islands region, the Court went on to observe that: " where the coastlines of two opposite States are themselves approximately equal in their relation to the continental shelf not only should the boundary in normal circumstances be the median line but the areas of shelf left to each Party on either side of the median line should be broadly equal or at least broadly comparable." [78]

Acknowledging that the presence of the Channel Islands disturbed " the balance of the geographical circumstances," [79] the Court felt that the question to be decided was whether and, if so, in what manner this should affect the " legal framework " [80] within which the boundary has to be delimited.

(iii) The Court found that the legal framework was " that of two opposite States one of which possesses island territories close to the coast of the other State." [81] It added that the size and importance of the Channel Islands might properly be taken into account in balancing the equities in the region.[82]

Also part of this legal framework were the 12-mile fishery limits of France and the United Kingdom, the 12-mile territorial sea of France and the three-mile and potential 12-mile territorial sea limits of the United Kingdom.[83]

Finally, " other elements in the framework " [84] were the various equitable considerations invoked by the parties regarding their navigational, defence and security interests. The Court found that, in the circumstances of the case, these considerations carried little weight and might simply " support and strengthen, but [could not] negative, any conclusions that are already indicated by the geographical, political and legal circumstances of the region which the Court has identified." [85] In the Court's view they tended to evidence

---

[76] *Ibid.* para. 181.   [77] *Ibid.*   [78] *Ibid.* para. 182.
[79] *Ibid.* para. 183.   [80] *Ibid.*   [81] *Ibid.* para. 187.
[82] *Ibid.*   [83] *Ibid.*   [84] *Ibid.* para. 188.
[85] *Ibid.*

the predominant interests of the French Republic in the southern areas of the English Channel.

(iv) Following its consideration of the natural prolongation doctrine, the Court went on to hold that, " Any ground of equity . . . is . . . to be looked for in the particular circumstances of the present case and in the particular equality of the two States in their geographical relation to the continental shelf of the Channel." [86]

The Court found that to give full effect to the Islands would result in a substantial diminution of the area of the shelf which would otherwise accrue to France; that this fact was prima facie creative of inequity; that the presence of the islands would, prima facie, constitute a " special circumstance " if Article 6 were applicable. Prima facie, therefore, a departure from the median line seemed to be justified. It was necessary to show, however, that a departure from the median line would be " equitable " or " justified " also in relation to the United Kingdom and in the light of all the relevant circumstances. [87]

The court accepted that a certain weight should be attached to the equitable considerations invoked by the United Kingdom—the political and economic character of the islands; their close ties with the United Kingdom and the latter's responsibility for their defence and security; and the fact that they had the possibility of enjoying an appreciable area of continental shelf only to their west and north. [88]

(v) Weighing the various equities in the balance, the Court decided that the primary element was the fact that the Channel Islands region formed part of the English Channel, throughout the whole length of which the parties faced each other as opposite States having almost equal coastlines. [89] In the Court's view the equitable considerations invoked by the United Kingdom invalidated the French proposal for a six-mile enclave for the Channel Islands but did not justify the adoption of the United Kingdom's proposals. [90] As has been seen, the Court drew two lines, a median line between the two mainlands and a second 12-mile line to the north and west of the Islands.

Whether viewed as the application of international customary law or as indicative of what the Court's findings would have been if Article 6 had been directly applicable, the Court's ruling in this region seems hard to justify. No one, probably, would quarrel with the Court's finding that the presence of the islands constituted special circumstances or a factor creative of inequity. However, it seems difficult to regard as other than the creation of a different inequity, a decision which adopts a median line, unmodified to

---

[86] *Ibid.* para. 195.   [87] *Ibid.* para. 197.   [88] *Ibid.* para. 198.
[89] *Ibid.* para. 199.   [90] *Ibid.* para. 198.

compensate the United Kingdom for its virtual loss of all the continental shelf around the islands, and at the same time purports to reflect equitable considerations invoked by the United Kingdom by awarding the islands an area of continental shelf which the United Kingdom could have secured, independently of the arbitration, by claiming the same breadth of territorial sea as has been claimed by France since 1971. Such a delimitation seems almost to deny that islands are entitled to a continental shelf, though of course such a denial would be difficult to square with Article 1 of the Geneva Convention on the Continental Shelf and its endorsement by the ICJ as declaratory of international customary law.[91] It is all the more difficult to accept as a properly-balanced judgment of the equities when it is recalled that the islands comprise a land area of 195 square kilometres and support a population of 130,000. The Court's evaluation of the equities certainly seems less persuasive here than in relation to the Scilly Isles.

(2) THE SCILLY ISLES. The Court's treatment of the Scilly Isles offers an instructive example of an archipelago [92] on the " right " side of the median line constituting special circumstances. As the Court pointed out, the greater projection of the United Kingdom coast into the Atlantic region, though partly due to the fact that the United Kingdom mainland extends 1° further west than the French mainland, is also due to the greater extension westwards of the Scilly Isles beyond the United Kingdom mainland than that of Ushant beyond the French mainland. " Thus, at its nearest point, Ushant is only about 10 miles and at its most westerly point no more than 14·1 nautical miles from the coast of Finistère; the nearest point of the Scilly Isles, on the other hand, is some 21 nautical miles and their most westerly point some 31 miles distant from Land's End. As a result, even when account is taken of the slight south-westerly trend of the English Channel, the further extension south-westwards of the United Kingdom's coast has a tendency to make it obtrude upon the continental shelf situated to seawards of the more westerly facing coast of the French Republic in that region." [93]

As the Court indicated in a later passage, " The effect of the presence of the Scilly Isles west-south-west of Cornwall is to deflect the equidistance line on a considerably more south-westerly course than would be the case if it were to be delimited from the baselines of the English mainland. The difference in the angle is 16°36'14"; and the extent of the additional area of shelf accruing to the United Kingdom, and correspondingly not accruing to the French Republic,

[91] See *ICJ Reports 1969.* para. 63.
[92] The Scillies group consists of 48 islands, six of which are inhabited, with a total population (in 1971) of 2,428 (*Decision*, para. 4).
[93] *Decision*, para. 235.

in the Atlantic region eastwards of the 1,000 metre isobath is approximately 4,000 square miles.[94]

The Court did of course acknowledge that this fact of nature did not in itself justify a departure from an equidistance line drawn by reference to the Scillies. The question was rather to decide whether " in the light of all the pertinent geographical circumstances, that fact amounts to an inequitable distortion of the equidistance line producing disproportionate effects on the areas of shelf accruing to the two States." [95]

The Court decided that it did. In its view, " the further projection westwards of the Scilly Isles, when superadded to the greater projection of the Cornish mainland westwards beyond Finistère, is of much the same nature for present purposes, and has much the same tendency to distortion of the equidistance line, as the projection of an exceptionally long promontory, which is generally recognized to be one of the potential forms of ' special circumstances '." [96]

As noted above, the Court held that to give " half effect " to the Scillies would bring about an appropriate abatement of the disproportionate effects of this " considerable projection onto the Atlantic continental shelf of a somewhat attentuated portion of the coast of the United Kingdom." [97]

III—Conclusions

Drawing together the various sections of Part II, what contribution has the Decision of the Court of Arbitration made to the elucidation of the concept of special circumstances and of the relationship between Article 6 of the Geneva Convention and the corresponding rules of international customary law?

(a) *Relationship between Article 6 and rules of international customary law*

It was concluded, on the basis of the analysis of " special circumstances " summarised in section (a), that this concept was much more limited in scope and less open to arbitrary and subjective concretisation than the principle of equity as interpreted by the ICJ in the *North Sea Continental Shelf* cases—also summarised in section (a). The Court of Arbitration would not appear to share this view and has gone a considerable way towards identifying " special circumstances " in the meaning of Article 6 with the equitable factors identified by the ICJ in the *North Sea* cases. The conclusion was reached that, in Professor Briggs' words, the Court of Arbitration's interpretation of Article 6 " constitutes some threat that the rule of positive law expressed in Article 6 will be eroded by its identification

---

[94] *Ibid.* para. 243.   [95] *Ibid.*   [96] *Ibid.* para. 244.   [97] *Ibid.* para. 249.

with subjective equitable principles, permitting attempts by the Court to redress the inequities of geography."

(b) *Status of equidistance rule and burden of proof of special circumstances*

In section (b), the opinion was expressed that a review of the *travaux préparatoires* of Article 6 indicated that it was the intention of the parties to the Geneva Convention that the equidistance rule should be regarded as the general or residual rule and that the onus of proof lay upon those pleading special circumstances to prove their existence. It was concluded that the contrary view adopted by the Court—that, strictly speaking, there was no burden of proof—was not only contrary to the intention of the parties, but was open to the same objection as the Court's view of the relationship between Article 6 and international customary law.

(c) *No legal limit to considerations which may be taken into account to ensure the application of equitable principles*

The Court's restrictive interpretation of this somewhat ambiguous dictum from the ICJ's Judgment will, it may be hoped, discourage States from reading it too literally and invoking as equitable considerations matters which, in law, clearly cannot properly be so considered.

(d) *Proportionality factor*

It was concluded in section (b) (iv) that the Court of Arbitration's reinterpretation of the significance of the so-called proportionality factor had placed it in its proper perspective and had established that it is simply a criterion which may be called in aid to determine whether a particular geographical feature does constitute special circumstances because of its unjust distorting effects.

(e) *Opposite-State and adjacent-State situations*

There are many situations in the world where the coasts of neighbouring States are not clearly classifiable as either opposite or adjacent. The Court's sensible and practicable interpretation of Article 6 will facilitate its application in such cases.

(f) *Islands and archipelagos as special circumstances*

On the basis of an examination of the Court's treatment of the archipelagos of the Channel Islands and the Scilly Isles, it seems reasonable to conclude that less than justice was done to the United Kingdom in relation to the Channel Islands. This part of the Court's Decision seems difficult to justify either in terms of the application of the special circumstances rule to a substantial group of islands or in terms of a comparison with its treatment of the Scilly Isles.

TRENDS IN THE LAW OF THE SEA

FROM *LEVIATHAN* TO *JAWS*?

By

GEORG SCHWARZENBERGER

THE marathon efforts of the Third United Nations Diplomatic Conference on the Law of the Sea (1973–   ) make it timely to review these protracted attempts in a wider perspective. The paper also offers an opportunity to re-examine the more general analyses of long-range trends offered and forecasts made three years ago when the Conference was slowly moving towards its likely anticlimax.[1]

I—FUNDAMENTALS

Two deceptively simple questions may provide a commensurate answer to the issue of the scope and limits of international law-making in the turbulent area of the high seas.

The first question is whether it is justifiable to describe past and present legal régimes of the high seas—or of hydrospace, as Professor Brown puts it [2]—in terms of maritime international orders. The second is whether current trends in the law of the sea permit the prognosis that we are moving towards a world maritime order or, at least, a plurality of regional maritime orders.

The techniques and methods applied in this paper are

(1) an inductive approach to the rules governing the international law of the sea from which the principle of the freedom of the seas is abstracted;

(2) an inter-disciplinary study of the evolution and functions of these rules in their social environment;

(3) a relativist treatment of the available patterns *de lege ferenda* for the further development of the Law of the Sea.

1—The Rules to be Examined

For purposes of studying the law of the sea from the angle of international order, it is advisable to distinguish between international

---

[1] See the lecture course entitled *World Maritime Order? Interdisciplinary Perspectives* (published in 7 *Thesaurus Acroasium*—1976 session) on which this paper is based. The lectures were given at the *Symposium on the Law of the Sea,* held at the Institute of Public International Law and International Relations at the University of Thessaloniki.

I would also like to acknowledge my indebtedness to my friend and colleague, Professor E. D. Brown, for his valuable comments on this paper.

[2] *The Legal Régime of Hydrospace (Library of World Affairs*—Stevens, London—No. 70—1971).

maritime law in unorganised international society, international societies on the confederate pattern of the League of Nations and United Nations, and more closely integrated groupings such as the European Economic Community.

Seven classical rules—in essentials, developed in pre-1914 international society—constitute the core of the contemporary international *customary* law of the sea:

(1) In a state of *peace*, each subject of international law exercises exclusive jurisdiction on the high seas over all ships which are entitled to fly its flag but, subject to narrow exceptions, not over those of any other subject of international law.

(2) In a state of intermediacy (*status mixtus*) between peace and war, subjects of international law may interfere with each other's shipping by way of reprisal.

(3) Permissible interference in *armed conflicts* with enemy and neutral shipping is regulated by the rules of sea warfare and prize law.

(4) The high seas, the air space above them, the sea-bed and subsoil may be used for any purpose which is not prohibited by international law.

(5) Foreign merchant ships have the right of innocent passage through the territorial seas of coastal States, and ships in distress have free access to maritime ports.

(6) Acts of piracy on the high seas are prohibited, and State territory may not be used as a base of piratical operations.

Warships or other public ships of any sovereign State may arrest pirate ships, and any sovereign State may exercise criminal and civil jurisdiction over crew and vessel under its own municipal law.

(7) The assumption of exclusive jurisdiction by any subject of international law over any portion of the surface of the high seas— as distinct from the sea-bed and subsoil—is prohibited.

The ensemble of these rules constitutes an international quasi-order, as distinct from an international order proper. In different words, these rules are as much *jus dispositivum* as any other rules of international customary law. To term them *jus cogens* in unorganised international society would be meaningless.

Some of these rules, if *developed* in codifications such as those of the 1958 Conventions on the Law of the Sea, are binding only on the parties to these Conventions.

2—*Basic Facts and Perspectives*

(a) *Basic Facts*

In any inter-disciplinary treatment of the Law of the Sea, three basic facts have to be borne in mind:

(1) Over 70 per cent. of the surface of the earth is covered by the sea.

(2) All the world's oceans are inter-linked.

(3) Nearly four-fifths of the world's sovereign States have maritime seaboards.

(b) *Perspectives*

History reveals three typical perspectives in which to view the sea:

(1) the *coastal* perspective, that is, a view of the sea primarily in relation to, and from the point of view of, the land bordering on it as, for instance, for purposes of inshore fishery or communication from one place on land to another on the same coast;

(2) the *lake* perspective, that is, a view of the sea formed under the overriding influence of an enclosed or semi-enclosed sea such as the Mediterranean or the Indian Ocean;

(3) the *oceanic* perspective, that is, a view of the sea as an inter-linking chain of the world's oceans.

It is possible to relate some of these perspectives to particular types of ship available (in their pristine prototypes, hollowed tree trunks, rafts, baskets, and contrast them with, for instance, square-rigged caravels as more suitable means of traversing oceans); to the invention of the mariner's compass, the sextant and the plumb-line; to the use of increasingly reliable marine charts, and to sea-orientated attitudes of discoverers and explorers.

For our purposes, it is unnecessary to become involved in an unavoidably inconclusive discussion on the supposed *causa causans* in ever varying situations of interaction. What is more relevant is that, for instance, the international law of both ancient Greece and Rome was essentially moulded by the lake view of the Mediterranean and, in contrast, that, since the sixteenth century, the oceanic perspective of the sea has become an essential characteristic of inter-national maritime law.

In Western countries, motivations which have brought about a transformation of the lake view of the law of the sea into the oceanic perspective are of the same complexity as those which have led to the expansion of European society into a world society. In international environments ultimately controlled by power—and this applies as much to the European society of the reconnaissance period as to the subsequent ages of discovery and imperialist expansion—it would be idle to speculate on the primacy of the political, military or economic element in this process. All three are different facets of power, and those actively involved in the worldwide expansion of Europe have known how to use the operative motivations of indi-vidual discoverers and explorers: their sense of adventure, greed for gold, jewels and spices, curiosity, and even nostalgic dreams of past—and undivided—worlds.

3—The Models Approach

The models approach to international law makes it possible to take more fully into account the richness of the storehouse of history, but in a form that reduces the likelihood of losing one's bearings through preoccupation with atypical detail. It reveals oceanic international law as one of the five basic types of international law across three millenia.

For closer examination of the law of the sea as a vital part of contemporary international law it is advisable to combine the models approach with the application of the order-test. It provides insights of especial relevance at a time when the actual division of the oceans has become technologically feasible but, as yet, a world order under any type of community law in the technical meaning of the term appears remote.

The application of the order-test yields three basic models for consideration: the anarchy model, the quasi-order model and the order model.

4—Key Words

Community: social group which is more highly integrated than a society (*q.v.*).

Dynamics: motion, for instance, law in motion. See also under *Statics*.

Inter-disciplinary approach: making use of any facet of a phenomenon that, in relation to any particular problem, is of special significance.

Ideology: idea or argument, employed to disguise in terms of abstract ideas or principles undisclosed interests, for instance, alleged concern for mankind as an excuse to curtail the rights of other sovereign States.

Jus aequum: legal system in which rights are relative and must be exercised reasonably and in good faith.

Jus cogens: law binding irrespective of the will of individual parties.

Jus dispositivum: law capable of being modified by consensual engagements.

Jus strictum: legal system in which rights are absolute and may be exercised irrespective of equitable considerations.

Legal order: legal system, embodying a *de facto* order (*q.v.*) and endowing it with the dignity of law.

Legal régime: system of legal rules which are reasonably coherent but are too specialised or subordinate to qualify as a legal order (*q.v.*).

Legitimation: recognition, confirmation, acceptance or justification of an existing or desired and, essentially, factual state of affairs.

Lex ferenda: law which it is desired to establish.

Lex lata: law in force.

Model: intended to represent simply but accurately a particular facet of reality.

Order: state of affairs characterised by the effective control of those subject to such a system by an essentially factual rather than normative apparatus of force and power. See also under *Legal order*.

Organised international society: international society on the level of, for instance, the confederate organisation of the United Nations and its Specialised Agencies.

Power: the mean between influence and force. Power distinguishes itself from *influence* by reliance on external pressure as a background threat, and from *force* by preference for achieving its ends without the actual use of physical pressure.

Pseudo-order: a pretended order which lacks the sanctions sustaining any true society or community order (*q.v.*).

Quasi-order: an order which, like the League of Nations, is too weak or precarious to achieve its appointed task.

Statics: state of rest, for instance, of law at any particular moment. See also under *Dynamics*.

Universalist: aiming at universality.

Unorganised international society: international society, lacking significant institutional superstructures.

Utopia: proposal *de lege ferenda* (*q.v.*), incompatible with an existing political or social order (see also under *Ideology*).

II—THE ANARCHY MODEL

The formative phase of European international law suggests three initial historical hypotheses: in the absence of agreement to the contrary, war—unrestrained by legal rules—as the state of normalcy, the rightlessness of foreigners, and the sea as no man's " land."

These inductively verifiable—and, in relation to West European practice, partly verified—hypotheses come remarkably close to the corresponding speculative deductions of Hobbes and Spinoza, based as they were on intuitive powers of insight into typical springs of human action.

1—The Model Illustrated

Three groups of incident will illustrate the anarchy model: one chosen from the formative period of European maritime law and two selected from the border-area between the contemporary maritime quasi-order and relapses into pristine anarchy.

(a) *The Britanny Incident*

The first case in point is a clash in the late thirteenth century between Norman and English sailors. In all likelihood, it took place not at Bayonne but in Britanny and well illustrates the anarchy model. It is described in Hume's *History of England* [3]:

" A Norman and an English vessel met off the coast near Bayonne; and both of them having occasion for water, they sent their boats to land, and the several crews came at the same time to the same spring: there ensued a quarrel for the preference: a Norman, drawing his dagger, attempted to stab an Englishman; who, grappling with him, threw his adversary on the ground; and the Norman, as was pretended, falling on his own dagger, was slain. This scuffle between two seamen about water soon kindled a bloody war between the two nations and involved a great part of Europe in the quarrel. The mariners of the Norman ship carried their complaints to the French king: Philip, without inquiring into the facts, without demanding redress, bade them take revenge and trouble him no more about the matter. The Normans, who had been more regular than usual in applying to the Crown, needed but this hint to proceed to immediate violence. They seized an English ship in the channel; and hanging, along with some dogs, several of the crew on the yardarm, in presence of their companions, dismissed the vessel; and bade the mariners inform their countrymen that vengeance was now taken for the blood of the Norman killed at Bayonne. This injury, accompanied with so general and deliberate an insult, was resented by the mariners of the Cinque-Ports, who, without carrying any complaint to the king, or waiting for redress, retaliated by committing like barbarities on all French vessels without distinction. The French, provoked by their losses, preyed on the ships of all Edward's subjects, whether English or Gascon; the sea became a scene of piracy between the nations; the sovereigns, without either seconding or repressing the violence of their subjects, seemed to remain indifferent spectators; the English made private associations with the Irish and Dutch seamen; the French with the Flemish and Genoese; and the animosities of the people on both sides became every day more violent and barbarous. A fleet of two hundred Norman vessels set sail to the south for wine and other commodities; and in their passage seized all the English ships which they met with; hanged the seamen, and seized the goods. The inhabitants of the English seaports, informed of this incident, fitted out a fleet of sixty sail, stronger and better manned than the others, and awaited the enemy on their return. After an obstinate battle, they put them to rout, and sunk, destroyed, or took the greater part of them. No quarter was given; and it is

---

[3] Vol. II (1810), pp. 486 *et seq.*

pretended that the loss of the French amounted to fifteen thousand men: which is accounted for by this circumstance, that the Norman fleet was employed in transporting a considerable body of soldiers from the south."

(b) *Cod War Incidents 1975–76*

Incidents in the 1975–76 Cod War between Iceland and the United Kingdom show quaint similarities to these acts of thirteenth-century lawlessness. Extracts from one report of such encounters will suffice to illustrate a type of twentieth-century naval confrontation which only just falls short of the use of armed force.[4]

The report is from a correspondent on board one of the United Kingdom support ships[5]: " An Icelandic gunboat again slipped through the Royal Navy protection net off south-east Iceland yesterday and harassed a trawler after a 28-knot chase that left British protection vessels helpless. The gunboat *Thor* then tried to harass a second trawler but was headed-off by the ocean-going tug *Lloydsman*. Later, Captain John Tait, the tactical commander of the Royal Navy's cod war operation, signalled commanders of protection vessels to cool it after angry exchanges during the heat of the battle between the captain of the *Thor* and Commander N. I. C. Nick Kettlewell, of the frigate *Brighton*. A collision seemed at one time certain between the *Lloydsman* and the *Thor*, and the two vessels were once within 6 ft. of each other before the *Thor* slipped away. The Royal Navy afterwards described the eventual heading-off of the *Thor* as the first major victory for the protection force. The Icelandic gunboat took advantage of the appalling weather, heavy snowstorms and a force-eight gale, to make its latest killing. As before, a decoy was used to tie up the protection vessels. The *Odin* went close to the south of the trawler pack early in the night, taking a passive role, but occupying the frigate *Falmouth* and the tug *Star Aquarius*. Then the *Thor* steamed south towards the pack under the cover of the snowstorm. The *Star Aquarius* moved in from the west to intercept and was forced by the weather conditions to come in close to make a positive identification. As soon as it did, the *Thor* put on speed and outpaced it. The frigate *Brighton* and the tugs *Euroman* and *Lloydsman* converged on the *Thor*. But the gunboat already had its cutter out and beat the protection vessels to the Grimsby trawler *Ross Ramillies*, cutting one warp. The *Thor* then sped towards another Grimsby trawler, the *Black Watch*, but it had already hauled the net in. By then the protection vessels were able to force the *Thor* away. Captain Tait signalled protection vessel

---

[4] For further extracts, see *loc. cit.* above, note 1.
[5] *The Times* (London), December 6, 1975.

commanders later, telling them that their role was simply peace in our time, and good fishing. . . . The Foreign Office has instructed Mr. Kenneth East, the British Ambassador in Reykjavik, to protest about the actions of the Icelandic gunboat *Thor* yesterday."

(c) *The Cay Salzbank Incident*

The last illustration of the anarchy model is taken from the Western Hemisphere. According to a Cuban Note, sent to the Department of State of the United States of America through the Czechoslovak Embassy in Washington in April 1976,[6] two Cuban fishing boats were attacked 80 miles off the central coast of Cuba by a launch armed with machine guns. The first boat was machine-gunned for over 45 minutes. The five Cubans on board, three of them wounded, escaped in a lifeboat. The launch then turned on the second Cuban boat, killing one crew member. Cuban exile groups in Miami claimed responsibility for the attack.

2—*Significance of the Anarchy Model*

The Brittany, Cod War and Cay Salzbank incidents can be distinguished on several grounds. The Brittany incident may be described as pertaining to a prelegal phase in the evolution of European society in which, in the absence of consensual engagements to the contrary between the sovereigns concerned, violence unlimited was lawful, that is, everybody realised that the high seas were in a state of pristine lawlessness.

In contrast, Icelandic and United Kingdom actions in the 1975–76 Cod War can be viewed as assertions of contested rights under governmental control in the triple consensual framework of the United Nations, the North Atlantic Treaty Organisation and the Council of Europe.

These and other differences between the two types of incident should not be minimised. Yet, one significant similarity remains: the continuing possibility of confrontations of the Cod War and Cay Salzbank types underlines the thinness of the border-line between peaceful relations in existing international law and a relapse into the anarchy pattern.

It is also possible to rationalise the Cod War from the angle of peaceful change. In different ways, apologists of either side may credit their government with a foresight (or guile) which, for the time being, it would be hard to verify. It is arguable that, by its unilateral assertion of an, in principle, exclusive 200-mile zone, the Icelandic Government was but hastening a process of consensus on a rule of maritime law to this effect and, thus, paving the way for an, at least,

---

[6] *The Times* (London), April 12, 1976.

partial success at the Third United Nations Conference on the Law of the Sea.

Similarly, the United Kingdom Government, benevolent observers may think, merely appeared to be drifting into a controlled escalation of its dispute with Iceland. Actually, they may consider that it reacted as it did to the Icelandic challenge so as to prepare public opinion at home and abroad for the inevitable acceptance, with gentlemanly reluctance, of an entirely acceptable 200-mile exclusive or preferential zone as a generally agreed rule of the law of the sea.

Different from the Cod War incident described above, the Cay Salzbank incident falls into the category of piracy *jure gentium*, and the navies of Cuba or any other sovereign State would have been fully entitled to take appropriate action. An official version of the United States reaction must still be awaited. Yet, if the assertion of the Cuban exile groups in Miami that they were responsible for the attack proved correct, this would raise the issue of United States responsibility for the illegal use by the Cuban exiles concerned of United States territory as a base for their hostile operations.

From the point of view of a models approach to the law of the sea, it matters little which interpretation of, by and large, uncontroversial factual situations in the Cod War and Cay Salzbank incidents is adopted. These factual substrata suggest, at least as a working hypothesis, the precariousness of the existing international maritime order and its proximity to the anarchy model, notwithstanding relevant confederate superstructures such as the United Nations, the North Atlantic Treaty Organisation and the Organisation of American States.

III—The Quasi-Order Model

A quasi-order model distinguishes itself from any order model, properly so-called, by its more precarious character.

In an impressionist way, the three Cod Wars between Iceland and the United Kingdom alone suggest that the existing international maritime order is a mere quasi-order. The fact that the parties are not only fellow-members of the United Nations—another mere quasi-order—but also belong to more closely knit political and military organisations and, nevertheless, can slide back into confrontations falling only just short of armed conflicts cannot but strengthen this preliminary finding.

In a wider historical perspective, the contemporary international maritime quasi-order which constitutes the framework of the Cod Wars is a late manifestation of this model which has two primary variants: the municipal law variant and the international law variant.

1—The Municipal Law Variant

In a world State—federal or unitary—the successful subjection of the oceans to control by a world government would transform this model into an order model proper.

Short of consummation of this process, attempts at establishing a public order on the basis of municipal law are, at most, of a universalist character. They lack the element of objective universality.

The Roman Law solution of the problem belongs to this category: the high seas as *res communis*,[7] and so does the dictum attributed to Emperor Antoninus Pius: " I am the ruler of the world [sometimes translated as " land "], but the Rhodian Sea law is the mistress of the sea." [8] Similarly, access from ports to the high seas and vice versa was regulated by Roman public law.

If sovereigns limit their exclusive claims under municipal law to portions of the high seas adjacent to their territories, they accept, by implication, the pluralist character of their claims. At this point, the universalist variant of the municipal-law model shades off into the imperialist variant.

Thus, in King John's Ordinance of March 30, 1201,[9] English overlordship is asserted in the Narrow Seas, including the Bristol Channel and the Irish Sea, and, at a later date, in *maribus Britannicis*.

Perhaps the most flamboyant assertion of claims to sovereignty over a part of the high seas was the annual ceremony in which the Doge of Venice was rowed in a State barge to the Channel of the Lido. There he threw a ring into the water as a symbol of Venice's espousal of the sea, reciting "We espouse thee, o sea, in sign of a real and perpetual dominion." [10]

, To the same category belong the attempts, made from time to time by one or the other Power, to establish special régimes in semi-enclosed seas such as the Baltic, the Black Sea, the Irish Sea, the Persian (Arab) Gulf and the Red Sea.

2—The International Law Variant

The object of the international-law variant of the quasi-order model is either to strengthen the municipal-law variant or provide a more acceptable alternative. While the former will be discussed in this Section, the latter will be treated below under IV.

The oldest known treaties to sustain the municipal law variant of the international quasi-order model are those between Carthage and Rome, variously dated between 508 and 306 B.C. and described by Livius as " *foedera vetusta*." Under these treaties, Roman freedom

---

[7] Celsus, *Dig*. 43.8.3. [8] *Dig*. 14.2.9.
[9] Selden, *Mare Clausum seu de Dominio Maris* (1636), Bk. II, Chap. 26.
[10] A. Justice, *A General Treatise of the Dominion and Laws of the Sea* (1705), p. 73.

of navigation in the Mediterranean was severely limited. Carthage permitted Roman ships to navigate only up to Cape Farina (the "beautiful promontory") and, in Italy, Rome was allowed to protect only Latium and specified towns on the Italian west coast, but without any corresponding limitation of Carthaginian freedom of movement.[11]

Similarly, the Papal Bull prohibiting navigation by others than Portugal on seas adjoining West Africa (A.D. 1455), and subsequent Bulls, purporting to grant exclusive rights on the high seas to Portugal and Spain, created rights not only between the Holy See and each of the countries so privileged.[12] In international law, these Bulls became effective between Portugal and Spain by the express or implied incorporation in treaties between the two countries such as the Treaty of Tordesillas (June 7, 1494).

To a limited extent, the British claims to sovereignty in adjacent seas also received international recognition as, for instance, in Article 13 of the Treaty of April 15, 1654, between the Commonwealth and the United Provinces of the Netherlands: " That the ships and vessels of the said United Provinces, as well those of War as others, which meet any of the Men of War of the Republic of England in the British Seas, shall strike the Flag to them in the same manner as was ever observed at any time heretofore under any former Government." Yet, by then, other forms of establishing an international quasi-order on the high seas had proved more generally acceptable.

IV—THE QUASI-ORDER MODEL
(continued)

Three factors significantly affected the search for alternative solutions in international law to the problem of an international maritime order: the increasing number of maritime Powers; growing consciousness of the oceanic and global character of the high seas, and the expansion of European society into a world society.

This situation made recognition of, or acquiescence in, exclusive claims regarding other than adjacent waters appear to be both presumptuous and impracticable. The alternative was search for a maritime order with a wider appeal.

In a pluralist international society which, for most other purposes, had accepted the principle of equality before the law as the basis of international relations between sovereign States, the rules of the new maritime order in the making had to comply with corresponding assumptions.

---

[11] H. Bengtson, *Die Verträge der griechisch-römischen Welt von 700 bis 338 v. Chr.* (1962), pp. 16 *et seq.*

[12] Selden, *op. cit.* above, note 9, Bk. I, Chap. 17.

1—The Naturalist Sub-Model

Given the situation outlined in the introductory paragraphs of this Section, deductively argued systems and rules of natural law provided apparently perfect answers. Derived as they were from supposedly immutable rules of primary natural law, these propositions applied equally to all mankind. The fact that the principle of reciprocity was an in-built element of these rules could but increase their attractiveness. Moreover, these rules of primary international law held out other inestimable advantages. They were there all the time. Thus, they merely required to be made articulate, and compliance with them could be demanded automatically as a matter of right. Moreover, addressed as these rules were to the conscience of all concerned, they were self-executing.

It merely required the linking of the " immutable " rules of, at least, primary natural law with the interests of particular maritime Powers to reveal the weaknesses of these supposedly automatic and self-executing maritime orders. Deductive reasonings could be put to any desired use, especially by emphasis, as required, on the character of controversial rules as rules of primary or secondary natural law, the formulation, as opportune, of the just titles of resort to war (*jus ad bellum*), and the selective use of evidence drawn from the most disparate sources: the Bible, classical writers, mythical and historical incidents, and dicta borrowed from Roman and Canon Law.

In the realities of seventeenth-century politics, the propositions put forward by naturalist writers from Alberico Gentili, Hugo Grotius, Franciscus Seraphinus de Freitas and Julius Pacius to Sir John Boroughs, John Selden and William Welwood hardly imposed onerous legal restraints on any maritime Power. They served, however, as handy—and, on occasion, made to measure—ideologies of policies pursued or political aspirations yet to be realised. Thus, these naturalist maritime orders were little more than pseudo-orders which but thinly covered the continuation of the anarchy pattern in actual State practice.

The origins and timing by the sponsors of the full or partial publication of major works in this category such as Grotius's *De Jure Praedae* and Selden's *Mare Clausum*, and Grotius's " *volte de face* " (Verzijl) at the Anglo-Dutch Conferences of 1613 and 1615 are of more than antiquarian interest. While the reasonings of the naturalist writers may have become dated, the uses to which their services were put have lessons of more enduring significance to teach: the basic incompatibility of the functions of legal advocacy and scholarship, and the self-neutralising character of doctrinal efforts made—to put it in the words of a famous letter by Hugo Grotius to

his brother [13]—" *optimo . . . in patriam animo* " or in the interest of
any other vested interest, national, international or multinational.

2—The Classical Sub-Model

If it suited any particular State to claim rights which, otherwise, it
could not claim, it was able to put to its advantage the potentialities
of naturalist reasoning on issues of international maritime order as
on any other matter in controversy. Yet, if it was not a question of
asking for something from somebody else but subjecting oneself to
legal duties, State practice showed a pronounced preference for
evidence of a, primarily, consensual character.

(a) *Genesis of the Classical Rules*

Over centuries, rules such as those relating to shipwreck or piracy
were embodied in treaties. When, gradually, they were taken for
granted by the core of European States, they came to be recognised
rules of an automatically binding international customary law. If such
rules belonged to the sphere of maritime law, it was the views of the
chief maritime Powers that were decisive on this transformation.

In fields such as those of the duties of maritime Powers in waters
adjoining their land territories and safety at sea, leading maritime
Powers took the initiative by unilateral action in their own national
and territorial seas or in relation to ships entitled to sail under their
flags. Similar to corresponding developments in the laws and
customs of land warfare, others followed suit because they recognised
the usefulness of the national codifications concerned or because
they desired to emulate the examples set by the leading Power.
Again, on an essentially consensual footing, further nourishing
grounds for rules of international customary law were created. Such
consensus also provided a firm basis for multilateral conventions,
codifying and developing the existing law. The prehistory of the
Brussels Conventions of 1910 on Collision and Assistance at Sea
illustrates this proposition.

The rules on this footing of reciprocity and increasingly general
acceptability, outlined above, constitute the bulk of the contemporary
international customary law of the sea.

(b) *The Order-Element in the Classical Rules*

What requires further examination is the order-element in classical
maritime law.

It will assist in isolating the order-element in these rules to distinguish between the rules applicable in a state of peace, a state of
intermediacy between peace and war, and in a state of war.

---

[13] *Epistolae*, Nr. 705.

State of Peace. The rules governing adjacent waters prove that, in areas capable of control by the coastal State, its interests prevail. The cannon-shot rule provided a persuasive *ex post* generalisation of this situation. If, in the pre-1914 and pre-1939 periods, the growth of this area of exclusive control did not keep pace with technological possibilities, the reason was not necessarily respect for the freedom of the seas. Strong naval Powers and other home States of deep-sea fishing fleets had every interest in keeping the size of national and territorial seas in check. Moreover, the replies to the League questionnaires on the territorial sea revealed greater discrepancies in actual State practice than would-be codifiers in the late twenties had imagined.

For the rest, such international order as was established in matters maritime was attained on the lines of least resistance: limitation, in principle, to the flag State of control of ships on the high seas; freedom of user of the high seas by any subject of international law for any purpose, softened in the 1958 High Seas Convention by infusion of an element of *jus aequum* (" reasonable use "). What, subsequently, was to prove more significant than could be realised in the formative stages of these rules was the exclusion of the sea-bed and subsoil from applicable rules; for this meant continuing freedom of appropriation of both, subject to non-interference with the user of the high seas by others.

The classical maritime law of peace left unsettled at least seven major issues:

(1) The *status of the territorial sea*, assimilated by the 1958 Convention to the national sea. What, in 1952, appeared to be an illegal annexation of an epicontinental 200-mile zone by Chile, Ecuador and Peru, retrospectively proved to be the shape of things to come.

(2) *The breadth of the territorial sea*, a subject on which, at the 1958 and 1960 Geneva Conferences on the Law of the Sea, it proved impossible to reach consensus.

(3) The legitimacy and scope of *protective zones* beyond the territorial sea for an increasing number of purposes in the national interest of coastal States. This matter is settled only between Parties to the 1958 Geneva Convention on the Territorial Sea and the Contiguous Zone (Art. 24).

(4) Exclusive rights in *continental shelves*, in the wake of the Truman Declaration of 1945, claimed unilaterally by a growing number of States and accepted in the 1958 Convention on the Continental Shelf to a depth of 200 metres or, beyond, to a variable limit of technical exploitability.

(5) The status of *artificial structures*, erected or anchored on the high seas.

(6) The status of *archipelagos*.

(7) The status of *semi-enclosed seas*, in the wake of the 1857 Treaty of Copenhagen in which, for a consideration, Denmark agreed to cease levying a toll for passage through the Sound, connecting the Kattegat and the Baltic.

Considering the unsettled character of so many major issues, the impossibility of settling any of them otherwise than by consent,[14] and the marked trend in the 1958 Geneva Conventions to accommodate the growing appetites of coastal States, it would be difficult to describe the peace-time maritime order of classical international law, including the achievements of the 1958 Geneva Conference, otherwise than in terms of an international quasi-order.

State of Intermediacy. So-called pacific blockades were symbolic of the open-endedness of the international public order of classical international law in the ambiguous zone created by the legitimacy of forcible reprisals in relations falling short of war between sovereign States. Neither the League Covenant nor the Kellogg Pact conclusively settled the matter. It was only by Article 2 (4) of the United Nations Charter that, otherwise than in compliance with the seven Purposes of the United Nations, the threat or use of force between, and by, member-States and, under Article 2 (6), by non-member States was unequivocally prohibited.

State of War. The high seas as the arena of simultaneous peaceful and non-peaceful users and as an area not subject to exclusive control by any one State or group of States offered opportunities to interfere not only with enemy naval forces but also with any other maritime activities carried on by the enemy and with those of States not involved in a particular armed conflict. Thus, it was tempting for naval Powers to aim at as complete control of the high seas as was attainable. In this sense, naval warfare in its widest sense (that is, including the control of neutral commerce) always tended to veer towards total, including economic, warfare.

In relations between belligerents, restraints imposed depended primarily on the effects, if more than negligible, on neutral Powers of naval action against, for instance, enemy merchant ships with neutral cargoes or enemy cargoes with neutral destinations. Even more so did such considerations determine direct interference with neutral maritime trade.

In both types of situation, it would be rash to equate self-restraint with law-abidingness. Especially in armed conflicts between sea and

---

[14] By December 31, 1977, the status of the 1958 Geneva Conventions, including ratifications, accessions and notifications of succession, subject to reservations and declarations, was as follows: I (Territorial Sea) 45; II (High Seas) 56; III (Fishing and Conservation of Living Resources) 35; IV (Continental Shelf) 53; V (Optional Protocol on Disputes) 37.

land Powers with relatively weak navies, compliance with strict rules such as the prohibition, in principle, of the destruction of neutral prize on the high seas offered considerable tactical advantages in influencing public opinion in neutral countries.

Even so, naval warfare in the post-Napoleonic period proves that the rules of maritime warfare and neutrality were most scrupulously observed in duel wars between secondary Powers, with the major Powers on the sidelines. Other rules—as happened with the contraband rules in the Paris Declaration of 1856—were first developed as compromises between maritime allies and, subject to an implied but practically unlimited right of disregard by way of reprisal, gradually adopted by third Powers.

In major wars, it pays strong naval powers to leave the responsibility for the escalating process of reprisals and counter-reprisals to the enemy. To achieve this end, it is necessary to keep commanders and diplomatic missions on the spot on a tight bureaucratic rein and leave controversial decisions which may involve breaches of international law or carefully reasoned departures from the rules on grounds of reprisal to the central authorities. The way in which decisions in this category were made in the United Kingdom in the initial phase of the Second World War is well depicted in Professor O'Connell's instructive Melland Schill Lectures on *The Influence of Law on Sea Power* (1975).

Yet, in the end, naval warfare in the First and Second World Wars confirms a general trend in major wars: the capture or, if this is impracticable, the destruction of all enemy shipping, determined efforts to deprive the enemy of access to the high seas, including strangulation of his export trade, and tight control of enemy trade with and through neutral coastal States. In the final stages of such major wars, the *ipse-dixitism* of reprisals and counter-reprisals and the use of the latest available means of technology in sea and air warfare tend towards almost unlimited total naval warfare.

These trends are dramatically summarised in Umpire Parker's Opinion on *War-Risk Insurance Premium Claims*.[15] It was awareness of the realities of maritime warfare in the Atlantic and Pacific during the Second World War that, in the case of Doenitz, induced the International Military Tribunal of Nuremberg to treat the facts proved regarding Allied practice as mitigating circumstances.

In the critical stages of major wars, such border-lines between international quasi-orders as may be thought to have existed in pre-war periods or initial phases of wars to the finish become so blurred as to amount to a thinly disguised relapse into the anarchy model.

---

[15] 1923—18 A.J.I.L. (1924), pp. 581–584.

Thus, viewing classical international maritime law and its derivatives as a whole, it appears charitable to describe it in terms of an international quasi-order.

V—THE ORDER MODEL

To whatever international maritime order a world society may aspire, such an order remains sectoral. Thus, it is unlikely to be stronger than that attained by world society itself.

In determining the likely maximal scope of the maritime order attainable in the United Nations, it may assist to examine earlier efforts to improve particular aspects of the overall maritime quasi-order prevailing at the time.

Three experiments deserve closer examination: British initiatives in the post-1815 period to police the oceans for purposes of outlawing the slave trade; the efforts to settle the status of the Straits and, thus, by implication, the Black Sea, and the endeavours of the Hague Peace Conferences of 1899 and 1907 to codify and develop the laws of maritime warfare and neutrality.

1—Outlawry of the Slave Trade

For our purposes, it must suffice to tabulate five lessons to be learned from the efforts made since the Napoleonic Wars to embody the prohibition of the slave trade in rules of international law:

(1) In a Separate Article to the First Paris Peace Treaty, agreed on May 30, 1814, between Great Britain and France, the Parties agreed that the colonial slave trade was " repugnant to the principles of natural justice and of the enlightened age in which we live."

Both Powers expressed their determination, at the Vienna Congress, to induce " all the Powers of Christendom to decree the abolition of the slave trade, so that the said Trade shall cease universally." In the Declaration of the Eight Powers of February 8, 1815, on the Universal Abolition of the Slave Trade, Austria, France, Great Britain, Portugal, Prussia, Russia, Spain and Sweden agreed to put an end to a " scourge which has so long desolated Africa, degraded Europe and afflicted humanity " and accepted the principle laid down in the Separate Article of the British-French Treaty. Yet, they admitted that the timing of the universal abolition of the slave trade was a matter of negotiation between the Powers concerned.

" The laws of Religion and of Nature " [16] notwithstanding, the prohibition was to be attained on a consensual basis. There was no question of the greater Powers forcing otherwise than by political and economic pressure new rules of international law on any sovereign State. In 1818, Austria, Prussia and Russia formally rejected a

---

[16] Additional Article of the Second Paris Peace Treaty, November 20, 1815.

suggested short-cut of solemnly assimilating the slave trade to piracy *jure gentium.*

(2) Judgments of English and United States courts eloquently reaffirmed the position under international customary law. In the absence of consensual arrangements to the contrary, warships had no right of visit and search on the high seas of ships of other sovereign States which were suspected of being engaged in the slave trade.

In refusing to treat slave-trading as piracy or as being otherwise illegal under international customary law, Sir William Scott held in the *Le Louis* case (1817) [17] that " to press forward to a great principle by breaking through every other great principle that stands in the way of its establishment; to force the way to the liberation of Africa by trampling on the independence of other States in Europe; in short, to procure an eminent good by means that are unlawful, is as little consonant to private morality as to public justice."

Similarly, in the *Antelope* case (U.S. Supreme Court, 1825),[18] Chief Justice Marshall found that the slave trade remained lawful to those whose government had not forbidden it. Thus, " if it be consistent with the law of nations, it cannot in itself be piracy," and foreign ships engaged in the slave trade, captured on the high seas by United States cruisers and brought into United States ports for adjudication, had to be restored to their owners.

Thus, two courts, manned by judges of the highest calibre, refused to bend the law to powerful pressures of public opinion and " develop " the law by techniques best left to " sea lawyers " or their terrestrial counterparts.

(3) Then, as now, means of legitimate but more cumbersome reform of the law were at hand: bilateral and multilateral treaties. With patience, and by the exercise of persuasive powers which included all the means employed to maintain *Pax Britannica,* successive British Governments gradually persuaded most of the States that mattered to join in these humanitarian efforts.

(4) If these treaties, culminating in the multilateral London Treaty of December 20, 1841, between Austria, France, Great Britain, Prussia and Russia, increasingly received general approbation, it was because they were based on the principle of reciprocity, including the exercise of the right of visit and search on the high seas of vessels suspected of slave-trading. Although, in practice, this meant that the British Navy—at the British taxpayer's expense—acted almost single-handed as the world's naval policeman in upholding the newly agreed standards, application of the reciprocity principle as the working principle behind these and other relevant

---

[17] 2 Dodson 210.   [18] 10 Wheaton 66.

conventions duly assuaged the sovereignty-complexes of the smaller Contracting Parties.

(5) When, in the League of Nations and United Nations eras, it was taken for granted that the outlawry of the slave-trade had become part of generally accepted international law, it was tempting to draw unwarranted conclusions from this, in itself, acceptable proposition.

(a) It was assumed that it was safe to whittle down the policing machinery under the 1841 Treaty. Actually, the view that, by and large, all parties to the relevant treaties of the League of Nations and United Nations periods would be anxious to assist in good faith in the application and execution of the 1926 Slave-Trade Convention and the 1956 Protocol covered a less creditable reality: awareness of the fact that some of the States most in need of effective supervision were not prepared to accept too rigid controls of their treaty observance.

(b) Moreover, official enthusiasm for these rare rules of a demonstrable *jus cogens*, especially in the International Law Commission and at the 1968–69 Vienna Conference on the Law of Treaties, was little affected by the growing irrelevance of these rules of international *jus cogens*. While the slave-trade had been largely reduced to the supply of status symbols in the form of spoilt domestic pets to Near and Middle Eastern potentates, new forms of mass servitude in authoritarian and totalitarian States had grown up which neither required imports across the seas nor were covered by effective rules of international law.

(c) Actually, the description of the prohibition of slave-trading in terms of *jus cogens* tends to be misleading. To the extent to which the relevant multilateral treaties are binding on individual parties, they cannot liberate themselves from these obligations in relation to third parties otherwise than in accordance with the provisions of these or any other multilateral treaties. In this sense, the anti-slave trade treaties are as much or as little *jus cogens* as, on a consensual basis, the parties intend them to be. If, as may be granted, the parties intend these treaties to be viewed as *jus cogens*, the scope *ratione personae* of these treaties as general (if consensual) international law can be further extended by devices such as recognition of new States on the assumption of their acceptance of the rules of general international law, including generally accepted humanitarian treaties, and the estoppels created by such acts.

If States decide to opt out of such engagements, legally or illegally, and they are allowed to do so without, apparently, detrimental consequences, this merely proves the limited significance of the distinction between *jus dispositivum* and *jus cogens* on a confederate level and the character of this type of world confederation as a mere quasi-order.

If any confirmation of this characterisation were required, it would be furnished by the formulation of the relevant rule in Article 13 of the 1958 High Seas Convention: " Every State shall adopt effective measures to prevent and punish the transport of slaves in ships authorised to fly its flag." Similarly, in a heterogeneous world in which democratic (in the Western sense), authoritarian and totalitarian States co-exist in universalist organisations such as the United Nations and its Related Agencies, the further stimulation, embodied in Article 13, of automatic emancipation of any slave taking refuge on board any ship is as relative as anybody's freedom in the flag State in question.

2—*The Straits*

The Judgment of the International Court of Justice in the *Corfu Channel* (*Merits*) case (1949) supports a general proposition: if a strait—that is, a natural and navigable waterway connecting two parts of the high seas—is situated in the territorial sea of a coastal State, foreign merchant ships and warships are entitled to innocent passage.

In a state of intermediacy between peace and war, and in war, the rule is limited by overriding security requirements of the littoral State. Moreover, as is shown by reservations made by a number of States to Articles 14–20 of the Territorial Sea Convention of 1958, even in a state of peace, these States do not extend the right of innocent passage to warships, but make the passage of warships dependent on prior authorisation. Finally, corresponding to growing demands for a larger breadth of the territorial sea, an increasing number of formerly international straits tend to be claimed as part of the territorial seas or as part of national waters.

It is at these points where the rules on territorial sovereignty and the freedom of the seas intersect that the uncertainties of the law of the sea are greatest, and professional advocacy on behalf of conflicting vested interests produces noteworthy illustrations of international law as a weapon of ideological warfare.

The limited consensus on the legal position of straits means that States are faced with the alternative of continuous confrontations and the establishment of more stable régimes regarding access to and navigation through Straits. In particular, this applies to semi-enclosed seas such as the Mediterranean, the Black Sea and the Baltic.

From the angle of international order, the changes through the ages in the international status of the Straits linking the Aegean and

Black Seas (including the Dardanelles, the Sea of Marmara and the Bosphorus) are especially instructive.

(a) *The Anarchy Model in Operation*

Since the legendary days of the Argonauts and the siege of Troy, the Hellespont, as the Straits were known in Antiquity, offers a splendid illustration of the anarchy pattern. Yet, the area also was the scene of one of the earliest known arbitrations by Periandros on the ownership of the town of Sigeon between Athens and Mytilene (*c.* 600 B.C.).[19]

Similarly, in days of the Byzantine Empire, the Straits were formally under the Emperor's sovereignty. Actually, with changing fortunes, Genoa and Venice continuously fought over the control of Constantinople and access to the Black Sea.

(b) *The Quasi-Order Model in Operation*

Since the establishment of the Ottoman Empire until Russian penetration to the Black Sea in the late seventeenth century, the status of the Straits and the Black Sea as being under the sovereignty of the Sublime Porte was generally accepted in Europe. Such changes as, gradually, were to secure free passage through the Straits between the Porte and other Powers (Russia: 1702 and 1774; Austria: 1784; Great Britain: 1799; France: 1802, and Prussia: 1806) rested on bilateral treaties.

The character of the multilateral régimes established in 1840–41, the 1923 Peace Treaty of Lausanne and the 1936 Straits Convention of Montreux varied according to the relations of the Western Powers with Turkey and Russia. If, at the time, Turkey was an ally in a policy of containing the expansion of Russia, the emphasis was on the maintenance of Turkish sovereignty, subject to innocent passage of merchant ships of all nations which, of necessity, included those of the anti-Russian Powers. If, as in the abortive Peace Treaty of Sèvres of 1920, Russia could be ignored, and Turkey as a defeated enemy had to be reintegrated into a Western-dominated international society, international control was the key-note.

Thus, in the London Convention on the Straits of 1841 between Austria, France, Great Britain, Prussia, Russia and the Ottoman Empire, the Powers affirmed their " unanimous determination to conform to the ancient rule of the Ottoman Empire, according to which the passage of the Straits of the Dardanelles and of the Bosphorus is always closed to foreign ships of war, so long as the Porte is at peace."

This formulation left it open whether the same ancient Turkish practice, if only on the basis of treaty obligations, regulated naviga-

---

[19] Herodotos, V, 95; Aristoteles, *Rhetoric* 1. 15.

tion in the Straits and access to the Black Sea regarding any foreign merchant ships while the Porte was in a state of peace with the flag States concerned. By 1841, it would probably have been premature to argue that a rule of international customary law on freedom of innocent passage through straits, especially in national waters, had come into existence.

Although the international régime envisaged in the 1920 Peace Treaty of Sèvres never came into operation, it is of major interest as an extreme power variant of the quasi-order model. It provided for the cession of a large area in the contempolated Zone of the Straits to Greece, a friendly neutral of the victorious First World War coalition; the demilitarisation of the whole Zone under the supervision of a Straits Commission, dominated by the former Allied and Associated Powers, and complete freedom of navigation for merchant ships and warships of all nations without flag discrimination and, similarly, complete freedom of the air. Whatever the intention, this régime would have exposed the southern flank of Russia to attack in an especially sensitive area: the Russian oil fields.

As a consequence of the change in the international position of Turkey prior to and during the elaboration of the 1923 Peace Treaty of Lausanne, the area of the demilitarised zone and the powers of the Straits Commission were considerably scaled down. Moreover, Turkey was to preside over the Commission. Similarly, detailed rules provided for sea and air passage of the various categories of ship and aircraft through the Straits while Turkey was in a state of peace, war or neutrality.

During the negotiations for the Lausanne Peace Treaty, the hands of Turkish diplomats were considerably strengthened by the then existing alternative to a settlement with the West: her Treaty of Friendship of 1921 with the Soviet Union. The Treaty envisaged a Straits settlement by a conference of Black Sea littoral States and safeguards for the " full sovereignty " of Turkey and the " security of Constantinople, her capital." [20]

By the middle Thirties, the Western Powers, the Soviet Union and Turkey were ready for a new settlement. The 1936 Straits Convention of Montreux—provisionally concluded for 20 years but, afterwards, of indefinite duration, subject to a right of denunciation by each Contracting Party (Article 28)—was indicative of basic changes that had taken place in the international kaleidoscope.

The principles of freedom of transit and navigation in the Straits, but only by sea, were reaffirmed and to remain unaffected by any denunciation of the Convention. Meanwhile, the Soviet Union, since

---

[20] Art. V—reiterated in Art. IV of the Russo-Turkish Treaty of Amity and Fraternity of 1922.

1934 a member of the League of Nations and, like the Western Powers, primarily anxious about the expansionism of Fascist Italy and Nazi Germany, put her trust in Kemal Pasha's Turkey. Thus, Turkey was permitted to refortify the Straits. The powers of the Straits Commission under the Lausanne Peace Treaty were transferred to Turkey, and the more detailed provisions for the application of the principles of freedom of transit and navigation in the Straits were revised in favour of Turkey and the Black Sea Powers.

Turkish neutrality until nearly the end of the Second World War and renewed Russian appetites for exclusive control of the Straits made it unlikely that the Montreux Convention would survive long into the post-war era. Yet, the swift transition from Allied wartime unity to the Cold War and Turkey's integration in the Western security system made all Parties concerned chary of denouncing the Convention and enabled Turkey to maintain her vigil of the Straits under the Montreux Convention.

(c) *Evaluation*

Five points of general significance emerge from the diplomatic history of the successive Straits and Black Sea settlements:

(1) *Constants*. The constant element in the international position of the Straits ever since Antiquity is the key position of the Straits area in two directions: it controls access to, and egress from, the Black Sea, and movements in either direction between Asia Minor and Europe.

(2) The chief *variables* in the various Straits settlements are the strength of the territorial entity or entities in the Straits area and of the other Powers interested in either or both of the control functions of the Straits.

(3) The successive multilateral Straits settlements of the nineteenth and twentieth centuries are closely linked with the changing fortunes of the individual greater Powers involved and the influence exercised at any particular time by groupings of Powers such as the Concert of Europe or wartime Allies in subsequent post- and pre-war periods. Thus, the regional régimes of the Straits tend to be as precarious as the wider quasi-orders in systems of open power politics or power politics in disguise. What, on the surface, may appear as greater resilience of some of these settlements is due rather to defeat of challengers of the pre-war *status quo* by Powers in favour of its maintenance.

(4) The consensual superstructures regulating freedom of navigation in and transit through the Straits since the early eighteenth century conform to the general pattern of the international law of the time:

(a) If a local territorial sovereign such as the Ottoman Empire exists as an effective independent entity or is propped up as such, the starting point of any internationally guaranteed freedom of navigation or transit is, as in relation to any other territory under the jurisdiction of a sovereign State, the consent of the local sovereign. At least in form, the European Powers paid scrupulous attention to this point in the 1840 and 1841 Conventions with the Porte.

(b) In some of the relevant treaties,[21] Contracting Parties purport to settle matters "in perpetuity" or "without limit of time." Yet unilateral denunciations such as that by Russia in 1870 of the Black Sea clauses of the 1856 Peace Treaty of Paris prove that such " permanent " solutions are hardly more stable than the shifting power relations on which they rest. If such relations are in danger of degenerating into " cold " peaces or wars between former allies as happened in the post-1945 period between the Western Allies and the Soviet Union, the very precariousness of such relations may counsel caution. Thus, notwithstanding the tight-rope diplomacy of Turkey during the Second World War and continuous rumblings from Moscow since the Yalta Conference of 1945, the Soviet Union considered it inadvisable to denounce the 1936 Montreux Convention as, for most purposes, it was entitled to do since 1954 (Art. 28).

(c) The changes in contracting parties to the various settlements, and the apparent imperviousness of the leading Powers to the reactions of potential dissidents among contracting parties to previous conventions, may prove something. They hardly furnish evidence of general acceptance of the majority principle for purposes of change-over from one system to another or revision of any particular convention otherwise than, for limited purposes, on a purely consensual footing (as, for instance, in Article 29 of the 1936 Montreux Convention). They are, however, in line with a gradual decline since the First World War in the standards of international *courtoisie* and respect for the rights of minorities in the international aristocracy of sovereign States. Yet such rough and ready practices leave the legal rights of dissidents unaffected, and changes made without their consent are opposable to them only on grounds of acquiescence.

(5) The international régime contemplated in the abortive 1920 Peace Treaty of Sèvres is instructive in its extremeness. It was based on the short-lived assumption of the possibility of treating the Soviet Union and Turkey as *quantités négligeables*. Thus, not only was the Black Sea opened to warships of all nations but also the contemplated Straits Commission and the devices of demilitarisation and institutionalisation were employed for purposes of underpinning

---

[21] Art. IX of the 1856 Paris Peace Treaty and Art. 28 (2) of the 1936 Montreux Convention.

the temporary hegemony in the area of the former Western Allied Powers in the First World War.

A comparison of the relevant provisions in the Sèvres Peace Treaty with the Lausanne Peace Treaty and Straits Convention of 1923 and the 1936 Montreux Convention drives home the difference made by the resurgence of the Soviet Union and Turkey. The hand-over to Turkey of the presidency of an enlarged and scaled-down Straits Commission symbolises the renewed significance attached to the element of territorial sovereignty in the Straits area.

3—*Taming the God of War?*

The occurrence of the First and, even more so, the Second World War conclusively proved that the attempts made at the Hague Conferences of 1899 and 1907 to tighten up the then existing international quasi-order were incommensurate to maintain general peace and obviate " as far as possible " recourses to force in the relations between States.[22]

Nonetheless, from the point of view of an effective international maritime order, two aspects of the Hague efforts at codifying and developing the international law of armed conflict continue to deserve attention: the treatment of the state of intermediacy (*status mixtus*) between peace and war, and the techniques employed at the two Conferences to paper over gaps in the international maritime order to be created.

(a) *Status mixtus*

So-called pacific blockades, that is, blockades in times of peace by naval forces of the shipping of the State against which these reprisals were directed, and other forms of the application of force falling short of war, were considered lawful prior to the 1907 Hague Peace Conference. In response to the protests raised by the " developing " —or, more accurately, capital-importing—countries of the time, especially in Latin America, Hague Convention II of 1907, subsequently named the Porter Convention after the chief United States delegate at the 1907 Hague Peace Conference, was devised. It was not limited to naval reprisals but also applied to other forms of armed force for the recovery of contract debts which the government of one country claimed from that of another as being due to its nationals.

Under the Porter Convention, the obligation of home States of creditors to refrain from resort to force was made dependent on willingness of the debtor State to arbitrate the issue at stake and submit to any award rendered. Yet, hardly any of the capital-importing States were prepared or, on grounds of internal politics, able to

---

[22] Heading of Part I and Art. 1, Hague Convention I, 1907.

offer more than token signatures, never to be followed by ratification of the Convention.

(b) *Naval Warfare*

It must suffice to provide three illustrations of the ways in which differences between land and sea Powers on major differences in matters of naval warfare were overcome:

(1) Sea Powers have an obvious interest in limiting the places where merchant ships may be converted into warships and precluding the reconversion of warships into merchant ships while the war lasts. The typical interests of land Powers are to the opposite effect.

In 12 Articles of Hague Convention VII, the Hague Peace Conference of 1907 attempted to codify the subject. Yet it had to admit in the Preamble that the Contracting Powers had been unable to reach agreement on the question of whether the conversion of a merchant ship into a warship was permissible on the high seas. Thus, the question of the place where such conversion and reconversion could lawfully be made remained " outside the scope " of the Convention, that is, as unsettled as it had been before, and so did the issue of the legality of reconversion during the war of a warship into a merchant ship.

(2) It is debatable whether the invention of the submarine or of automatic submarine contact mines was the most devastating contribution of pre-1914 technology to naval warfare. What is clear is that Hague Convention VIII of 1907 on Submarine Contact Mines permits every Contracting Party to contract out of all substantive obligations it may, on the surface, be considered to have undertaken under the Convention.

Probably, the first prize for formulating legal obligations with open-ended contracting-out clauses ought to be awarded to the authors of Article 6 of Hague Convention VIII: " The Contracting Parties which do not, at present, own perfected mines of the pattern contemplated in the present Convention, and which, consequently, could not, at present, carry out the rules laid down in Articles 1 and 3, undertake to convert the *matériel* of their mines as soon as possible so as to bring it into conformity with the foregoing requirements."

(3) Hague Convention IX of 1907 on Bombardment by Naval Forces in Time of War calls for attention for a reason of its own. The draftsmen succeeded in putting the clock back behind international customary law as it stood prior to this codification. They hedged round by exceptions and reservations the broad rules of international customary law as it had been judicially developed in a number of arbitration cases between 1883 and 1903. They introduced previously unknown distinctions between land and

sea warfare, resulting in relaxations of formerly applicable general rules, and weakened accepted restraints of the standard of civilisation by reformulating relevant rules—such as that on prior notice of bombardment in appropriate cases—as purely admonitory rules and, thus, reducing them to *lex imperfecta*.

(c) *Maritime Neutrality*

The evolution of the international law of maritime neutrality abounds in revealing insights into the operative reasons behind the equilibria achieved from time to time between belligerents and neutral Powers and the reversal of the policies of such Powers when they happened to be neutrals or themselves became belligerents.

It must suffice to recall the remarkable attempts made in Hague Convention XII of 1907 to create an international prize court, and, in the complementary London Declaration of 1909, to codify the substantive law to be applied by the court.

The object of Convention XII was to create an international court of redress (*recours*) against judgments of national prize courts, rather than a court of appeal in the technical sense.

The International Prize Court was to have jurisdiction in three types of case: (1) if the judgment of a national prize court concerned the property of a neutral State or national; (2) if it concerned enemy cargo on a neutral ship, an enemy ship captured in neutral waters and not the subject of a claim through diplomatic channels; (3) if the capture was alleged to be contrary to conventions in force between belligerents or legal rules laid down by the captor State.

Redress was to be available to neutral States and, subject to reservations, their nationals and those of enemy States.

The International Prize Court was to consist of 15 members. They were to be appointed by each of the Contracting Parties for a term of six years. Nine judges were to constitute a quorum. While those of the eight greater Powers enumerated were always to be summoned to sit, the others were to be called upon according to an annual rota annexed to the Convention.

The International Prize Court was to pronounce the capture of the ship or cargo to be valid or to be null and void. In the latter case, it was authorised to fix the amount of damages due.

In accordance with Article 7 of Hague Convention XII, the International Prize Court was to apply, first, applicable treaties, secondly, generally recognised rules of international law and, thirdly, the general principles of justice and equity. In its Final Act, the 1907 Hague Peace Conference recommended codification at a further conference of the laws and customs of naval war. This conference assembled in London in 1908 and produced the 1909 Declaration on Laws of Naval Warfare.

Most Contracting Powers had considered their signatures of Hague Convention XII as dependent on consensus on the rules of substance to be applied 'by the International Prize Court. Thus, it fell to Nicaragua to become the only State to ratify the Convention.

Bearing in mind the relative character of most tales of success and failure, it would be rash to dismiss this double failure out of hand. It may claim a continued relevance on, at least, three grounds:

(1) The purpose of the International Prize Court was to reassure potential neutral Powers that their grievances would receive due consideration not only in the national prize courts of belligerents but also in an impartial international organ with powers of redress. The fact that both the British and German delegations at the Second Hague Peace Conference put forward drafts for an International Prize Court, and these Powers, together with France and the United States of America, consolidated their proposals in a joint draft, proves the awareness of the tactical usefulness each of these countries attached to the sponsorship of the project.

(2) The protests of smaller States against the preponderance of judges appointed by the greater Powers in the contemplated International Prize Court stimulated further thinking on a fairer composition of international courts in general. Thus, a generally acceptable solution of the issue could be found more speedily than, otherwise, would have been likely when it came to drafting the Statute of the Permanent Court of International Justice.

(3) The necessity to court public opinion in neutral countries— with or without ratification of the London Declaration—made it advisable for belligerents on both sides in the First World War to choose as righteous a starting point as possible. Thus, subject to significant reservations, the Allied Powers and Germany announced that, on a basis of reciprocity, they would apply the Declaration. Yet, as discussed previously in this paper, these laudable intentions soon became submerged in a crescendo of reprisals and counter-reprisals against alleged breaches of the law of maritime warfare by the other side, and naval warfare degenerated into almost total warfare with unrestricted submarine warfare, unanchored submarine mines and long-distance blockades of enemy shores.

If Hague Convention XII and the London Declaration had been in force, the position would hardly have differed. Both Conventions were subject to all-participation clauses,[23] that is, they were operative only if all belligerents happened to be Contracting Parties to each of the Conventions.

---

[23] Art. 51 (1), Hague Convention XII, 1907; Art. 66, London Declaration, 1909.

VI—THE ORDER MODEL
(*continued*)

It remains to consider a growing number of relevant resolutions on the high seas, passed by the General Assembly since 1967, and some pointers in United Nations practice.

1—*Community Vistas*

The resolutions adopted since 1967 by the United Nations General Assembly on various aspects of the law of the sea have a, at first sight, surprising feature in common. They tend to be adopted unanimously, with, occasionally, a small number of member-States abstaining.

(a) *Status of the Resolutions*

To assess the legal significance of these Resolutions, it is advisable to recall that, in principle, these—like any other—substantive resolutions of a non-organisational character are but recommendations to member-States and other organs of the United Nations. By itself, neither unanimity nor reiteration changes their recommendatory character under the United Nations Charter. Unanimity may provide evidence of a consensus on objectives (or " goal values "—McDougal) and ways of approach. Yet, before any estoppel is read into " declarations," passed by the General Assembly in quasi-legislative language, such declarations require careful analysis.

Thus, the Declaration of Principles governing the Sea-Bed and the Ocean Floor, and the Subsoil thereof, beyond the limits of National Jurisdiction, was adopted by the General Assembly by 108 votes, none against, with 14 abstentions.[24] Yet any estoppel regarding rights under existing international law was expressly ruled out by the reservation in the Declaration that " States shall act in the area in accordance with the applicable principles and rules of international law." Moreover, a number of member-States stated their reservations regarding various principles contained in the Declaration. Furthermore, they refrained from putting forward amendments only on the clear understanding that they did not wish to disturb the delicate balance attained in the Declaration, and that the Declaration was not legally binding.

It is awareness of the non-committal character of this type of resolution which, at least at plenary meetings of the General Assembly, allows the illusion of a near-unanimous consensus to be created.

(b) *Common Heritage of Mankind?*

Two terms which appear with increasing frequency in the repertoire

---

[24] Resolution 2749 (XXV), December 17, 1970.

of General Assembly resolutions on the law of the sea and the preliminary texts of the Third United Nations Conference on the Law of the Sea require consideration. The sea-bed and subsoil thereof are described as the " common heritage of mankind," and activities in this area are to be carried out " for the benefit of mankind as a whole." [25]

In a deeply divided and heterogeneous world society, whose equipoise rests on fear of nuclear co-extermination, and which is barely contained in the weak confederate framework of the United Nations, references to an unstructured mankind sound quaint. They are reminiscent of the optimistic variant of eighteenth-century natural law and the misdescription—with all the emotive undertones associated with the notion—of contemporary world society as an " international community."

On land, it may be taken, the General Assembly accepts that the " common heritage " has been divided up in a continuous process of segmentation that can hardly be described in terms of an international community. Similarly, the use for wartime purposes of the high seas, over-fishing and maritime pollution suggest, at best, a squandering of such a common heritage as might have been left to mankind (one might ask, by whom?). Actually, what, so far, appears to have preserved the " common heritage " below the seas is less community-spirited self-denial than limitations of marine technology.

Thus, if terms such as " common heritage of mankind " and " exploitation of the sea-bed and sea floor in the interest of mankind " have any meaning, they must be viewed as community postulates. *De lege ferenda*, they are unobjectionable. Yet, if the use of the present tense in declarations is to mean that, in law, these submerged areas *are* a common heritage, we pass from advocacy and rhetoric to an unacceptable form of conceptualist law-making under the counter.

2—*Pointers in United Nations Practice*

More accurately than from General Assembly resolutions, such consensus as actually exists among members of the United Nations can be assessed from the hard and fast treaty obligations into which these members are prepared to enter.

It must suffice to choose three fields which, it is hoped, have been fairly selected: access to the sea for land-locked States, marine pollution, and régimes of common user of the high seas.

(a) *Access to the Sea*

Under the international customary law of unorganised international

---

[25] See *e.g.* Art. 136 and 140 of the Informal Composite Negotiating Text (A/COMF. 62/WP. 10).

society, no right of access to the sea by land-locked States exists. If such a right is to come into existence, it must be established on a consensual basis.

In the 1958 Convention on the High Seas, this position is reaffirmed as the law under the international quasi-order of the United Nations. Any supposed right of access to the sea is described in terms of " should " but not " shall ": " In order to enjoy the freedom of the seas on equal terms with coastal States, States having no sea-coast should have free access to the sea." [26] Yet, it is expressly stated that a legal duty to grant free transit through the territories of coastal States to States having no sea-coast exists only " in conformity with existing international conventions " and can be created only " by common agreement." [27]

At the first UNCTAD Conference (1964), the principle of free access to the sea was incorporated as one of the eight Principles adopted by the Conference. Yet, with a preponderance of coastal States among the " new " States, the principle of free access to the sea was formulated exactly as it had been by " old " States, that is, with all the reservations contained in Article 3 of the 1958 Convention on the High Seas.

The 1965 Convention on Transit Trade provides a multilateral framework on the subject but, otherwise, does not take matters any further. Thus, coastal States, " old " and " new " alike, do not appear to go out of their way in providing their land-locked co-inheritors with access to the " common heritage of mankind."

(b) *Marine Pollution*

That marine pollution on any but a negligible scale is incompatible with the long-range interests of any coastal State or, if it were preferred, mankind at large, is hardly in doubt. Thus, the degree of self-restraint shown or restraint imposed by legal rules is a reliable indicator of the actual willingness of States to limit for the common good short-term interests in causing pollution.

It is arguable that the formulation of the freedom of the seas as *jus aequum* in the 1958 Convention on the High Seas (Article 2) contains all that is needed by way of legal prescription. It may be thought to imply that any appreciable maritime pollution which originates in national waters or the territorial sea or takes place on the high seas constitutes an abuse of the freedom of the seas and amounts to an international tort. The *ratio* behind the *Trail Smelter* case (1938; 1941) between Canada and the United States of America could well be extended to all three types of situation.

This position has been weakened by two provisions on maritime

---

[26] Art. 3 (1).   [27] *Ibid*.

pollution in the 1958 Convention. It is left to every State to draw up regulations to prevent pollution of the seas by the discharge of oil from ships or resulting from exploration and exploitation of the sea-bed and its subsoil.[28] Similarly, every State is to take measures to prevent pollution of the seas by activities with radioactive materials or other harmful agents or by the dumping of radioactive waste.[29]

Similarly, the lengthening series of conventions on various aspects of maritime pollution—initiated by a bilateral treaty of 1942 between the United Kingdom and Venezuela on the Submarine Area of the Gulf of Paria [30] and followed by a series of multilateral conventions since 1954—suggests three inferences:

(1) States do not consider the prevention of marine pollution as a duty incumbent on them under any prior rule of international customary law.

(2) The suspension and denunciation clauses contained in the treaties make it difficult to argue that these and other relevant treaties confirm the subsequent evolution of a relevant rule of international customary law.

(3) The regional efforts made so far on the prevention of maritime pollution as, for instance, the 1969 Agreement for Co-operation in dealing with Pollution of the North Sea by Oil do not suggest greater intensity of effort or more effective supervision of observance of the Covention to a degree that would permit considering such efforts as consensual regional orders.

(c) *Régimes of Common User*

Under the umbrella of a municipal order such as that of the Roman Empire, it appears to follow "naturally" from the character of the high seas as *res communis* that, like the air, the use of the sea is common to all men.[31] It is not surprising that, especially in countries with a Roman-Law tradition, reminiscences of common user in Roman Law should have lingered on as a kind of inarticulate natural law.

Actually, international customary law does not know of any user of the territorial sea to be shared with third States other than that of innocent passage. Conversely, on the high seas it recognises an unlimited common user for all subjects of international law, subject to the few limitations accepted as being inherent in a rule *juris aequi*.

Thus, any common user in the territorial sea or limitation of user on the high seas rests on a consensual basis. Whether, and in whose favour, such user is preferential or is on a footing of equality depends on the consensual engagement in question. It is on the extension of the discrimination against others *beyond* the territorial sea in favour

[28] Art. 24.   [29] Art. 25.   [30] Art. 7.   [31] *Dig.* 47.10.13, para. 7.

of a coastal State " in a situation of special dependence on its coastal fisheries " in further " adjacent waters " under a supposed rule of international customary law (" crystallised . . . in recent years ") that the Judgments of the International Court of Justice in the *Fisheries Jurisdiction* cases appear to go well beyond *lex lata*.[32]

As, in the *Minquiers and Ecrehos* case,[33] the International Court of Justice observed, an " agreed common fishery zone " was established already in the 1839 Fisheries Convention between France and Great Britain. Moreover, in the two multilateral Conventions of 1882 and 1887 to be discussed below, policing of the North Sea attained a degree of international integration between participant States that, even in the days of the Council of Europe and the European Communities, has remained unsurpassed.

It is in the degree of submission to effective control that the degree of good faith of sovereign States and international integration actually achieved have to be measured. From this angle, the 1882 North Sea Policing of Fisheries Convention and the supplementary 1887 Convention on Liquor Traffic in the North Sea (not ratified by France) may claim topical interest. The " outrages "—to use the term of the title of a British Government enquiry [34]—committed by seamen against each other in the best tradition of the anarchy model and intensified by the free enterprise of liquor boats plying between fishing boats had given rise to these quasi-legislative efforts.

Under the 1882 Convention, cruisers of the Contracting Parties (all North Sea Powers except Norway and Sweden, then still united) were authorised to authenticate infractions of the major regulations prescribed by the Convention and all offences relating to fishing operations, " whichever may be the nation to which the fishermen guilty of such infractions may belong." [35]

For purposes of establishing the nationality of a fishing boat and obtaining proof of an offence, the cruisers were granted the right of visit and search of boats, including those of other than their own nationality.[36] They were further authorised to take the offending boat into a port of her own nationality and temporarily detain part of the crew of the fishing boat on one of the cruisers.[37] Resistance was equated with resistance to the authority of the nation of the fishing boat.[38]

In the case of non-serious contraventions of the Convention which caused damage to any fisherman, commanders of cruisers were permitted to arbitrate at sea between parties willing to agree to such arbitration, and fix the compensation to be paid.[39]

---

[32] *I.C.J. Reports* (1974), pp. 23 and 192.   [33] *Ibid.* (1953), p. 58.
[34] C. 2878, 1881.   [35] Art. XXVIII.   [36] Art. XXIX.
[37] Art. XXX.   [38] Art. XXXII.   [39] Art. XXXIII.

The 1882 and 1887 Conventions invite comparison with the 1943 draft Convention to replace the 1882 Convention,[40] the 1964 European Fisheries Convention, the Resolution on the Policing of Fisheries, adopted by the 1964 Fisheries Conference (January 17, 1964) and the 1970 Fisheries Regulation of the European Economic Community.[41]

Neither the 1964 Convention nor the 1970 Regulation—nor the aspirations of the 1943 draft Convention and the 1964 Resolution—came anywhere near the level of integration in policing matters which had been reached nearly a century ago.

VII—TOWARDS A MARITIME WORLD ORDER?

In conclusion, it may be helpful to consider some trends in the law of the sea and features in the United Nations law of the sea in the making which are directly relevant from the angle of international maritime order.

1—Trends

It would be tempting to use or, more accurately, abuse the models approach to international law in general, and the law of the sea in particular, to view the evolution of international law and the law of the sea in terms of progress from the anarchy model via the quasi-order model to—or, at least, towards—the order model.

If the emphasis is put on hard law, as distinct from mere blueprints, there is little evidence to substantiate any such teleological interpretation of the historical process. If anything, the evidence points to retrogression in the effectiveness, although not the quantity and deliberative superstructures, of international co-operation since the Anti-Slave Trade Treaty of 1841 and the North Sea Conventions of 1882 and 1887.

Trends in three fields can be readily identified and verified: changes in the forms of evolution of the law of the sea, the relation between the rules governing the principles of State sovereignty and the freedom of the seas, and the relative significance of the three major models considered in this paper.

(a) Forms of Evolution

The evolution of the law of the sea from pristine anarchy via bilateral treaties to a growing body of international customary law corresponds to the general pattern of the evolution of international law in Europe. In the post-1815 era, a further change from bilateral treaties to multilateral treaties under the aegis of the Concert of

---

[40] Cmd. 6496, 1943.

[41] Reg. 2141, 1970; Arts. 100–103, Act of Accession, annexed to the 1972 Accession Treaty.

Europe is noticeable, and this change from bilateralism to multi-lateralism intensified in the post-1919 and post-1945 periods. For better or worse, small States and non-coastal States increasingly participated in the quasi-legislative efforts made at the various conferences.

A major qualification of the movement from bilateralism to multi-lateralism is necessary. It is necessary to avoid the impression that all that happened was a rationalisation of consensual arrangements, corresponding to the expansion in the number of " sovereign and equal " members of the United Nations and world society at large. There was a sharp rise in unilateral acts which, at the time, were hard to square with the law as it stood. They took the forms of unilateral extensions of the territorial sea for all or specified purposes and exclusive claims to the continental shelf.

(b) *Sovereignty versus Freedom of the Seas*

To appreciate the intensification of the trend towards unilateralism in our time, it helps to compare it with the reactions of the Powers to earlier attempts at flouting what they considered to be settled rules of international law.

When, in 1870, Russia denounced the Black Sea clauses of the Paris Peace Treaty of 1856, she knew that, because of France's involvement in war with Germany, the risk of war with the Western Powers was remote. Yet, the very choice of this moment indicates Russia's awareness of the seriousness of her challenge. The London Conference of 1871 acquiesced in Russia's *fait accompli*, but insisted on Russia reaffirming, in concert with the other European Powers, the principle of the sanctity of international treaties.

Similarly, the unilateral extension in 1935 by Norway of her fisheries zones and, by implication, her territorial sea by drawing straight base lines between fixed points on the mainland, islands and rocks was on a scale that was difficult to reconcile with general inter-national law as it then stood. It led to a prolonged diplomatic dispute between Norway and the United Kingdom and, in the end, the Judgment of the International Court of Justice in the *Anglo-Norwegian Fisheries* case (1951).

During the proceedings before the Court, the United Kingdom conceded the Norwegian claim to a four-mile limit of her territorial sea. It merely contested the treatment of the *skjaergaard* (rock rampart), rather than the mainland, as the coast line and the Nor-wegian construction of the base lines. The Court decided the case in favour of Norway, but it did so on factual grounds which emphasised the supposedly unique character of the Norwegian coast. Moreover, by supporting its reasoning with metalegal considerations such as the "vital needs of the population," [42] the Court opened the door to arguments which, in the *North Sea Continental Shelf* cases (1969) and the *Fisheries Jurisdiction* cases (1974), were to bestow retrospective respectability on even more questionable exercises of the Court in judicial law-making.

With its 1951 Judgment, the International Court of Justice gave further impetus to a movement that, since the Roosevelt and Panama Declarations of 1939 and the Truman Proclamations of 1945 regarding Fishing and the Continental Shelf, could rely on precedents created or supported by the United States. In 1952, the Court's Judgment was followed by the Santiago Declaration of Chile, Ecuador and Peru on their " international maritime policy," asserting " sole jurisdiction and sovereignty " in a 200-mile maritime zone. Thus, the pace quickened and, under the " progressive " banners of conservation and environment protection, an increasing number of States pushed outwards their claims to exclusive control of vast areas of the high seas. What, at the Second United Nations Conference on the Law of the Sea of 1960, would still have been considered preposterous became an acceptable part of the package deals prepared at the Caracas (1975) and New York (1976) Sessions of the Third United Nations Conference on the Law of the Sea.

Whether termed epicontinental sea, patrimonial sea or exclusive economic zone, the overall trend is unmistakable. In the continuous contest between State sovereignty and freedom of the seas, the movement is increasingly towards massive extensions of the territorial sovereignty of coastal States and a corresponding shrinkage of the oceans.

The strength of this expansionism lies in the preponderance of local land power in the contiguous areas of the high seas and the restraints on sea power imposed by the international quasi-order of the United Nations. While it leaves coastal States free to refuse the judicial settlement of their claims, it prohibits maritime Powers from the threat or use of force in the interest of the freedom of the seas and suggests to them the easier alternative of following in the foot-steps of—as may be preferred—small-Power law-breakers or pace-makers for a " new " international law.

It was awareness of this tactical situation which enabled Iceland to ignore the adverse Judgments of the International Court of Justice in the *Icelandic Fisheries Jurisdiction* cases (1974), and, by playing the trump card of the threat to close the NATO base in Iceland, win the 1975–76 Cod War with the United Kingdom.

(c) *An Inter-Disciplinary Presumption*
Analysis of the evolution of the law of the sea in terms of models

[42] *I.C.J. Reports* (1951), p. 142.

furnishes a strong inter-disciplinary presumption: unless convincing evidence to the contrary is forthcoming, it may be assumed that, deceptive trappings notwithstanding, any international order apparently concurred in by the Powers is but an international quas-order or fulfils the functions of a mere quasi-order. Similarly, in the prevailing international environment, any blueprint for a maritime world order is prima facie suspect of being part of an ideological smoke-screen, if only for purposes of international one-upmanship.

From this angle, regional settlements such as those made since 1841 regarding the Straits are especially instructive. They belong to the variant of regional arrangements in which Powers strangers to the region are involved. They tend to reflect faithfully the relative strength of the primary Powers concerned and to be linked closely with the wider and overriding international system of the time. So long as this is one of open power politics or power politics in disguise, the, apparently, genuinely international and, especially, institutional superstructures of the regional arrangements in question matter little. What does matter are the positions taken up by the individual regional Powers in relation to the alignments concerned.

Similarly, in a power-dominated overall environment, preferences of major regional Powers for regional settlements exclusive to coastal States of particular regions such as the Black Sea, the Baltic or the Mediterranean are probably best understood as means for the attainment or maintenance of hegemonial relations in, at least, the local area affected.

If, in any particular case, such sceptical interpretation should do injustice to the purely functional intentions of the parties, they are free to rebut by deeds the presumption suggested in this Section.

A special word of warning on conventions and schemes couched in moralising terms appears apposite. Whether it is conservation of resources, protection of the environment or, what is least credible, activities to be carried out for the benefit of mankind as a whole—whether conceived unstructured or elevated into a subject of inter-national law of its own—any such demonstration of concern with international interests of a long-range character on the part of diplo-matic or other mayflies calls for immunisation by a stronger than normal dose of polite reserve and scepticism.

It is well to reflect on the wisdom expressed by Thomas Hobbes in *De Corpore Politico* [43]: " Right of all men to all things is in effect no better than if no man had right to anything." In this as in so many other respects, the realities underlying the anarchy and quasi-order models differ but little.

---

[43] 3rd ed., 1684—I, Chap. I, para. 10.

2—Blueprints Examined

In a comprehensive treatment of the subject, it would be necessary to systematise the chief proposals put forward in the post-1945 period for the development of the law of the sea from the angle of international order and study the attitudes taken towards them by the various Powers.

In the context of this paper, it must suffice to throw out the suggestion as an idea to be taken up by anybody keen on this type of inter-disciplinary research, and select three proposals which, from the point of view of international order, may claim to be representative of current trends. They are taken from the Informal Composite Negotiating Text of July 15, 1977, of the Third United Nations Conference on the Law of the Sea [44] and concern the exclusive economic zone, the International Sea-Bed Authority, and the settlement of disputes.

(a) *The Exclusive Economic Zone*

In accordance with the Negotiating Text, coastal States are to have a territorial sea of 12 miles, a further contiguous zone of up to 24 miles for preventing and punishing infringements of their customs, fiscal, immigration or sanitary regulations, and an exclusive economic zone *sui generis* of 200 miles, beyond and adjacent to the territorial sea.

In the exclusive economic zone, the coastal State is to be granted " sovereign rights " regarding the conservation and exploitation of the actual resources of the sea-bed and subsoil and the superjacent waters, and exclusive jurisdiction regarding the establishment and use of artificial islands, installations and structures, other activities for the economic exploitation of the zone, and pollution control.

Other States are limited in the exclusive zone to rights of navigation, overflight and communication, but subject to control by the coastal State in safety zones around artificial islands, installations and structures. Like land-locked States in the region, other States may participate in the exploitation of the living resources of the zone only under agreements with the coastal State.

In assessing the significance of the proposal for an exclusive economic zone, it is advisable to bear in mind two aspects of the matter:

(1) The area to be enclosed in exclusive economic zones of coastal States covers more than one-third of the total area of the high seas, and 10 countries would receive 30 per cent. of the area to be appropriated. Combined with the rules on international straits proposed in the Convention, it is estimated that, on a consensual basis,

[44] U.N. Doc. A/CONF. 62/WP.10.

four-fifths of world fishing and nearly all exploitable off-shore oil would come under the control of coastal States.[45]

(2) In the *Fisheries Jurisdiction* cases between the United Kingdom and Iceland and between Germany and Iceland (1974), the International Court of Justice considered it to be generally accepted that, independently of its territorial sea, a coastal State may claim an exclusive fishery zone up to 12 miles. The Court leaned over backwards even further (and beyond *lex lata* as it then stood) to accommodate any coastal State " in a situation of special dependence on its coastal fisheries." It held that, in an undefined zone beyond the 12-mile limit, other States had to recognise the preferential rights of coastal States in this particular category, and that both were legally bound to negotiate equitable settlements on the basis of the recognition of the preferential, but not exclusive, rights of coastal States.

The Court's pronouncements are hard to square with international law or the proper exercise of the international judicial function. It required courage for a member of the Court to disclose, as did Judge Ignazio Pinto, the inarticulate *arrière-pensées* of the majority of the members of the Court and point out the excessiveness of their " dynamic " approach to international law.[46] Yet the gap between the law as, in 1974, even the Court felt constrained to " declare " it and the appetites of coastal States appears to have grown to propensities which are perhaps best symbolised by *Jaws*, the shark of sharks.

(b) *The International Sea-Bed Authority*

Under the Informal Composite Negotiating Text, the sea-bed and the subsoil thereof in the area beyond national jurisdiction (abbreviated as the Area)—territorial sea, exclusive economic zone and continental shelf to the outer edge of the continental margin—are to be the common heritage of mankind, and activities there are to be regulated and controlled by an International Sea-Bed Authority. Activities in the Area are to be carried out for the benefit of mankind as a whole, taking into particular consideration the interests and needs of the " developing " countries (not defined in the Convention). The area is to be used exclusively for peaceful purposes (also left undefined). Moreover, the Authority and Parties to the Convention are to co-operate in promoting the transfer to " developing " countries of technology and scientific knowledge relating to the area.

All Parties to the Convention are to be members of the Authority. Its primary organs are to be an Assembly, a Council, an Enterprise and a Secretariat.

The *Assembly* is to be the supreme policy-making organ of the

[45] *The Economist* (London), March 19, 1976, pp. 13–14.
[46] *I.C.J. Reports* (1974), pp. 37 and 210.

Authority. It has power to lay down general guidelines, issue general policy directions to other organs, elect the members of the Council, select the members of the Sea-bed Disputes Chamber of a Law of the Sea Tribunal, and, on the recommendations of the Council, appoint the members of the Governing Board of the Enterprise. The Assembly is also to approve the budget of the Authority on its submission by the Council. Voting in the Assembly on questions of substance, including whether a question is one of substance or procedure, is by a two-thirds majority of the members present and voting. Such a majority must include a majority of the members of the Authority.

The *Council* is to consist of 36 members elected by the Assembly, half of these members to be elected in accordance with the principle of equitable geographical representation and the other half with a view to the representation of special interests. It is to be the executive organ of the Authority and supervise the activities of the *Enterprise*, which conducts activities in the Area. Finally, the Council is to decide questions of substance by a three-quarters majority. Decisions on matters of procedure, including whether an issue is one of substance or procedure, are to be made by a majority of the members present and voting.

(c) *Settlement of Disputes*

A settlement of disputes system is provided in Part XV of the Informal Composite Negotiating Text. States parties to the Convention are to accept a general obligation to settle by peaceful means of their own choice any dispute on the interpretation or application of the Convention. If a dispute cannot be settled in this way, any such dispute, at the request of any party to the dispute, is to be submitted to arbitration or judicial settlement by one of a number of institutions, the decision of which is binding on the parties.

Proposals in the Negotiating Text on limited access to the contemplated Law of the Sea Tribunal by other than Contracting Parties and on limited appellate supervision of organs under special procedures provided in the Convention may cause problems of their own. Yet the crucial issue will be the scope of the automatic jurisdiction to be granted to international judicial organs concerning the exclusive economic zone.

The fulsome contracting-out clause for Contracting Parties under earlier versions of the Negotiating Text has been severely limited in the latest version.[47] Yet it remains to be seen whether this formulation will be acceptable to the proponents of the exclusive economic zone as part of the sovereign domain of coastal States.

---

[47] Art. 296 and 297.

(d) *Evaluation*

In any evaluation of the Informal Composite Negotiating Text, it is essential to bear in mind the fundamental assumption made in the Negotiating Text: that the four Parts should constitute an inseparable package deal.

On this basis, it is possible to argue that, if a comprehensive Convention came into force and received general support, especially from the greater majority of coastal States, the Convention would go a long way towards a workable international maritime order.

Until the degree of general support which the disputes-settlement system will attract is clarified, doubts on the order-character of the contemplated package deal will persist.

Even the assumption of an indivisible package deal may be sacrificed to the desire of attaining formal consensus. In this eventuality, selective acceptance of the Convention, especially the Part on the Territorial Sea and the Contiguous Zone, might be welcomed as a, however spurious, legitimation of policies of coastal States, eagerly waiting to annex at the earliest moment the exclusive economic zones which it is intended to grant them as part of the envisaged package deal. The consensus attained at the September 1978 Session on the need to strengthen the powers of coastal States against pollution dangers in an area of 200 miles seawards is likely to prove another move—unavoidably on the lines of least resistance—towards the " nationalisation," rather than the cleansing of the high seas.

It would also not be surprising if, in selective reliance on existing international law regarding the sea-bed and subsoil thereof, national enterprises and multinational consortia in possession of the requisite capital and technology sprang into action. They may be expected to race one another to the manganese nodules and other minerals in the " Area," intended under the Convention to be treated as the heritage of mankind and to be husbanded for the benefit of what is supposed to be *homo sapiens*.

In conclusion, the hope may be expressed (October 1978) that the 1979 and 1980 Sessions of the United Nations Conference on the Law of the Sea will confound the more sceptical prognoses advanced in this analysis of long-range trends.

SUGGESTIONS
FOR
INTER-DISCIPLINARY READING

I—General

Alexandrowicz, C. H.: *An Introduction to the History of the Law of Nations in the East Indies* (1967)

Anstey, R.: *The Atlantic Slave Trade and British Abolition 1760–1810* (1975)

Bowett, D. W.: *The Law of the Sea* (1967)

Brown, E. D.: *The Legal Régime of Hydrospace* (1971)

Brownley, I.: *Principles of Public International Law* (Part IV—1973)

Chauveau, P.: *Traité de droit maritime* (1958)

Colombos, C. J.: *The International Law of the Sea* (1967)

Fahl, G.: *Der Grundsatz der Freiheit der Meere in der Staatenpraxis von 1493 bis 1648* (1969)

Ferron, O. de: *Le droit international de la mer*, 2 vols. (1958–60)

Fulton, T. W.: *The Sovereignty of the Sea* (1911)

Gidel, G.: *Le droit international public de la mer*, 4 vols. (1932–34)

Jados, S. S.: *Consulate of the Sea and Related Documents* (1975)

Johnson, D. H. N.: *The Geneva Conference on the Law of the Sea*, 13 *Year Book of World Affairs* (1959)

Johnson, D. M.: *The International Law of Fisheries* (1965)

Lachs, F.: *Die Meeresfreiheit, Versuch einer Problemstellung*, 15 *Zeitschrift für oeffentliches Recht* (1935)

McDougal, M. S., and Burke, W. T.: *The Public Order of the Oceans* (1962)

Mitsides, Th.: *Consolato del Mare*, 22 *Revue Hellénique de Droit International* (1969)

O'Connell, D. P.: *International Law*, 2 vols. (1970)

Oppenheim, L. (ed. H. Lauterpacht): *International Law*, 2 vols. (1952–55)

Parry, J. H.: *The Discovery of the Seas* (1975)

Pleionis, L.: *The Influence of the Rhodian Sea Law on the other Maritime Codes*, 20 *Revue Hellénique de Droit International* (1967)

Queneudec, J.-P.: *Droit Maritime International* (1971)

Schwarzenberger, G.: *International Law as Applied by International Courts and Tribunals*, 3 vols. (1957–76)

Smith, H. A.: *Great Britain and the Law of Nations*, Vol. II (1935)

——: *The Law and Custom of the Sea* (1959)

Sørensen, M.: *Law of the Sea*, 520 *International Conciliation* (1958)

Tunkin, G. I.: *Voelkerrechtstheorie* (1972)

Verdross, A.: *Voelkerrecht* (1964)

Verzijl, J. H. W.: *International Law in Historical Perspective*, Vol. IV (1971)

II—Special Aspects

Alexander, L. M.: *Offshore Claims and Fisheries in North-West Europe*, 14 *Year Book of World Affairs* (1960)

Ballenger, J.: *La pollution en droit international* (1975)

Barros, J., and Johnston, D. M.: *The International Law of Pollution* (1974)

Bennouna, M.: *Le fond des mers et des océans au dela des juridictions nationales* (7 *Thesaurus Acroasium*—1976 Session)

Bouchez, L. J.: *The Régime of Bays in International Law* (1961)

Brown, E. D.: *Passage through the Territorial Sea, Straits used for International Navigation and Archipelagos* (1974)

——: *Deep-Sea Mining,* 22 *Year Book of World Affairs* (1968)

——: *British Fisheries and the Common Market,* 25 *Current Legal Problems* (1972)

Bruel, E.: *International Straits,* 2 vols. (1947)

Butler, W. E.: *The Law of Soviet Territorial Waters* (1961)

Govindaraj, V. C.: *Land-locked States and their Right of Access to the Sea,* 14 *Indian Journal of International Law* (1974)

Graham, C.: *Ice islands in international law* (7 *Thesaurus Acroasium*—1976 Session)

Gray, E.: *The Devil's Device. The Story of Robert Whitehead, Inventor of the Torpedo* (1975)

Green, L. C.: *The Continental Shelf,* 4 *Current Legal Problems* (1951)

Guliano, M.: *The Régime of Straits in General International Law,* 1 *Italian Yearbook of International Law* (1975)

Jennings, R. Y.: *The Limits of Continental Shelf Jurisdiction,* 18 *International and Comparative Law Quarterly* (1969)

Johnson, D. H. N.: *Artificial Islands,* 4 *International Law Quarterly* (1951)

——: *The Anglo-Norwegian Fisheries Case,* 1 *International and Comparative Law Quarterly* (1952)

——: *The Legal Status of the Sea-Bed and Subsoil,* 16 *Zeitschrift für ausländisches öffentliches Recht und Völkerrecht* (1956)

Koulouris, M.: *Les droits souverains sur le plateau continental,* 24 *Revue Hellénique de Droit International* (1971)

Lapidoth, R.: *Les Détroits en Droit International* (1972)

Lauterpacht, H.: *Sovereignty over Submarine Areas,* 27 *British Year Book of International Law* (1950)

O'Connell, D. P.: *Mid-Ocean Archipelagos in International Law,* 45 *British Year Book of International Law* (1975)

——: *Innocent Passage of Warships* (7 *Thesaurus Acroasium*—1976 Session)

Oudenijk, J. K.: *Status and Extent of Adjacent Waters* (1970)

Pharand, D.: *International Straits* (7 *Thesaurus Acroasium*—1976 Session)

Rangel, V. M.: *Le Droit de la Mer dans la Jurisprudence de la Cour Internationale de Justice* (7 *Thesaurus Acroasium*—1976 Session)

Read, J. E.: *The Trail Smelter Dispute,* 1 *Canadian Yearbook of International Law* (1963)

Rubin, A.: *Evolution and Self-Defence at Sea* (7 *Thesaurus Acroasium*—1976 Session)

——: *Piracy, Paramountcy and Protectorates* (1974)

Schinas, J. G.: *L'affaire du " Torrey Canyon,"* 26–27 *Revue Hellénique de Droit International* (1973–74)

Schwarzenberger, G.: *Economic World Order?* (1970)

———: *International Law and Order* (1971)

Smith, H. A.: *The Anglo-Norwegian Fisheries Case*, 7 *Year Book of World Affairs* (1953)

United Nations Legislative Series: *Law and Regulations on the Régime of the High Seas* (1951–59)

———: *Laws concerning the Nationality of Ships* (1955–59)

———: *Laws and Regulations on the Régime of the Territorial Sea* (1957)

———: *National Legislation and Treaties relating to the Territorial Sea* etc. (1970)

———: *National Legislation and Treaties relating to the Law of the Sea* (1974–75)

Vallat, F. A.: *The Continental Shelf*, 23 *British Year Book of International Law* (1946)

Waldock, C. H. M.: *The Legal Basis of Claims to the Continental Shelf*, 36 *Grotius Society Transactions* (1950)

Yates, G. T., and Young, H. J.: *Limits to National Jurisdiction over the Sea* (1974)

Zemanek, K.: *Dardanellen* in Strupp-Schlochauer, *Wörterbuch des Voelkerrechts*, Vol. I (1960)

III—Current Trends and Problems

Adede, A. O.: *The System for Exploitation of the " Common Heritage of Mankind " at the Caracas Conference*, 69 *American Journal of International Law* (1975)

Bouchez, L. J., and Kaijen, L. (eds.): *The Future of the Law of the Sea* (1973)

Brown, E. D.: *The Legal Régime of Inner Space: Military Aspects*, 22 *Current Legal Problems* (1969)

———: *The Continental Shelf and the Exclusive Economic Zone*, 4 *Maritime Policy and Management* (1977)

Canadian Council on International Law: *Avoiding International Conflicts: Law of the Sea Issues* (1977)

Caflisch, L.: *Land-locked and Geographically Disadvantaged States and the New Law of the Sea* (7 *Thesaurus Acroasium*—1976 Session)

Centre des Hautes Etudes Internationales, Université de Téhéran: *Le nouveau droit de la mer* (1975–76)

Christy, F. T., and Others (eds.): *Law of the Sea. Caracas and Beyond* (1975)

Churchill, R., and Others (eds.): *New Directions in the Law of the Sea*, 4 vols. (1973–78)

Clement, M. O., and Others: *Who Protects the Ocean?* (1975)

Cohen, Maxwell: The Régime of Boundary Waters—*The Canadian and United States Experience* (Recueil, Hague Academy of International Law, 1975)

Conforti, B.: *Does Freedom of the Seas Still Exist?*, 1 *Italian Yearbook of International Law* (1975)

Dickstein, H. L.: *International Law and the Environment: Evolving Concepts*, 26 *Year Book of World Affairs* (1972)

Dupuy, R.-J.: *The Law of the Sea: Current Problems* (1974)

Falk, R. A.: *A Study of Future Worlds* (1975)

Frankowska, M. (ed.): *Scientific and Technological Revolution and the Law of the Sea* (1974)

Friedmann, W.: *The Future of the Oceans* (1971)

Garcia-Amador, F. V.: *The Latin American Contribution to the Development of the Law of the Sea*, 68 *American Journal of International Law* (1974)

Glassner, M. I.: *Access to the Sea for Developing Land-Locked States* (1970)

Hambro, E.: *The Human Environment: Stockholm and After*, 28 *Year Book of World Affairs* (1974)

Henkin, L.: *Law for the Sea's Mineral Resources* (1967)

Hollick, A. L., and Osgood, R. E.: *New Era of Ocean Politics* (1974)

Hurst, Sir Cecil: *Whose is the Bed of the Sea?*, 4 *British Year Book of International Law* (1923–24)

Ibler, V.: *The Settlement of Disputes arising from the Interpretation and Application of the Sea Law Convention* (7 *Thesaurus Acroasium*—1976 Session)

Jenks, C. W.: *The Common Law of Mankind* (1958)

Kalshoven, F.: *Belligerent Reprisals* (1971)

Knight, H. G. (ed.): *The Future of International Fisheries Management* (1975)

—— and Others: *Policy Issues in Ocean Law* (1975)

Kuehne, E. W.: *Das Voelkerrecht und die militaerische Nutzung des Meeresbodens* (1975)

Lachs, M.: *Some Reflections on Science, Technology and International Law*, in M. K. Nawaz (ed.), *Essays in International Law in Honour of Krishna Rao* (1975)

Law of the Sea Institute, University of Rhode Island: *Law of the Sea: Caracas and Beyond* (9th Annual Conference, 1975)

Luttwak, E. N.: *The Political Uses of Modern Sea Power* (1975)

Mancke, D., and Schwarz, H.-P. (eds.): *Seemacht und Aussenpolitik* (1974)

McWhinney, E.: *The Codifying Conference as an Instrument of International Law-Making: From the " Old" Law of the Sea to the " New,"* 3 *Syracuse Journal of International Law and Commerce* (1975)

Moore, J. N.: *The Common Interest in the Oceans* (7 *Thesaurus Acroasium* —1976 Session)

Mouton, M. W.: *The Impact of Science on International Law*, Recueil, *Hague Academy of International Law*, Vol. 119 (1966)

Myrdal, A.: *Preserving the Oceans for Peaceful Purposes*, Recueil, *Hague Academy of International Law*, Vol. 133 (1971)

O'Connell, D. P.: *The Influence of Law on Sea Power* (1975)

Oda, S.: *The International Law of Ocean Development. Basic Documents*, 2 vols. (1972–75)

Owen, D.: *Western Naval Strategy for the Eighties*, 28 *Year Book of World Affairs* (1974)

Pastor Ridruejo, J. A.: *La Explotacion de los Fondes Marinos Mas Alla de la Jurisdiccion Nadional* (1975)

Piquemal, A.: *Le fonds de mer. Patrimoine commun de l'humanité* (1973)

Poch, A.: *La Actual Revision del Derecho del Mar. Una Perspectiva Espanola*, 4 vols. (1975)

Rao, P. S.: *The Public Order of Ocean Resources* (1975)

Rosenne, S.: *The Third United Nations Conference on the Law of the Sea*, 11 *Israel Law Review* (1976)

Ruester, B., and Simma, B.: *International Protection of the Environment*, 2 vols. (1975)

Saxena, S. K.: *United Nations Documents on the Law of the Sea, 1955–1975*, 15 *Indian Journal of International Law* (1975)

Scerni, M.: *La zone économique exclusive* (7 *Thesaurus Acroasium*—1976 Session)

Schramm, G. G.: *The Case for Coastal State Jurisdiction*, 44 *Nordisk Tidskrift for International Ret* (1974–75)

Schwarzenberger, G.: *The Dynamics of International Law* (1976)

Sibthorp, M. M. (ed.): *The North Sea. Challenge and Opportunity* (1975)

Soubeyrol, J.: *Les Conventions de lutte contre la pollution de mer de 1954 à 1976* (7 *Thesaurus Acroasium*—1976 Session)

Stavropoulos, C. A.: *Procedural Problems of the Third Conference on the Law of the Sea*, 6 *UNITAR News* (1974)

Stein, E.: *The Impact of New Weapons Technology on International Law*, Recueil, *Hague Academy of International Law*, Vol. 132 (1971)

Stevenson, J. R., and Oxman, B. H.: *The Third United Nations Conference on the Law of the Sea: the 1975 Geneva Session*, 69 *American Journal of International Law* (1975)

Stryam, M.: *International Straits and Ocean Law*, 15 *Indian Journal of International Law* (1975)

UNCTAD: *Implications of the Exploitation of the Mineral Resources of the International Area of the Sea-bed* (TD/B/C. 1/170—1975)

Zacklin, R. (ed.): *The Changing Law of the Sea: Western Hemisphere Perspectives* (1974)

For further bibliographic information, especially relevant treaties and decisions of national and international judicial organs, see Schwarzenberger-Brown, *A Manual of International Law* (6th ed., 2nd rev. impression 1978—Professional Books, Abingdon, Oxon), Part II: *Study Outlines* under V (Nos. 3–10) and VII (No. 20).

INDEX

375